The CAR Book

2017

by

Jack Gillis

and

Amy Curran
Richard Eckman

with

Carl E. Nash, Ph.D.

Foreword by

Michael Brooks
Center for Auto Safety

A Center for Auto Safety Publication

229627386

ACKNOWLEDGMENTS

Co-author, Richard "Ricky" Eckman again did an extraordinary job of managing and organizing this 37th edition of *The Car Book*. It is a monumental effort as, literally, thousands of data points go into compiling the book and all of its ratings. As a 26 year veteran of *The Car Book*, Amy Curran prepared all of the graphics necessary to clearly present the data and managed the logistics necessary to get a printed book in the hands of the public. For the second year, important new safety advice and content was provided by noted auto safety expert and former NHTSA official, Dr. Carl Nash. Thanks to Amy, Ricky, and the team, consumers have the information they need to make a smart, sensible new car choice.

For 36 years, this effort would not have been possible without the essential contributions from the late Clarence Ditlow and the staff of the Center for Auto Safety, including Michael Brooks and Jon Robinson.

As always, the most important factor in being able to bring this information to the American car buyer for 37 years is the encouragement, support, and love from my brilliant and beautiful wife, Marilyn Mohrman-Gillis. For her and our four terrific children–Katie, John, Brian and Brennan–I am eternally grateful.

—*J.G.*

This edition of The Car Book is dedicated to the memory of
Clarence M. Ditlow, III
One of the Most Effective Safety Advocates in America's History
A True Friend and Great Mentor Who Saved Inumerable Lives

On November 10, 2016, America lost one of the most effective consumer advocates in its history with the death of Clarence M. Ditlow, III. He played a key role in the remarkable history of *The Car Book*. When first published by the National Highway Traffic Safety Administration in 1980, it became one of the most popular publications in the history of the government's Pueblo, Colorado distribution center. I was responsible for developing the publication under the Carter Administration. When the Reagan Administration took over, the government cancelled the publication under pressure from the car companies who didn't like the fact that consumers could tell which cars were the safer and which were not. In 1981, because he believed the information in *The Car Book* to be so important to consumers, Clarence Ditlow came to me and suggested that I publish it privately with the Center for Auto Safety. After consulting with attorneys and with the assistance of Joel Makower of Tilden Press and the unconditional support of my wife, Marilyn Mohrman-Gillis, I set out to collect the data and continue to make this important information available to the American public. In part, due to Clarence's prodding, insight, and determination, *The Car Book*, throughout the years, had many more publication "firsts" than could be listed here. During the past 36 years, Clarence and I developed a deep and lasting friendship. He was both my partner and mentor. I learned much from this man, who for over four decades, fought tirelessly to stem the toll that automobiles take on American society. In addition, he was one of the first to understand how the environmental impact of the automobile could be tamed. Clarence Ditlow was likely responsible for saving more lives than anyone else in the auto safety community. His efforts were monumental, his effectiveness unmatched, and his dedication to public service was a beacon for hundreds of advocates. His death is a tragic blow to public safety at a time when consumer protections are at such great risk. I worked with Clarence, almost daily, for 36 years and, like many, knew him as an uncompromising advocate, a true compass for what's right, and a loyal friend. He will be dearly missed.

Contents

MICHAEL BROOKS, CENTER FOR AUTO SAFETY

Until recently, motor vehicle crashes were one of the leading causes of death and injury in the U.S. and they remain a major factor. Serious regulation of vehicle safety began a half century ago with passage of the National Traffic and Motor Vehicle Safety Act. At that time, there were nearly 26 road fatalities per hundred thousand population. In 2014 that number was down to just above 10. Had the earlier rate continued, 83,000 people would have died in vehicle crashes in 2014. Unfortunately, traffic deaths rose 7 percent to 35,072 in 2015, and 2016, preliminary data shows a 10.4 percent increase in traffic fatalities over 2015, a projected 38,700 deaths!

The National Highway Traffic Safety Administration was given reasonably strong authority to set safety standards and require safety defect recalls. This was because the auto industry, concerned that states were passing conflicting safety standards, was willing to accept a stronger agency in order to give the Federal government authority to pre-empt state standards. Unfortunately, the agency has been kept small and underfunded, and its political leadership has often been reluctant or tardy in taking bold action for safety. The industry successfully fought against a provision for criminal penalties for violating the Safety Act that could have put their executives behind bars for selling vehicles they knew were unsafe. Drunk drivers that kill innocent motorists can be put in jail, but not auto executives.

Automakers have been assessed fines approaching or exceeding $1 billion by the Department of Justice for violations of federal law, which may have a moderate deterrent effect on future behavior. However, civil penalties available to NHTSA are capped at $35 million per violation, which is nothing more than a slap on the wrist for companies making billions of dollars per year in profits. Even after setting the record for recalls in one year, and buying its way out of prosecution for $900 million on the deadly ignition switch defect, GM placed the blame on a rogue engineer, retaining most of the upper-level staff whose actions contributed to the cover-up, and their profits are now as strong as ever.

Industry practices that result in compromised safety do not always result in stronger Federal standards. For years, weak roofs on rollover-prone vehicles saved the auto industry hundreds of millions of dollars every year while thousands of consumers died because those roofs collapsed in rollovers. Ironically, in 1970, NHTSA proposed a roof crush standard that would have had the same effect as the standard that was finally adopted nearly 40 years later and that could have saved many thousands of lives and prevented an even greater number of injuries. Along with two other rollover standards, one requiring electronic stability control (to reduce the likelihood of a rollover) and one that is substantially reducing ejection in rollovers, rollover fatalities in new vehicles are now down by roughly 75 percent. In numerous lawsuits, General Motors and Ford produced phony research and tests that supposedly showed no connection between roof crush and occupant injuries. They have yet to apologize to the American public for their deceptive position.

Collapsing seatbacks have been killing and injuring children in rear crashes for decades, during which time automakers have continually fought an upgrade to the federal seat strength standard. While some European manufacturers have made adequately strong front seatbacks, showing that it is feasible, NHTSA has failed to respond positively to recent petitions from the Center for Auto Safety and others to strengthen the seatback standard.

Two recent defect cases demonstrate that automakers do not take NHTSA too seriously. Takata made defective air bag inflators that send shrapnel into the faces of crash victims, and conducted a campaign of misinformation for years, because they could underprice other suppliers by using a cheaper propellant that was not stable over time. For several years after their own engineers recognized a problem, GM installed ignition switches that would suddenly shut off engines, power steering and brakes, and air bags. Crashes of cars with these switches killed more than 200 people and injured many more, until the efforts of the Center for Auto Safety exposed this serious defect.

New cars are likely to continue to be produced with marginal safety performance and various defects. *The Car Book*'s comprehensive crash protection safety ratings and listings of advanced, optional safety features can direct you toward safer new vehicles.

The Center for Auto Safety endorses a national goal of Zero Traffic Deaths by 2050. Your concern for vehicle safety, both in your choice of a vehicle and in your communications with NHTSA and Congress on safety issues, will help us achieve that goal. Your active support of CAS will support our work on your behalf toward safer, more reliable vehicles. In addition to using *The Car Book*, go to www.autosafety.org to learn more about auto safety and how you can support the Center.

JACK GILLIS

Years ago when safety belts were introduced, and later airbags, vehicle safety was transformed. Today, the new safety features in many of the 2017 models could have an even bigger impact on keeping occupants safe. In order to make you both a smarter and safer car buyer, *The Car Book* documents these improvements and puts them at your fingertips. By rating the 2017s for the number of safety features they have, you can easily find the top performers among the models you are considering. The good news is that many of the new, life-saving features are becoming available on the less expensive vehicles.

Amazingly, this is the 37th year we've been bringing consumers the information they need to make a smart and safe vehicle choice. For 36 of those 37 years, a key reason why we've been able to do this is the support we've received from Clarence Ditlow, Executive Director of the Center for Auto Safety. Sadly, Clarence died in November, 2016. Nevertheless, his spirt lives on as we redouble our efforts to both fight for safer, better performing vehicles and give you the tools to find and buy them. Clarence believed that educating consumers was one of the best ways to improve the safety of vehicles. He has been America's primary advocate in bringing media, consumer and Congressional attention to the many serious auto defects that have been in the news. His efforts have saved lives and brought about important changes in auto company practices and government regulations. Clarence believed that consumers want safer, better performing vehicles and worked to insure that *The Car Book* helped make that happen. For a tribute to Clarence

from Ralph Nader, see page 59. For my own comments, see the Acknowledgements on page 2.

This year, in keeping with Clarence's forward-looking approach, we have expanded our section at the end of the book on 24 new electric vehicles. Based on family size and driving needs of the typical family, EVs would work for nearly half of Americans! EVs work like your cell phone—imagine plugging them in each night and then gliding silently and smoothly throughout your driving day in a high-tech, low maintenance vehicle.

Not only are vehicles getting better, so is the buying experience. More dealers are abandoning the difficult negotiation process in favor of a straightforward posted price. So with lots of new electronics, improved safety features, and some improvements in the showroom, *The Car Book* is ready to guide you to a great new 2017 vehicle!

Working closely with the Center for Auto Safety, our goal is to sift through the myriad of government and industry data on cars and present the information so you can actually use it. Thirty seven years ago, *The Car Book* was the first publication to give you the ability to make an informed choice on one of the most important and complex items that you will ever purchase. In setting out to change the way people buy their cars, *The Car Book* was able to change the way car companies made them.

In keeping with *The Car Book's* philosophy of making it as easy as possible to identify the truly good performers in the government crash tests, we provide a unique Car Book Combined Crash Test Rating which

combines all of the complex government testing into a simple, straightforward number. In addition, we take the step of comparing the vehicles on a relative basis to each other so you can easily tell the best performers from the worst.

Before *The Car Book*, consumers had no idea which warranties were better, what you could expect to pay for typical repairs, which cars cost the most and least to insure, or how they stacked up in government complaints. Now you have this information all in one place.

Our exclusive car-by-car ratings at the end of the book provide an overview of all the criteria you need to make a good choice. Here, you'll be able to quickly assess key features and see how the car you're interested in stacks up against its competition so you can make sure your selection is the best car for you.

While the choices get better each year, it's still a challenge to separate the lemons from the peaches. There are differences in how cars protect you in a crash, how much they cost to maintain, and the benefits of their warranties. Nevertheless, by using *The Car Book*, there's no reason why your next car shouldn't last at least 150,000 miles. Finally, our "Showroom Strategies" section will give you the keys to getting the best deal.

The information in *The Car Book* is based on data collected and developed by our staff, the U.S. Department of Transportation, and the Center for Auto Safety. With all of this information in hand, you'll find some great choices for 2017.

—*Jack*

USING THE BUYING GUIDE

The "Buying Guide" provides a quick comparison of the 2017 cars in terms of their safety, warranty, fuel economy, complaint rating, and price range—arranged by size class. To fully understand the information in the charts, it is important to read the related section in the book.

Overall Rating: This shows how well this car stacks up on a scale of 1 to 10 when compared to all others on the market. Because safety is the most important component of our ratings, cars with no crash test results at the time of printing are not given an overall rating.

Combined Crash Test Rating: This indicates how well the car performed in the government's frontal and side crash test programs compared to this year's vehicles tested to date. See pages 19-27 for details.

Safety Feature Rating: This is an evaluation of how many extra safety features are available in comparison to all the vehicles. See pages 76-80.

Warranty Rating: This is an overall comparative assessment of the car's warranty. See pages 35-37.

Fuel Economy: This is the EPA city/highway mpg for, what is expected to be, the most popular version of each model.

Complaint Rating: This is based on complaints received by the U.S. Department of Transportation. If not rated, the vehicle is too new to have a complaint rating. See page 54.

Price Range: This will give you a general idea of the "sticker," or manufacturer's suggested retail price (MSRP).

 Indicates a *Car Book* Best Bet. See pages 13-18.

 ### ABOUT THE CAR BOOK BEST BETS

It is important to consult the specific chapters to learn more about how *The Car Book* ratings are developed and to look on the car pages, beginning on page 81, for more details on these vehicles. In order to be considered as a "Best Bet" the vehicle must have a crash test rating as safety is a critical factor in gaining that recognition. *Vehicles with "Poor" (3 or 4) or "Very Poor" (1 or 2) in Combined Crash Tests, or Front or Side Crash Test Ratings, or an additional injury warning will not qualify as a "Best Bet." In addition, vehicles with a poor or very poor safety feature rating will not qualify as a "Best Bet."* Because most people are considering vehicles in the same size category, the "Best Bets" beginning on page 13 are by size—indicating how these vehicles compared against others in the same size class.

You will note that some of our "Best Bets" have some "not so good" ratings on the next pages. Nevertheless, these vehicles still rise to the top in their size class. This points to the trade offs we often make when buying a new vehicle.

Vehicle	Pg #	Overall Rating	Combined Crash Test Rating	Safety Features Rating	Warranty Rating	Fuel Economy Rating	Complaint Rating	Price Range
Subcompact								
BMW i3	97			Average	Very Good	Very Good	Very Good	$43-47,000
Chevrolet Sonic	120	9	Very Good	Good	Average	Good	Average	$15-21,000
Chevrolet Spark	121	6	Very Poor	Good	Average	Very Good	Very Good	$13-17,000
Fiat 500	134	2	Very Poor	Very Poor	Average	Good	Very Poor	$15-20,000
Ford Fiesta	142	3	Poor	Poor	Poor	Good	Very Poor	$14-18,000
Honda Fit	155	8	Very Good	Poor	Very Poor	Very Good	Average	$15-21,000
Hyundai Accent	159	6	Poor	Very Poor	Very Good	Good	Very Good	$14-17,000
Hyundai Veloster	166	5	Poor	Poor	Very Good	Good	Very Poor	$18-23,000
Kia Rio	181	5	Very Poor	Very Poor	Very Good	Good	Good	$14-20,000
Kia Soul	184	8	Very Good	Average	Very Good	Average	Average	$15-35,000
Mazda MX-5	204			Very Poor	Very Poor	Good	Poor	$24-31,000
Mini Cooper	214	5	Poor	Poor	Very Good	Good	Good	$20-30,000
Mini Countryman	215			Poor	Very Good	Good	Very Good	$22-35,000
Mitsubishi Mirage	217	3	Very Poor	Very Poor	Very Good	Very Good	Very Poor	$12-16,000
Nissan Versa	233	2	Very Poor	Very Poor	Very Poor	Very Good	Average	$11-17,000
Smart ForTwo	236			Very Poor	Poor	Very Good	Very Poor	$14-20,000
Toyota Prius C	252	7	Poor	Poor	Very Poor	Very Good	Very Good	$19-24,000
Toyota Yaris	259	5	Poor	Very Poor	Very Poor	Good	Very Good	$15-18,000
Toyota Yaris iA	260			Poor	Very Poor	Very Good		$15-17,000
Compact								
Acura ILX	81	8	Average	Good	Average	Average	Poor	$27-34,000
Audi A3	85	7	Average	Good	Good	Average	Good	$30-48,000
Audi A4	86			Average	Good	Average		$37-48,000
BMW 2 Series	92			Good	Very Good	Average	Very Good	$32-46,000
BMW 3 Series	93	7	Good	Good	Very Good	Average	Good	$33-45,000
BMW 4 Series	94			Good	Very Good	Average	Good	$41-58,000
Buick Cascada	102			Very Poor	Good	Poor		$33-37,000
Buick Verano	107	10	Very Good	Good	Good	Average	Average	$21-27,000
Cadillac ATS	108	8	Good	Very Good	Very Good	Average	Poor	$34-48,000
Chevrolet Cruze	115			Very Good	Average	Good	Good	$16-23,000
Chevrolet Volt	126			Very Good	Average	Very Good	Poor	$33-37,000
Dodge Dart	132	4	Very Good	Very Poor	Poor	Average	Very Poor	$16-24,000
Ford C-MAX	136	5	Poor	Average	Poor	Very Good	Very Poor	$24-30,000
Ford Focus	144	6	Very Good	Poor	Poor	Good	Very Poor	$16-29,000

Vehicle	Pg #	Overall Rating	Combined Crash Test Rating	Safety Features Rating	Warranty Rating	Fuel Economy Rating	Complaint Rating	Price Range
Compact (cont.)								
Honda Civic	153	8	Average	Good	Very Poor	Very Good	Poor	$19-26,000
Hyundai Elantra	161	6	Poor	Good	Very Good	Good		$17-22,000
Kia Forte	179	6	Poor	Poor	Very Good	Good	Poor	$16-21,000
Lexus CT	189			Poor	Good	Very Good	Average	$31-31,000
Lexus IS	193	6	Poor	Very Good	Good	Poor	Very Good	$37-43,000
Lexus RC	195			Very Good	Good	Average		$39-62,000
Mazda Mazda3	202	8	Average	Good	Very Poor	Very Good	Very Good	$17-26,000
Merc.-Benz B-Class	205			Average	Poor	Very Good		$39-39,000
Merc.-Benz C-Class	206	3	Poor	Very Good	Poor	Average	Average	$39-67,000
Merc.-Benz CLA-Class	207			Very Good	Poor	Good	Very Poor	$32-49,000
Mitsubishi Lancer	216	4	Very Poor	Very Poor	Very Good	Good	Average	$17-23,000
Nissan 370Z	220			Very Poor	Very Poor	Poor	Poor	$29-49,000
Nissan Leaf	225	4	Very Poor	Very Poor	Very Poor	Very Good	Very Poor	$29-36,000
Nissan Sentra	231	5	Poor	Poor	Very Poor	Good	Good	$16-21,000
Subaru Impreza	239			Very Good	Poor	Poor		$18-23,000
Toyota 86	245			Poor	Very Poor	Good		$26-26,000
Toyota Corolla	248	8	Average	Very Good	Very Poor	Good	Very Good	$18-22,000
Toyota Corolla iM	249			Average	Very Poor	Good		$18-19,000
Toyota Prius	251	7	Average	Good	Very Poor	Very Good	Average	$24-30,000
Toyota Prius V	253	8	Good	Average	Very Poor	Very Good	Very Good	$26-30,000
Volkswagen Beetle	261	1	Poor	Very Poor	Average	Average	Average	$19-36,000
Volkswagen Golf	262	4	Average	Average	Average	Good	Very Poor	$20-29,000
Volkswagen Jetta	263	5	Good	Poor	Average	Good	Average	$17-24,000
Intermediate								
Acura TLX	84	9	Very Good	Very Good	Average	Poor	Very Poor	$31-44,000
Audi A5	87			Very Poor	Good	Average		$41-50,000
Audi A6	88	6	Good	Good	Good	Poor	Good	$46-63,000
BMW 5 Series	95	6	Poor	Good	Very Good	Average	Average	$50-62,000
Buick Regal	106	4	Average	Average	Good	Poor	Average	$27-36,000
Cadillac CTS	109	9	Good	Good	Very Good	Poor	Good	$45-70,000
Chevrolet Camaro	112	5	Good	Average	Average	Poor	Good	$26-41,000
Chevrolet Corvette	114			Very Poor	Average	Very Poor	Good	$55-$83,000
Chevrolet Malibu	118	10	Average	Very Good	Average	Good	Very Good	$21-27,000
Chrysler 200	127	9	Good	Very Good	Poor	Average	Very Poor	$21-31,000
Ford Fusion	145	6	Poor	Very Good	Poor	Average	Average	$22-36,000
Ford Fusion Energi	146	9	Good	Very Good	Poor	Very Good	Average	$33- 41,000
Ford Mustang	147	7	Good	Poor	Poor	Poor	Average	$24-54,000
Honda Accord	152	9	Very Good	Good	Very Poor	Good	Average	$22-34,000

Vehicle	Pg #	Overall Rating	Combined Crash Test Rating	Safety Features Rating	Warranty Rating	Fuel Economy Rating	Complaint Rating	Price Range
Intermediate (cont.)								
Hyundai Azera	160			Average	Very Good	Poor	Poor	$34-39,000
Hyundai Sonata	164	10	Very Good	Good	Very Good	Good	Average	$21-34,000
Infiniti Q50	167	6	Average	Average	Good	Poor	Very Good	$33-49,000
Infiniti Q70	168			Good	Good	Very Poor	Poor	$49-65,000
Kia Cadenza	178			Very Good	Very Good	Poor		$32-44,000
Kia Optima	180	9	Good	Good	Very Good	Average	Good	$22-36,000
Lexus ES	190	7	Good	Very Good	Good	Poor	Good	$38-41,000
Lexus GS	191			Very Good	Good	Poor	Very Good	$45-63,000
Lincoln MKZ	199	5	Poor	Very Good	Very Good	Very Poor	Good	$35-49,000
Mazda Mazda6	203	8	Good	Average	Very Poor	Good	Poor	$21-30,000
Nissan Altima	221	5	Good	Poor	Very Poor	Good	Average	$22-32,000
Nissan Maxima	226	4	Good	Poor	Very Poor	Average	Poor	$32-39,000
Subaru Legacy	240	6	Very Good	Very Good	Poor	Good	Poor	$21-31,000
Toyota Avalon	246	7	Good	Very Good	Very Poor	Poor	Average	$33-42,000
Toyota Camry	247	8	Good	Very Good	Very Poor	Good	Very Good	$23-31,000
Volkswagen Passat	264	3	Average	Poor	Average	Good	Poor	$22-30,000
Volvo S60	266	10	Good	Good	Good	Good	Good	$34-47,000
Volvo V60	267			Good	Good	Good	Very Poor	$36-49,000
Large								
BMW 7 Series	96			Very Good	Very Good	Poor	Good	$81-94,000
Buick LaCrosse	105	6	Average	Very Good	Good	Poor		$32-41,000
Cadillac XTS	111	9	Very Good	Good	Very Good	Poor	Good	$45-72,000
Chevrolet Impala	117	7	Good	Good	Average	Poor	Good	$27-40,000
Chrysler 300	128	2	Poor	Average	Poor	Poor	Very Poor	$32-45,000
Dodge Challenger	130	5	Good	Poor	Poor	Poor	Average	$26-62,000
Dodge Charger	131	3	Poor	Average	Poor	Poor	Very Poor	$27-65,000
Ford Taurus	148	4	Good	Average	Poor	Poor	Average	$27-42,000
Genesis G80	149			Very Good	No Index	Poor		$41-$54,000
Lincoln Continental	197			Very Good	Very Good	Very Poor		$44-64,000
Mercedes-Benz E-Class	208			Very Good	Poor	Poor		$52-69,000
Mercedes-Benz S-Class	213			Very Good	Poor	Very Poor	Poor	$96-170,000
Tesla Model S	242	10	Very Good	Very Good	Very Good	Very Good	Very Poor	$68-134,000
Minivan								
Chrysler Pacifica	129	9	Good	Good	Poor	Poor		$28-42,000
Honda Odyssey	157	8	Good	Good	Very Poor	Poor	Average	$29-42,000
Kia Sedona	182	7	Good	Average	Very Good	Very Poor	Average	$26-39,000
Nissan Quest	229			Very Poor	Very Poor	Poor	Average	$26-43,000
Toyota Sienna	256	2	Average	Good	Very Poor	Very Poor	Poor	$29-47,000

Vehicle	Pg #	Overall Rating	Combined Crash Test Rating	Safety Features Rating	Warranty Rating	Fuel Economy Rating	Complaint Rating	Price Range
Small SUV								
Acura RDX	83	9	Very Good	Good	Average	Poor	Average	$35-40,000
Audi Q3	89			Poor	Good	Poor	Very Good	$33-40,000
BMW X1	98			Average	Very Good	Average	Good	$32-34,000
Buick Encore	104	10	Very Good	Good	Good	Average	Very Good	$24-31,000
Chevrolet Trax	125	8	Very Good	Good	Average	Average	Very Good	$21-27,000
Fiat 500X	135			Average	Average	Average		$20-25,000
Ford Escape	138	7	Good	Good	Poor	Average	Average	$23-30,000
Honda CR-V	154			Good	Very Poor	Good		$23-33,000
Honda HR-V	156	5	Poor	Poor	Very Poor	Good	Poor	$19-26,000
Hyundai Tucson	165	6	Poor	Very Good	Very Good	Average	Very Poor	$22-31,000
Infiniti QX50	169			Poor	Good	Very Poor	Very Poor	$34-35,000
Jeep Compass	173	3	Very Poor	Poor	Poor	Very Poor	Poor	$19-26,000
Jeep Patriot	175	2	Very Poor	Poor	Poor	Very Poor	Poor	$17-25,000
Jeep Renegade	176	2	Poor	Average	Poor	Poor	Very Poor	$17-27,000
Jeep Wrangler	177			Very Poor	Poor	Very Poor	Very Poor	$23-37,000
Kia Sportage	185	8	Good	Good	Very Good	Poor	Very Good	$22-34,000
Land Rvr RRover Evoque	187			Good	Good	Poor	Good	$41-53,000
Lexus NX	194	6	Good	Very Good	Good	Poor	Very Good	$34-41,000
Lincoln MKC	198	5	Poor	Average	Very Good	Poor	Good	$32-47,000
Mazda CX-5	200	3	Poor	Average	Very Poor	Good	Poor	$21-29,000
Merc.-Benz GLA-Class	209			Very Good	Poor	Average	Good	$32-49,000
Merc.-Benz GLC-Class	210			Very Good	Poor	Very Poor	Poor	$39-54,000
Mitsu. Outlander Sport	219	4	Poor	Very Poor	Very Good	Average	Average	$19-27,000
Nissan Juke	224	2	Very Poor	Poor	Very Poor	Average	Good	$20-30,000
Subaru Crosstrek	237	6	Average	Good	Poor	Good	Very Good	$21-29,000
Subaru Forester	238	4	Average	Good	Poor	Average	Average	$22-34,000
Toyota RAV4	254	6	Good	Very Good	Very Poor	Poor	Very Good	$24-36,000
Volkswagen Tiguan	265	1	Very Poor	Very Poor	Average	Poor	Poor	$24-36,000
Mid-Size SUV								
Acura MDX	82	8	Very Good	Very Good	Average	Very Poor	Very Poor	$43-57,000
Audi Q5	90	3	Poor	Poor	Good	Poor	Good	$40-55,000
Audi Q7	91			Very Good	Good	Very Poor	Very Good	$54-64,000
BMW X3	99	7	Average	Good	Very Good	Poor	Good	$38-47,000
BMW X5	100	6	Good	Very Good	Very Good	Very Poor	Very Good	$55-72,000
Cadillac XT5	110	5	Poor	Good	Very Good	Very Poor		$39-62,000
Chevrolet Equinox	116	2	Very Poor	Poor	Average	Average	Poor	$23-31,000
Dodge Journey	133	1	Very Poor	Poor	Poor	Very Poor	Very Poor	$20-33,000
Ford Edge	137	8	Very Good	Very Good	Poor	Poor	Poor	$28-40,000

Vehicle	Pg #	Overall Rating	Combined Crash Test Rating	Safety Features Rating	Warranty Rating	Fuel Economy Rating	Complaint Rating	Price Range
Mid-Size SUV (cont.)								
Ford Explorer	140	3	Average	Good	Poor	Very Poor	Very Poor	$31-53,000
GMC Terrain	116	2	Very Poor	Poor	Average	Average	Poor	$23-31,000
Honda Pilot	158	8	Very Good	Good	Very Poor	Poor	Very Poor	$29-42,000
Hyundai Santa Fe	162			Good	Very Good	Very Poor	Poor	$30-41,000
Hyundai Santa Fe Sport	163	7	Good	Good	Very Good	Poor		$25-38,000
Infiniti QX60	170	3	Average	Good	Good	Poor	Poor	$42-53,000
Jeep Cherokee	172	5	Average	Good	Poor	Poor	Very Poor	$23-31,000
Jeep Grand Cherokee	174	4	Average	Good	Poor	Very Poor	Very Poor	$30-47,000
Kia Sorento	183	6	Good	Average	Very Good	Poor	Poor	$26-45,000
Land Rvr RRover Sport	188			Average	Good	Very Poor	Good	$64-93,000
Lexus RX	196	5	Average	Very Good	Good	Poor	Good	$41-53,000
Mazda CX-9	201			Average	Very Poor	Poor		$31-44,000
Merc.-Benz GLE-Class	212			Very Good	Poor	Very Poor	Very Good	$52-101,000
Mitsubishi Outlander	218	4	Average	Average	Very Good	Average	Very Poor	$23-31,000
Nissan Murano	227	4	Poor	Average	Very Poor	Poor	Average	$29-40,000
Nissan Pathfinder	228	2	Average	Poor	Very Poor	Poor	Very Poor	$29-43,000
Nissan Rogue	230	2	Very Poor	Average	Very Poor	Average	Good	$23-30,000
Porsche Macan	234			Good	Average	Very Poor	Very Good	$47-76,000
Subaru Outback	241	7	Very Good	Good	Poor	Average	Poor	$25-34,000
Tesla Model X	243			Very Good	Very Good	Very Good		$88-138,000
Volvo XC60	268			Average	Good	Average		$36-51,000
Volvo XC70	269			Poor	Good	Average	Average	$37-48,000
Large SUV								
BMW X6	101			Very Good	Very Good	Very Poor	Poor	$61-102,000
Buick Enclave	103	6	Very Good	Poor	Good	Very Poor	Poor	$39-49,000
Cadillac Escalade	123	5	Very Good	Good	Average	Very Poor	Poor	$47-65,000
Cadillac Escalade ESV	122	4	Average	Good	Average	Very Poor	Poor	$49-67,000
Chevrolet Suburban	122	4	Average	Average	Average	Very Poor	Poor	$49-67,000
Chevrolet Tahoe	123	5	Very Good	Average	Average	Very Poor	Poor	$47-65,000
Chevrolet Traverse	124	6	Very Good	Poor	Average	Very Poor	Poor	$31-44,000
Ford Expedition	139	7	Very Good	Poor	Poor	Very Poor	Good	$41-66,000
Ford Flex	143			Poor	Poor	Very Poor	Very Poor	$30-43,000
GMC Acadia	150			Good	Average	Very Poor		$32-46,000
GMC Yukon	123	5	Very Good	Average	Average	Very Poor	Poor	$47-65,000
GMC Yukon XL	122	4	Average	Average	Average	Very Poor	Poor	$49-67,000
Infiniti QX80	171			Good	Good	Very Poor	Average	$63-88,000
Land Rvr Range Rover	186			Average	Good	Very Poor	Average	$84-139,000
Lexus GX	192			Very Good	Good	Very Poor	Very Good	$51-62,000

Vehicle	Pg #	Overall Rating	Combined Crash Test Rating	Safety Features Rating	Warranty Rating	Fuel Economy Rating	Complaint Rating	Price Range
Large SUV (cont.)								
Lincoln Navigator	139	7	Very Good	Poor	Poor	Very Poor	Good	$41-66,000
Merc.-Benz GL-Class	211			Very Good	Poor	Poor	Very Good	$63-119,000
Nissan Armada	222			Good	Very Poor	Very Poor		$44-59,000
Toyota 4Runner	244	2	Very Poor	Average	Very Poor	Very Poor	Very Good	$33-43,000
Toyota Highlander	250	7	Very Good	Very Good	Very Poor	Very Poor	Very Good	$29-50,000
Toyota Sequoia	255			Average	Very Poor	Very Poor	Good	$44-64,000
Volvo XC90	270			Very Good	Good	Poor	Very Poor	$43-70,000
Compact Pickup								
Chevrolet Colorado	113	3	Poor	Poor	Average	Poor	Poor	$20-34,000
GMC Canyon	113	3	Poor	Poor	Average	Poor	Poor	$20-34,000
Nissan Frontier	223			Very Poor	Very Poor	Very Poor	Average	$18-34,000
Toyota Tacoma	257	2	Very Poor	Average	Very Poor	Very Poor	Average	$24-35,000
Standard Pickup								
Chevrolet Silverado	119	5	Good	Poor	Average	Very Poor	Good	$27-54,000
Ford F-150	141	8	Very Good	Average	Poor	Very Poor	Good	$26-56,000
GMC Sierra	151	5	Good	Poor	Average	Very Poor	Average	$28-55,000
Nissan Titan	232			Very Poor	Very Poor	Very Poor	Average	$35-55,000
Ram 1500	235	4	Average	Very Poor	Very Poor	Very Poor	Poor	$26-52,000
Toyota Tundra	258			Good	Very Poor	Very Poor	Very Good	$30-50,000

BEST BETS

 ollowing is our list of the highest rated 2017 vehicles in each size category. The ratings are based on expected performance in nine important categories–Combined Crash Rating, Safety Features, Rollover, Preventive Maintenance, Repair Costs, Warranty, Fuel Economy, Complaints, and Insurance Costs–with the heaviest emphasis placed on safety. (See box on page 6.)

CHEVROLET SONIC — SUBCOMPACT

Combo Crash Tests	9	Warranty	6
Safety Features	7	Fuel Economy	7
Rollover	5	Complaints	5
PM	10	Insurance	1
Repair Costs	9	**OVERALL RATING**	**9**

Page 120

KIA SOUL — SUBCOMPACT

Combo Crash Tests	9	Warranty	10
Safety Features	5	Fuel Economy	5
Rollover	4	Complaints	5
PM	5	Insurance	1
Repair Costs	9	**OVERALL RATING**	**8**

Page 184

AUDI A3 — COMPACT

Combo Crash Tests	6	Warranty	7
Safety Features	8	Fuel Economy	6
Rollover	7	Complaints	7
PM	1	Insurance	8
Repair Costs	5	**OVERALL RATING**	**7**

Page 85

BMW 3 SERIES — COMPACT

Combo Crash Tests	7	Warranty	9
Safety Features	7	Fuel Economy	6
Rollover	8	Complaints	7
PM	5	Insurance	5
Repair Costs	2	**OVERALL RATING**	**7**

Page 93

BUICK VERANO — COMPACT

Combo Crash Tests 10	Warranty 8
Safety Features 8	Fuel Economy 5
Rollover 6	Complaints 6
PM 8	Insurance 8
Repair Costs 7	**OVERALL RATING . . 10**

Page 107

TOYOTA PRIUS — COMPACT

Combo Crash Tests 5	Warranty 2
Safety Features 8	Fuel Economy 10
Rollover 7	Complaints 6
PM 9	Insurance 5
Repair Costs 5	**OVERALL RATING . . . 7**

Page 251

ACURA TLX — INTERMEDIATE

Combo Crash Tests 10	Warranty 6
Safety Features 9	Fuel Economy 4
Rollover 8	Complaints 1
PM 5	Insurance 10
Repair Costs 6	**OVERALL RATING . . . 9**

Page 84

CHRYSLER 200 — INTERMEDIATE

Combo Crash Tests 8	Warranty 4
Safety Features 9	Fuel Economy 6
Rollover 7	Complaints 1
PM 9	Insurance 8
Repair Costs 8	**OVERALL RATING . . . 9**

Page 127

HONDA ACCORD — INTERMEDIATE

Combo Crash Tests 9	Warranty 2
Safety Features 7	Fuel Economy 8
Rollover 8	Complaints 6
PM 10	Insurance 5
Repair Costs 7	**OVERALL RATING . . . 9**

Page 152

HYUNDAI SONATA
BEST CAR BET   INTERMEDIATE

Page 164

Combo Crash Tests 9	Warranty 10
Safety Features 7	Fuel Economy 7
Rollover 7	Complaints 5
PM 6	Insurance 3
Repair Costs 9	**OVERALL RATING . . 10**

MAZDA MAZDA6
BEST CAR BET   INTERMEDIATE

Page 203

Combo Crash Tests 8	Warranty 1
Safety Features 6	Fuel Economy 8
Rollover 7	Complaints 4
PM 7	Insurance 5
Repair Costs 9	**OVERALL RATING . . . 8**

TOYOTA AVALON
BEST CAR BET   INTERMEDIATE

Page 246

Combo Crash Tests 8	Warranty 2
Safety Features 10	Fuel Economy 4
Rollover 7	Complaints 6
PM 6	Insurance 8
Repair Costs 4	**OVERALL RATING . . . 7**

TOYOTA CAMRY
BEST CAR BET   INTERMEDIATE

Page 247

Combo Crash Tests 7	Warranty 2
Safety Features 10	Fuel Economy 7
Rollover 6	Complaints 9
PM 6	Insurance 5
Repair Costs 4	**OVERALL RATING . . . 8**

CADILLAC XTS
BEST CAR BET   LARGE

Page 111

Combo Crash Tests 10	Warranty 9
Safety Features 8	Fuel Economy 3
Rollover 5	Complaints 7
PM 2	Insurance 8
Repair Costs 4	**OVERALL RATING . . . 9**

TESLA MODEL S — LARGE

Page 242

Combo Crash Tests 10	Warranty 10
Safety Features 10	Fuel Economy. 10
Rollover 10	Complaints 1
PM 5	Insurance 5
Repair Costs. 5	**OVERALL RATING. . 10**

HONDA ODYSSEY — MINIVAN

Page 157

Combo Crash Tests 8	Warranty 2
Safety Features 7	Fuel Economy. 3
Rollover 5	Complaints 5
PM 9	Insurance 10
Repair Costs. 8	**OVERALL RATING. . . 8**

ACURA RDX — SMALL SUV

Page 83

Combo Crash Tests 10	Warranty 6
Safety Features 8	Fuel Economy. 3
Rollover 3	Complaints 5
PM 5	Insurance 10
Repair Costs. 6	**OVERALL RATING. . . 9**

BUICK ENCORE — SMALL SUV

Page 104

Combo Crash Tests 9	Warranty 8
Safety Features 8	Fuel Economy. 5
Rollover 2	Complaints 9
PM 8	Insurance 8
Repair Costs. 8	**OVERALL RATING. . 10**

CHEVROLET TRAX — SMALL SUV

Page 125

Combo Crash Tests 9	Warranty 6
Safety Features 8	Fuel Economy. 5
Rollover 2	Complaints 9
PM 4	Insurance 8
Repair Costs. 5	**OVERALL RATING. . . 8**

FORD ESCAPE — BEST CAR Book BET — SMALL SUV

Page 138

Combo Crash Tests	8	Warranty	4
Safety Features	7	Fuel Economy	5
Rollover	2	Complaints	5
PM	6	Insurance	5
Repair Costs	9	**OVERALL RATING**	**7**

KIA SPORTAGE — BEST CAR Book BET — SMALL SUV

Page 185

Combo Crash Tests	7	Warranty	10
Safety Features	7	Fuel Economy	4
Rollover	4	Complaints	9
PM	5	Insurance	5
Repair Costs	7	**OVERALL RATING**	**8**

ACURA MDX — BEST CAR Book BET — MID-SIZE SUV

Page 82

Combo Crash Tests	9	Warranty	6
Safety Features	10	Fuel Economy	2
Rollover	3	Complaints	2
PM	5	Insurance	10
Repair Costs	6	**OVERALL RATING**	**8**

FORD EDGE — BEST CAR Book BET — MID-SIZE SUV

Page 137

Combo Crash Tests	10	Warranty	4
Safety Features	9	Fuel Economy	4
Rollover	3	Complaints	4
PM	7	Insurance	8
Repair Costs	5	**OVERALL RATING**	**8**

HONDA PILOT — BEST CAR Book BET — MID-SIZE SUV

Page 158

Combo Crash Tests	9	Warranty	2
Safety Features	7	Fuel Economy	3
Rollover	3	Complaints	2
PM	10	Insurance	10
Repair Costs	7	**OVERALL RATING**	**8**

HYUNDAI SANTA FE SPORT — MID-SIZE SUV

Page 163

Combo Crash Tests	7	Warranty	10
Safety Features	7	Fuel Economy	3
Rollover	3	Complaints	5
PM	4	Insurance	5
Repair Costs	8	**OVERALL RATING...**	**7**

SUBARU OUTBACK — MID-SIZE SUV

Page 241

Combo Crash Tests	10	Warranty	3
Safety Features	8	Fuel Economy	7
Rollover	2	Complaints	3
PM	1	Insurance	1
Repair Costs	10	**OVERALL RATING...**	**7**

TOYOTA HIGHLANDER — LARGE SUV

Page 250

Combo Crash Tests	9	Warranty	2
Safety Features	9	Fuel Economy	2
Rollover	3	Complaints	10
PM	8	Insurance	8
Repair Costs	1	**OVERALL RATING...**	**7**

FORD F-150 — STANDARD PICKUP

Page 141

Combo Crash Tests	10	Warranty	4
Safety Features	5	Fuel Economy	2
Rollover	2	Complaints	8
PM	8	Insurance	8
Repair Costs	7	**OVERALL RATING...**	**8**

CRASH TESTS

Safety is likely the most important factor that most of us consider when choosing a new car. In the past, evaluating safety was difficult. Now, thanks to the information in *The Car Book*, it's much easier to pick a safe vehicle. The bottom line: For the greatest protection, you'll want the maximum number of safety features (See Safety Checklist, pages 78-80) and good crash test results (the following tables).

A key factor in occupant protection is how well the car protects you in a crash. This depends on its ability to absorb the force of the impact rather than transfer it to the occupant.

In the frontal test, the vehicle impacts a solid barrier at 35 mph. In the side test, a moving barrier is crashed into the side of the vehicle at 38.5 mph. A second side test simulates hitting a tree or roadside pole by smashing a vehicle onto a vertical pole at the driver's door at 20 mph. The only occupant in this side pole test is a small female dummy in the driver seat.

The dummies measure the impact on the head, chest, neck and thighs.

Not all 2017 vehicles have undergone a crash test. The good news is that by carrying forward previous tests from cars that haven't changed, we have results for 136 2017 models. The bad news is that there are 61 models for which we don't have crash test results.

How the Cars are Rated: The combined crash test ratings are based on the *relative* performance of the 2017 vehicles tested to date. *This is a big difference from the government's "star" program.* Rather than large groups of undifferentiated vehicles in the government's star ratings, *The Car Book* rates them from best to worst. This means that those manufacturers really working on safety each year will rise to the top.

The first column provides *The Car Book's* Combined Crash Test Rating. The cars are rated from 10 Best to 1 Worst. The front is weighted 60%, the side 36%, and the pole test 4% with results compared among all new 2017 crash tests to date.

Next are the individual front and side tests. Again, relative to all other 2017 vehicles with crash test results, we indicate if the vehicle was Very Good, Good, Average, Poor or Very Poor. For side tests, the cars are rated separately from the trucks. Because of their construction, the dynamics of a side test are different in cars and light trucks.

The next five columns indicate the likelihood of the occupant sustaining a life-threatening injury. The percent likelihood is listed for the driver and front passenger in the front test, the driver and rear passenger in the side test, and the driver in the side pole test. Lower percentages mean a lower likelihood of being seriously injured if there is a crash test of this type. This information is taken directly from the government's analysis of the crash test results.

USING CRASH TEST DATA

TIP

One of the most important results of our being the first to publish crash test data, and later develop our relative comparative ratings, is that it has put enormous pressure on the manufacturers to improve. Whereas years ago, when competition was based on style and horsepower, thanks to *The Car Book*, today's manufacturers are feverously competing on safety features. While the most important factors in evaluating the safety of today's vehicles are crash test performance and advanced safety features, size and weight do play a role. It is important to compare vehicles in the size classes that follow. For example, in a frontal collision between a subcompact and SUV rated 'Very Good," you'll be better off in the SUV. Nevertheless, selecting the best performers in whatever size class you are buying, is fundamental to protecting yourself. And remember, these tests are conducted with fully belted dummies, if you are not wearing your safety belt, then test results do not really apply.

Crash Tests

Crash Test Performance (10=Best, 1=Worst)	Combined Car Book Crash Test Rating	Test Type	Car Book Crash Test Rating-Index (Lower numbers are better)	Likelihood of Life Threatening Injury				
				Front Fixed Barrier		Side Moving Barrier		Side Pole
				Front Driver	Front Pass.	Side Driver	Side Pass.	Pole Driver
Subcompact								
Chevrolet Sonic	9	Front	Very Good-166	8.7%	8.7%			
		Side	Average-113			7.0%	4.6%	7.1%
Chevrolet Spark	2	Front	Very Poor-228	13.6%	10.7%			
		Side	Poor-147			9.2%	6.8%	5.6%
Fiat 500	1	Front	Very Poor-256	11.4%	16.0%			
		Side	Poor-148			5.3%	8.0%	15.8%
Ford Fiesta	4	Front	Average-199	8.2%	12.8%			
		Side	Poor-154			8.9%	8.2%	3.6%
Honda Fit	9	Front	Good-175	9.2%	9.1%			
		Side	Good-85			6.8%	2.5%	3.5%
Hyundai Accent	3	Front	Poor-209	9.2%	12.8%			
		Side	Very Poor-234			8.6%	17.0%	4.3%
Hyundai Veloster	4	Front	Poor-205	12.4%	9.2%			
		Side	Poor-131			6.9%	7.8%	1.5%
Kia Rio	2	Front	Very Poor-230	10.8%	13.7%			
		Side	Very Poor-177			13.5%	7.0%	3.5%
Kia Soul	9	Front	Good-180	7.6%	11.2%			
		Side	Very Good-81			4.7%	4.0%	2.6%
Mini Cooper	4	Front	Average-194	10.7%	9.7%			
		Side	Very Poor-250			7.5%	18.7%	8.6%
Mitsubishi Mirage	2	Front	Poor-218	12.6%	10.5%			
		Side	Very Poor-210			7.5%	11.8%	22.1%
Nissan Versa	1	Front	Very Poor-244	10.2%	15.8%			
		Side	Very Poor-206			11.2%	12.1%	3.5%
Toyota Prius C	3	Front	Poor-206	11.7%	10.1%			
		Side	Very Poor-239			14.7%	12.1%	8.1%
Toyota Yaris	3	Front	Poor-217	9.9%	13.1%			
		Side	Poor-159			7.3%	8.7%	10.1%
Compact								
Acura ILX	5	Front	Poor-209	9.5%	12.5%			
		Side	Good-105			5.6%	4.4%	9.5%
Audi A3	6	Front	Average-197	11.2%	9.6%			
		Side	Average-113			7.0%	5.1%	4.2%
BMW 3 Series	7	Front	Average-194	11.6%	8.9%			
		Side	Good-108			7.9%	4.3%	2.3%

CRASH TESTS

Crash Test Performance (10=Best, 1=Worst)	Combined Car Book Crash Test Rating	Test Type	Car Book Crash Test Rating-Index (Lower numbers are better)	Likelihood of Life Threatening Injury				
				Front Fixed Barrier		Side Moving Barrier		Side Pole
				Front Driver	Front Pass.	Side Driver	Side Pass.	Pole Driver
Compact (cont.)								
Buick Verano	10	Front	Very Good-155	7.5%	8.7%			
		Side	Very Good-75			6.1%	1.9%	4.3%
Cadillac ATS	8	Front	Very Good-162	8.2%	8.7%			
		Side	Poor-138			7.5%	7.4%	4.8%
Dodge Dart	9	Front	Good-188	9.2%	10.6%			
		Side	Very Good-78			4.1%	4.1%	2.4%
Ford C-MAX	4	Front	Poor-212	10.3%	12.2%			
		Side	Poor-129			9.2%	4.1%	9.1%
Ford Focus	9	Front	Good-178	8.4%	10.3%			
		Side	Good-95			6.7%	3.9%	2.6%
Honda Civic	5	Front	Average-197	9.3%	11.5%			
		Side	Poor-153			4.9%	10.0%	9.6%
Hyundai Elantra	3	Front	Poor-211	12.1%	10.3%			
		Side	Poor-163			5.5%	11.7%	4.1%
Kia Forte	3	Front	Poor-208	10.1%	11.9%			
		Side	Poor-156			9.0%	8.4%	2.7%
Lexus IS	4	Front	Very Poor-226	10.8%	13.2%			
		Side	Good-85			5.4%	3.2%	5.9%
Mazda Mazda3	6	Front	Good-185	8.5%	10.9%			
		Side	Poor-119			11.5%	2.4%	2.8%
Mercedes-Benz C-Class	4	Front	Average-203	7.8%	13.6%			
		Side	Very Poor-170			5.7%	12.2%	4.8%
Mitsubishi Lancer	2	Front	Poor-214	9.4%	13.3%			
		Side	Very Poor-199			4.0%	16.4%	5.6%
Nissan Leaf	1	Front	Very Poor-229	9.2%	15.1%			
		Side	Very Poor-215			5.6%	17.0%	5.0%
Nissan Sentra	3	Front	Very Poor-242	11.8%	14.0%			
		Side	Poor-118			6.6%	6.5%	1.7%
Toyota Corolla	5	Front	Poor-217	9.6%	13.4%			
		Side	Good-105			3.6%	6.7%	5.6%
Toyota Prius	5	Front	Average-203	10.3%	11.1%			
		Side	Average-116			6.5%	2.0%	23.2%
Toyota Prius V	7	Front	Poor-211	10.3%	12.0%			
		Side	Very Good-70			4.3%	1.5%	10.5%
Volkswagen Beetle	3	Front	Average-198	9.6%	13.2%			
		Side	Average-116			7.3%	6.0%	5.3%

CRASH TESTS

Crash Test Performance (10=Best, 1=Worst)	Combined Car Book Crash Test Rating	Test Type	Car Book Crash Test Rating-Index (Lower numbers are better)	Likelihood of Life Threatening Injury				
				Front Fixed Barrier		Side Moving Barrier		Side Pole
				Front Driver	Front Pass.	Side Driver	Side Pass.	Pole Driver
Compact (cont.)								
Volkswagen Golf	5	Front	Poor-216	9.8%	11.1%			
		Side	Poor-125			9.1%	3.9%	3.6%
Volkswagen Jetta	7	Front	Average-200	10.0%	11.1%			
		Side	Very Good-78			4.2%	3.9%	3.8%
Intermediate								
Acura TLX	10	Front	Very Good-156	7.3%	8.9%			
		Side	Very Good-58			4.4%	1.7%	3.4%
Audi A6	8	Front	Very Good-163	9.3%	7.7%			
		Side	Average-115			8.1%	3.9%	7.0%
BMW 5 Series	4	Front	Very Poor-233	13.1%	11.7%			
		Side	Good-85			8.4%	0.8%	5.5%
Buick Regal	5	Front	Average-199	9.9%	11.1%			
		Side	Average-116			4.1%	7.8%	4.3%
Cadillac CTS	8	Front	Good-184	8.1%	11.2%			
		Side	Good-102			6.9%	3.3%	7.9%
Chevrolet Camaro	7	Front	Average-201	10.7%	10.5%			
		Side	Very Good-78			5.9%	2.3%	4.7%
Chevrolet Malibu	6	Front	Poor-223	10.4%	13.3%			
		Side	Very Good-73			6.0%	1.2%	6.4%
Chrysler 200	8	Front	Very Good-173	8.3%	9.9%			
		Side	Average-116			4.7%	7.0%	5.9%
Ford Fusion	3	Front	Very Poor-226	8.7%	15.2%			
		Side	Poor-117			6.3%	6.2%	4.1%
Ford Fusion Energi	7	Front	Very Good-154	7.3%	8.7%			
		Side	Poor-158			14.6%	3.6%	4.7%
Ford Mustang	8	Front	Very Good-162	7.0%	9.9%			
		Side	Poor-140			3.3%	10.4%	7.0%
Honda Accord	9	Front	Very Good-169	8.7%	8.9%			
		Side	Good-104			2.9%	7.7%	3.0%
Hyundai Sonata	9	Front	Very Good-147	7.5%	7.8%			
		Side	Average-114			5.8%	6.2%	4.6%
Infiniti Q50	5	Front	Very Poor-246	10.7%	15.6%			
		Side	Very Good-68			6.5%	1.2%	2.6%
Kia Optima	7	Front	Good-175	7.3%	11.0%			
		Side	Poor-128			4.2%	9.3%	2.2%
Lexus ES	8	Front	Good-190	9.5%	10.5%			
		Side	Good-96			5.5%	3.3%	10.5%

CRASH TESTS

Crash Test Performance (10=Best, 1=Worst)	Combined Car Book Crash Test Rating	Test Type	Car Book Crash Test Rating-Index (Lower numbers are better)	Likelihood of Life Threatening Injury				
				Front Fixed Barrier		Side Moving Barrier		Side Pole
				Front Driver	Front Pass.	Side Driver	Side Pass.	Pole Driver
Intermediate (cont.)								
Lincoln MKZ	3	Front	Very Poor-226	8.7%	15.2%			
		Side	Poor-117			6.3%	6.2%	4.1%
Mazda Mazda6	8	Front	Good-185	7.6%	11.7%			
		Side	Good-96			8.2%	2.5%	3.5%
Nissan Altima	7	Front	Very Good-165	7.2%	10.0%			
		Side	Very Poor-189			17.7%	4.4%	4.9%
Nissan Maxima	7	Front	Good-185	8.7%	10.8%			
		Side	Average-111			6.0%	4.3%	11.4%
Subaru Legacy	10	Front	Very Good-161	8.9%	7.9%			
		Side	Very Good-80			3.3%	4.7%	4.0%
Toyota Avalon	8	Front	Average-194	10.1%	10.4%			
		Side	Very Good-63			4.1%	1.2%	9.1%
Toyota Camry	7	Front	Average-195	11.2%	9.4%			
		Side	Good-107			6.1%	3.8%	11.3%
Volkswagen Passat	5	Front	Very Poor-238	12.6%	12.8%			
		Side	Very Good-76			4.4%	3.1%	5.3%
Volvo S60	8	Front	Very Good-157	8.3%	8.1%			
		Side	Poor-153			9.5%	7.6%	3.8%
Large								
Buick LaCrosse	5	Front	Good-188	8.1%	11.6%			
		Side	Very Poor-168			11.6%	7.7%	2.9%
Cadillac XTS	10	Front	Very Good-160	7.6%	9.1%			
		Side	Good-88			4.2%	4.3%	6.7%
Chevrolet Impala	7	Front	Very Good-173	7.5%	10.6%			
		Side	Poor-142			10.1%	6.1%	2.9%
Chrysler 300	2	Front	Very Poor-236	12.7%	12.5%			
		Side	Poor-120			12.9%	0.8%	5.1%
Dodge Challenger	8	Front	Average-204	11.7%	9.8%			
		Side	Very Good-56			4.7%	1.4%	2.6%
Dodge Charger	4	Front	Very Poor-232	14.3%	10.4%			
		Side	Good-110			12.2%	0.6%	3.8%
Ford Taurus	7	Front	Very Good-164	8.4%	8.7%			
		Side	Poor-154			8.3%	8.3%	5.8%
Lincoln MKS	7	Front	Very Good-164	8.4%	8.7%			
		Side	Poor-154			8.3%	8.3%	5.8%
Tesla Model S	10	Front	Good-180	9.4%	9.5%			
		Side	Very Good-58			3.5%	1.5%	7.9%

CRASH TESTS

Crash Test Performance (10=Best, 1=Worst)	Combined Car Book Crash Test Rating	Test Type	Car Book Crash Test Rating-Index (Lower numbers are better)	Likelihood of Life Threatening Injury				
				Front Fixed Barrier		Side Moving Barrier		Side Pole
				Front Driver	Front Pass.	Side Driver	Side Pass.	Pole Driver
Minivan								
Chrysler Pacifica	8	Front	Very Good-159	8.7%	7.9%			
		Side	Poor-93			5.8%	4.3%	3.2%
Honda Odyssey	8	Front	Good-187	9.9%	9.8%			
		Side	Good-57			2.9%	2.3%	5.6%
Kia Sedona	7	Front	Very Good-153	7.7%	8.3%			
		Side	Very Poor-108			10.9%	0.9%	6.5%
Toyota Sienna	6	Front	Average-197	8.6%	12.1%			
		Side	Average-71			2.9%	4.0%	4.5%
Small SUV								
Acura RDX	10	Front	Very Good-149	7.0%	8.5%			
		Side	Good-62			2.2%	2.9%	7.9%
Buick Encore	9	Front	Very Good-165	8.3%	9.0%			
		Side	Average-66			3.3%	3.0%	5.4%
Chevrolet Trax	9	Front	Very Good-165	8.3%	9.0%			
		Side	Average-66			3.3%	3.0%	5.4%
Ford Escape	8	Front	Good-179	8.3%	10.5%			
		Side	Good-60			2.0%	3.5%	5.0%
Honda HR-V	4	Front	Poor-214	11.9%	10.8%			
		Side	Average-70			4.4%	2.6%	5.1%
Hyundai Tucson	4	Front	Poor-210	11.2%	11.1%			
		Side	Average-72			3.7%	1.7%	12.8%
Jeep Compass	1	Front	Very Poor-314	17.4%	17.0%			
		Side	Very Poor-106			9.3%	2.4%	4.8%
Jeep Patriot	1	Front	Very Poor-295	18.6%	13.4%			
		Side	Very Poor-106			4.2%	5.6%	9.4%
Jeep Renegade	3	Front	Poor-207	10.4%	11.6%			
		Side	Very Poor-187			3.8%	15.8%	2.4%
Kia Sportage	7	Front	Average-195	10.9%	9.6%			
		Side	Good-59			3.5%	1.6%	7.4%
Lexus NX	7	Front	Very Good-153	7.7%	8.3%			
		Side	Very Poor-108			10.9%	0.9%	6.5%
Lincoln MKC	3	Front	Poor-213	8.9%	13.7%			
		Side	Poor-84			2.5%	5.8%	3.4%
Mazda CX-5	3	Front	Very Poor-227	7.3%	16.7%			
		Side	Average-64			2.2%	3.4%	7.0%
Mitsubishi Outlander Sport	4	Front	Average-203	10.0%	11.3%			
		Side	Very Poor-97			2.8%	6.3%	6.8%

CRASH TESTS

Crash Test Performance (10=Best, 1=Worst)	Combined Car Book Crash Test Rating	Test Type	Car Book Crash Test Rating-Index (Lower numbers are better)	Likelihood of Life Threatening Injury				
				Front Fixed Barrier		Side Moving Barrier		Side Pole
				Front Driver	Front Pass.	Side Driver	Side Pass.	Pole Driver
Small SUV (cont.)								
Nissan Juke	1	Front	Very Poor-289	12.5%	18.7%			
		Side	Very Poor-185			11.7%	9.1%	4.8%
Subaru Crosstrek	5	Front	Poor-205	10.4%	10.7%			
		Side	Good-56			3.8%	2.8%	12.8%
Subaru Forester	6	Front	Average-200	9.0%	12.7%			
		Side	Poor-82			3.1%	2.6%	2.9%
Toyota RAV4	7	Front	Average-204	10.6%	10.9%			
		Side	Very Good-49			3.2%	1.1%	6.5%
Volkswagen Tiguan	1	Front	Very Poor-287	13.2%	17.9%			
		Side	Poor-86			3.3%	4.2%	10.0%
Mid-Size SUV								
Acura MDX	9	Front	Very Good-168	8.3%	9.2%			
		Side	Average-68			2.5%	4.2%	3.6%
Audi Q5	3	Front	Very Poor-230	14.6%	9.9%			
		Side	Poor-74			2.7%	4.4%	4.9%
BMW X3	6	Front	Good-188	8.8%	11.0%			
		Side	Poor-75			4.9%	3.5%	.9%
BMW X5	8	Front	Good-177	8.9%	9.7%			
		Side	Good-62			2.4%	3.1%	6.7%
Cadillac XT5	4	Front	Average-199	8.2%	12.7%			
		Side	Very Poor-104			4.7%	5.6%	7.2%
Chevrolet Equinox	2	Front	Poor-216	9.5%	13.4%			
		Side	Very Poor-120			11.7%	2.0%	4.5%
Dodge Journey	2	Front	Poor-222	9.6%	14.0%			
		Side	Very Poor-154			5.7%	9.7%	9.1%
Ford Edge	10	Front	Very Good-161	8.3%	8.5%			
		Side	Very Good-53			2.6%	2.7%	2.9%
Ford Explorer	6	Front	Good-183	10.4%	8.8%			
		Side	Poor-94			5.1%	3.5%	9.9%
GMC Terrain	2	Front	Poor-216	9.5%	13.4%			
		Side	Very Poor-120			11.7%	2.0%	4.5%
Honda Pilot	9	Front	Good-189	9.9%	10.0%			
		Side	Very Good-46			2.5%	1.0%	8.1%
Hyundai Santa Fe Sport	7	Front	Good-184	9.2%	10.1%			
		Side	Average-71			3.6%	3.2%	6.3%
Infiniti QX60	6	Front	Average-196	11.2%	9.5%			
		Side	Average-64			4.9%	1.8%	4.2%

CRASH TESTS

Crash Test Performance (10=Best, 1=Worst)	Combined Car Book Crash Test Rating	Test Type	Car Book Crash Test Rating-Index (Lower numbers are better)	Likelihood of Life Threatening Injury				
				Front Fixed Barrier		Side Moving Barrier		Side Pole
				Front Driver	Front Pass.	Side Driver	Side Pass.	Pole Driver
Mid-Size SUV (cont.)								
Jeep Cherokee	5	Front	Very Poor-228	11.2%	13.1%			
		Side	Very Good-45			3.2%	1.7%	1.6%
Jeep Grand Cherokee	6	Front	Good-178	9.4%	9.3%			
		Side	Poor-93			8.3%	2.3%	2.4%
Kia Sorento	7	Front	Good-177	8.8%	9.7%			
		Side	Poor-84			3.2%	5.3%	3.7%
Lexus RX	5	Front	Very Poor-237	14.5%	10.8%			
		Side	Very Good-54			3.1%	2.2%	3.7%
Mitsubishi Outlander	5	Front	Average-195	12.4%	8.0%			
		Side	Poor-91			3.8%	4.7%	7.8%
Nissan Murano	3	Front	Very Poor-261	9.9%	18.0%			
		Side	Average-66			6.1%	0.9%	4.3%
Nissan Pathfinder	6	Front	Average-196	11.2%	9.5%			
		Side	Average-64			4.9%	1.8%	4.2%
Nissan Rogue	1	Front	Very Poor-240	10.5%	15.0%			
		Side	Very Poor-116			6.5%	4.6%	10.4%
Subaru Outback	10	Front	Very Good-161	8.9%	7.9%			
		Side	Very Good-50			2.9%	1.9%	4.0%
Large SUV								
Buick Enclave	9	Front	Good-181	9.6%	9.3%			
		Side	Good-57			2.1%	3.4%	3.8%
Cadillac Escalade		Front	No Index					
		Side	Very Good-45			3.0%	0.4%	8.6%
Cadillac Escalade ESV		Front	No Index					
		Side	Average-69			4.5%	1.0%	12.2%
Chevrolet Suburban	6	Front	Average-195	10.4%	10.2%			
		Side	Average-69			4.5%	1.0%	12.2%
Chevrolet Tahoe	9	Front	Good-185	9.7%	9.7%			
		Side	Very Good-45			3.0%	0.4%	8.6%
Chevrolet Traverse	9	Front	Good-181	9.6%	9.3%			
		Side	Good-57			2.1%	3.4%	3.8%
Ford Expedition	10	Front	Very Good-167	9.1%	8.4%			
		Side	Very Good-37			2.5%	0.5%	6.5%
GMC Yukon	9	Front	Good-185	9.7%	9.7%			
		Side	Very Good-45			3.0%	0.4%	8.6%
GMC Yukon XL	6	Front	Average-195	10.4%	10.2%			
		Side	Average-69			4.5%	1.0%	12.2%
Lincoln Navigator	10	Front	Very Good-167	9.1%	8.4%			
		Side	Very Good-37			2.5%	0.5%	6.5%
Toyota 4Runner	1	Front	Very Poor-255	11.9%	15.5%			
		Side	Poor-88			7.1%	0.9%	11.7%

CRASH TESTS

Crash Test Performance (10=Best, 1=Worst)	Combined Car Book Crash Test Rating	Test Type	Car Book Crash Test Rating-Index (Lower numbers are better)	Likelihood of Life Threatening Injury				
				Front Fixed Barrier		Side Moving Barrier		Side Pole
				Front Driver	Front Pass.	Side Driver	Side Pass.	Pole Driver
Large SUV (cont.)								
Toyota Highlander	9	Front	Good-192	11.2%	9.0%			
		Side	Very Good-45			2.4%	1.1%	7.3%
Compact Pickup								
Chevrolet Colorado	3	Front	Poor-223	10.4%	13.3%			
		Side	Average-73			6.0%	1.2%	6.4%
GMC Canyon	3	Front	Poor-223	10.4%	13.3%			
		Side	Average-73			6.0%	1.2%	6.4%
Toyota Tacoma	1	Front	Very Poor-258	14.2%	13.5%			
		Side	Very Poor-115			10.1%	1.0%	12.7%
Standard Pickup								
Chevrolet Silverado	8	Front	Very Good-156	8.1%	8.1%			
		Side	Poor-80			2.7%	3.7%	11.7%
Ford F-150	10	Front	Very Good-167	8.1%	9.4%			
		Side	Very Good-43			3.6%	0.7%	3.9%
GMC Sierra	8	Front	Very Good-150	8.3%	7.3%			
		Side	Poor-80			2.7%	3.7%	11.7%
Ram 1500	5	Front	Poor-214	10.8%	11.9%			
		Side	Good-59			5.2%	0.3%	7.3%
Toyota Tundra		Front	Very Poor-236	12.0%	13.2%			
		Side	No Index			2.7%		7.5%

CHILD SAFETY

Incorrect Child Safety Seat Installation: Surveys show up to 85 percent of parents do not install their child seats properly. Incorrect installation of a child safety seat can deny the child lifesaving protection and may even contribute to further injuring the child. Read the installation instructions carefully. If you have any questions about the correct installation in your particular car, go to www.safercar.gov/parents. There you will find a list of inspection stations near you where you can go for a free check up and advice by trained experts.

Child Safety Seat Recalls: Manufacturers are required to put address cards in child seat packages. Mail the registration card as soon as you open the box! You can also register your own seat at www.safercars.gov/parents for notification about recalls on your particular seat(s).These are the only ways you will receive notification of a seat recall. Keep a copy of the manufacturer's address and contact the manufacturer if you move. To find out if the seat you are using has ever been recalled go to www-odi.nhtsa.dot.gov/owners/SearchSafety Issues. You can also contact the Auto Safety Hotline at 800-424-9393.

Seat Belts for Kids: How long should young children use car seats? For children, a car seat is twice as effective in preventing injury as an adult lap and shoulder harness, so use it for as long as possible. Most children can start using seat belts at 4'9" or tall enough for the shoulder belt to cross the chest, not the neck. The lap section of the belt should be snug and as low on the hips as possible. If the shoulder belt crosses the face or neck, use a booster seat.

AUTOMATIC SAFETY PROTECTION

The concept of automatic safety protection is not new. Automatic fire sprinklers in public buildings, oxygen masks in airplanes, purification of drinking water, and pasteurization of milk are all commonly accepted forms of automatic safety protection. Airbags and other new safety features provide automatic crash protection in cars.

Automatic crash protection protects people from what is called the "second collision," when the occupant collides with the interior of the vehicle. Because the "second collision" occurs in less than a tenth of a second, providing automatic, rather than manual, protection dramatically improves the chances of escaping injury.

Automatic crash protection comes in two basic forms, airbags and automatic control of safety features.

Since airbags were introduced over 30 years ago, they have been so successful in saving lives that car makers now include a variety of types which deploy from as many as 10 different areas of the interior.

The automatic control of safety features was first introduced with anti-lock brakes. Today, Electronic Stability Control (ESC) and other automatic functions such as Collision Avoidance Braking and Lane Departure Warnings are improving the safety of new cars.

Electronic Stability Control (ESC) takes advantage of anti-lock brake technology and helps minimize the loss of control. Each car maker will have its own name for this feature, but they all work in a similar fashion.

ESC, which is now required in all light vehicles, uses speed sensors on each wheel to determine if one or more of the wheels is locking up or skidding. ESC then uses these speed sensors, and a unit that determines the steering angle, to monitor what's happening with the vehicle. A special control device measures the steering and rotation of the tires in order to detect when a vehicle is about to go in a direction different from the one indicated by the steering wheel—or out of control! This will typically occur during a hard turn or on slippery surfaces. The control unit will sense whether the car is over-steering (turning sharper than you intended resulting in the back wheels slipping sideways) or under-steering (continuing to move forward despite your intended turn). When either of these events occur, the control unit will automatically apply the brakes to the appropriate wheels to correct the situation and, in some cases, automatically slow down the engine.

ESC will not keep the vehicle under control in severely out of control situations nor does it work as well on curvey roads as on straight roads. Nevertheless, according to the Insurance Institute for Highway Safety, ESC can reduce the chance of a single vehicle crash by over 50% and is particularly effective in reducing rollovers. Its benefit is that it will prevent more typical losses of control from escalating into a crash. For more details on key automatic safety features, see pages 78-80.

⚠ TELEMATICS ⚠

Telematic systems are subscription-based services ($100-$300 per year) that use a combination of cellular technology and global positioning systems to provide a variety of safety and convenience features. The main safety feature is automatic crash notification (ACN) which connects the vehicle's occupants to a call center that directs emergency medical teams to the car. ACN is activated by pressing a button on the dash or rear view mirror or automatically activates if the airbag deploys. The call center receives the exact location of your vehicle and notifies a local emergency response team. This can reduce the time it takes for an emergency team to reach your vehicle. Other safety features can include roadside assistance, remote door unlocking, stolen vehicle tracking, and driving directions.

Caution! Some manufacturers are adding cell phone capability to the ACN system. Talking on the ACN, or any cell phone, while driving increases the risk of a crash by 4 times—about the same effect as drinking and driving.

WHAT'S COMING IN THE FUTURE

CRASHWORTHINESS AND OCCUPANT PROTECTION

Among the great successes in auto safety are the improved occupant protection from air bags and better designed safety belts. Recently, new regulations and technologies have resulted in a dramatic reduction in rollover casualties. Rollovers, especially SUVs and pickups, had been responsible for one third of all road fatalities.

Today, all new light vehicles under 10,000 pounds have electronic stability control systems to keep them under better control, much stronger roofs, and side curtain air bags with improved designs to control ejection even when one is not wearing a safety belt. As a consequence, rollover fatalities in recent models have dropped by about 70%.

REAR END COLLISIONS

Although the crashworthiness of new vehicles is dramatically better than in cars of the past, there is still a problem in rear impacts. The front seat and backs of some vehicles are still so weak that they will collapse and cause even belted occupants to slide into the rear seat or even out the back window when a vehicle is hit from behind. Children in the rear seat – which is where they should be – are, tragically, right in the path of a collapsing front seat. While it is important to carry children in the rear seat for their safety, if possible the child should be placed behind an unoccupied seat or behind the seat occupied by the smallest adult.

Research and testing has shown how to design seating systems that can protect both the people in these seats, and the kids sitting behind them. Unfortunately, we have little data on which vehicles have strong seatbacks. We do know that Mercedes-Benz and BMW vehicles do have strong seatbacks. The Insurance Institute for Highway Safety (iihs.org) has ratings of head restraints in some vehicles for rear impact safety of a seat occupant that can differentiate relatively safe from unsafe vehicles in rear impacts.

WHAT'S NEXT?

Three major changes are occurring in motor vehicle design. First, the fuel economy standards are becoming more rigorous. Cars in 2025 will have to go twice as far on a gallon of gas as they did only a few years ago. Second, advances in electronics, sensors and computing power are being used to both improve safety and take over more of the driving. Third, electric vehicle are breaking into showrooms.

While current safety improvements have been to protect people when crashes occur, most future technology will be devoted to reducing the potential that a crash will even occur. Advanced sensors, electronics and computers will either warn a driver of a potential collision or actually take over control of the vehicle to avoid a crash.

Unquestionably, the self-driving car is coming, but today's vehicles are already "computers on wheels". Computers control emissions, transmissions, crash sensing, braking and many other critical actions. Manufacturers now offer systems that not only *warn* about vehicles in your blind spot, inadvertent lane changing or upcoming crashes, but actually *take action* to avoid collisions.

Lane Keeping Assist monitors the location of the vehicle within a lane and makes an automatic correction if the vehicle drifts out of the center. It also warns if a driver attempts to change lanes when it is not safe to do so.

Smart cruise control, which can vary travel speeds automatically according to traffic conditions, is becoming common.

Automatic braking, that will slow or stop a car when a potential rear end collision or pedestrian is sensed, is available in many cars.

Because of the popularity of these life-saving devices, manufacturers are rushing systems, with varying degrees of effectiveness and reliability, to market. Both NHTSA and IIHS are developing tests and ratings for the performance of such systems. For some of these features, back up cameras, lane changing and forward crash warnings, NHTSA has voluntary standards which define good performance. We've indicated which of these features do and do not meet the government performance standards on the car rating pages.

The good news is that more and more of this technology is becoming available in the cars most of us buy. Unfortunately, too many times these important safety features come with options you may not want, but have to pay for, to get the safety feature. Nevertheless, whether buying for yourself or your new teenage driver, we believe taking advantage of the safety features in today's new vehicles is critically important.

ROLLOVER

Until a few years ago, more than 10,000 people died in rollovers every year. Half of these casualties were thrown out of the vehicle during the rollover and many others suffered head and neck injuries from collapsing roofs. The auto industry denied that anything could be done to reduce this toll even though the 2003 Volvo XC90 had several features that offered rollover occupant protection.

The risk that a vehicle will rollover is a significant safety challenge, especially with sport utility vehicles pickups and vans. Because of their relatively high center of gravity, they are less stable than most passenger cars. As a result, they are more likely to roll over on a sharp turn or if they go out of control.

There are a few reasons why rollovers occur: drifting off the side of the road where the vehicle "trips" on an obstacle and rolls; responding with a major steering correction in this situation; or, over-steering–making too sharp a turn and having your rear wheels skid out, turning the vehicle sideways.

As a result of a major campaign by the Center for Auto Safety and others, the government is finally requiring new vehicles to have certain rollover protections including:

Electronic Stability Control: ESC automatically applies braking to wheels selectively when a vehicle is on the verge of going out of control. (See page 28.) This can keep the vehicle from sliding and rotating sideways, making it vulnerable to rolling over. ESC has substantially reduced the likelihood of a rollover.

Ejection Control: This feature is designed to keep passengers in the car, even if they are not wearing their safety belts. Ejection control includes improved designs that keep the glass in place even when the window breaks and window curtain air bags that cover the side windows in a rollover. These air curtains cushion the occupant and reduce the chances that they will be ejected.

Roof Strength: Until recently, roof strength requirements were weak and few manufacturers designed roofs that could hold up when a vehicle rolled over. Prodded by the rollover roof crush tests sponsored by the Center for Auto Safety, the government doubled the force that a roof must sustain when the front corner is pushed down at an angle, and required that the test be conducted sequentially on both sides. The result: Most new vehicle roofs can withstand a force of more than four times the weight of the vehicle.

Padding in the Roof: This standard requires energy absorbing padding and helps reduce the likelihood of a concussion or other head injury if your head strikes the roof.

ROLLOVER ESTIMATES

Electronic stability control has dramatically reduced the incidences of rollover by preventing a vehicle from getting into a position where it could rollover. Nevertheless, there are still situations in which a vehicle could find itself in a position where a rollover could occur. A rollover position generally occurs when the vehicle turns sideways and continues to move in a sideways direction. When the ESC fails to prevent a vehicle from getting in this position, the likelihood of an actual rollover is directly related to the vehicle's center of gravity. The higher the center of gravity, the more likely the vehicle is to rollover when in a rollover position.

To approximate a vehicle's center of gravity, the government uses a formula, called the Static Stability Index. It is based on the ratio of the height of the car's center of gravity to half of its track width (the lateral distance between two wheels). Using the SSI the government further develops a "risk of rollover" percentage. The higher the percentage, the more likely the vehicle is to rollover, if in a rollover position.

You can't use this information to exactly predict rollovers. However, all things being equal, if two vehicles are in the same rollover situation, the one with the lower percentage is less likely to roll over. Because this formula doesn't consider such things as driver behavior, vehicle weight, and the effectiveness of the vehicle's ESC, experts do not believe it tells the whole story. We agree, and have urged the government to provide an even better rollover rating system.

The good news: In buying a new vehicle, you can be reasonably confident, thanks to the new standards, that it will have a reasonable level of rollover resistance and, should it roll over, good protection in most situations.

STATIC STABILITY INDEX

Vehicle	SSI (High=Better)	Chance of Rollover	Vehicle	SSI (High=Better)	Chance of Rollover	Vehicle	SSI (High=Better)	Chance of Rollover
Acura ILX	10.7%	Low	Ford Flex	15.5%*	High	Mercedes-Benz C-Class	11.1%	Moderate
Acura MDX	15.5%	High	Ford Focus	11.6%	Moderate	Mercedes-Benz CLA-Class	10.5%*	Low
Acura RDX	15.5%	High	Ford Fusion	10.9%	Low	Mercedes-Benz E-Class	9.5%*	Low
Acura TLX	9.9%	Low	Ford Fusion Energi	10.9%	Low	Mercedes-Benz GLA-Class	12.1%*	Moderate
Audi A3	10.9%	Low	Ford Mustang	8.0%	Very Low	Mercedes-Benz GLC-Class	16.4%*	High
Audi A4	9.9%*	Low	Ford Taurus	11.3%	Moderate	Mercedes-Benz GL-Class	17.4%*	Very High
Audi A5	8.6%	Very Low	GMC Acadia	15.9%	High	Mercedes-Benz GLE Class	16.4%*	High
Audi A6	9.0%	Very Low	GMC Sierra	17.4%	Very High	Mercedes-Benz S-Class	9.9%*	Low
Audi Q3	13.3%	Moderate	Honda Accord	9.9%	Low	Mini Cooper	11.1%	Moderate
Audi Q5	15.1%	High	Honda Civic	9.3%	Very Low	Mini Countryman	13.6%*	High
Audi Q7	14.3%*	High	Honda CR-V	16.9%*	High	Mitsubishi Lancer	12.1%	Moderate
BMW 2 Series	10.1%*	Low	Honda Fit	14.7%	High	Mitsubishi Mirage	16.4%	High
BMW 3 Series	9.5%	Low	Honda HR-V	13.3%	Moderate	Mitsubishi Outlander	16.4%	High
BMW 4 Series	8.9%*	Very Low	Honda Odyssey	12.7%	Moderate	Mitsubishi Outlander Sport	16.9%	High
BMW 5 Series	9.3%	Very Low	Honda Pilot	16.4%	High	Nissan 370Z	7.9%	Very Low
BMW 7 Series	9.7%*	Low	Hyundai Accent	12.4%	Moderate	Nissan Altima	10.3%	Low
BMW i3	13.0%*	Moderate	Hyundai Azera	9.9%*	Low	Nissan Armada	21.2%*	Very High
BMW X1	13.6%*	High	Hyundai Elantra	10.7%	Low	Nissan Frontier	19.8%*	Very High
BMW X3	16.4%	High	Hyundai Santa Fe	14.3%*	High	Nissan Juke	15.1%	High
BMW X5	17.9%	Very High	Hyundai Santa Fe Sport	15.1%	High	Nissan Leaf	10.9%	Low
BMW X6	15.9%*	High	Hyundai Sonata	10.5%	Low	Nissan Maxima	9.5%	Low
Buick Cascada	9.7%*	Low	Hyundai Tucson	16.4%	High	Nissan Murano	15.5%	High
Buick Enclave	15.5%	High	Hyundai Veloster	10.5%	Low	Nissan Pathfinder	17.9%	Very High
Buick Encore	17.9%	Very High	Infiniti Q50	9.7%	Low	Nissan Quest	15.1%*	High
Buick LaCrosse	9.9%*	Low	Infiniti Q70	13%*	Moderate	Nissan Rogue	16.4%	High
Buick Regal	10.9%	Low	Infiniti QX50	14.3%*	High	Nissan Sentra	11.8%	Moderate
Buick Verano	11.3%	Moderate	Infiniti QX60	17.9%	Very High	Nissan Versa	14.3%	High
Cadillac ATS	10.1%	Low	Infiniti QX80	19.1%	Very High	Ram 1500	21.9%	Very High
Cadillac CTS	10.1%	Low	Jeep Cherokee	17.4%	Very High	Smart ForTwo	16.4%*	High
Cadillac XT5	15.1%	High	Jeep Compass	18.5%	Very High	Subaru Crosstrek	15.1%	High
Cadillac XTS	11.8%	Moderate	Jeep Grand Cherokee	20.4%	Very High	Subaru Forester	16.9%	High
Chevrolet Camaro	8.0%*	Very Low	Jeep Patriot	21.9%	Very High	Subaru Legacy	10.1%	Low
Chevrolet Colorado	21.2%	Very High	Jeep Renegade	17.9%	Very High	Subaru Outback	17.4%	Very High
Chevrolet Corvette	6.6%*	Very Low	Jeep Wrangler	21.2%*	Very High	Tesla Model S	5.7%	Very Low
Chevrolet Cruze	11.1%*	Moderate	Kia Cadenza	11.3%*	Moderate	Tesla Model X	8.3%*	Very Low
Chevrolet Equinox	17.4%	Very High	Kia Forte	10.3%	Low	Toyota 4Runner	24.6%	Very High
Chevrolet Impala	12.1%	Moderate	Kia Optima	9.9%	Low	Toyota 86	7.9%*	Very Low
Chevrolet Malibu	10.3%	Low	Kia Rio	11.6%	Moderate	Toyota Avalon	10.7%	Low
Chevrolet Silverado	17.4%	Very High	Kia Sedona	13.0%	Moderate	Toyota Camry	11.1%	Moderate
Chevrolet Sonic	12.7%	Moderate	Kia Sorento	15.1%	High	Toyota Corolla	11.8%	Moderate
Chevrolet Spark	17.9%	Very High	Kia Soul	14.7%	High	Toyota Corolla iM	10.5%*	Low
Chevrolet Suburban	20.4%	Very High	Kia Sportage	14.7%	High	Toyota Highlander	16.9%	High
Chevrolet Tahoe	21.9%	Very High	Land Rvr Rng Rover	17.4%*	Very High	Toyota Prius	10.7%	Low
Chevrolet Traverse	15.5%	High	Land Rver Rng Rvr Evoque	13.0%*	Moderate	Toyota Prius C	11.8%	Moderate
Chevrolet Trax	17.9%	Very High	Land Rng Rvr Sport	15.5%*	High	Toyota Prius V	13.6%	High
Chevrolet Volt	10.1%*	Low	Lexus CT	11.3%*	Moderate	Toyota RAV4	16.9%	High
Chrysler 200	10.7%	Low	Lexus ES	11.1%	Moderate	Toyota Sequoia	17.4%*	Very High
Chrysler 300	11.3%	Moderate	Lexus GS	10.1%*	Low	Toyota Sienna	14.0%	High
Chrysler Pacifica	11.6%	Moderate	Lexus GX	10.1%*	Low	Toyota Tacoma	14.7%	High
Dodge Challenger	11.1%	Moderate	Lexus IS	9.5%	Low	Toyota Tundra	19.8%	Very High
Dodge Charger	10.1%	Low	Lexus NX	15.9%	High	Toyota Yaris	13.6%	High
Dodge Dart	10.7%	Low	Lexus RC	9.0%*	Very Low	Toyota Yaris iA	12.4%	Moderate
Dodge Journey	17.9%	Very High	Lexus RX	16.9%	High	Volkswagen Beetle	10.5%	Low
Fiat 500	14.3%	High	Lincoln Continental	10.1%*	:pw	Volkswagen Golf	13.3%	Moderate
Fiat 500X	14.3%*	High	Lincoln MKC	16.9%	High	Volkswagen Jetta	11.1%	Moderate
Ford C-MAX	14.7%	High	Lincoln MKZ	10.9%	Low	Volkswagen Passat	10.7%	Low
Ford Edge	15.5%	High	Mazda CX-5	17.4%	Very High	Volkswagen Tiguan	17.4%	Very High
Ford Escape	19.1%	Very High	Mazda CX-9	15.5%*	High	Volvo S60	10.1%	Low
Ford Expedition	19.8%	Very High	Mazda Mazda3	10.5%	Low	Volvo V60	10.7%*	Low
Ford Explorer	17.4%	Very High	Mazda Mazda6	10.3%	Low	Volvo XC60	15.1%*	High
Ford F-150	19.1%	Very High	Mazda MX-5 Miata	7.5%*	Very Low	Volvo XC70	13.0%*	Moderate
Ford Fiesta	14.3%	High	Mercedes-Benz B-Class	14.5%*	High	*Calculated		

As gas prices bounce up and down, regular driving still takes a big bite out of our pocketbooks. Even at today's lower gas prices, the average household spends $1,500 a year on gasonline. The good news is that higher fuel efficiency standards are forcing car companies to provide more fuel efficient vehicles. Buying right and practicing more fuel efficient driving will make a huge difference in your vehicle's operating costs. With the current low gas prices, many consumers are buying fuel inefficient vehicles. Beware, when gas prices go back up, and they will, you'll be stuck with a budget-busting gas guzzler.

Using the EPA ratings is the best way to incorporate fuel efficiency in selecting a new car. By comparing these ratings, even among cars of the same size, you'll find that fuel efficiency varies greatly. One compact car might get 36 miles per gallon (mpg) while another compact gets only 22 mpg. If you drive 15,000 miles a year and you pay $2.15 per gallon for fuel, the 36 mpg car will save you $570 a year over the "gas guzzler." Imagine what's going to happen when gas prices go back up!

Today, thanks to changes in the way the EPA estimates miles per gallon, the numbers more closely match what you can expect from the vehicle.

Octane Ratings: Once you've purchased your car, you'll be faced with choosing the right gasoline. Oil companies spend millions of dollars trying to get you to buy so-called higher performance or high octane fuels. Using high octane fuel can add considerably to your gas bill, and the vast majority of vehicles do not need it. Check your owner's manual and only use the recommended octane rating, which is usually 87. Very few vehicles require "premium" gasoline.

The octane rating of a gasoline is not a measure of power or quality. It is simply a measure of the gas' resistance to engine knock, which is the pinging sound you hear when the air and fuel mixture in your engine ignites prematurely during acceleration.

Your engine may knock when accelerating a heavily loaded car uphill or when the humidity is low. This is normal and does not mean you need a higher-octane gasoline. When buying, consider the impact of a high octane gas car. It will increase your fuel costs by around 25%.

FIVE FACTORS AFFECTING FUEL ECONOMY

1. Engine Power: The smaller the engine the better your fuel efficiency. A 10% increase in the size of your engine can increase your fuel consumption rate by 6%. Smaller engines can be cheaper to maintain as well. With new engine designs and turbocharging, manufacturers can get more power out of smaller engines.

2. Transmission: Most automatic transmissions today can achieve as high a fuel economy as a manual transmission. Well-designed transmissions with more gears and continuously variable transmissions will generally achieve better fuel economy.

3. Cruise Control: Using cruise control can save fuel because driving at a constant speed uses less fuel than changing speeds frequently.

4. Hybrids: Most manufacturers offer hybrid vehicles that have both gasoline and electric engines. Hybrids can offer 30% better fuel economy and lower emissions.

5. Electrics: All-electric vehicles can keep you out of the gas station altogether. See our new section on page 271.

TWELVE WAYS TO SAVE MONEY AT THE PUMP

Here are a few simple things you can do that will save you a lot of money. Specific savings are based on gas at $2.15.

1. Pump 'Em Up: 27% of vehicles have tires that are under-inflated. Properly inflated tires can improve mileage by 3%, which is like getting 6 cents off a gallon of gas. Check the label on your door or glove box to find out what the pressure range should be for your tires. Don't use the "max pressure" written on your tire. Electronic gauges are fast, easy to use and accurate. Don't rely on the numbers on the air pump. The good news–all new cars must have a low tire pressure warning on the dash.

2. Check Your Air Filter: A dirty air filter by itself can rob a car by as much as 10% percent of its mileage. If an engine doesn't get enough air, it will burn too much gasoline. Replacing a dirty filter can in effect knock up to 22 cents off a gallon of gas.

3. Straighten Out: Not only does poor wheel alignment cause your tires to wear out faster and cause poor handling, but it can cause your engine to work harder and reduce your fuel efficiency by 10%.

4. Be A Regular: Check your owner's manual. Very, very few cars actually need high-octane gas. Using 87-octane (regular) gas can save you over 28 cents per gallon over mid-grade and 53 cents over premium.

5. Tune Up: A properly tuned engine is a fuel saver. Have a trusted mechanic tune your engine to factory specifications and you could save up to 8 cents a gallon.

6. Check Your Cap: It is estimated that nearly 15% of the cars on the road have broken or missing gasoline caps. This hurts your mileage and can harm the environment by allowing your gasoline to evaporate. Many Ford products have a capless gas filler, which is a great convenience.

7. Don't Speed: A car moving at 55 mph gets better fuel economy than the same car at 65 mph. For every 5 mph you reduce your highway speed, you can reduce fuel consumption by 7%, which is like getting 15 cents off a gallon of gas.

8. Don't Idle: An idling car gets 0 mpg. Cars with larger engines typically waste more gas at idle than cars with smaller engines. If you're stopped for more than a minute, consider turning your engine off. Some new cars do that automatically.

9. Drive Smoother: The smoother your accelerations and decelerations, the better your mileage. A smooth foot can save 38 cents a gallon.

10. Combo Trips: Short trips can be expensive because they usually involve a "cold" vehicle. For the first mile or two before the engine gets warmed up, a cold vehicle only gets 30 to 40% of the mileage it gets at full efficiency. Combine your trips.

11. Lose Weight: For every 100 pounds you carry around, you lose 1 to 2% in fuel efficiency. Remove extra items from your trunk or the rear of your SUV. Empty your roof rack—50% of engine power, traveling at highway speed, is used in overcoming aerodynamic drag or wind resistance.

12. Choose Your Gas Miser: If you own more than one vehicle, choosing to drive the one with better gas mileage will save you money. If you drive 15,000 miles per year, half in a vehicle with 20 mpg and half with a 30 mpg vehicle and switch to driving 75% of your trips in the 30 mpg vehicle, you will save $134.50 annually with gas at $2.15.

FUEL ECONOMY

Get up-to-date information about fuel economy at www.fueleconomy.gov, a website created by the Department of Energy and the EPA. There you'll find the EPA's Fuel Economy Guide, allowing you to compare fuel economy estimates for today's models and back to 1985. You'll also find out about the latest technological advances pertaining to fuel efficiency. The site is extremely useful and easy to navigate. Also, see the Fuel Factor section on our car rating pages.

FUEL ECONOMY MISERS AND GUZZLERS

Because the success of the EPA program depends on consumers' ability to compare the fuel economy ratings easily, we have included key mileage figures on our ratings pages. Listed below are the best and worst of this year's ratings according to annual fuel cost. The complete EPA fuel economy guide is available at www.fueleconomy.gov.

FUEL ECONOMY MISERS AND GUZZLERS			
Vehicle	**Specifications**	**MPG (city/hwy)**	**Annual Fuel Cost**
THE BEST			
Electric Vehicles (EV)*			
BMW I3 BEV	Automatic, RWD	137/111	$550
Chevrolet Bolt EV	Automatic, FWD	128/110	$550
Fiat 500e	Automatic, FWD	121/103	$600
Nissan LEAF	Automatic, FWD	124/101	$600
KiaSoul Electric	Automatic, FWD	120/92	$600
Plug In Hybrid Electric Vehicles (PHEVs)*			
Chevrolet Volt	1.5L, 4 cyl., Continuously Variable, FWD	43/42	$650
Ford Fusion Energi Plug-in Hybrid	2.0L, 4 cyl., Continuously Variable, FWD	43/41	$800
Hyundai Sonata Plug-in Hybrid	2.0L, 4 cyl., 6-sp. Automated Manual, FWD	38/40	$800
Audi A3 e-tron ultra	1.4L, 4 cyl., 6-sp. Automated Manual - Selectable, FWD	33/36	$1,050
Gas			
Toyota Prius Eco	1.8L, 4 cyl., Continuously Variable, FWD	58/53	$578
Toyota Prius	1.8L, 4 cyl., Continuously Variable, FWD	54/50	$618
Honda Accord	2.0L, 4 cyl., Continuously Variable, FWD	49/47	$670
Chevrolet Malibu	1.8L, 4 cyl., Continuously Variable, FWD	49/43	$697
Kia Optima Hybrid	2.0L, 4 cyl., 6-sp. Automated Manual, FWD	39/46	$765
Ford Fusion Hybrid	2.0L, 4 cyl., Continuously Variable, FWD	43/41	$766
Hyundai Sonata Hybrid SE	2.0L, 4 cyl., 6-sp. Automated Manual, FWD	39/45	$773
Lexus CT 200h	1.8L, 4 cyl., Continuously Variable, FWD	43/40	$774
Toyota Prius v	1.8L, 4 cyl., Continuously Variable, FWD	43/39	$783
Hyundai Sonata Hybrid	2.0L, 4 cyl., 6-sp. Automated Manual, FWD	38/43	$801
Toyota Camry Hybrid LE	2.5L, 4 cyl., Continuously Variable, FWD	42/38	$802
Lincoln MKZ Hybrid	2.0L, 4 cyl., Continuously Variable, FWD	41/38	$813
Lexus ES 300h	2.5L, 4 cyl., 6-sp. Selectable Continuously Var., FWD	40/39	$815
Toyota Avalon Hybrid	2.5L, 4 cyl., 6-sp. Selectable Continuously Var., FWD	40/39	$815
Mitsubishi Mirage	1.2L, 3 cyl., Continuously Variable, FWD	37/43	$812
Toyota Camry Hybrid XLE/SE	2.5L, 4 cyl., Continuously Variable, FWD	40/37	$834
Honda Fit	1.5L, 4 cyl., Continuously Variable, FWD	33/40	$892
Honda Civic	1.5L, 4 cyl., Continuously Variable, FWD	32/42	$884
Toyota Yaris iA	1.5L, 4 cyl., 6-sp. Semi-Automatic, FWD	32/40	$906
Mazda Mazda2	1.5L, 4 cyl., 6-sp. Semi-Automatic, FWD	32/40	$906
THE WORST**			
Mercedes-Benz AMG S 65 Coupe	6.0L, 12 cyl., 7-sp. Automatic, 4WD	11/13	$3,366
Mercedes-Benz AMG G 63	5.5L, 8 cyl., 7-sp. Automatic, 4WD	12/14	$3,105
Mercedes-Benz GLS 550 4Matic	4.7L, 8 cyl., 9-sp. Automatic, 4WD	14/18	$2,626
Lexus LX 570	5.7L, 8 cyl., 8-sp. Semi-Automatic, 4WD	13/18	$2,626
Jeep Grand Cherokee SRT	6.4L, 8 cyl., 7-sp. Semi-Automatic, AWD	13/19	$2,551
Lexus GX 460	4.6L, 8 cyl., 6-sp. Semi-Automatic, 4WD	15/18	$2,450
Dodge Challenger SRT8	6.2L, 8 cyl., 8-sp. Manual, RWD	13/21	$2,413
Chevrolet Camaro	6.2L, 8 cyl., 8-sp. Manual, RWD	14/20	$2,398
Dodge Charger SRT	6.2L, 8 cyl., 8-sp. Automatic, RWD	13/22	$2,349
Ford Mustang GT350	5.2L, 8 cyl., 6-sp. Manual, RWD	14/21	$2,335
Infiniti QX80	5.6L, 8 cyl., 7-sp. Automatic, 4WD	13/19	$2,245
Toyota Tundra	5.7L, 8 cyl., 6-sp. Semi-Automatic, 4WD	13/17	$2,179
Toyota Sequoia	5.7L, 8 cyl., 6-sp. Semi-Automatic, 4WD	13/17	$2,179
Nissan Armada	5.6L, 8 cyl., 7-sp. Semi-Automatic, 4WD	13/18	$2,115
Toyota Tundra	5.7L, 8 cyl., 6-sp. Automatic, RWD	13/18	$2,115
Toyota Land Cruiser	5.7L, 8 cyl., 8-sp. Semi-Automatic, 4WD	13/18	$2,115
RAM 1500	5.7L, 8 cyl., 6-sp. Automatic, 4WD	13/19	$2,054
GMC Canyon	3.6L, 6 cyl., 8-sp. Automatic, RWD	15/17	$2,028
Chevrolet Colorado	3.6L, 6 cyl., 8-sp. Automatic, RWD	15/17	$2,028
Ford F150	L5.0, 8 cyl., 6-sp. Semi-Automatic, RWD	14/20	$1,931

Note: 2017 annual fuel cost based on driving 15,000 miles and a projected regular gas price of $2.15; #=Premium Required; *=Fuel Economy rating based on hybrid function only; annual cost based on epa estimate for gas and electric use; **=Low volume exotic vehicles (over $120,000) and cargo vans were excluded.

COMPARING WARRANTIES

After buying your car, maintenance will be a significant portion of your operating costs. The strength of your warranty and the cost of repairs after the warranty expires will determine these costs. Comparing warranties and repair costs, before you buy, can save you thousands of dollars down the road.

Along with your new car comes a warranty which is a promise from the manufacturer that the car will perform as it should. Most of us never read the warranty until it is too late. In fact, because warranties are often difficult to read and understand, most of us don't really know what our warranty covers.

To keep your warranty in effect, you must operate and maintain your car according to the instructions in your owner's manual. It is important to keep a record of all maintenance performed on your car.

Do not confuse a warranty with a service contract. A service contract must be purchased separately while a warranty is yours at no extra cost when you buy the car.

Warranties are difficult to compare because they contain fine print and confusing language. The following table will help you compare this year's warranties. Because the table does not contain all the details about each warranty, review the actual warranty to understand its fine points. You have the right to inspect a warranty before you buy—it's the law.

The table provides information on five critical items in a warranty:

The **Basic Warranty** covers most parts against manufacturer's defects. Tires, batteries, and items added to the car at the time of sale are covered under separate warranties. The table describes coverage in terms of months and miles. For example, 48/50 means the warranty is good for 48 months or 50,000 miles, whichever comes first. This is the most important part of your warranty because it covers the items most likely to fail. We give the basic warranty the most weight.

The **Power Train Warranty** often lasts longer than the basic warranty. Because each manufacturer's definition of the power train is different, it is important to find out exactly what your warranty will cover. Power train coverage should include the engine, transmission, and drive train. Some luxury cars will cover additional systems such as steering, suspension, and electrical systems. We give the powertrain warranty less weight than the basic because it doesn't cover as much as the basic warranty. Even with less weight in our rating, it can have a lot of influence in the overall index if it is very long.

The **Corrosion Warranty** usually applies only to actual holes due to rust. Read this section carefully because many corrosion warranties do not apply to what the manufacturer may describe as cosmetic rust or bad paint.

The **Roadside Assistance** column indicates whether or not the manufacturer offers a program for helping with break-downs, lockouts, jump starts, flat tires, running out of gas, and towing. Some have special limitations or added features. Because each one is different, check yours carefully.

The **Scheduled Maint. (Free)** column indicates whether or not free scheduled maintenance is included and for how long. These programs cover parts scheduled to be replaced such as filters. If there is an asterisk next to the coverage, that means the manufacturer also covers the cost of <u>any</u> parts that need to be replaced because of wear. Covering the cost of "wear" parts is a terrific feature and offered by very few manufacturers.

The last column, the **Warranty Rating Index**, provides an overall assessment of this year's warranties. **The higher the Index number, the better the warranty.** We give the most weight to the basic and power train components of the warranties. Roadside assistance was weighted somewhat less, and the corrosion warranty received the least weight.

Finally, we also considered special features such as extra coverage on batteries or wheel alignment. These benefits added to the overall ratings, whereas certain limitations (shortened transferability) took away from the rating.

The best ratings are in *BOLD*.

WARRANTY COMPARISON

Manufacturer	Basic Warranty	Power Train Warranty	Corrosion Warranty	Roadside Assistance	Scheduled Maint. (Free)	Index	Warranty Rating
Acura[1]	48/50	72/70	60/75	48/50		1106	Average
Audi	48/50	48/50	144/180	48/Unlimited	12/5	1203	Good
BMW	**48/50**	**48/50**	**144/180**	**48/Unlimited**	**48/50[1]**	**1288**	**Very Good**
Buick	48/50	72/70	72/90	72/70	24/24	1229	Good
Cadillac[2]	**48/50**	**72/70**	**72/90[3]**	**72/70**	**48/50**	**1320**	**Very Good**
Chevrolet	36/36	60/60	72/90[4]	60/60	24/24	1062	Average
Chrysler[5]	36/36	60/60	60/75[6]	60/60		1010	Poor
Dodge[7]	36/36	60/60	60/75[8]	60/60		1010	Poor
Fiat[9]	48/50	48/50	60/75[10]	48/50		1014	Average
Ford[11]	36/36	60/60	60/Unlimited	60/60		989	Poor
Genesis[12]	**60/60**	**120/100[13]**	**84/Unlimited**	**60/Unlimited**		**1469**	**Very Good**
GMC	36/36	60/60	72/90	60/60	24/24	1026	Average
Honda[14]	36/36	60/60	60/Unlimited	36/36		912	Very Poor
Hyundai[15]	**60/60**	**120/100[16]**	**84/Unlimited**	**60/Unlimited**		**1469**	**Very Good**
Infiniti[17]	48/60	72/70	84/Unlimited	48/Unlimited		1248	Good
Jeep[18]	36/36	60/60	36/Unlimited[19]	60/60		964	Poor
Kia[20]	**60/60**	**120/100[21]**	**60/100**	**60/60**		**1366**	**Very Good**
Land Rover	60/60	60/60	72/Unlimited	36/50	12/15	1169	Good
Lexus[22]	48/50	72/70	72/Unlimited	48/Unlimited	12/10	1200	Good
Lincoln[23]	**48/50**	**72/70**	**60/Unlimited**	**72/70[24]**	**24/24**	**1271**	**Very Good**
Mazda	36/36	60/60	36/Unlimited	36/36		846	Very Poor
Mercedes-Benz[25]	48/50	48/50	48/50	48/50		937	Poor
Mini	**48/50**	**48/50**	**144/Unlimited**	**48/Unlimited**	**36/36**	**1280**	**Very Good**
Mitsubishi	**60/60**	**120/100**	**84/100**	**60/Unlimited**		**1429**	**Very Good**
Nissan	36/36	60/60	60/Unlimited			798	Very Poor
Porsche	48/50	48/50	144/180	48/50		1157	Average
Ram	60/60	60/60	36/Unlimited			930	Very Poor
Smart[26]	48/50	48/50	48/50	48/50		937	Poor
Subaru[27]	36/36	60/60	60/Unlimited	48/50		972	Poor
Tesla	**48/50**	**96/Unlimited**	**48/50**	**48/50**		**1357**	**Very Good**
Toyota	36/36	60/60	60/Unlimited	24/Unlimited	24/25	925	Very Poor
Volkswagen	36/36	60/60	120/120	36/36	12/12	1014	Average
Volvo	48/50	48/50	120/Unlimited	48/Unlimited	36/36	1220	Good

[1] Wheel Alignment and Balancing 12/12
[2] Wheel Alignment and Balancing 12/7.5
[3] All Corrosion 48/50
[4] All Corrosion 36/36
[5] Wheel Alignment and Balancing 12/12
[6] All Corrosion 36/Unlimited
[7] Wheel Alignment and Balancing 12/12
[8] All Corrosion 36/Unlimited
[9] Wheel Alignment and Balancing 12/12
[10] All Corrosion 36/Unlimited

[11] Wheel Alignment and Balancing 12/12; Brake Pads 12/18
[12] Wheel Alignment and Balancing 12/12; Wear Items 12/12
[13] Only transferable up to 60/60
[14] Wheel Alignment and Balancing 12/12
[15] Wheel Alignment and Balancing 12/12; Wear Items 12/12
[16] Only transferable up to 60/60
[17] Wheel Alignment and Balancing 12/12
[18] Wheel Alignment and Balancing 12/12

[19] All Corrosion 36/Unlimited
[20] Wheel Alignment and Balancing 12/12
[21] Transferable only to 60/60
[22] Wheel Alignement and Balancing 12/12
[23] Wheel Alignment and Balancing 12/12; Brake Pads 12/18
[24] Lifetime for original owner
[25] Wheel Alignment and Balancing 12/12
[26] Wheel Alignment and Balancing 12/12
[27] Wear Items 36/36

SECRET WARRANTIES

If dealers report a number of complaints about a certain part or system and the manufacturer determines that the problem is due to faulty design or assembly, the manufacturer may permit dealers to repair the problem at no charge to the customer, even though the warranty is expired. In the past, this practice was often reserved for customers who made a big fuss. The availability of the free repair was never publicized, which is why we call these "secret warranties."

Manufacturers deny the existence of secret warranties. They call these free repairs "policy adjustments" or "goodwill service." Whatever they are called, most consumers never hear about them.

Many secret warranties are disclosed in service bulletins that the manufacturers send to dealers. These bulletins outline free repair or reimbursement programs, as well as other problems and their possible causes and solutions.

Service bulletins from manufacturers must, by law, be sent to, and be on file at, the National Highway Traffic Safety Administration. You can visit www.nhtsa.gov to access NHTSA's Service Bulletin database.

If you find that a secret warranty is in effect and repairs are being made at no charge after the warranty has expired, contact the Center for Auto Safety, 1825 Connecticut Ave. NW, #330, Washington, DC 20009, www.autosafety.org. They will publish the information so others can benefit.

Disclosure Laws: Spurred by the proliferation of secret warranties and the failure of the FTC to take action, California, Connecticut, Virginia, Wisconsin, and Maryland have passed legislation that requires consumers to be notified of secret warranties on their cars. Several other states have introduced similar warranty bills. You can find out more online at your state's website.

Typically, the laws require the following: direct notice to consumers within a specified time after the adoption of a warranty adjustment policy; notice of the disclosure law to new car buyers; reimbursement within a number of years after payment to owners who paid for covered repairs before they learned of the extended warranty service; and dealers must inform consumers who complain about a covered defect that it is eligible for repair under warranty.

If you live in a state with a secret warranty law already in effect, write your state attorney general's office (in care of your state capital) for information. To encourage passage of such a bill, contact your state representatives (in care of your state capital).

Some state lemon laws require dealers and manufacturers to give you copies of Technical Service Bulletins on problems affecting your vehicle. These bulletins may alert you to a secret warranty on your vehicle or help you make the case for a free repair if there isn't a secret warranty. See page 59 for an overview of your state's lemon law. If you would like to see the complete law, go to www.autosafety.org to view your state's lemon laws.

LITTLE SECRETS OF THE AUTO INDUSTRY

TIP

Every auto company makes mistakes building cars. When they do, they often issue technical service bulletins telling dealers how to fix the problem. Rarely do they publicize these fixes, many of which are offered for free, called secret warranties. The Center for Auto Safety has published a book called *Little Secrets of the Auto Industry*, a consumer guide to secret warranties and has finally gotten NHTSA to make them available on their website. This book explains how to find out about secret warranties, offers tips for going to small claims court and getting federal and state assistance, and lists information on state secret warranty laws. To order a copy, send $17.50 to: Center for Auto Safety, Pub. Dept. CB, 1825 Connecticut Ave. NW, Suite 330, Washington, DC 20009.

KEEPING IT GOING

Comparing maintenance costs before you buy can help decide which car to purchase. These costs include preventive maintenance servicing—such as changing the oil and filters—as well as the cost of repairs after your warranty expires. The following tables enable you to compare the costs of preventive maintenance and nine likely repairs.

Preventive Maintenance: The first column in the table is the periodic servicing, specified by the manufacturer, that keeps your car running properly. For example, regularly changing the oil and oil filter. Every owner's manual specifies a schedule of recommended servicing for at least the first 60,000 miles and many now go to 100,000 miles. The tables on the following pages estimate the labor cost of following this preventive maintenance schedule for 60,000 miles, the length of a typical warranty. Service parts are not included in this total.

Repair Costs: The tables also list the costs for nine repairs that typically occur during the first 100,000 miles. There is no precise way to predict exactly when a repair will be needed. But if you keep a car for 75,000 to 100,000 miles, it is likely that you will experience many of these repairs at least once. The last column provides a relative indication of how expensive these nine repairs are for many cars. Repair cost is rated as Very Good if the total for nine repairs is in the lowest fifth of all the cars rated, and

Very Poor if the total is in the highest fifth.

Most repair shops use "flat-rate manuals" to estimate repair costs. These manuals list the approximate time required for repairing many items. Each automobile manufacturer publishes its own manual and there are several independent manuals as well. For many repairs, the time varies from one manual to another. Some repair shops even use different manuals for different repairs. To determine a repair bill, a shop multiplies the time listed in its manual by its hourly labor rate and then adds the cost of parts.

Some dealers and repair shops create their own maintenance schedules which call for more frequent (and thus more expensive) servicing than the manufacturer's recommendations. If the service recom-

mended by your dealer or repair shop doesn't match what the manufacturer recommends, make sure you understand and agree to the extra items. Our cost estimates are based on published repair times multiplied by a nationwide average labor rate of $90 per hour and include the cost of replaced parts and related adjustments.

Prices in the following tables may not predict the exact costs of these repairs. For example, labor rates for your area may be more or less than the national average. However, the prices will provide you with a relative comparison of costs for various automobiles.

Finally, for many of the electric vehicles you'll see a $0. That's because the EV doesn't have that part. This is one reason why EVs can be less expensive to maintain.

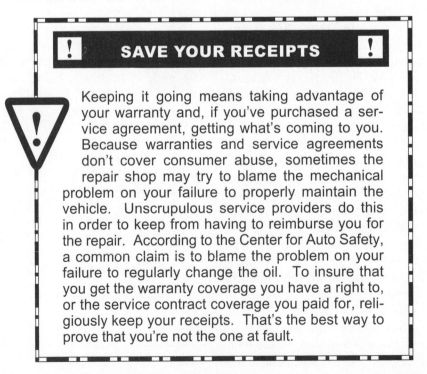

! SAVE YOUR RECEIPTS !

Keeping it going means taking advantage of your warranty and, if you've purchased a service agreement, getting what's coming to you. Because warranties and service agreements don't cover consumer abuse, sometimes the repair shop may try to blame the mechanical problem on your failure to properly maintain the vehicle. Unscrupulous service providers do this in order to keep from having to reimburse you for the repair. According to the Center for Auto Safety, a common claim is to blame the problem on your failure to regularly change the oil. To insure that you get the warranty coverage you have a right to, or the service contract coverage you paid for, religiously keep your receipts. That's the best way to prove that you're not the one at fault.

	PM Costs to 60,000 Miles	REPAIR COSTS									
		Front Brake Pads	Starter	Fuel Injector	Fuel Pump	Struts/ Shocks	Timing Belt/Chain	Water Pump	Muffler	Headlamps	Relative Repair Cost*
Subcompact											
BMW i3	882	153	0	0	0	233	0	853	0	1256	Vry. Gd.
Chevrolet Sonic	504	196	377	82	386	169	276	324	620	785	Vry. Gd.
Chevrolet Spark	540	196	315	139	443	161	457	293	431	894	Vry. Gd.
Fiat 500	630	169	310	398	558	89	364	446	283	756	Vry. Gd.
Ford Fiesta	828	129	456	105	514	161	379	314	475	640	Vry. Gd.
Honda Fit	477	145	634	219	495	382	577	283	245	877	Good
Hyundai Accent	864	121	432	175	464	176	389	309	358	283	Vry. Gd.
Hyundai Veloster	882	162	353	139	431	321	536	345	401	698	Vry. Gd.
Kia Rio	774	128	423	205	360	225	377	303	411	639	Vry. Gd.
Kia Soul	954	128	427	214	313	267	354	305	434	1021	Vry. Gd.
Mazda MX-5	864	189	343	221	480	363	473	257	622	980	Average
Mini Cooper	1161	204	553	200	628	359	1029	444	501	1298	Poor
Mini Countryman	1161	219	464	204	425	366	1029	420	630	847	Average
Mitsubishi Mirage	612	198	852	310	132	344	619	574	430	809	Average
Nissan Versa	594	189	403	278	522	190	436	207	322	670	Vry. Gd.
Smart ForTwo	1035	97	465	200	438	512	1432	468	968	762	Poor
Toyota Prius C	558	137	0	266	467	213	501	624	274	859	Vry. Gd.
Toyota Yaris	486	138	395	225	460	287	502	237	248	683	Vry. Gd.
Toyota Yaris iA	536	138	395	225	460	287	502	234	248	683	Vry. Gd.
Compact											
Acura ILX	576	141	594	157	506	448	549	385	621	1090	Average
Audi A3	1177	188	409	251	440	679	738	627	639	852	Average
Audi A4	855	229	788	514	700	713	528	790	639	977	Poor
BMW 2 Series	999	240	588	423	473	350	1332	750	671	1167	Vry. Pr.
BMW 3 Series	945	240	588	423	474	350	1288	725	682	1194	Vry. Pr.
BMW 4 Series	945	241	658	218	500	391	1063	767	867	1141	Vry. Pr.
Buick Cascada	1251	271	348	331	352	747	506	574	1071	1073	Poor
Buick Verano	720	291	353	428	514	213	587	618	272	1011	Good
Cadillac ATS	1179	199	581	416	406	452	492	414	1140	1066	Average
Chevrolet Cruze	963	196	260	232	524	174	775	430	621	599	Good
Chevrolet Volt	1080	173	0	120	380	140	1250	447	570	1000	Good
Dodge Dart	630	176	229	395	573	236	605	312	505	701	Average
Ford C-MAX	594	180	289	137	342	250	628	177	262	638	Vry. Gd.
Ford Focus	882	147	422	291	479	122	693	240	312	665	Vry. Gd.
Honda Civic	423	141	558	220	443	210	639	251	303	743	Good
Hyundai Elantra	981	148	360	175	285	209	420	258	367	764	Vry. Gd.
Kia Forte	585	164	237	196	332	211	542	287	330	532	Vry. Gd.
Lexus CT	558	142	0	449	455	245	1702	698	596	1368	Poor
Lexus IS	756	155	945	640	414	492	1930	529	862	1339	Vry. Pr.
Lexus RC	729	139	759	391	474	241	1851	1189	1292	1161	Vry. Pr.
Mazda Mazda3	792	176	335	308	580	205	451	290	427	708	Vry. Gd.
Mercedes-Benz B-Class	864	177	0	0	0	442	0	0	0	1070	Vry. Gd.
Mercedes-Benz C-Class	1287	181	722	331	1060	489	407	723	928	1138	Vry. Pr.
Mercedes-Benz CLA-Class	1269	151	1065	628	686	260	422	484	655	1041	Poor
Mitsubishi Lancer	504	186	874	357	628	335	614	565	421	1294	Poor
Nissan 370Z	594	174	505	362	525	568	761	673	602	1105	Poor
Nissan Leaf	666	150	0	0	0	225	0	710	0	1352	Vry. Gd.
Nissan Sentra	702	154	346	360	562	176	590	232	406	646	Vry. Gd.
Subaru Impreza	1008	153	507	232	453	622	392	453	403	820	Good
AVERAGE OF ALL VEHICLES	$877	$195	$461	$306	$518	$367	$869	$478	$622	$938	

	PM Costs to 60,000 Miles	REPAIR COSTS									Relative Repair Cost*
		Front Brake Pads	Starter	Fuel Injector	Fuel Pump	Struts/Shocks	Timing Belt/Chain	Water Pump	Muffler	Headlamps	
Compact (cont.)											
Toyota 86	972	184	640	581	692	356	646	387	616	979	Average
Toyota Corolla	549	151	469	312	427	334	638	257	386	530	Good
Toyota Corolla iM	513	151	469	312	427	334	638	257	386	530	Good
Toyota Prius	558	137	0	449	429	352	1661	691	284	857	Average
Toyota Prius V	558	165	0	447	467	352	1691	453	270	860	Average
Volkswagen Beetle	918	184	555	301	430	328	983	474	897	1101	Poor
Volkswagen Golf	1089	179	687	208	364	417	549	451	457	603	Good
Volkswagen Jetta	918	160	673	417	535	422	598	659	719	766	Average
Intermediate											
Acura TLX	936	141	606	138	441	300	451	218	709	1513	Average
Audi A5	972	206	783	424	476	484	523	772	1492	1301	Vry. Pr.
Audi A6	972	228	936	536	684	550	670	497	748	1121	Vry. Pr.
BMW 5 Series	567	257	649	291	663	705	788	728	971	1342	Vry. Pr.
Buick Regal	1251	280	353	340	359	747	542	616	1062	1053	Poor
Cadillac CTS	1179	269	335	241	911	424	743	415	1266	1016	Poor
Chevrolet Camaro	1251	470	289	377	632	352	660	432	632	506	Average
Chevrolet Corvette	1062	544	588	351	1477	204	872	451	844	1378	Vry. Pr.
Chevrolet Malibu	711	280	353	468	529	390	614	629	478	510	Good
Chrysler 200	585	125	245	110	422	204	538	220	587	1075	Good
Ford Fusion	684	162	193	126	301	123	594	203	401	1015	Vry. Gd.
Ford Fusion Energi	846	162	0	126	301	123	594	202	401	1015	Vry. Gd.
Ford Mustang	603	151	176	193	399	156	887	269	300	744	Vry. Gd.
Honda Accord	504	149	509	471	476	263	493	223	456	1074	Good
Hyundai Azera	972	112	422	163	457	176	344	311	367	283	Vry. Gd.
Hyundai Sonata	891	148	286	189	327	281	188	372	643	745	Vry. Gd.
Infiniti Q50	882	167	458	412	494	558	1342	682	629	1408	Vry. Pr.
Infiniti Q70	702	246	444	371	458	849	1342	680	692	1487	Vry. Pr.
Kia Cadenza	972	105	253	199	112	219	551	288	887	531	Vry. Gd.
Kia Optima	864	169	237	196	332	211	524	289	330	532	Vry. Gd.
Lexus ES	864	133	491	431	434	868	1836	451	459	1311	Vry. Pr.
Lexus GS	657	164	719	549	468	417	1915	364	832	1491	Vry. Pr.
Lincoln MKZ	684	166	437	175	338	791	1444	878	435	1595	Vry. Pr.
Mazda Mazda6	799	183	241	226	535	233	540	216	359	696	Vry. Gd.
Nissan Altima	954	147	374	338	449	312	650	273	407	692	Good
Nissan Maxima	828	150	409	416	472	239	981	401	662	877	Average
Subaru Legacy	1268	162	560	205	417	539	317	418	383	885	Good
Toyota Avalon	864	137	478	359	466	535	1852	366	376	906	Poor
Toyota Camry	864	137	491	331	434	562	1662	310	404	896	Poor
Volkswagen Passat	918	170	710	253	480	384	1709	465	704	677	Poor
Volvo S60	909	194	451	314	801	264	567	449	676	499	Good
Volvo V60	1116	194	451	323	792	264	433	448	667	499	Good
Large											
BMW 7 Series	585	144	649	541	528	2087	1270	727	739	1302	Vry. Pr.
Buick LaCrosse	1251	271	435	394	490	773	1299	419	605	1099	Poor
Cadillac XTS	1242	300	417	394	548	280	779	419	835	1385	Poor
Chevrolet Impala	958	261	412	312	711	196	542	620	611	610	Good
Chrysler 300	630	220	228	181	365	141	735	353	968	1230	Average
Dodge Challenger	630	220	220	181	242	136	733	162	974	679	Good
Dodge Charger	630	229	220	181	244	138	724	246	1081	671	Good
Ford Taurus	909	156	401	215	342	172	1089	976	686	1351	Poor
AVERAGE OF ALL VEHICLES	**$877**	**$195**	**$461**	**$306**	**$518**	**$367**	**$869**	**$478**	**$622**	**$938**	

	PM Costs to 60,000 Miles	REPAIR COSTS									Relative Repair Cost*
		Front Brake Pads	Starter	Fuel Injector	Fuel Pump	Struts/ Shocks	Timing Belt/ Chain	Water Pump	Muffler	Headlamps	
Large (cont.)											
Genesis G80	1044	231	453	217	431	342	1430	368	573	1045	Poor
Lincoln Continental	900	168	410	166	482	180	1026	1089	632	1481	Poor
Mercedes-Benz E-Class	1017	186	804	589	488	495	1124	761	1136	1297	Vry. Pr.
Mercedes-Benz S-Class	1017	296	744	446	518	2018	373	948	1471	1625	Vry. Pr.
Minivan											
Chrysler Pacifica	504	266	410	392	542	157	898	265	566	533	Good
Honda Odyssey	540	157	492	102	415	192	378	419	654	713	Good
Kia Sedona	990	159	249	347	372	336	1274	369	537	327	Good
Nissan Quest	702	154	513	304	521	377	1015	274	606	770	Average
Toyota Sienna	1116	148	506	406	1051	297	1475	349	408	1028	Vry. Pr.
Small SUV											
Acura RDX	909	167	515	238	480	293	288	441	357	1594	Average
Audi Q3	972	211	761	324	639	484	532	771	650	1179	Poor
BMW X1	783	236	588	441	581	522	1339	712	741	1109	Vry. Pr.
Buick Encore	720	309	269	112	433	199	721	356	605	661	Good
Chevrolet Trax	974	297	390	316	544	220	1191	492	619	1036	Average
Fiat 500X	630	169	310	398	558	91	366	451	283	756	Vry. Gd.
Ford Escape	855	147	225	95	369	173	711	213	309	954	Vry. Gd.
Honda CR-V	504	141	594	167	341	407	558	218	397	756	Good
Honda HR-V	747	149	581	178	362	429	576	142	394	792	Good
Hyundai Tucson	972	130	369	144	336	217	456	420	576	577	Vry. Gd.
Infiniti QX50	594	165	426	374	471	688	1658	684	685	1630	Vry. Pr.
Jeep Compass	450	154	397	111	351	234	552	251	566	1001	Good
Jeep Patriot	450	116	285	111	342	177	471	254	570	433	Vry. Gd.
Jeep Renegade	540	130	289	89	348	241	538	238	570	443	Vry. Gd.
Jeep Wrangler	369	210	249	263	530	114	852	366	356	372	Vry. Gd.
Kia Sportage	927	155	237	225	349	269	556	400	631	1411	Good
Land Rover Range Rover Evoque	774	278	578	516	688	707	531	294	713	529	Average
Lexus NX	931	143	749	387	474	244	1454	886	663	1153	Vry. Pr.
Lincoln MKC	855	171	419	167	499	189	981	879	492	1674	Poor
Mazda CX-5	792	164	385	354	331	225	395	236	462	624	Vry. Gd.
Mercedes-Benz GLA-Class	486	317	776	557	546	622	323	882	828	1383	Vry. Pr.
Mercedes-Benz GLC-Class	962	330	754	579	546	592	317	833	828	1383	Vry. Pr.
Mitsubishi Outlander Sport	792	275	911	364	780	485	621	527	458	1470	Poor
Nissan Juke	945	150	518	346	501	288	1428	307	361	609	Average
Subaru Crosstrek	1008	162	552	269	468	492	736	429	403	820	Average
Subaru Forester	1026	153	552	241	417	539	664	457	356	836	Good
Toyota RAV4	963	177	469	322	693	247	1832	254	893	687	Poor
Volkswagen Tiguan	1053	179	673	464	414	416	907	798	430	929	Average
Mid-Size SUV											
Acura MDX	936	160	547	186	442	258	396	466	654	1501	Average
Audi Q5	972	211	761	324	684	484	559	765	650	1181	Poor
Audi Q7	1080	268	758	599	829	1739	1590	390	1064	1273	Vry. Pr.
BMW X3	1242	240	588	273	617	578	892	642	953	348	Average
BMW X5	1053	296	622	570	518	563	932	796	1476	1495	Vry. Pr.
Cadillac XT5	1251	200	381	421	434	189	752	397	932	1157	Average
Chevrolet Equinox	1278	293	371	286	870	196	542	619	632	921	Average
Dodge Journey	423	214	415	190	702	345	1042	268	1416	653	Poor
Ford Edge	756	183	410	194	456	244	1121	1063	610	919	Average
AVERAGE OF ALL VEHICLES	**$877**	**$195**	**$461**	**$306**	**$518**	**$367**	**$869**	**$478**	**$622**	**$938**	

	PM Costs to 60,000 Miles	Front Brake Pads	Starter	Fuel Injector	Fuel Pump	Struts/ Shocks	Timing Belt/ Chain	Water Pump	Muffler	Headlamps	Relative Repair Cost*
Mid-Size SUV (cont.)											
Ford Explorer	909	156	401	310	686	293	1049	1024	900	1358	Vry. Pr.
Honda Pilot	504	157	516	211	495	210	378	508	653	826	Good
Hyundai Santa Fe	972	173	259	139	410	261	509	318	570	1095	Good
Hyundai Santa Fe Sport	972	173	259	139	455	261	510	318	570	1102	Good
Infiniti QX60	1040	154	421	394	458	676	1656	675	676	1691	Vry. Pr.
Jeep Cherokee	270	222	338	257	726	193	852	236	841	787	Average
Jeep Grand Cherokee	630	222	338	257	726	193	852	236	841	787	Average
Kia Sorento	936	145	254	315	473	270	1848	459	672	914	Poor
Land Rover Range Rover Sport	1258	240	663	648	631	794	1255	378	475	294	Vry. Pr.
Lexus RX	900	150	757	382	476	191	1854	1187	1203	1165	Vry. Pr.
Mazda CX-9	774	188	310	229	568	309	1098	1187	600	866	Poor
Mercedes-Benz GLE-Class	1053	325	774	578	556	610	369	898	845	1392	Vry. Pr.
Mitsubishi Outlander	981	186	319	269	758	234	621	519	412	779	Good
Nissan Murano	702	192	457	389	526	265	1096	454	511	832	Average
Nissan Pathfinder	1140	172	460	412	508	190	1094	484	610	963	Average
Nissan Rogue	1053	154	378	367	747	199	1120	338	621	1602	Poor
Porsche Macan	1080	377	600	428	579	1411	1305	501	1750	1011	Vry. Pr.
Subaru Outback	1242	162	560	205	417	539	287	420	293	288	Vry. Gd.
Volvo XC60	909	268	443	246	731	235	628	397	591	539	Good
Volvo XC70	738	278	417	248	734	242	646	402	609	567	Good
Large SUV											
BMW X6	1107	293	622	533	518	563	932	582	1363	1539	Vry. Pr.
Buick Enclave	1206	282	381	325	652	177	1381	458	632	1342	Poor
Chevrolet Suburban	1278	281	320	286	697	194	863	525	737	627	Average
Chevrolet Tahoe	1278	281	320	295	920	224	863	520	1122	627	Average
Chevrolet Traverse	1206	282	381	325	559	223	1389	456	619	727	Average
Ford Expedition	1098	175	302	174	578	260	922	273	625	604	Good
Ford Flex	801	147	401	193	430	200	1094	998	732	1451	Poor
GMC Acadia	1206	282	381	325	559	177	1299	458	619	1213	Poor
Infiniti QX80	1080	172	526	303	523	515	1423	283	377	1631	Poor
Land Rover Range Rover	837	240	663	648	631	794	1255	377	475	294	Vry. Pr.
Lexus GX	819	154	893	449	623	155	1284	590	532	1049	Poor
Mercedes-Benz GL-Class	1062	317	758	625	551	601	368	863	828	1383	Vry. Pr.
Nissan Armada	1080	163	498	303	530	375	1711	292	624	912	Poor
Toyota 4Runner	558	150	540	354	632	240	1863	447	511	838	Poor
Toyota Highlander	720	143	501	402	986	646	1888	559	1176	679	Vry. Pr.
Toyota Sequoia	819	301	868	377	757	392	1226	517	506	831	Poor
Volvo XC90	1044	205	452	356	655	344	665	370	609	585	Good
Compact Pickup											
Chevrolet Colorado	1278	281	383	295	650	210	863	496	897	701	Average
Nissan Frontier	1080	163	441	367	558	201	853	301	406	721	Good
Toyota Tacoma	558	147	525	348	816	172	1428	249	465	763	Average
Standard Pickup											
Chevrolet Silverado	1092	281	383	295	651	210	863	494	897	702	Average
Ford F-150	612	183	461	523	621	127	809	266	472	583	Good
GMC Sierra	1278	281	383	295	650	210	814	494	718	702	Average
Nissan Titan	1620	163	580	303	563	200	810	307	590	749	Poor
Ram 1500	576	151	295	141	406	163	518	399	399	453	Vry. Gd.
Toyota Tundra	819	167	830	320	859	221	1013	447	506	831	Average
AVERAGE OF ALL VEHICLES	$877	$195	$461	$306	$518	$367	$869	$478	$622	$938	

42

SERVICE CONTRACTS

Service contracts are one of the most expensive options you can buy. In fact, service contracts are a major profit source for many dealers.

A service contract is not a warranty. It is more like an insurance plan that, in theory, covers repairs that are not covered by your warranty or that occur after the warranty runs out. They are often inaccurately referred to as "extended warranties."

Service contracts are generally a poor value. The companies who sell contracts are very sure that, on average, your repairs will cost considerably less than what you pay for the contract—if not, they wouldn't be in business.

Here are some important questions to ask before buying a service contract:

How reputable is the company responsible for the contract? If the company offering the contract goes out of business, you will be out of luck. The company may be required to be insured, but find out if they actually are and by whom. Check with your Better Business Bureau or office of consumer affairs if you are not sure of a company's reputation. Service contracts from car and insurance companies are more likely to remain in effect than those from independent companies.

Exactly what does the contract cover and for how long? Service contracts vary considerably—different items are covered and different time limits are offered. This is true even among service contracts offered by the same company. For example, one company has plans that range from 4 years/36,000 miles maximum coverage to 6 years/100,000 miles maximum coverage, with other options for only power train coverage. Make sure you know what components are covered because if a breakdown occurs on a part that is not covered, you are responsible for the repairs.

If you plan to resell your car in a few years, you won't want to purchase a long-running service contract. Some service contracts automatically cancel when you resell the car, while others require a hefty transfer fee before extending privileges to the new owner. Check out the transferability of the service contract.

Some automakers offer a "menu" format, which lets you pick the items you want covered in your service contract. Find out if the contract pays for preventive maintenance, towing, and rental car expenses. If not written into the contract, assume they are not covered.

Make sure the contract clearly specifies how you can reach the company. Knowing this before you purchase a service contract can save you time and aggravation in the future.

How will the repair bills be paid? It is best to have the service contractor pay bills directly. Some contracts require you to pay the repair bill, and reimburse you later. This can be a major hassle.

Where can the car be serviced? Can you take the car to any mechanic if you have trouble on the road? What if you move?

What other costs can be expected? Most service contracts will have a deductible expense, which means you will have to pay part of the repair cost. Compare deductibles on various plans. Also, some companies charge the deductible for each individual repair while other companies pay per visit, regardless of the number of repairs being made.

What are your responsibilities? Make sure you know what you have to do to uphold the contract. For example if you have to follow the manufacturer's recommended maintenance, keep detailed records or the contract could be voided. You will find your specific responsibilities in the contact. Be sure to have the seller point them out.

SERVICE CONTRACTS VS. SAVINGS ACCOUNT

TIP

One alternative to buying a service contract is to deposit the cost of the contract into a savings account. If the car needs a major repair not covered by your warranty, the money in your account is likely to cover the cost. Most likely, you'll be building up a down payment for your next car!

TIPS FOR DEALING WITH A MECHANIC

Call around. Don't choose a shop simply because it's nearby. Calling a few shops may turn up estimates cheaper by half.

Don't necessarily go for the lowest price. A good rule is to eliminate the highest and lowest estimates; the mechanic with the highest estimate is probably charging too much, and the lowest may be cutting too many corners.

Check the shop's reputation. While internet reviews need to be considered with some skepticism, see what others are saying about the shop. Your local consumer agency and the BBB may have unfavorable reports that would disqualify shops you may be considering.

Look for certification. Mechanics can be certified by the National Institute for Automotive Service Excellence, an industry yardstick for competence. Certification is offered in eight areas of repair and shops with certified mechanics are allowed to advertise this fact. However, make sure the mechanic working on your car is certified for the repair you need.

Take a look around. A well-kept shop reflects pride in workmanship. A skilled and efficient mechanic would probably not work in a messy shop.

Don't sign a blank check. The service order you sign should have specific instructions or describe your vehicle's symptoms. Avoid signing a vague work order. Be sure you are called for final approval before the shop does extra work. Many states require a written estimate signed by you and require that the shop get your permission for repairs that exceed the estimate by 10%.

Show interest. Ask about the repair. But don't act like an expert if you don't really understand what's wrong. Express your satisfaction. If you're happy with the work, compliment the mechanic and ask for him or her the next time you come in. You will get to know each other and the mechanic will get to know your vehicle.

Take a test-drive. Before you pay for a major repair, you should take the car for a test-drive. The few extra minutes you spend checking out the repair could save you a trip back to the mechanic. If you find that the problem still exists, there will be no question that the repair wasn't properly completed.

REPAIR PROTECTION BY CREDIT CARD

Paying your auto repair bills by credit card can provide a much needed recourse if you are having problems with an auto mechanic. According to federal law, you have the right to withhold payment for sloppy or incorrect repairs.

In order to use this right, you should first try to work out the problem with the mechanic. Also, unless the credit card company owns the repair shop (this might be the case with gasoline credit cards used at gas stations), two other conditions must be met. First, the repair shop must be in your home state (or within 100 miles of your current address), and second, the cost of repairs must be over $50. Until the problem is settled or resolved in court, the credit card company cannot charge you interest or penalties on the amount in dispute.

If you decide to take action, send a letter to the credit card company and a copy to the repair shop, explaining the details of the problem and what you want as settlement. Send the letter by certified mail with a return receipt requested.

Sometimes the credit card company or repair shop will attempt to put a "bad mark" on your credit record if you use this tactic. Legally, you can't be reported as delinquent if you've given the credit card company notice of your dispute, but a creditor can report that you are disputing your bill, which goes in your record. However, you have the right to challenge any incorrect information and add your side of the story to your file.

For more information, contact the Federal Trade Commission, Credit Practices Division, 601 Pennsylvania Avenue, NW, Washington, DC 20580 or at www.FTC.gov.

TIRE RATINGS

Buying tires has become an infrequent task because today's radial tires last much longer than the tires of the past. Surprisingly, a tire has to perform more functions simultaneously than any other part of the car (steering, bearing the load, cushioning the ride, and stopping).

Because comparing tires is difficult, many consumers mistakenly use price and brand name to determine quality. As there are hundreds of tire lines to choose from, and only a few tire manufacturers, the difference in many tires may only be the brand name.

But there is help. The government requires tires to be rated according to their safety and expected mileage.

Treadwear, traction, and heat resistance grades are printed on the sidewall and are attached to the tire on a paper label. Ask the dealer for the grades of the tires they sell. Using this rating system, a sampling of top rated tires follows on page 48.

Treadwear: The treadwear grade gives you an idea of the mileage you can expect from a tire. It is shown in numbers–720, 700, 680, 660, and so forth. Higher numbers mean longer tire life. A tire with a grade of 600 should give you twice as much mileage as one rated 300. Use the treadwear grade as a relative basis of comparison.

Traction: Traction grades of AA, A, B, and C describe the tire's ability to stop on wet surfaces. Tires graded AA will stop on a wet road in a shorter distance than tires graded B or C. Tires rated C have poor traction.

Heat Resistance: Heat resistance is graded A, B, and C. An A rating means the tire will run cooler than one rated B or C and be less likely to fail if driven over long distances at highway speeds. Tires that run cooler tend to have lower rolling resistance contributing to better fuel economy. Hot-running tires can result in blow-outs or tread separation.

TIRE CARE

Pump 'em Up: An estimated one-third of us are driving on underinflated tires. Because even good tires lose air, it is important to check your tire pressure monthly. Underinflated tires can be dangerous, use more fuel and cause premature tire failure. When checking your tires, be sure to use an accurate gauge and inflate to the pressure indicated in your owner's manual, not the maximum pressure printed on your tire. The good news, because of the importance of proper tire inflation, cars have built-in tire pressure monitoring but you should check tire pressure regularly even if the warning doesn't light up.

When to Replace: If all of Lincoln's head is visible when you insert the top of a penny into a tread groove, it's time to replace the tire. While this old rule of thumb is still valid, today's tires also have a built-in wear indicator. A series of horizontal bars appear across the surface when the tread depth reaches the danger zone.

GETTING THE BEST PRICE

The price of the same tire can vary depending on where you shop so shopping around is vital to finding a good buy. You are most likely to find the best prices at independent tire dealers who carry a variety of tire brands.

The price of a tire is based on its size, and tires come in as many as nine sizes. For example, the list price of the same tire can range from $74.20 to $134.35, depending on its size. To get the best buy:

1. Check to see which manufacturer makes the least expensive "off brand." Only a few manufacturers produce the over 1,800 types of tires sold in the U.S.

2. Don't forget to compare balancing and mounting costs. These extra charges can add up to more than $25 or be offered at no cost.

3. Never pay list price for a tire. A good rule of thumb is to pay at least 30-40 percent off the suggested list price.

4. Use the treadwear grade the same way you would the "unit price" in a supermarket. The tire with the lowest cost per grade point is the best value. For example, if tire A costs $100 and has a treadwear grade of 600, and tire B costs $80 and has a treadwear grade of 300, tire A is the better buy, even though its initial cost is more.

Tire A: $100÷600=$0.17 per point
Tire B: $80÷300=$0.27 per point

Where you live is a factor in how long your tires will last. Tire wear is affected by the level of abrasive material in the road surface. Generally, the road surfaces of the West Coast, Great Lakes region, and northern New England are easiest on tires. The Applachian and Rocky Mountain areas are usually the hardest.

HOW TO READ A TIRE

Tire Type and Size: The most important information on a tire are the letters and the numbers indicating its type and size.

1. Tire Type: The P at the beginning of the tire size indicates that the tire is a passenger vehicle tire. LT indicates light truck tire, and T indicates a temporary or spare tire.

2. Tire Width is the first part of the number and is measured in millimeters, from sidewall to sidewall.

3. Tire Height is the next number and tells you the height of the tire from the bead to the tread. This is described as a percentage of the tire width. In our example, the tire's height is 65 percent of its width. The smaller the aspect ratio, the wider the tire in relation to its height.

4. Tire Construction designates how the tire was made. R indicates radial construction which is the most common type. Older tires were made using diagonal bias D or bias belted B construction, but these tire types are no longer used on passenger vehicles.

5. Wheel Diameter identifies the wheel rim diameter (in inches-15) needed for this tire.

6. Load Index: The load rating indicates the maximum load for that tire. A higher number indicates a higher load capacity. The rating 95, for example, corresponds to a load capacity of 1521 pounds. Larger vehicles, SUVs and pickups need tires with a higher load capacity.

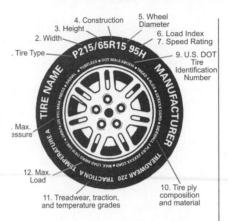

7. Speed Rating indicates the maximum speed that the tire can sustain a ten minute endurance test without being in danger. All passenger car tires are rated at least S and pass the test at speeds up to 112 mph. Other ratings are as follows: T up to 118 mph, H up to 130 mph, V up to 149 mph and Z 150 mph or higher. Other types of tires, temporary spares and snow tires are lower on the rating scale.

8. Severe Conditions: M+S indicates the tire meets the Rubber Manufacturers Association's definition of a mud and snow tire. There are no performance tests for this standard. If the tire has an M+S and a "mountain and snowflake" symbol then the traction is at least 10% better than the regular version of the tire. These symbols are not in the above example.

9. Tire Identification Number
Example: DOT NJ HR 2AF 5212
The letters DOT certify compliance with all applicable safety standards established by the U.S. Department of Transportation. The next four characters is a code where the first two characters indicate the manufacturer and the second two characters indicate the plant where the tire was made.

For a guide to plant codes, go to www.tiresafetygroup.com.

Next you may see an optional string of three to four characters. Most manufacturers use these to record company specific information they use to identify their products or that can be used to identify tires in the market for recall purposes.

The last four digits determine the week and year the tire was made. The digits 5212 would signify that the tire was made during the 52nd week of 2012. Don't buy tires more than a year old. Tires naturally degrade with age, so you want the newest possible tires for the longest life (and safe operation.)

10. Tire Ply Composition and Material indicates the type of cord (polyester or steel) and number of plies in the tire, 4-ply, 6-ply, 8-ply, for both the tread and the sidewall.

11. Treadwear, Traction and Temperature Grades are three performance grades assigned to the tire and are the best way to truly evaluate the tires expected performance in these three critical areas. See page 46 for more information.

12. Max Load Limit tells you the cold inflation load limit in lbs. (pounds) and in kg (kilograms). The number corresponds to the load index.

13. Max Pressure is the maximum recommended pressure in psi (pounds per square inch) and in kPa (kilopascals). However, this is not the tire pressure for your car. You must check your owner's manual for the proper tire pressure for the tires on your car.

A Sampling of Top Rated Tires

Brand Name	Model	Description	Traction	Heat	Treadwear
Michelin	DEFENDER	All Sizes	A	B	820
Bridgestone	DUELER H/L ALENZA PLUS "H" & "V" Spd Rtd	All Sizes	A	A	800
Toyo	TOYO ULTRA Z900 (H-rated)	All sizes	A	A	800
Bridgestone	DUELER H/L ALENZA PLUS "T" Spd Rtd	All Sizes	A	B	800
Mastercraft	Avenger Touring LSR (TR)	15"-18"	A	A	780
Cooper	CS5 Grand Touring	All sizes	A	B	780
Big O	EURO TOUR (T RATED)	All sizes	A	A	740
Bridgestone	TURANZA SERENITY "H" Spd Rtd	All sizes	A	A	740
Cooper	Discoverer SRX (H)	All sizes	A	A	740
Goodyear	ASSURANCE COMFORTRED TOURING (T&H)	All sizes	A	B	740
Hankook	Optimo H725 (OE)	P235/60R17	A	B	740
Maxxis	MA-T1 Escapade	All sizes	A	A	720
Michelin	LTX M/S2	All Sizes	A	A	720
Big O	LEGACY TOUR PLUS (S & T RATED)	All sizes	A	B	720
Falken	SN211	All sizes	A	B	720
Michelin	LATITUDE TOUR	All Sizes except	A	B	720
Michelin	X RADIAL LT2	All Sizes	A	B	720
Vogue	CUSTOM BUILT IX (S)	P225/60R16	A	B	720
Vogue	WIDE TRAC TOURING II (S)	All sizes	A	B	720
Nokian	Nokian eNTYRE	All sizes	A	A	700
Big O	LEGACY TOUR PLUS	P205,215,225 & 235/70R15 T	A	B	700
Bridgestone	DUELER H/L ALENZA "T" Spd Rtd	All sizes	A	B	700
Bridgestone	TURANZA LS-T	All sizes	A	B	700
Co-op	GOLDENMARK LUXURY TOURING (T)	All sizes	A	B	700
Cooper	Discoverer CTS (T-rated)	All sizes	A	B	700
Cordovan	CENTURY	All sizes	A	B	700
Cordovan	GRAND SPIRIT TOURING LS	All sizes	A	B	700
Delta	ESTEEM XLE	P235/75R15	A	B	700
Goodyear	ASSURANCE COMFORTRED	All sizes	A	B	700
Hankook	DynaPro HT	All sizes	A	B	700
Hankook	Optimo H725	All sizes	A	B	700
Hankook	ROADHANDLER	All sizes	A	B	700
Hankook	Route Master UH70	All sizes	A	B	700
Laramie	GRANDEUR TOURING GT 60/65/70 ser.	14 -16	A	B	700
Mentor	VANTAGE TOURING LE	All sizes	A	B	700
Monarch	ULTRA TOUR LS	All sizes	A	B	700
Multi-Mile	EXCEL	All sizes	A	B	700
National	OVATION	P235/75R15	A	B	700
Spartan	AVISTA	P205/65R16 94T	A	B	700
Spartan	AVISTA (S & T)	ALL EXCEPT	A	B	700
Sumitomo	Enhance L/X (T-Rated)	All sizes	A	B	700
Sumitomo	TOURING LST	All sizes	A	B	700
Toyo	VERSADO LX	T	A	B	700
Toyo	TOUREVO LS	T	A	B	700
Toyo	800 ULTRA	ALL	A	B	700
Yokohama	AVID TRZ	P195/70R14 90T	A	B	700
Hankook	DynaPro HT (OE)	265/60R18, 265/60R18	B	A	700
Hankook	veNtus S1 noble2 (OE)	235/55R17, 235/55ZR17	B	A	700
Bridgestone	DUELER H/L ALENZA "S" Spd Rtd	All sizes	B	B	700
Cordovan	TOUR PLUS LST (T rated)	All sizes	A	A	680
Eldorado	LEGEND TOUR (T rated)	All sizes	A	A	680
Hercules	ROADTOUR XUV	235/60R17T, 235/65R18T, P255/65R18T	A	A	680
Jetzon	GENESIS LST (T rated)	All sizes	A	A	680
Multi-Mile	GRAND TOUR LS (T rated)	All sizes	A	A	680
Sigma	REGENT TOURING LS (T rated)	All sizes	A	A	680
Telstar	ECHELON ULTRA LST (T rated)	All sizes	A	A	680
Vanderbilt	TOURING LSE (T rated)	All sizes	A	A	680

For a complete listing of all the tires on the market, you can call the Auto Safety Hot Line toll free, at 888-327-4236 or 800-424-9153(TTY). Or, go to www.safercar.gov/tires

WARNING

As tires age, they naturally dry out and can become potentially dangerous. Some experts recommend getting rid of a six-year-old tire no matter what condition it is in. Recently, a national news organization went undercover and found 12 year old tires for sale, so be sure to check a tire's manufacture date listed as part of the tire identification number before purchasing. Ask for tires that are less than one year old.

Insurance is a big part of ownership expenses, yet it's often forgotten in the show-room. As you shop, remember that the car's design and accident history may affect your insurance rates. Some cars cost less to insure because experience has shown that they are damaged less, less expensive to fix after a collision, or stolen less.

Auto insurance covers different aspects of damage and injury. The term "first party" means you and "third party" means someone else who was involved in a crash with your vehicle. The critical parts of your insurance are:

Liability (third party): This pays for damage or injury you or your vehicle may inflict on others. It is generally limited (in some cases to only $10,000 but may be several hundred thousand dollars) so that if you severely or fatally injure someone, the liability insurance will not be adequate to pay the costs. For minor or moderate damage or injury, insurance companies generally negotiate payments, but for major ones, there may be lawsuits.

Collision Damage (first party): This pays for crash damage to your own car when no other party is found to be at fault for the accident. If you lease your vehicle or have an outstanding loan on it, you will be required to have collision damage insurance.

Uninsured or Underinsured drivers: This pays your expenses when someone else is at fault, but lacks sufficient insurance or personal resources to pay for the damage or injury. The amount typically covers property damage, but may not cover serious injuries.

Comprehensive (first party): This covers the cost of some types of damage not related to crashes including theft.

Supplementary Insurance: Additional forms of insurance that may apply when auto insurance doesn't cover loss are health insurance, which may pay the cost of more serious injuries, life insurance which pays if you are killed in a crash and umbrella policy insurance which may pay liability costs beyond what is covered by your auto policy. An umbrella policy may be important if you want to protect assets such as savings, your house or business, or other major assets.

Shop Around: You can save hundreds of dollars by shopping around for insurance.

There are a number of factors that determine what coverage will cost you. A car's design can affect both the chances and severity of an accident. For example, a well-designed bumper, which few cars have, may escape damage in a low-speed crash. Some cars are easier to repair than others or may have less expensive parts. Cars with four doors tend to be damaged less than cars with two doors.

Other factors that affect your insurance costs include:

Your Annual Mileage: The more you drive, the more your vehicle will be "exposed" to a potential accident. Driving less than 5,000 to 7,500 miles per year often gets a discount. Ask your insurer if they offer this option.

Where You Drive and Park: If you regularly drive and park in the city, you will most likely pay more than if you drive in rural areas. You may get a discount if you garage your car.

Youthful Drivers: Usually the highest premiums are paid by male drivers under the age of 25. Whether or not the under-25-year-old male is married also affects insurance rates. (Married males pay less.) As the driver gets older, and if he or she has good driving record, rates are lowered.

Insurance discounts and surcharges depend upon the way a vehicle is traditionally driven. Sports cars, for example, are usually surcharged due, in part, to the typical driving habits of their owners. Four-door sedans and station wagons generally merit discounts. Not all companies offer discounts or surcharges, and many cars receive neither. Some companies offer a discount or impose a surcharge on collision premiums only. Others apply discounts and surcharges on both collision and comprehensive coverage. Discounts and surcharges usually range from 10 to 30 percent. Remember that

REDUCING INSURANCE COSTS

one company may offer a discount on a particular car while another may not.

Major crashes are rare events for individuals, but more than 35,000 people are killed and double that number suffer serious injuries in crashes each year. In a very severe crash with major injury or death, the limits on first and third party auto insurance will be inadequate to cover the costs. NHTSA estimates that the economic cost of a fatality may range from several million to more than ten million dollars, and injuries such as quadriplegia and serious brain damage could easily have a lifetime cost of ten million dollars for each individual. If a crash is not deemed to be the fault of another motorist (such as with a single vehicle crash), your health insurance may cover the cost of your injuries, but is unlikely to cover such things as long-term rehabilitation and loss of income.

Get Your Discounts: After you have shopped around and found the best deal by comparing the costs of different coverages, be sure you get all the discounts you are entitled to.

Most insurance companies offer discounts of 5 to 30 percent on various parts of your insurance bill. Ask your insurance company for a complete list of the discounts that it offers. These can vary by company and from state to state.

Here are some of the most common insurance discounts:

Driver Education/Defensive Driving Courses: Discounts for completing a state-approved driver education course can mean a $40 reduction in the cost of coverage. Discounts of 5 to 15 percent are available in some states to those who complete a defensive driving course.

Good Student Discounts of up to 25 percent for full-time high school or college students who are in the upper 20 percent of their class, on the dean's list, or have a B or better grade point average.

Good Driver Discounts are available to drivers with an accident and violation-free record, (or no incidents in the past 3 years).

Mature Driver Credit: Drivers ages 50 and older may qualify for up to a 10 percent discount or a lower price bracket.

Sole Female Driver: Some companies offer discounts of 10 percent for females, ages 30 to 64, who are the only driver in a household.

Non-Drinkers and Non-Smokers: A few companies offer incentives ranging from 10–25 percent to those who abstain.

Farmer Discounts: Many companies offer farmers either a 10 to 30 percent discount or a lower price bracket.

Car Pooling: Commuters sharing driving may qualify for discounts of 5 to 25 percent or a lower price bracket.

Children away at school don't drive the family car very often, so if they're on your policy and they're at school, let your company know. If you insure them separately,

! DON'T SPEED !

Besides endangering the lives of your passengers and other drivers, speeding tickets will increase your insurance premium. It only takes one speeding ticket to lose your "preferred" or "good driver" discount, which requires a clean driving record. Two or more speeding tickets or accidents can increase your premium by 40% to 200%. Some insurers may simply drop your coverage. According to the Insurance Institute for Highway Safety (IIHS), you are 17% more likely to be in an accident if you have just one speeding ticket. Insurance companies know this and will charge you for it.

discounts of 10–40 percent or a lower price bracket are available.

Desirable Cars: Premiums are usually much higher for cars that are the favorite target of thieves.

Anti-Theft Device Credits: Discounts of 5-15 percent are offered in some states for cars equipped with a hood lock and an alarm or a disabling device (active or passive) that prevents the car from being started without a key.

Multi-policy and Multicar Policy Discount: Some companies offer discounts of up to 10–20 percent for insuring your home and auto with the same company, or more than one car.

First Accident Allowance: Some insurers offer a "first accident allowance," which guarantees that if a customer achieves a certain number of accident-free years, his or her rates won't go up after the first at-fault accident.

Deductibles: Opting for the largest deductible you're comfortable with will reduce your premiums. Increasing your deductible to $500 from $200 could cut your collision premium about 20 percent. Raising the deductible to $1,000 from $200 could lower your premium about 45 percent. The discounts may vary by company.

Collision Coverage: The older the car, the less the need for collision insurance. Consider dropping collision insurance entirely on an older car. Regardless of how much coverage you carry, the insurance company will only pay up to the car's "book value." For example, if your car requires $1,000 in repairs, but its "book value" is only $500, the insurance company is required to pay only $500.

Organizations: If you are a member of AARP, AAA, the military, a union, a professional group, an alumni association, or similar organization, you may be able to get lower cost insurance or a discount.

YOUNG DRIVERS

Each year, teenagers account for about 15 percent of highway deaths. According to the Insurance Institute for Highway Safety (IIHS), the highest driver death rate per 100,000 people is among 18-year-olds. Parents need to make sure their children are fully prepared to be competent, safe drivers before letting them out on the road. All states issue learner's permits. However, only 35 states and the District of Columbia require permits before getting a driver's license. It isn't difficult for teenagers to get a license and only 14 states prohibit teenagers from driving during night and early morning. Call your state's MVA for young driver laws.

Because of the challenges in learning how to drive safely, parents should not to let their teenagers drive an older SUV, very small car, or one without airbags.

LOW-SPEED COLLISION DAMAGE

The main purpose of a bumper is to protect your car in low-speed collisions. Unfortunately, the bumpers on today's cars and light trucks mostly fail to prevent or minimize such damage. That leaves many of us victims of a $500 to $5,000 repair bill after a minor impact, and the possibility of an increased insurance bill.

For a few years prior to 1982, the federal government required that new cars have bumpers capable of withstanding impacts of up to 5 with no damage. Under the anti-regulatory fervor of the early 1980s, the government rolled back this along with some safety requirements. (The requirement for air bags was initially a victim of deregulation, but a Supreme Court ruling followed by a creative rulemaking gave us both air bags and safety belt use laws.)

Today, the federal law only requires that bumpers protect the safety features of cars in 2.5 mph collisions: less than a walking pace. This standard also requires that passenger *car* bumpers match each other in height to reduce the likelihood of underride in a collision.

Unfortunately, the matching bumper requirement does not apply to SUVs, pickups, and vans. With such a high percentage of these vehicles on the road, bumper mismatches in crashes are quite common which results in excessive damage and costly repairs. The rollback of the bumper standard enabled car companies to sell lots of expensive parts, and has cost consumers millions of dollars in increased insurance premiums and repair costs.

California requires that companies disclose which bumpers meet the old 5 mph standard; but few, if any manufacturers disclose this information.

In order to see how well bumpers actually protect our vehicles, the Insurance Institute for Highway Safety used to conduct low-speed collision damage tests. It was shocking how poorly the bumpers of recent models protected them. IIHS found that repairs after a 10 mph rear end collisions between a car and an SUV from the same manufacturer, repairs would cost as much as $6,000 per vehicle, with the average being around $3,000 (see below). Despite the fact that IIHS is funded by the insurance industry, there has been no interest in continuing this test program.

Consumers Union, which also used to conduct bumper tests and report on the results in Consumer Reports has also discontinued these tests. The result is that consumers are left with neither an effective bumper standard nor consumer information on low speed crash protection.

Bumpers on most contemporary vehicles are mostly minor structures covered by plastic facings. Styling is a more important criterion for bumper design than protection. Now that bumpers contain many of the important sensing devices, they are vulnerable to even more expensive repairs. Until we demand that all cars and light trucks provide better low speed collision protection, car owners will be stuck with the consequent repair bills and high insurance costs.

DAMAGE REPAIR COSTS IN 10 MPH FRONT-INTO-REAR CRASH TESTS

Source: Insurance Institute for Highway Safety

SUV INTO CAR	SUV Damage	Car Damage	Total Damage
Honda CR-V into Honda Civic	$1,721	$1,274	$2,995
Toyota RAV4 into Toyota Corolla	$1,434	$2,327	$3,761
Hyundai Tucson into Kia Forte	$850	$3,223	$4,073
Volkswagen Tiguan into Volkswagen Golf	$2,329	$2,058	$4,387
Jeep Patriot into Dodge Caliber	$1,415	$3,095	$4,510
Ford Escape into Ford Focus	$1,470	$3,386	$4,856
Nissan Rogue into Nissan Sentra	$2,884	$4,560	$7,444

CAR INTO SUV	Car Damage	SUV Damage	Total Damage
Kia Forte into Hyundai Tucson	$1,510	$2,091	$3,601
Dodge Caliber into Jeep Patriot	$2,559	$1,338	$3,897
Honda Civic into Honda CR-V	$4,921	$1,053	$5,974
Volkswagen Golf into Volkswagen Tiguan	$4,555	$1,872	$6,427
Nissan Sentra into Nissan Rogue	$5,114	$1,428	$6,542
Ford Focus into Ford Escape	$5,203	$2,208	$7,411
Corolla into Toyota RAV4	$3,852	$6,015	$9,867

See www.IIHS.org

CENTER FOR AUTO SAFETY

Every year automobile manufacturers spend millions of dollars making their voices heard in government decision making. For example, General Motors, Ford, and other major automakers have large staffs in Detroit and Washington that work solely to influence government activity. But who looks out for the consumer?

For over 45 years, the non-profit Center for Auto Safety (CAS) has told the consumer's story to government agencies, to Congress, and to the courts. Along with countless recalls of defective vehicles, CAS achievements include airbags in every car and lemon laws in every state.

CAS was established in 1970 by Ralph Nader and Consumers Union, publishers of *Consumer Reports*. As consumer concerns about auto safety issues expanded, so did the work of CAS. CAS' activities include:

Initiating Safety Recalls: CAS analyzes over 20,000 consumer complaints each year. CAS requests government investigations and recalls of defective vehicles. CAS advocacy has resulted in the recall of millions of vehicles, most recently GM faulty ignition switches, Jeep fuel tank fires, and exploding Takata airbags.

Representing the Consumer in Washington: CAS follows the activities of federal agencies and Congress to ensure that they carry out their responsibilities to the American taxpayer. CAS brings a consumer's point of view to vehicle safety policies and rule-making. Since 1970, CAS has submitted more than 500 petitions and comments on federal safety standards. Additionally, CAS has testified over 50 times before Congressional Committees on auto safety, warranties and service bulletins, air pollution, consumer protection, and fuel economy.

One major effort on safety standards has been the successful fight to get airbags in every car. CAS also worked to strengthen weak roofs that crush in rollovers. Since 2013, vehicles have had roofs more than twice as strong as before, and deaths and injuries due to rollovers have been dramatically reduced.

Exposing Secret Warranties: CAS played a prominent role in the disclosure of secret warranties, "policy adjustments," as they are called by manufacturers. These occur when an automaker agrees to pay for repair of certain defects beyond the warranty period but refuses to notify consumers.

Lemon Laws: CAS' work on Lemon Laws aided in the enactment of state laws which make it easier to return a defective new automobile and get money back. Prior to the arrival of Lemon Laws, automakers only bought back a few hundred vehicles per year. Today, they are forced to buy back tens of thousands of bad cars each year.

Tire Ratings: Consumers have reliable treadwear ratings to help them get the most miles for their dollar thanks to a CAS' lawsuit overturning DOT's revocation of this valuable tire information program.

Legal Action: When CAS has exhausted other means of obtaining relief for consumer problems, it initiates legal action. The Center recently succeeded in a lawsuit against DOT Secretary Anthony Foxx, forcing the government to make public all manufacturer communications to dealers regarding safety issues. CAS also challenges class action settlements that don't deliver for consumers.

CAS is your safety and lemon insurance, and depends on public support to do all its good work. Annual membership is $40. All contributions are tax-deductible. To contribute by credit card, go to the CAS website at: www.autosafety.org/make-donation/.

To contribute by mail, send a check to: Center for Auto Safety, 1825 Connecticut Ave., NW #330, Washington, DC 20009-5708.

CENTER FOR AUTO SAFETY ONLINE

The Center for Auto Safety has a website at www.autosafety.org to provide information to consumers and to organize consumer campaigns against auto companies on safety defects. Detailed information and advice on defects in specific makes and models are on CAS' website. Consumers with lemons can file online complaints with CAS and get referred to lemon lawyers.

WWW.AUTOSAFETY.ORG

A TRIBUTE TO CLARENCE M. DITLOW, III FROM RALPH NADER

America lost one of the most formidable advocates in its history when Clarence Ditlow died last November. For over 40 years, Clarence served tirelessly as the Executive Director of the Center for Auto Safety.

Clarence came to Washington, D.C. in June 1971 to work on auto safety issues with Ralph Nader and Joan Claybrook (who later became NHTSA Administrator) at Nader's Public Interest Research Group. Over the course of the next five decades, he monitored the National Highway Traffic Safety Administration's activities, helped to inform Congress on auto safety, fuel economy and emissions issues, and exposed the auto industry when it failed to serve its customers.

At the Center, Clarence got important Federal legislation and motor vehicle safety standards passed, got unsafe vehicles recalled, and kept the public informed on safety issues.

Ralph Nader described him as:

"Calm, deliberate and a man of few words, this graduate of Lehigh, Georgetown Law and Harvard Law School bore down on wrongdoing, negligence and bureaucratic passivity with jack-hammer intensity year in and year out. While culpable auto executives were on the golf links, he was at his office on weekends assembling evidence about the causes of crashes and their human casualties, and preparing formal petitions and lawsuits demanding action."

"I recruited this remarkable man about 45 years ago to work on auto safety. It took no more than fifteen minutes for me to invite him to work with us full-time. That's the kind of first impression he made. He was serious, committed and answered every question with clarity and brevity. His ability to distill and convey information resulted in reporters regularly tapping him for television, radio, and newspaper interviews."

"Over the years he was the 'go-to' person for hundreds of reporters, columnists, editorial writers, researchers, and legislative staff. Patiently, he would walk them through the details of motor vehicle failures and engineering deficiencies, the derelictions of management and the inaction of government regulators not doing their job. He took his work beyond auto safety to include fuel efficiencies, emitted pollutants, and sloppy vehicle construction and design."

"You could hardly have imagined a more perfect blend of knowledge, compassion, persistence, resilience, extraordinary strategic and communication abilities and factual diligence as was embodied in such an amiable man. He was a civic personality par excellence who never wavered in his many fights with wayward corporate adversaries."

Clarence's extensive efforts resulted in numerous changes in federal law and policy. These changes have been greatly responsible for the dramatic reduction in motor vehicle deaths on our nation's highways, and have prevented an even greater number of injuries. The Center for Auto Safety has evaluated Clarence's work on seat belts, airbags, rollover, child seats and other critical safety standards, and estimates that his efforts contributed to saving the lives of over 330,000 people during the past 40 years.

Clarence labored to achieve auto safety victories both large and small. On the heels of his efforts to expose the most widespread safety defect in history, exploding Takata airbags that have resulted in over 70 million vehicles recalled worldwide, he was also focused on the smallest of those among us. One of Clarence's final campaigns was an attempt to persuade NHTSA to promulgate a stronger standard for seatback strength. He documented dozens of cases where children, who were otherwise properly restrained in rear seats, were injured or killed after a front seatback failed under the weight of its occupant. It would be a tribute to him for NHTSA to upgrade this standard.

The full story of Clarence Ditlow remains to be told, as his work lives on in the form of stronger vehicle safety protections that will continue to prevent deaths and mitigate injuries well into the foreseeable future.

Americans spend billions of dollars on vehicle repairs every year. While many of those repairs are satisfactory, there are times when getting your vehicle fixed can be a very difficult process. In fact, vehicle defects and repairs are the number one cause of consumer complaints, according to the Federal Trade Commission. This chapter is designed to help you if you have a complaint, whether it's for a new vehicle still under warranty or for one you've had for years. In addition, we offer a guide to arbitration, the names and addresses of consumer groups, federal agencies, and the manufacturers themselves. Finally, we tell you how to take the important step of registering your complaint, particularly if it involves safety, with the U.S. Department of Transportation.

No matter what your complaint, keep accurate records. Copies of the following items are indispensable in helping to resolve your problems:

☑ your original purchase papers

☑ your service invoices

☑ bills you have paid

☑ letters you have written to the manufacturer or the repair facility owner

☑ written repair estimates from your independent mechanic.

☑ notes on discussion with company representatives including names and dates.

RESOLVING COMPLAINTS

Here are some basic steps to help you resolve your problem:

1 First, return your vehicle to the repair facility that did the work. Bring a written list of the problems and make sure that you keep a copy of the list. Give the repair facility a reasonable opportunity to examine your vehicle and attempt to fix it. Speak directly to the service manager (not to the service writer who wrote up your repair order), and ask him or her to test drive the vehicle with you so that you can point out the problem.

2 If that doesn't resolve the problem, take the vehicle to a diagnostic center or another mechanic for an independent examination. This may cost $45 to $60. Get a written statement defining the problem and outlining how it may be fixed. Give your repair shop a copy. If your vehicle is under warranty, do not allow any warranty repair by an independent mechanic; you may not be reimbursed by the manufacturer.

3 If your repair shop does not respond to the independent assessment, present your problem to an arbitration panel. These panels hear both sides of the story and try to come to a resolution.

If the problem is with a new vehicle dealer, or if you feel that the manufacturer is responsible, you may be able to use one of the manufacturer's arbitration programs.

If the problem is solely with an independent dealer, a local Better Business Bureau (BBB) may be able to mediate your complaint. It may also offer an arbitration hearing. In any case, the BBB should enter your complaint into its files on that establishment.

When contacting any arbitration program, determine how long the process takes, who makes the final decision, whether you are bound by that decision, and whether the program handles all problems or only warranty complaints.

Beware of "binding arbitration" because you give up your right to later pursue legal action.

4 If there are no arbitration programs in your area, contact private consumer groups, local government agencies, or your local "action line" newspaper columnist, newspaper editor, or radio/TV broadcaster. A phone call or letter from them may persuade a repair facility to take action. Send a copy of your letter to the repair shop.

5 One of your last resorts is to bring a lawsuit against the dealer, manufacturer, or repair facility in small claims court. The fee for filing such an action is usually small, and you generally act as your own attorney, saving attorney's fees. There is a monetary limit on the amount you can claim, which varies from state to state. Your local consumer affairs office, state attorney general's office, or the clerk of the court can tell you how to file such a suit.

6 Finally, talk with an attorney. It's best to select an attorney who is familiar with handling automotive problems and has no ties to the local business community. Lawyer referral services can provide names of attorneys who deal with automobile problems. If you can't afford an attorney, contact the Legal Aid Society.

WARRANTY COMPLAINTS

If your vehicle is under warranty or you are having problems with a factory-authorized dealership, here are some guidelines:

1 Have the warranty available to show the dealer. Make sure you call the problem to the dealer's attention before the end of the warranty period.

2 If you are still dissatisfied after giving the dealer a reasonable opportunity to fix your vehicle, contact the manufacturer's representative (also called the zone representative) in your area. This person can authorize the dealer to make repairs or take other steps to resolve the dispute. Your dealer will have your zone representative's name and telephone number. Explain the problem and ask for a meeting and a personal inspection of your vehicle.

3 If you can't get satisfaction from the zone representative, call or write the manufacturer's owner relations department. Your owner's manual contains this phone number and address. In each case, as you move up the chain, indicate the steps you have already taken and keep careful records of your efforts.

4 Your next option is to present your problem to a complaint handling arbitration program. Beware of "binding arbitration" because you give up your right to later pursue legal action and beware of arbitrators selected by a manufacturer, dealer or repair shop.

If you complain of a problem during the warranty period, you have a right to have the problem fixed even after the warranty runs out. If your warranty has not been honored, you may be able to "revoke acceptance," which means that you return the vehicle to the dealer. If you are successful, you may be entitled to a replacement vehicle or to a full refund of the purchase price and reimbursement of legal fees under the Magnuson-Moss Warranty Act. Or, if you are covered by one of the state lemon laws, you may be able to return the vehicle and receive a refund or replacement from the manufacturer.

NEED HELP?

If you need legal assistance with your repair problem, the Center for Auto Safety has a list of lawyers who specialize in helping consumers with auto repair problems. For the names of attorneys in your area, send a stamped, self-addressed envelope to: Center for Auto Safety, 1825 Connecticut Ave. NW, Suite 330, Washington, DC 20009. Check their website at www.autosafety.org for a shorter list of lemon law attorneys. The Center has also published *The Lemon Book*, a detailed guide to resolving automobile complaints, available for $17.50 directly from the Center.

Attorneys Take Note: For information on litigation assistance provided by the Center for Auto Safety, including *The Lemon Law Litigation Manual*, please contact the Center for Auto Safety at the above address.

VEHICLE SAFETY HOT LINE: 800-424-9393
TTY FOR HEARING IMPAIRED: 800-424-9153
WWW.SAFERCAR.GOV

The toll-free Auto Safety Hot Line can provide information on recalls, record information about safety problems, and refer you to the appropriate government experts on other vehicle related problems. You can even have recall information mailed to you within 24 hours of your call at no charge. Most importantly, you can call the hot line to report safety problems which will become part of the National Highway - Traffic Safety Administration's complaint database. If you have access to the internet, www.safercar.gov is a more efficient way to register complaints and obtain recall and safety information. You can also look up the individual complaints about a particular vehicle.

COMPLAINT INDEX

Thanks to the efforts of the Center for Auto Safety, we are able to provide you with a car by car index of vehicle complaints on file with the National Highway Traffic Safety Administration (NHTSA). Each year, thousands of Americans file online, or call the government, to register complaints about their vehicles.

The Car Book Complaint Index is the result of our analysis of these complaints. It is based on a ratio of the number of complaints for each vehicle to the sales of that vehicle. In order to predict the expected complaint performance of the 2017 models, we have examined the complaint history of that car's series. The term series refers to the fact that when a manufacturer introduces a new model, that vehicle remains essentially unchanged, on average, for four to six years. For example, the Ford Explorer was redesigned in 2011 and remains essentially the same car for 2017. As such, we have compiled the complaint experience for that series in order to give you some information to use in deciding which car to buy. For vehicles introduced or significantly changed in 2017, we do not yet have enough data to develop a complaint index.

The following table presents the projected best and worst complaint ratings for the 2017 models for which we can develop ratings. Higher index numbers mean the vehicle generated a greater number of complaints. Lower numbers indicate fewer complaints.

2017 PROJECTED COMPLAINT INDEX

THE BEST	INDEX*
Audi Q7	636
Mercedes-Benz GL-Class	675
Toyota Prius C	719
Infiniti Q50	801
Chevrolet Malibu	804
Lexus GS	819
Toyota Yaris	892
Mini Countryman	977
Subaru Crosstrek	1005
BMW X5	1016
Toyota Corolla	1026
Lexus NX	1029
Audi Q3	1112
Toyota Highlander	1122
Mercedes-Benz GLE-Class	1190
Lexus IS	1210
Mazda Mazda3	1231
Toyota Prius V	1244
BMW 2 Series	1270
Kia Sportage	1274
Lexus GX	1326

THE WORST	INDEX*
Hyundai Tucson	>20,000
Tesla Model S	>20,000
Volvo XC90	18,510
Chrysler 200	17,737
Infiniti QX50	15,125
Jeep Cherokee	15,035
Dodge Journey	11,302
Smart ForTwo	10,945
Jeep Grand Cherokee	10,774
Ford Focus	10,063
Ford Fiesta	9,959
Jeep Wrangler	9,449
Acura TLX	9,345
Volvo V60	9,053
Dodge Dart	8,913
Jeep Renegade	8,574
Fiat 500	8,501
Volkswagen Golf	7,943
Honda Pilot	7,758
Nissan Pathfinder	7,507

*IMPORTANT NOTE: The numbers represent relative index scores, not the number of complaints received. The complaint index score considers sales volume and years on the road. Lower index numbers are better. We capped the complaint index at 20,000 for excessively high complaint indices.

Consumer Groups and Government Contacts

Advocates for Highway and Auto Safety
750 First St., NE, Suite 1130
Washington, DC 20002
(202) 408-1711/408-1699 fax
www.saferoads.org
An alliance of consumer, health and safety groups and insurance companies. A great resource for state laws governing auto safety. A leading organization fighting for safer cars before the U.S. Congress and the National Highway Traffic Safety Administration.

Consumer Action
1170 Market St., Suite 500
San Francisco, CA 94102
(415) 777-9635
www.consumer-action.org
Complaint handling and advocacy related to consumer rights. A great resource for non-English consumer information.

Consumers for Auto Reliability and Safety
1303 J St., Suite 270
Sacramento, CA 95814
(530) 759-9440
www.carconsumers.org
Auto safety, airbags, and lemon laws. A leader in exposing the sale and rental of cars with open safety recalls.

KIDS AND CARS
(816) 216-7085
www.kidsandcars.org
email@kidsandcars.org
Safety and advocacy related to protecting children in and around motor vehicles. They lead the effort to require already available technology to prevent the death of unattended children in hot cars or from tragic back over accidents.

SafetyBelt Safe, U.S.A.
P.O. Box 553
Altadena, CA 91003
(800) 745-SAFE
www.carseat.org
stombrella@carseat.org
Excellent information and training on child safety seats and safety belt usage. The majority of parents do not use child seats correctly.

National Highway Traffic Safety Administration
1200 New Jersey Ave., SE, West Bldg.
Washington, DC 20590
(888) 327-4236
www.nhtsa.gov
www.safercar.gov
NHTSA issues safety and fuel economy standards for new motor vehicles; investigates safety defects and enforces recall of defective vehicles and equipment; conducts research and demonstration programs on vehicle safety, fuel economy, driver safety, and automobile inspection and repair; provides grants for state highway safety programs in areas such as police traffic services, driver education and licensing, emergency medical services, pedestrian safety, and alcohol abuse.

In addition with the EPA, they are in charge of setting fuel economy standards. They have a huge job, are woefully underfunded and need consumers to support their efforts in Congress.

Environmental Protection Agency
1200 Pennsylvania Ave., NW
Washington, DC 20460
(202) 272-0167/www.epa.gov
www.fueleconomy.gov
EPA's responsibilities include setting and enforcing air and noise emission standards for motor vehicles and measuring fuel economy in new vehicles (EPA Fuel Economy Guide).

Federal Trade Commission
600 Pennsylvania Ave., NW
Washington, DC 20580
(202) 326-2222
www.ftc.gov
The FTC regulates advertising, credit practices, marketing abuses, and professional services and ensures that products are properly labeled (as in fuel economy ratings). The commission covers unfair or deceptive trade practices in motor vehicle sales and repairs, as well as non-safety defects.

U.S. Department of Justice
Civil Division
950 Pennsylvania Ave., NW
Washington, DC 20530
(202) 307-0066
www.justice.gov/civil
feedback@doj.gov
The DOJ enforces federal law that requires manufacturers to label new automobiles and forbids removal or alteration of labels before delivery to consumers. Labels must contain make, model, vehicle identification number, dealer's name, suggested base price, manufacturer option costs, and manufacturer's suggested retail price.

AUTOMOBILE MANUFACTURERS

Acura (Division of Honda)
John Ikeda, Vice President-General Manager
See Honda for address
Customer Relations: 800-382-2238

Audi (Division of Volkswagen)
Scott Keogh, President
See Volkswagen for address
Customer Relations: 800-822-2834

BMW
Ludwig Willisch, President and CEO
300 Chestnut Ridge Road
Woodcliff Lake, NJ 07677-7731
Customer Relations: 800-831-1117

Buick (Division of General Motors)
P.O. Box 33136
Detroit, MI 48232-5136
Customer Relations: 800-521-7300

Cadillac (Division of General Motors)
P.O. Box 33169
Detroit, MI 48232-5169
Customer Relations: 800-458-8006

Chevrolet (Division of General Motors)
P.O. Box 33136
Detroit, MI 48323-5136
Customer Relations: 800-222-1020

Chrysler (Chrysler, Dodge, Fiat, Jeep, Ram)
Sergio Marchionne, CEO
1000 Chrysler Drive
Auburn Hills, MI 48326
Customer Relations: 800-247-9753

Dodge (Division of Chrysler)
P.O. Box 21-8004
Auburn Hills, MI 48321-8004
Customer Relations: 800-423-6343

Fiat (Division of Chrysler)
P.O. Box 21-8004
Auburn Hills, MI 48321-8004
Customer Relations: 888-242-6342

Ford (Ford, Lincoln)
Mark Fields, President and CEO
P.O. Box 6248
Dearborn, MI 48126
Customer Relations 800-392-3673

General Motors (Buick, Cadillac, Chev., GMC)
Mary Barra, Chairman and CEO
300 Renaisance Center
Detorit, MI 48265

Genesis (Division of Hyundai)
Erwin Raphael, General Manager
10550 Talbert Ave.
Fountain Valley, CA 92708
Customer Relations: 844-340-9741

GMC (Division of General Motors)
P.O. Box 33172
Detroit, MI 48232
Customer Relations: 800-462-8782

Honda (Honda, Acura)
Toshiaki Mikoshiba, President and CEO
1919 Torrance Blvd.
Torrance, CA 90501
Customer Relations: 800-999-1009

Hyundai (Hyundai, Genesis)
David Zuchowski, President and CEO
P.O. Box 20850
Fountain Valley, CA 92728-0850
Customer Relations: 800-633-5151
Email: consumeraffairs@hmausa.com

Infiniti (Division of Nissan)
Roland Krueger, President
See Nissan for address
Customer Relations: 800-662-6200

Jaguar, Land Rover
Joachim Eberhardt, President
555 MacArthur Blvd.
Mahwah, NJ 07430
Jaguar Customer Relations: 800-452-4827
Land Rover Cust. Relations: 800-637-6837

Jeep (Division of Chrysler)
P.O. Box 21-8004
Auburn Hills, MI 48321-8004
Customer Relations: 877-426-5337

Kia
Jang Won Sohn, President and CEO
P.O. Box 52410
Irvine, CA 92619-2410
Customer Relations: 800-333-4542

Lexus (Division of Toyota)
Jeff Bracken, Vice President and General Manager
P.O. Box 2991-Mail Drop L201
Torrance, CA 90509-2991
Customer Relations: 800-255-3987

Lincoln (Division of Ford)
Kumar Galhotra, President
See Ford for address
Customer Relations: 800-521-4140

Mazda
Masahiro Moro, President and CEO
P.O. Box 19734
Irvine, CA 92623-9734
Customer Relations: 800-222-5500

Mercedes-Benz
Dietmar Exler, President and CEO
1 Mercedes Drive
Montvale, NJ 07645
Customer Relations 800-367-6372

Mini (Division of BMW)
Thomas Felbermair, Vice President
See BMW for address
Customer Relations: 866-275-6464

Mitsubishi
Ryujiro Kobashi, President and CEO
P.O. Box 6400
Cypress, CA 90630-9998
Customer Reloations: 800-648-7820

Nissan
Carlos Ghosn, President and CEO
P.O. Box 685003
Franklin, TN 37068-5003
Customer Relations: 800-647-7261

Porsche
Klaus Zellmer, President and CEO
980 Hammond Dr., Suite 1000
Atlanta, GA 30328
Customer Relations: 800-767-7243

Ram (Division of Chrysler)
P.O. Box 21-8007
Auburn Hills, MI 48321-8004
Customer Relations: 866-726-4636

Smart (Division of Mercedes-Benz)
Mike Nolte, General Manager
1 Mercedes Drive
Montvale, NJ 07645
Customer Relations 800-762-2466

Subaru
Tomomi Nakamura, Chairman and CEO
P.O. Box 6000
Cherry Hill, NJ 08034-6000
Customer Relations: 800-782-2783

Telsa
Elon Musk, Chairman and CEO
3500 Deer Creek
Palo Alto, CA 94304
Customer Relations: 877-798-3752

Toyota (Toyota, Lexus)
Jim Lentz, President and CEO
19001 South Western Ave. Dept. WC11
Torrance, CA 90501
Customer Relations: 800-331-4331

Volkswagen
Hinrich Woebcken, President and CEO
2200 Ferdinand Porsche Dr.
Herndon, VA 20171
Customer Relations: 800-822-8987

Volvo
Lex Kerssemakers, President and CEO
One Volvo Drive
P.O. Box 914
Rockleigh, NJ 07647
Customer Relations: 800-458-1552

LEMON LAWS

Sometimes, despite our best efforts, we buy a vehicle that just doesn't work right. There may be little problem after little problem, or perhaps one big problem that the dealer cannot seem to fix. Because of the "sour" taste that such vehicles leave in the mouths of consumers who buy them, these vehicles are known as "lemons."

In the past, it was difficult to obtain a refund or replacement if a vehicle was a lemon. The burden of proof was left to the consumer. Because it is hard to define exactly what constitutes a lemon, many lemon owners were unable to win a case against a manufacturer. And when they won, consumers had to pay for their attorneys giving them less than if they had traded in their lemon.

Thanks to "Lemon Laws" passed by all states, lemon-aide is available when consumers get stuck with a lemon. Although there are some important state-to-state variations, all of the laws have similarities: They establish a period of coverage, usually two years from delivery or the written warranty period, whichever is shorter; they may require some form of noncourt arbitration; and most importantly they define a lemon. In most states a new car, truck, or van is "presumed" to be a lemon when it has been taken back to the shop 3 to 4 times for the same problem or is out of service for a total of 30 days during the covered period. This time does not mean consecutive days and can be for different problems. 15 states have safety lemon provisions which presume a vehicle is a lemon after only 1 to 2 repairs of a defect likely to cause death or serious injury. Be sure to keep careful records of your repairs since some states now require only one of the repairs to be within the specified time period. Thirty-three states provide for the award of attorney fees with the other 17 relying on the Federal lemon law for fees. A vehicle may be covered by the lemon law even though it doesn't meet the specific state requirements.

Specific information about your state's law can be obtained from your state attorney general's office or at the Center for Auto Safety's website. The following table offers a general description of the Lemon Law in your state and what you need to do to set it in motion (Notification/Trigger). We indicate where state-run arbitration programs are available. State-run programs are the best type of arbitration. Be aware, a few state lemon laws are so bad consumers should only rely on the Federal lemon law (the Magnuson-Moss Warranty Act) and state contract law. We have marked these bad laws with a ☒ while the best laws have a ☑.

If you would like to see the complete law in your state, go to www.autosafety.org.

| ☑ **The Best Lemon Laws** |
| ☒ **The Worst Lemon Laws** |

Alabama	Qualification: 3 unsuccessful repairs or 30 calendar days within shorter of 24 months or 24,000 miles, provided 1 repair attempt or 1 day out of service is within shorter of 1 year or 12,000 miles. Notice/Trigger: Certified mail to manufacturer + opportunity for final repair attempt within 14 calendar days.
Alaska	Qualification: 3 unsuccessful repairs or 30 business days out of service within shorter of 1 year or warranty. Notice/Trigger: Certified mail to manufacturer + dealer (or repair agent) that problem has not been corrected in reasonable number of attempts + refund or replacement demanded within 60 days. Manufacturer has 30 calendar days for final repair attempt.
Arizona	Qualification: 4 unsuccessful repairs or 30 calendar days out of service within warranty period or shorter of 2 years or 24,000 miles. Notice/Trigger: Written notice + opportunity to repair to manufacturer.
Arkansas ☑ BEST	Qualification: 3 unsuccessful repairs, 5 total repairs of any nonconformity, or 1 unsuccessful repair of problem likely to cause death or serious bodily injury within longer of 24 months or 24,000 miles. Notice/Trigger: Certified or registered mail to manufacturer who has 10 days to notify consumer of repair facility. Facility has 10 days to repair.

L—Law specifically applies to leased vehicles; S-C—State has certified guidelines for arbitration; S-R—State-run arbitration mechanism available

California	Qualification: 4 repair attempts or 30 calendar days out of service or 2 repair attempts for defect likely to cause death or serious bodily injury within shorter of 18 months or 18,000 miles, or "reasonable" number of attempts during entire express warranty period. Notice/Trigger: Direct written notice to manufacturer at address clearly specified in owner's manual. Covers small businesses with up to 5 vehicles under 10,000 pounds GVWR.
☑ BEST	

Colorado	Qualification: 4 unsuccessful repairs or 30 business days out of service within shorter of 1 year or warranty. Notice/Trigger: Prior certified mail notice + opportunity to repair for manufacturer.
☒ WORST	

Connecticut	Qualification: 4 unsuccessful repairs or 30 calendar days out of service within shorter of 2 years or 24,000 miles, or 2 unsuccessful repairs of problem likely to cause death or serious bodily injury within warranty period or 1 year. Notice/Trigger: Report to manufacturer, agent, or dealer. Written notice to manufacturer only if required in owner's manual or warranty. S-R

Delaware	Qualification: 4 unsuccessful repairs or 30 calendar days out of service within shorter of 1 year or warranty. Notice/Trigger: Written notice + opportunity to repair to manufacturer.

D.C.	Qualification: 4 unsuccessful repairs or 30 calendar days out of service or 1 unsuccessful repair of safety-related defect, within shorter of 2 years or 18,000 miles. Notice/Trigger: Report to manufacturer, agent, or dealer.

Florida	Qualification: 3 unsuccessful repairs or 15 calendar days within 24 months from delivery. Notice/Trigger: Certified or express mail notice to manufacturer who has 10 days to notify consumer of repair facility plus 10 more calendar days for final repair attempt after delivery to designated dealer. S-R

Georgia	Qualification: 1 unsuccessful repair of serious safety defect or 3 unsuccessful repair attempts or 30 calendar days out of service within shorter of 24,000 miles or 24 months. Notification/Trigger: Overnight or certified mail notice return receipt requested. Manufacturer has 7 days to notify consumer of repair facility & consumer has 14 days from manufacturer receipt of original notice to deliver vehicle to repair facility. Facility has 28 calendar days from manufacturer receipt of original notice to repair. State-run arbitration mechanism available. Law specifically applies to leased vehicles.

Hawaii	Qualification: 3 unsuccessful repair attempts, or 1 unsuccessful repair attempt of defect likely to cause death or serious bodily injury, or out of service for total of 30 days within shorter of 2 years or 24,000 miles. Notice/Trigger: Written notice + opportunity to repair to manufacturer. S-R

Idaho	Qualification: 4 repair attempts or 30 business days out of service within shorter of 2 years or 24,000 miles, or 1 repair of complete failure of braking or steering likely to cause death or serious bodily injury. Notice/Trigger: Written notice to manufacturer or dealer + one opportunity to repair to manufacturer. S-R.

Illinois	Qualification: 4 unsuccessful repairs or 30 business days out of service within shorter of 1 year or 12,000 miles. Notice/Trigger: Written notice + opportunity to repair to manufacturer.

Indiana	Qualification: 4 unsuccessful repairs or 30 business days out of service within shorter of 18 months or 18,000 miles. Notice/Trigger: Written notice to manufacturer only if required in the warranty.
☒ WORST	

L—Law specifically applies to leased vehicles; S-C—State has certified guidelines for arbitration; S-R—State-run arbitration mechanism available

Iowa	Qualification: 3 unsuccessful repairs, or 1 unsuccessful repair of nonconformity likely to cause death or serious bodily injury, or 30 calendar days out of service within shorter of 2 years or 24,000 miles. Notice/Trigger: Certified registered mail + final opportunity to repair within 10 calendar days of receipt of notice to manufacturer.
Kansas	Qualification: 4 unsuccessful repairs or 30 calendar days out of service or 10 total repairs within shorter of 1 year or warranty. Notice/Trigger: Actual notice to manufacturer.
Kentucky	Qualification: 4 unsuccessful repairs or 30 calendar days out of service within shorter of 1 year or 12,000 miles. Notice/Trigger: Written notice to manufacturer.
Louisiana	Qualification: 4 unsuccessful repairs or 90 calendar days out of service within shorter of 1 year or warranty. Notice/Trigger: Report to manufacturer or dealer.
Maine	Qualification: 3 unsuccessful repairs (or 1 unsuccessful repair of serious failure of brakes or steering) or 15 business days out of service within shorter of warranty or 3 years or 18,000 miles. Applies to vehicles within first 18,000 miles or 3 years regardless of whether claimant is original owner. Notice/Trigger: Written notice to manufacturer or dealer. Manufacturer has 7 business days after receipt for final repair attempt. S-R
Maryland	Qualification: 4 unsuccessful repairs, 30 calendar days out of service or 1 unsuccessful repair of braking or steering system within shorter of 15 months or 15,000 miles. Notice/Trigger: Certified mail return receipt requested + opportunity to repair within 30 calendar days of receipt of notice to manufacturer or factory branch.
Massachusetts	Qualification: 3 unsuccessful repairs or 10 business days out of service within shorter of 1 year or 15,000 miles. Notice/Trigger: Notice to manufacturer or dealer who has 7 business days to attempt final repair. S-R
Michigan	Qualification: 4 unsuccessful repairs within 2 years from date of first unsuccessful repair or 30 calendar days within shorter of 1 year or warranty. Notice/Trigger: Certified mail return receipt requested to manufacturer who has 5 business days to repair after delivery. Consumer may notify manufacturer after third repair attempt.
Minnesota	Qualification: 4 unsuccessful repairs or 30 business days or 1 unsuccessful repair of total braking or steering loss likely to cause death or serious bodily injury within shorter of 2 years or warranty. Notice/Trigger: Written notice + opportunity to repair to manufacturer, agent, or dealer.
Mississippi	Qualification: 3 unsuccessful repairs or 15 business days out of service within shorter of 1 year or warranty. Notice/Trigger: Written notice to manufacturer who has 10 business days to repair after delivery to designated dealer.
Missouri	Qualification: 4 unsuccessful repairs or 30 business days out of service within shorter of 1 year or warranty. Notice/Trigger: Written notice to manufacturer who has 10 calendar days to repair after delivery to designated dealer.
Montana	Qualification: 4 unsuccessful repairs or 30 business days out of service after notice within shorter of 2 years or 18,000 miles. Notice/Trigger: Written notice + opportunity to repair to manufacturer. S-R
Nebraska	Qualification: 4 unsuccessful repairs or 40 calendar days out of service within shorter of 1 year or warranty. Notice/Trigger: Certified mail + opportunity to repair to manufacturer.

L—Law specifically applies to leased vehicles; S-C—State has certified guidelines for arbitration; S-R—State-run arbitration mechanism available

Nevada	Qualification: 4 unsuccessful repairs or 30 calendar days out of service within shorter of 1 year or warranty. Notice/Trigger: Written notice to manufacturer.
New Hampshire	Qualification: 3 unsuccessful repairs by same dealer or 30 business days out of service within warranty. Notice/Trigger: Report to manufacturer, distributor, agent, or dealer (on forms provided by manufacturer) + final opportunity to repair before arbitration. S-R
New Jersey ☑ BEST	Qualification: 3 Unsuccessful repairs or 20 calendar days out of service within shorter of 2 years or 24,000 miles; or 1 unsuccessful repair of a serious safety defect likely to cause death or serious bodily injury. Notice/Trigger: Certified mail notice, return receipt requested to manufacturer who has 10 days to repair. Consumer may notify manufacturer at any time after the second repair attempt, or after the first repair attempt in the case of a serious safety defect.
New Mexico ☒ WORST	Qualification: 4 unsuccessful repairs or 30 business days out of service within shorter of 1 year or warranty. Notice/Trigger: Written notice + opportunity to repair to manufacturer, agent, or dealer.
New York	Qualification: 4 unsuccessful repairs or 30 calendar days out of service within shorter of 2 years or 18,000 miles. Notice/Trigger: Notice to manufacturer, agent, or dealer.
North Carolina	Qualification: 4 unsuccessful repairs within shorter of 24 months, 24,000 miles or warranty or 20 business days out of service during any 12 month period of warranty. Notice/Trigger: Written notice to manufacturer + opportunity to repair within 15 calendar days of receipt only if required in warranty or owner's manual.
North Dakota ☒ WORST	Qualification: 3 unsuccessful repairs or 30 business days out of service within shorter of 1 year or warranty. Notice/Trigger: Direct written notice + opportunity to repair to manufacturer. (Manufacturer's informal arbitration process serves as prerequisite to consumer refund or replacement.)
Ohio ☑ BEST	Qualification: 3 unsuccessful repairs of same nonconformity, 30 calendar days out of service, 8 total repairs of any nonconformity, or 1 unsuccessful repair of problem likely to cause death or serious bodily injury within shorter of 1 year or 18,000 miles. Notice/Trigger: Report to manufacturer, its agent, or dealer.
Oklahoma	Qualification: 4 unsuccessful repairs or 30 calendar days out of service within shorter of 1 year or warranty. Notice/Trigger: Written notice + opportunity to repair to manufacturer.
Oregon	Qualification: 4 unsuccessful repairs or 30 business days within shorter of 1 year or 12,000 miles. Notice/Trigger: Direct written notice + opportunity to repair to manufacturer.
Pennsylvania	Qualification: 3 unsuccessful repairs or 30 calendar days within shorter of 1 year, 12,000 miles, or warranty. Notice/Trigger: Delivery to authorized service + repair facility. If delivery impossible, written notice to manufacturer or its repair facility obligates them to pay for delivery.
Rhode Island	Qualification: 4 unsuccessful repairs or 30 calendar days out of service within shorter of 1 year or 15,000 miles. Notice/Trigger: Report to dealer or manufacturer who has 7 days for final repair opportunity.

L—Law specifically applies to leased vehicles; S-C—State has certified guidelines for arbitration; S-R—State-run arbitration mechanism available

South Carolina	Qualification: 3 unsuccessful repairs or 30 calendar days out of service within shorter of 1 year or 12,000 miles. Notice/Trigger: Certified mail + opportunity to repair (not more than 10 business days) to manufacturer only if manufacturer informed consumer of such at time of sale.
South Dakota	Qualification: 4 unsuccessful repairs, 1 of which occurred during shorter of 1 year or 12,000 miles, or 30 calendar days out of service during shorter of 24 months or 24,000 miles. Notice/Trigger: Certified mail to manufacturer + final opportunity to repair + 7 calendar days to notify consumer of repair facility.
Tennessee	Qualification: 4 unsuccessful repairs or 30 calendar days out of service within shorter of 1 year or warranty. Notice/Trigger: Certified mail notice to manufacturer + final opportunity to repair within 10 calendar days.
Texas	Qualification: 4 unsuccessful repairs when 2 occurred within shorter of 1 year or 12,000 miles, + other 2 occur within shorter of 1 year or 12,000 miles immediately following second repair attempt; or 2 unsuccessful repairs of serious safety defect when 1 occurred within shorter of 1 year or 12,000 miles + other occurred within shorter of 1 year or 12,000 miles immediately following first repair; or 30 calendar days out of service within shorter of 2 years or 24,000 miles + at least 2 attempts were made within shorter of 1 year or 12,000 miles. Notice/Trigger: Written notice to manufacturer. S-R
Utah	Qualification: 4 unsuccessful repairs or 30 business days out of service within shorter of 1 year or warranty. Notice/Trigger: Report to manufacturer, agent, or dealer. S-R
Vermont	Qualification: 3 unsuccessful repairs when at least first repair was within warranty, or 30 calendar days out of service within warranty. Notice/Trigger: Written notice to manufacturer (on provided forms) after third repair attempt, or 30 days. Arbitration must be held within 45 days after notice, during which time manufacturer has 1 final repair. S-R Note: Repairs must been done by same authorized agent or dealer, unless consumer shows good cause for taking vehicle to different agent or dealer.
Virginia	Qualification: 3 unsuccessful repairs, or 1 repair attempt of serious safety defect, or 30 calendar days out of service within 18 months. Notice/Trigger: Written notice to manufacturer. If 3 unsuccessful repairs or 30 days already exhausted before notice, manufacturer has 1 more repair attempt not to exceed 15 days.
Washington	Qualification: 4 unsuccessful repairs, 30 calendar days out of service (15 during warranty period), or 2 repairs of serious safety defect, first reported within shorter of warranty or 24 months or 24,000 miles. One repair attempt + 15 of 30 days must fall within manufacturer's express warranty of at least 1 year of 12,000 miles. Notice/Trigger: Written notice to manufacturer. S-R Note: Consumer should receive replacement or refund within 40 calendar days of request.
West Virginia ☑ BEST	Qualification: 3 unsuccessful repairs or 30 calendar days out of service or 1 unsuccessful repair of problem likely to cause death or serious bodily injury within shorter of 1 year or warranty. Notice/Trigger: Written notice + opportunity to repair to manufacturer.
Wisconsin	Qualification: 4 unsuccessful repairs or 30 calendar days out of service within shorter of 1 year or warranty. Notice/Trigger: Report to manufacturer or dealer. Note: Consumer should receive replacement or refund within 30 calendar days after offer to return title.
Wyoming	Qualification: 3 unsuccessful repairs or 30 business days out of service within 1 year. Notice/Trigger: Direct written notice + opportunity to repair to manufacturer. S-R

L—Law specifically applies to leased vehicles; S-C—State has certified guidelines for arbitration; S-R—State-run arbitration mechanism available

5 BASIC STEPS TO CAR BUYING

Buying a car means matching wits with a seasoned professional. But if you know what to expect, you'll have a much better chance of getting a really good deal!

There's no question that buying a car can be an intimidating experience. But it doesn't have to be. First of all, you have in your hands all of the information you need to make an informed choice. Secondly, if you approach the purchase logically, you'll always maintain control of the decision. Start with the following basic steps:

1 Consider your needs and how you will use a vehicle, and based on that, narrow your choice down to a particular class of car—sports, station wagon, minivan, sedan, large luxury, SUV, truck, or economy car. These are general classifications and some cars may fit into more than one category. In most cases, The Car Book presents the vehicles by size class.

2 Determine what features are really important to you. Most buyers consider safety on the top of their list, which is why the "Safety Chapter" is right up front in The Car Book. Specifically items such as back up cameras, automatic braking, and lane keeping assist along with airbags, power options, the general size, fuel economy, number of passengers, as well as "hidden" elements such as maintenance and insurance costs, should be considered at this stage in your selection process.

3 Find three or four cars that meet the needs you outlined above and your pocketbook. It's important not to narrow your choice down to one car because then you lose all your bargaining power in the showroom. (Why? Because you might lose the psychological ability to walk away from a bad deal!) In fact, because cars today are more similar than dissimilar, it's not hard to keep three or four choices in mind. In the "Car Rating Pages" in the back of the book, we suggest some competitive choices for your consideration. For example, if you are interested in the Honda Accord, you should also consider the Toyota Camry, Ford Fusion, and Hyundai Sonata.

4 Make sure you take a good, long test drive. The biggest car buying mistake most of us make is to overlook those nagging problems that seem to surface only after we've brought the car home. Spend at least an hour driving the car and preferably without a salesperson. If a dealership won't allow you to test drive a car without a salesperson, go somewhere else. The test drive should include time on the highway, parking, taking the car in and out of your driveway or garage, sitting in the back seat, and using the trunk or storage area. Renting the car you're interested in for a day can be very insightful.

TIP: Whatever you do, don't talk price until you're ready to buy!

5 This is the stage most of us dread—negotiating the price. While price negotiation is a car buying tradition, a few dealers are trying to break tradition by offering so-called "no-haggle" or "posted" pricing. Since they're still in the minority and because it's very hard for an individual to establish true competition between dealers, we recommend avoiding negotiating altogether by using the nonprofit CarBargains pricing service described on page 68.

THE 180-DEGREE TURN

TIP

When buying a car, you have the most important tool in the bargaining process: the 180-degree turn. Be prepared to walk away from a deal, even at the risk of losing the "very best deal" your salesperson has ever offered, and you will be in the best position to get a real "best deal." Remember: Dealerships need you, the buyer, to survive.

IN THE SHOWROOM

Being prepared is the best way to turn a potentially intimidating showroom experience into a profitable one. Here's some advice on handling what you'll find in the showroom.

Beware of silence. Silence is often used to intimidate, so be prepared for long periods of time when the salesperson is "talking with the manager." This tactic is designed to make you want to "just get the negotiation over with." Instead of becoming a victim, do something that indicates you are serious about looking elsewhere. Bring the classified section of the newspaper and begin circling other cars or review brochures from other manufacturers. By sending the message that you have other options, you increase your bargaining power and speed up the process.

Don't fall in love with a car. Never look too interested in any particular car. Advise family members or friends who go with you against being too enthusiastic about any one car. Tip: Beat the dealers at their own game— bring along a friend who tells you that the price is "too much compared to the other deal," or "I really liked that other car much better," or "wasn't that other car much cheaper?"

Keep your wallet in your pocket. Don't leave a deposit, even if it's refundable. You'll feel pressure to rush your shopping, and you'll have to return and face the salesperson again before you are ready.

Shop at the end of the month. Salespeople anxious to meet sales goals are more willing to negotiate a lower price at this time.

Buy last year's model. The majority of new cars are the same as the previous year, with minor cosmetic changes. You can save considerably by buying in early fall when dealers are clearing space for "new" models. The important trade-off you make using this technique is that the carmaker may have added a new safety feature to an otherwise unchanged vehicle.

Buying from stock. You can often get a better deal on a car that the dealer has on the lot. However, these cars often have expensive options you may not want or need. Do not hesitate to ask the dealer to remove an option (and its accompanying charge) or sell you the car without charging for the option. The longer the car sits there, the more interest the dealer pays on the car, which increases the dealer's incentive to sell.

Ordering a car. Cars can be ordered from the manufacturer with exactly the options you want. Simply offering a fixed amount over invoice (see page 66 for more about the invoice price) may be attractive because it's a sure sale and the dealership has not invested in the car. All the salesperson has to do is take your order.

If you do order a car, make sure when it arrives that it includes only the options you requested. Don't fall for the trick where the dealer offers you unordered options at a "special price," because it was their mistake. If you didn't order an option, don't pay for it.

⚠ BEWARE OF MANDATORY ARBITRATION AGREEMENTS

More and more dealers are adding mandatory binding arbitration agreements, which they often call "dispute resolution mechanisms," to your purchase contract. What this means is that you waive the right to sue or appeal any problem you have with the vehicle. In addition, the dealer often gets to choose the arbitrator. Before you start negotiating the price, ask if the dealer requires Mandatory Binding Arbitration. If so, and they won't remove that requirement, you should buy elsewhere. Many dealers do not have this requirement.

GETTING THE BEST PRICE

One of the most difficult aspects of buying a new car is getting the best price. Most of us are at a disadvantage negotiating because we don't know how much the car actually cost the dealer. The difference between what the dealer paid and the sticker price represents the negotiable amount.

Beware, now that most savvy consumers know to check the so-called "dealer invoice," the industry has camouflaged this number. Special incentives, rebates, and kickbacks can account for $500 to $2,000 worth of extra profit to a dealer selling a car at "dealer invoice." The non-profit Center for the Study of Services recently discovered that in 37 percent of cases when dealers are forced to bid against each other, they offered the buyer a price below the "dealer invoice"—an unlikely event if the dealer was actually losing money. The bottom line is that "dealer invoice" doesn't really mean dealer cost.

You can't really negotiate with only one dealer, you need to get two or three bidding against each other. Introducing competition is the best way to get the lowest price on a new car. To do this you have to convince two or three dealers that you are, in fact, prepared to buy a car; that you have decided on the make, model, and features; and that your decision now rests solely on which dealer will give you the best price. You can try to do this by phone, but often dealers will not give you the best price, or will quote you a price over the phone that they will not honor later. Instead, you should try to do this in person. As anyone knows who has ventured into an auto showroom simply to get the best price, the process can be lengthy and terribly arduous. Nevertheless, if you can convince the dealer that you are serious and are willing to take the time to go to a number of dealers, it will pay off. Be sure the dealer knows that you simply want the best price for the particular make, model and options. Otherwise, we suggest you use the CarBargains service described on page 68.

Here are some other showroom strategies:

Shop away from home. If you find a big savings at a dealership far from your home or on the Internet, call a local dealer with the price. They may match it. If not, pick up the car from the distant dealer, knowing your trip has saved you hundreds of dollars. You can still bring it to your local dealer for warranty work and repairs.

Beware of misleading advertising. New car ads are meant to get you into the showroom. They usually promise low prices, big rebates, high trade-in, and spotless integrity—don't be deceived. Advertised prices are rarely the true selling price. They usually exclude transportation charges, service fees, or document fees. And always look out for the asterisk, both in advertisements and on invoices. It can be a signal that the advertiser has something to hide.

Don't talk price until you're ready to buy. On your first few trips to the showroom, simply look over the cars, decide what options you want, and do your test-driving.

Shop the corporate twins. Page 75 contains a list of corporate twins—nearly identical cars that carry different name plates. Check the price and options of the twins of the car you like. A higher-priced twin may have more options, so it may be a better deal than the lower-priced car with the added options you want.

Watch out for dealer preparation overcharges. Before paying the dealer to clean your car, make sure that preparation is not included in the basic price. The price sticker will state: "Manu-facturer's suggested retail price of this model includes dealer preparation."

If you must negotiate . . . negotiate up from the "invoice" price rather than down from the sticker price. Simply make an offer close to or at the "invoice" price. If the salesperson says that your offer is too low to make a profit, ask to see the factory invoice.

Don't trade in. Although it is more work, you can usually do better by selling your old car yourself than by trading it in. To determine what you'll gain by selling the car yourself, check the NADA Official Used Car Guide at your credit union or library. On the web, the Kelly Blue Book website at kbb.com is a good source for determining the value of your used car. The difference between the trade-in price (what the dealer will give you) and the retail price (what you typically can sell it for) is your extra payment for selling the car yourself. Another option is to get a bid for your car from one of the national used car chains, such as CarMax. They do buy used cars with no obligation for you to buy from them.

If you do decide to trade your car in at the dealership, keep the buying and selling separate. First, negotiate the best price for your new car, then find out how much the dealer will give you for your old car. Keeping the two deals separate ensures that you know what you're paying for your new car and simplifies the entire transaction.

Question everything the dealer writes down. Nothing is etched in stone. Because things are written down, we tend not to question them. This is wrong—always assume that anything written down, or printed, is negotiable.

BUYING FOR SAFETY

So how do you buy for safety? Many consumers mistakenly believe that handling and performance are the key elements in the safety of a car. While an extremely unresponsive car could cause an accident, most new cars have adequately safe handling. In fact, many people actually feel uncomfortable driving high performance cars because the highly responsive steering, acceleration, and suspension systems can be difficult to get used to. But the main reason handling is overrated as a safety measure is that automobile collisions are, by nature, accidents. Once they've begun, they are beyond human capacity to prevent, no matter how well your car handles. So the key to protecting yourself is to purchase a car that offers a high degree of crash protection and automatic crash avoidance features.

When it comes to crash protection there are amazing new features to look for which we describe in the Safety Chapter and in the Guide to the Ratings on pages 79-80.

Here's a general list of what you should look for:

Dynamic Head Restraints: They adjust to give better protection in an accident.

Air Belts: Belts that blow up like long, soft balloons in a crash. Just being introduced in rear seats on some Ford vehicles.

Lane Keeping Assist: Keeps you within the white lines.

Automatic Braking: Applies the brakes faster than you can.

Blind Spot Detection: Keeps you from hitting another vehicle that you may not see.

Rear View Camera: Keeps children behind your car safe and helps with parking.

Adaptive Cruise Control: Adjusts your speed based on surrounding highway traffic.

Roll Sensing Airbags: Offer extra protection in a rollover–standard in many new cars.

Bicycle Detection: Alerts you when a bicycle has been detected.

Left Turn Crash Avoidance: Prevents a crash if turning left into the path of another car.

Adaptive Headlights: Increases vision by turning headlights when steering wheel turns.

CARBARGAINS' BEST PRICE SERVICE

Even with the information that we provide you in this chapter of *The Car Book*, many of us still will not be comfortable negotiating for a fair price. In fact, as we indicated on the previous page, we believe it's really very difficult to negotiate the best price with a single dealer. The key to getting the best price is to get dealers to compete with each other.

CarBargains is a service of the non-profit Consumers' CHECK-BOOK, a consumer group that provides comparative price and quality information for many products and services.

CarBargains will "shop" the dealerships in your area and obtain at least five price quotes for the make and model of the car that you want to buy. The dealers who submit quotes know that they are competing with other area dealerships and have agreed to honor the prices that they submit. It is important to note that CarBargains is not an auto broker or "car buying" service; they have no affiliation with dealers.

Here's how the service works:
1. You provide CarBargains with the specific make, model, and style of car you wish to buy (Toyota Camry XLE, for example).
2. Within two weeks, CarBargains will send you dealer quote sheets from at least five local dealers who have bid against one another to sell you that car. Each dealer's offer is actually a commitment to a dollar amount above (or below) "factory invoice cost" for that model. You get the name and phone number of the manager responsible for handling the quote.

You will also receive a print-out that enables you to figure the exact cost for each available option you might want on the vehicle.
3. Determine which dealer offers the best price using the dealer quote sheets. Add up the cost including the specific options you want. Contact the sales manager of that dealership and arrange to purchase the car.

If a car with the options you want is not available on the dealer's lot, you can, in many cases, have the dealer order the car from the factory or from another dealer at the agreed price.

When you receive your quotes, you will also get some suggestions on low-cost sources of financing and a valuation of your used car (trade-in).

The price for this service ($250, or $225 if you become a member) may seem expensive, but when you consider the savings that will result by having dealers bid against each other, as well as the time and effort of trying to get these bids yourself, we believe it's a great value. The dealers know they have a bona fide buyer; they know they are bidding against 5-7 of their competitors; and, you have CarBargains' experts on your side.

To obtain CarBargains' competitive price quotes, call them at 800-475-7283 or visit their website at www.carbargains.org. Or, you can send a check for $250 to CarBargains, 1625 K St., NW, 8th Floor, Washington, DC 20006. Be sure to include your mailing address, phone number, and e-mail address (in case of questions), and the exact make, model, style, and year of the car you want to buy. You should receive your report within two weeks.

⚠️ AUTO BROKERS ⚠️

While CarBargains is a non-profit organization created to help you find the best price for the car you want to purchase, auto brokers are typically in the business to make money. As such, the price you end up paying for the car will include additional profit for the broker. There have been cases where the auto broker makes certain promises, takes your money, and you never hear from him again. While many brokers are legitimately trying to get their customers the best price, others have developed special relationships with certain dealers and may not do much shopping for you. As a consumer, it is difficult to tell which are which. This is why we recommend CarBargains. If CarBargains is not for you, then we suggest you consider using a buying service associated with your credit union or auto club. They can arrange for the purchase of a car at some fixed price over "dealer invoice."

FINANCING

You've done your test-drive, researched prices, studied crash tests, determined the options you want, and haggled to get the best price. Now you have to decide how to pay for the car.

If you have the cash, pay for the car right away. You avoid finance charges, you won't have a large debt haunting you, and the full value of the car is yours. You can then make the monthly payments to yourself to save up for your next car.

However, most of us cannot afford to pay cash for a car, which leaves two options: financing or leasing. While leasing may seem more affordable, financing will actually cost you less and give you flexibility. When you finance a car, you own it after you finish your payments. At the end of a lease, you have nothing. We don't recommend leasing, but if you want more information, see page 71.

Shop around for interest rates. Most banks and credit unions will knock off at least a quarter of a percent for their customers. Have these quotes handy when you talk financing with the dealer.

The higher your down payment, the less you'll have to finance. This will not only reduce your overall interest charges, but often qualifies you for a lower interest rate.

Avoid long car loans. The monthly payments are lower, but you'll pay far more in overall interest charges. For example, a two-year, $25,000 loan at 4 percent will cost you $1,055 in interest; the same amount at five years will cost you $2,625— well over twice as much!

Beware of manufacturer promotional rates—the 0 to 1 percent rates you see advertised. These low rates are usually only valid on two or three-year loans and only for the most credit-worthy customers.

Read everything you are asked to sign and ask questions about anything you don't fully understand.

Make sure that an extended warranty has not been added to the purchase price. Dealers will sometimes do this without telling you. Extended warranties are generally a bad value. See the "Warranties" chapter for more information.

Credit Unions vs. Banks: Credit unions generally charge fewer and lower fees and offer better rates than banks. In addition, credit unions offer counseling services where consumers can find pricing information on cars or compare monthly payments for financing. You can join a credit union either through your employer, an organization or club, or if you have a relative who is part of a credit union.

DON'T BE TONGUE-TIED

TIP

Beware of high-pressure phrases like "I've talked to the manager and this is really the best we can do. As it is, we're losing money on this deal." Rarely is this true. Dealers are in the business to make money and most do very well. Don't tolerate a take-it-or-leave-it attitude. Simply repeat that you will only buy when you see the deal you want and that you don't appreciate the dealer pressuring you. Threaten to leave if the dealer continues to pressure you to buy today.

Don't let the dealer answer your questions with a question. If you ask, "Can I get this same car with leather seats?" and the salesperson answers, "If I get you leather seats in this car, will you buy today?" this response tries to force you to decide to buy before you are ready. Ask the dealer to just answer your question and say that you'll buy when you're ready. It's the dealer's job to answer questions, not yours.

If you are having a difficult time getting what you want, ask the dealer: "Why won't you let me buy a car today?" Most salespeople will be thrown off by this phrase as they are often too busy trying to use it on you. If they respond in frustration, "OK, what do you want?" you can simply say "straightforward answers to simple questions."

Get a price; don't settle for: "If you're shopping price, go to the other dealers first and then come back." This technique ensures that they don't have to truly negotiate. Your best response is: "I only plan to come back if your price is the lowest, so that's what I need today, your lowest price."

TYPICAL OPERATING COSTS

Here are the annual operating costs for some popular vehicles. These costs include operating expenses (fuel, oil, maintenance, and tires) and ownership expenses (insurance, financing, taxes, depreciation, and licensing) and are based on keeping the vehicle for 3 years and driving 20,000 miles per year. This information is from Runzheimer International. Runzheimer evaluated thirty 2017 model cars, vans, SUVs, and light trucks and determined the most and least expensive to operate among those vehicles. (Source: www.runzheimer.com)

Projected Ownership and Operating Costs
Based on Driving 3 Years, 20,000 miles per Year

Select 2017 Cars

Most Expensive

Genesis G90 Premium 6-cyl. 3.3L	$22,587
Cadillac CTS Luxury 6-cyl. 3.6L	$19,657
Mercedes-Benz E300 4-cyl. 2.0L	$19,241
Ford Taurus Limited AWD 6-cyl. 3.5L	$15,734
Buick Lacrosse Essence 6-cyl. 3.6L	$15,267

Least Expensive

Nissan Altima S 4-cyl. 2.5L	$10,303
Mazda Mazda3 Touring 4-cyl. 2.0L	$9,736
Chevrolet Sonic LT 4-cyl. 1.8L	$9,197
Mazda Mazda3 Sport 4-cyl. 2.0L	$8,968
Toyota Corolla LE 4-cyl. 1.8L	$8,941

Select 2017 Trucks, Vans, and SUVs

Most Expensive

Chevrolet Tahoe LS 8-cyl. 5.3L	$17,261
Ford F250 XL 2WD 8FT 8-cyl. 6.2L	$14,838
Dodge Grand Caravan GT 6-cyl. 3.6L	$14,223
Chevrolet Silverado 1500 LS 6-cyl. 4.3L	$12,631
Jeep Grand Cherokee Laredo 6-cyl. 3.6L	$12,401

Least Expensive

Chevrolet Silverado 1500 Work 2WD 8FT 6-cyl. 4.3L	$11,975
Dodge Grand Caravan SE 6-cyl. 3.6L	$11,910
Chevrolet Silverado 1500 Work 2WD 6FT 6-cyl. 4.3L	$11,886
Ford Escape SE 4-cyl. 2.0L	$11,622
Toyota Tacoma SR5 4-cyl. 2.7L	$10,405

Runzheimer is providing the attached information for reference only. Any direct reproduction or publication of this data in its entirety without prior consent from Runzheimer is strictly forbidden. Founded in 1933, Runzheimer connects people, companies and their vehicles in ways that drive superior productivity and impactful business intelligence. Runzheimer is the leader in workforce mobility programs, designing and delivering fair, accurate and defensible™ business vehicle programs, relocation information services and business expense solutions.

DO YOU NEED A SECOND CAR?

TIP

Rather than invest in a second vehicle more and more consumers are depending on alternatives such as transit, cabs, Uber, Lyft, and other ride or car sharing programs and various types of vehicle rental including car sharing such as Zipcar and Car2Go. While paying for rides may seem uneconomical, when you consider how much you use the second vehicle, it's overall ownership, maintenance, depreciation and operating costs, your monthly cost for alternative transportation will undoubtedly be far less. Many millennials are skipping even first car ownership, having determined that the responsibility, cost, and housing of their own car far outweighs the use of alternative rides and public transportation. Another choice people are making is selecting a smaller, less expensive, more fuel efficient car, even though there are occasions when a big vehicle would be very useful and convenient. Instead, they are renting a pickup for that occasional trip to the Home Depot or garden center or renting an SUV for picking up or dropping off kids at college or weekend furniture runs.

LEASING VS. BUYING

About 25% of new car transactions are actually leases. Unfortunately, most leasees don't realize that, in spite of the low monthly payments, leasing costs more than buying.

When you pay cash or finance a car, you own an asset; leasing leaves you with nothing except all the headaches and responsibilities of ownership with none of the benefits. When you lease you pay a monthly fee for a predetermined time in exchange for the use of a car. However, you also pay for maintenance, insurance, and repairs as if you owned the car. Finally, when it comes time to turn in the car, it has to be in top shape—otherwise, you'll have to pay for repairs, clean up, or body work. One of the most important things to remember about a lease is that it is very difficult and expensive to end it early.

If you are considering a lease, here are some leasing terms you need to know and some tips to get you through the process:

Capitalized Cost is the price of the car on which the lease is based. Negotiate this as if you were buying the car. Capitalized Cost Reduction is your down payment.

Know the make and model of the vehicle you want. Tell the agent exactly how you want the car equipped. You don't have to pay for options you don't request. Decide in advance how long you will keep the car.

Find out the price of the options on which the lease is based. Typically, they will be full retail price. Their cost can be negotiated (albeit with some difficulty) before you settle on the monthly payment.

Find out how much you are required to pay at delivery. Most leases require at least the first month's payment. Others have a security deposit, registration fees, or other "hidden costs." When shopping around, make sure price quotes include security deposit and taxes—sales tax, monthly use tax, or gross receipt tax. Ask how the length of the lease affects your monthly cost.

Find out how the lease price was determined. Lease prices are generally based on the manufacturer's suggested retail price, less the predetermined residual value. (Residual value is how much the seller expects the vehicle to be worth at the end of the lease.) The best lease values are cars with a high expected residual value. To protect themselves, leasers tend to underestimate residual value, but there is little you can do about this estimate.

Find out the annual mileage limit. Don't accept a contract with a lower limit than you need. Most standard contracts allow 15,000 to 18,000 miles per year. If you go under the allowance one year, you can go over it the next. Watch out for excess mileage fees. If you go over, you'll get charged per mile.

Avoid "capitalized cost reduction" or "equity leases." Here the leaser offers to lower the monthly payment by asking you for more money up front—in other words, a down payment.

Ask about early termination. Between 30 and 40 percent of two-year leases are terminated early and 40–60 percent of four-year leases terminate early—this means expensive early termination fees. If you terminate the lease before it is up, what are the financial penalties? Typically, they are very high so watch out. Ask the dealer exactly what you would owe at the end of each year if you wanted out of the lease. Remember, if your car is stolen, the lease will typically be terminated. While your insurance should cover the value of

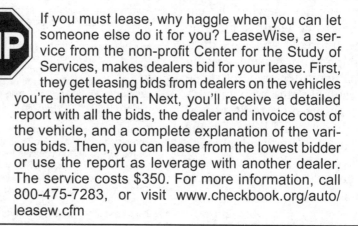

LEASEWISE

If you must lease, why haggle when you can let someone else do it for you? LeaseWise, a service from the non-profit Center for the Study of Services, makes dealers bid for your lease. First, they get leasing bids from dealers on the vehicles you're interested in. Next, you'll receive a detailed report with all the bids, the dealer and invoice cost of the vehicle, and a complete explanation of the various bids. Then, you can lease from the lowest bidder or use the report as leverage with another dealer. The service costs $350. For more information, call 800-475-7283, or visit www.checkbook.org/auto/leasew.cfm

the car, you still may owe additional amounts per your lease contract.

Avoid maintenance contracts. Getting work done privately is cheaper in the long run. And don't forget, this is a new car with a standard warranty.

Arrange for your own insurance. By shopping around, you can generally find less expensive insurance than what's offered by the lessor.

Ask how quickly you can expect delivery. If your agent can't deliver in a reasonable time, maybe he or she can't meet the price quoted.

Retain your option to buy the car at the end of the lease at a predetermined price. The price should equal the residual value; if it is more then the leaser is trying to make an additional profit. Regardless of how the end-of-lease value is determined, if you want the car, make an offer based on the current "Blue Book" value of the car at the end of the lease.

Again, residual value is the value of your car at the end of the lease. The Automotive Lease Guide is often used by leasing companies to determine the residual value. Because determining the residual value means predicting what the car is going to be worth some time in the future, it is a very difficult thing to do. As such, leasing companies often underestimate the residual value which means you'll absorb more of the cost of the vehicle in the lease. On the other hand, if the residual value at the end of the lease is very low, consider buying the vehicle for that amount.

LEASING VS. BUYING

The following table compares the costs of leasing vs. buying the same car over three and six years. Your actual costs may vary, but you can use this format to compare the cars you are considering. Our example assumes the residual value of the purchased vehicle to be 55 percent after three years and 40 percent after six years.

After 3 Years	36 month Lease	5 Yr Loan–3.25% Sell in 3 Yrs
MSRP	$33,500	$33,500
Lease Value/Purchase Price[1]	$30,150	$30,150
Initial Payment/Down Payment[2]	$3,015	$3,015
Loan Amount	$0	$27,135
Monthly Payments[3]	$320	$491
Total Payments (first 3 years of loan)[4]	$11,520	$17,662
Amount Left on Loan	$0	$11,385
Excess miles and disposition fees[5]	$480	$0
Total Cost[6]	$15,015	$32,062
Less Value of Vehicle .55 residual[7]	$0	$18,425
Overall Cost, first 3 years	**$15,015**	**$13,637**
Savings over Leasing 3 Years		**$1,378**

After 6 Years	2nd 3 Yr Lease	5 Yr Loan–3.25% Keep Car 6 yrs.
MSRP - 2nd Lease 5% increase in cost[8]	$35,175	$33,500
Lease Value/Purchase Cost of Car[1]	$31,658	$30,150
Initial Payment/Down Payment[2]	$3,166	$3,015
Loan Amount	$0	$27,135
Monthly Payment[9]	$340	$491
Total Payments[10]	$12,240	$29,436
Amount Left on Loan	$0	$0
Excess miles and disposition fees[5]	$480	$0
Total Cost of 2nd Lease[6]	$15,886	$0
Total Cost[11]	$30,901	$32,451
Less Value of Vehicle .40 residual 6 yrs[12]	$0	$13,400
Overall Cost, 6 years	**$30,901**	**$19,051**
Savings Over Leasing 6 Years		**$11,850**

1. Purchase price reflects that most buyer's pay about 90% of the MSRP.
2. Initial lease payment based on leases with 10% due at signing and loans with 10% down payment.
3. Monthly lease payments based on typical leases as reported by US News and World Report. Monthly finance payments based on a 5 year, 3.25% loan.
4. Total payments (lease and finance) paid for 3 years.
5. Average excess mileage fee of $480 based on a 12000 mile limit and averages 3 typical situations: 25% going 1500 mile over the limit at $0.15/mile; 50% pre-paying for 1500 in mile overages at $0.10/mile, and 25% not exceeding the mileage limit–plus a typical disposition fee of $350.
6. Total amount paid; includes down payment, monthly payments, and end of lease fees.
7. Three-year residual value of 55 percent based on average actual 36-month residual value for the top 10 selling vehicles for model year 2016.
8. Represents the expected 5% increase in the cost of a similar leased vehicle 3 years later.
9. Estimated increase in lease payment.
10. Total payments for the second 3 year lease and total payments for the 5 year loan at 3.25%.
11. Total cost of 2 3-year leases and total cost for 5 year loan purchase.
12. Six-year residual value of 40 percent based on average actual 72-month residual value for the top 10 selling vehicles for model year 2016.

USING THE INTERNET

The Internet is changing the way car buyers research and shop for cars. But the Internet should be used with caution. Anyone can publish a website with no guarantee concerning the accuracy of the information on it. We advise that you only visit websites that have a familiar non-web counterpart. A good example is the Center for Auto Safety's website at www.autosafety.org where you can find information on auto safety, including publications and newsletters which are typically mailed out to subscribers.

Use the Internet as an information resource. Unfortunately, most automaker websites are nothing more than sophisticated ads with little comparative information. However, many do include a "build your own" feature which you can use to get the MSRP for the cars you are considering. While you never want to pay MSRP, it's a good way to get a general sense of the cost.

There are also several online car shopping services that have launched. We view most of them with skepticism. Many online car shopping services are tied to a limited, often non-competitive, group of dealers. They may claim the lowest price, but you'll most likely have a dealer calling you with a price that is not much better than what you'd get if you went into a dealership.

Auto insurance and financing sites are sometimes no better. Don't rely solely on these online services; getting quotes from other sources is the only way to make sure you truly have the best deal.

Finally, clicking a mouse is no substitute for going out and test-driving a car. If you are shopping for a used car, you must check out the actual car before signing on the dotted line. Do not rely on online photos. In fact, online classifieds for cars are no more reliable than looking in a newspaper.

If you do use an online car shopping service, be sure to shop around on your own. Visit dealerships, get quotes from several car shopping services, and research the value of your used car (see www.nadaguides.com). Beware that if you give anyone online your phone number, or email address, you are opening yourself up to unwanted email, junk mail, and sales calls.

ON THE WEB

autosafety.org
The Center for Auto Safety (CAS) provides consumers with a voice for auto safety and quality in Washington and to help lemon owners fight back across the country.

carfax.com
Carfax collects information from numerous sources to provide a vehicle history on a specific vehicle, based on the Vehicle Identification Number (VIN). Carfax can help uncover costly and potentially dangerous hidden problems. Beware, however, a "clean" history may be because serious problems were never reported.

checkbook.org
The Center for the Study of Services (CSS) is an independent, nonprofit consumer organization and the creator of Consumers' CHECKBOOK. One of the few car buying services worth using, CHECKBOOK's CarBargains and LeaseWise service pits dealers against each other, keeping you from haggling, and using the power of competitive bidding to get you a great price.

safercar.gov
The National Highway Traffic Safety Administration (NHTSA) website contains useful information on safety standards, crash tests, recalls, technical service bulletins, child seats, and safety advisories.

fueleconomy.gov
This joint effort by the Department of Energy and the Environmental Protection Agency contains EPA fuel economy ratings for passenger cars and trucks from 1985 to the present, gas saving tips, greenhouse gas and air pollution ratings, energy impact scores, a downloadable Fuel Economy Guide, and a variety of other useful information in a very user-friendly format.

DEPRECIATION

Over the past 20 years, new vehicle depreciation costs have steadily increased. A study conducted by Runzheimer International shows that depreciation and interest now account for just over 50 percent of the costs of owning and operating a vehicle. Recently, however, the increasing cost of depreciation has slowed down. This is due to the increased prices of new vehicles and the stabilization in finance rates.

While there is no foolproof method for predicting retained vehicle value, your best bet is to purchase a popular vehicle model. Chances are, though not always, it will also be a popular used vehicle, meaning that it will retain more of its value when you go to sell it.

Most new cars are traded in within four years and are then available on the used car market. The priciest used cars may not be the highest quality. Supply and demand, as well as appearance, are important factors in determining used car prices.

The table indicates which of the top-selling 2013 cars held their value the best and which did not.

2013 VEHICLES WITH THE BEST AND WORST RESALE VALUE

THE BEST				THE WORST			
Model	2013 Price	2016 Price	Retain. Value	Model	2013 Price	2016 Price	Retain. Value
ToyotaTacoma	$28,185	$27,500	97.6%	Chevrolet Impala	$26,725	$13,975	52.3%
Jeep Wrangler	$29,995	$28,700	95.7%	Ford Focus	$17,295	$9,275	53.6%
Toyota 4Runner	$31,490	$27,550	87.5%	Chevrolet Malibu	$22,390	$12,025	53.7%
Toyota Tundra	$32,995	$27,650	83.8%	Dodge Avenger	$18,995	$10,475	55.2%
Chevrolet Equinox	$24,155	$20,125	83.3%	Chevrolet Cruze	$24,885	$13,750	55.3%
Jeep Patriot	$15,995	$12,875	80.5%	Chrysler 200	$18,995	$10,500	55.3%
Jeep Grand Cherokee	$28,795	$22,725	78.9%	Volkswagen Passat	$23,945	$13,250	55.3%
Nissan Murano	$30,340	$23,900	78.8%	Toyota Sienna	$30,135	$17,250	57.2%
Chevrolet Silverado	$29,314	$22,250	75.9%	Nissan Maxima	$31,550	$18,075	57.3%
GMC Acadia	$34,050	$25,400	74.6%	Ford Fusion	$21,700	$12,525	57.7%
Cadillac SRX	$37,155	$27,475	74.0%	Kia Forte	$15,900	$9,200	57.9%
Chevrolet Camaro	$23,345	$17,200	73.7%	Cadillac CTS	$39,095	$22,800	58.3%
BMW 3 Series	$43,150	$31,650	73.4%	Buick Enclave	$45,625	$26,925	59.0%
Subaru Forester	$21,995	$16,025	72.9%	Mini Cooper	$19,700	$11,850	60.2%
Honda CR-V	$22,795	$16,600	72.8%	Volkswagen Jetta	$17,775	$10,875	61.2%
Honda Accord	$21,680	$15,675	72.3%	Acura MDX	$43,280	$26,700	61.7%
Hyundai Santa Fe	$24,450	$17,550	71.8%	Nissan Altima	$21,500	$13,300	61.9%
Ford F-150	$29,744	$21,325	71.7%	Dodge Charger	$25,995	$16,125	62.0%
Toyota Prius	$24,200	$17,250	71.3%	Ford Explorer	$29,100	$18,050	62.0%
Toyota Highlander	$30,245	$21,400	70.8%	Subaru Legacy	$22,495	$13,975	62.1%
Ram Pickup	$29,235	$20,580	70.4%	Ford Taurus	$26,700	$16,625	62.3%
Nissan Frontier	$25,140	$17,600	70.0%	Buick LaCrosse	$31,660	$19,775	62.5%
Kia Rio	$13,600	$9,500	69.9%	Nissan Versa	$12,990	$8,150	62.7%
BMW X5	$47,500	$33,125	69.7%	Hyundai Elantra	$16,965	$10,650	62.8%
Toyota RAV4	$24,700	$17,175	69.5%	Toyota Corolla	$17,060	$10,750	63.0%

CORPORATE TWINS

"Corporate twins" refers to vehicles that have different names but share the same mechanics, drivetrain, and chassis. In many cases the vehicles are identical. Sometimes the difference is in body style, price, or options as with the Chevrolet Tahoe and the Cadillac Escalade.

While corporate twins share the same basic structure and running gear, some will drive and feel different because of the tuning of the suspension, the standard equipment and options available, and the the comfort and convenience features. One twin may stress a soft ride and luxury while another a tighter, sportier feel.

Historically, corporate twins have been limited mainly to domestic car companies. Today, several Asian and European car companies have started the practice.

CORPORATE TWINS

Chrysler
Chrysler 300
Dodge Charger

Ford
Ford Escape
Lincoln MKC

Ford Expedition
Lincoln Navigator

Ford Fusion
Lincoln MKZ

General Motors
Buick Encore
Chevrolet Trax

Buick LaCrosse
Cadillac XTS
Chevrolet Impala

Buick Verano
Chevrolet Cruze

Cadillac Escalade
Chevrolet Tahoe
GMC Yukon

General Motors (cont.)
Cadillac Escalade ESV
Chevrolet Suburban
GMC Yukon XL

Cadillac XT5
GMC Acadia

Chevrolet Colorado
GMC Canyon

Chevrolet Equinox
GMC Terrain

Chevrolet Silverado
GMC Sierra

Honda
Acura TLX
Honda Accord

Hyundai–Kia
Hyundai Accent
Kia Rio

Hyundai Azera
Kia Cadenza

Hyundai–Kia (cont.)
Hyundai Elantra
Kia Forte

Nissan
Nissan Pathfinder
Infiniti QX60

Toyota
Lexus ES
Toyota Avalon

Lexus NX
Toyota RAV4

Lexus GX
Toyota 4Runner

Volkswagen-Audi
Audi A3
Volkswagen Golf

Audi Q3
Volkswagen Tiguan

Cadillac Escalade

Chevrolet Tahoe

GMC Yukon

RATINGS

This section provides an overview of the most important features of this year's new models. Nearly all the information you'll need to make a smart choice is concisely presented on one page. (The data are collected for the model expected to be the most popular.) Here's what you'll find and how to interpret the data we've provided:

The Ratings

These are the ratings in nine important categories, as well as an overall comparative rating. We have adopted the Olympic rating system with "10" being the best.

Overall Crash Test: This rating represents a combination of the front and side crash test ratings and provides a relative comparison of how this year's models did against each other. We give the best performers a 10 and the worst a 1. Remember to compare crash test results relative to other cars in the same size class. For details, see page 19.

Safety Features: This is an evaluation of how much extra safety is built into the car. We give credit for torso and pelvis side airbags, roll-sensing side airbags, a knee bolster bag, crash imminent braking, daytime running lamps, adjustable upper seat belt anchorages, lane keeping assist, pedestrian crash avoidance, automatic crash notification, lane departure warning, dynamic brake support, and frontal collision warning. We also include dynamic head restraints, backup cameras and blind spot detection among other important safety features. See the "Safety Checklist" descriptions on the following pages.

Rollover: Electronic Stability Control has dramatically reduced the likelihood of rollovers (see page 30). Because of that, we've reduced the "weight" that the rollover rating has in the vehicle's overall rating. When ESC is not able to prevent the vehicle from getting into a position where a rollover is possible, the vehicle's center of gravity plays a major role in whether or not that vehicle will actually rollover. The government uses a formula which estimates the "risk of rollover" in percentages. (See page 31) Using those percentages, we rated the 2017 vehicles on a relative basis. Again, the good news is that ESC is often able to prevent a vehicle from getting into a position where it is likely to roll over.

Preventive Maintenance: Each manufacturer suggests a preventive maintenance schedule designed to keep the car in good shape and to protect your rights under the warranty. Those with the lowest estimated PM costs get a 10 and the highest a 1. See pages 39-43 for the estimated costs and more information.

Repair Costs: It is virtually impossible to predict exactly what any new car will cost you in repairs. As such, we take nine typical repairs that you are likely to experience after your warranty expires and compare those costs among this year's models. Those with the lowest cost get a 10 and the highest a 1. See pages 39-43 for specific part repair cost and more information.

Warranty: This is an overall assessment of the manufacturer's basic, powertrain, corrosion, and roadside assistance warranties compared to all other manufacturer warranties. We also give credit for perks like free scheduled maintenance. We give the highest-rated warranties a 10 and the lowest a 1. For details, see page 36.

Fuel Economy: Here we compare the EPA mileage ratings of each car. The misers get a 10 and the guzzlers get a 1. For the purposes of the overall rating we pick the fuel economy rating of what is expected to be the most popular engine and drive train configuration. See page 33 for more information.

Complaints: This is where you'll find how each vehicle stacks up against hundreds of others on the road, based on the U.S. government complaint data for that vehicle. If the car has not been around long enough to have developed a complaint history, it is given a 5 (average). The least complained about cars get a 10 and the most problematic a 1. See page 56 for details.

Insurance Costs: Insurance companies rate vehicles to determine how much they plan to charge for insurance. While each insurer may have slightly different methods of rating, vehicles typically get a discount (max and min), a surcharge (max and min) or neither (average or typical). We looked at data from the insurance rating program of the largest insurer in America. This rating can predict the cost of insuring that vehicle, however, your location, age, driving record, and other factors also play a significant role in your cost of insurance. (See The Insurance Section pages 48-51.) Vehicles with a low rating (1 or 3) are more expensive to insure than other vehicles in that class or category. On the other hand, vehicles with a high rating (8 or 10) would be less expensive to insure in that particular class of vehicles. Because insurance companies may rate vehicles differently, it's important to compare prices between companies before you buy the car.

Overall Rating: This is the "bottom line." Using a combination of all of the key ratings, this tells how this vehicle stacks up against the others on a scale of 1 to 10. Due to the importance of safety, the combined crash test rating is 20 percent of the overall rating while the other eight ratings are 10 percent each. Vehicles with no front or side crash test results, as of our publication date, cannot be given an overall rating. In other categories, if information is unavailable, an "average" is included in order to develop an overall rating.

At-a-Glance

Status: Here we tell you if a vehicle is all-new, unchanged, or has received appearance change. All-new vehicles (the minority) are brand new from the ground up. Unchanged vehicles are essentially the same, but could have some different color or feature options. Vehicles with an appearance change are those whose internal workings stayed essentially the same, but have updated body panels.

Year Series Started: Each year the model is made, the production usually improves and as a result there are fewer defects. Therefore, the longer a car has been made, the less likely you are to be plagued with manufacturing and design defects. On the other hand, the newer a car is, the more likely it is to have the latest in features and safety.

Twins: These are cars with different make and model names but share the same mechanics, drive train, and chassis. In some cases the vehicles are identical, in other cases the body style, pricing or options are different.

Body Styles: This is a listing of the various body styles available such as coupe, sedan, wagon, etc. SUVs and minivans are only offered in one body style. Data on the page are for the first style listed.

Seating: This is the number of seating positions in the most popular model. When more than one number is listed (for example, 5/6) it means that different seat configurations are available.

Anti-theft Device: This lists the anti-theft devices standard for the vehicle. An immobilizer is an electronic device fitted to an automobile which prevents the engine from running unless the correct key (or other token) is present. This prevents the car from being "hot-wired" and driven away. A car alarm is an electronic device that emits high-volume sound and can sometimes flash the vehicles headlights in an attempt to discourage theft of the vehicle itself, its contents, or both. Passive devices automatically enter an armed state after the ignition is turned off and doors are closed. Active devices require the user to perform some action like pressing a button to arm and disarm the system.

Parking Index Rating: Using the car's length, wheelbase, and turning circle, we have calculated how easy it will be to maneuver this car in tight spots. This rating of "very easy" to "very hard" is an indicator of how much difficulty you may have parking.

Where Made: Here we tell you where the car was assembled. You'll find that traditional domestic companies often build their vehicles in other countries. Also, many foreign companies build their cars in the U.S.

Fuel Factor

MPG Rating (city/hwy): This is the EPA-rated fuel economy for city and highway driving measured in miles per gallon. Most models have a variety of fuel economy ratings because of different engine and transmission options. We've selected the combination expected to be most popular.

Driving Range: Given the car's expected fuel economy and gas tank size, this value gives you an idea of the number of miles you can expect to go on a tank of gas.

Fuel: The type of fuel specified by the manufacturer: regular, premium, E85.

Annual Fuel Cost: This is an estimate based on driving 15,000 miles per year at $2.15/gallon for regular and $2.68/gallon for premium. If the vehicle takes E85 (85% ethanol and 15% gasoline) or gasoline we calculated the annual cost using regular gasoline.

Gas Guzzler Tax: Auto companies are required to pay a gas guzzler tax on the sale of cars with exceptionally low fuel economy. This tax does not apply to light trucks.

Greenhouse Gas Emissions: This shows the amount (in tons) of greenhouse gases (carbon dioxide, nitrous oxide, and methane) that a vehicle emits per year along with the CO_2 emitted in producing and distributing the fuel.

Barrels of Oil Used Per Year: This is the number of barrels of petroleum the vehicle will likely use each year. One barrel, once refined, makes about 19.5 gallons of gas.

Competition

Here we tell you how the car stacks up with some of its key competitors. Use this information to broaden your choice of new car possibilities. This list is only a guideline, not an all-inclusive list of every possible alternative.

Price Range

This box contains information on the MSRP. When available, we offer a variety of prices between the base and the most luxurious version of the car. The difference is often substantial. Usually the more expensive versions have fancy trim, larger engines, and lots of automatic equipment. The least expensive versions usually have manual transmissions and few extra features. In addition to the price range, we provide the estimated dealer markup. Remember, prices and dealer costs can

change during the year. Use these figures for general reference and comparisons, not as a precise indication of exactly how much the car you are interested in will cost. See page 68 for a buying service designed to ensure that you get the very best price.

Safety Checklist

Crash Tests

Frontal and Side Crash Test Ratings: Here's where we tell you if the front or side crash test index was very good, good,

average, poor or very poor when compared to 2017 cars tested to date. To provide this rating we use the crash test for the vehicles with the best available safety equipment among the models when multiple models were tested. Unfortunately, not all of the 2017 models have been crash tested. If the car has been previously tested and the 2017 model is unchanged, we can carry those results forward. For details about the crash test programs, see page 19.

Airbags

All vehicles have dual front airbags and head airbags that

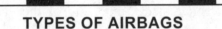

TYPES OF AIRBAGS

Airbags were introduced over 30 years ago and have been so successful in saving lives that car makers now include a variety of types. Here's a rundown of the basic types of airbags you'll find in today's vehicles. Manufacturers have various marketing names for these airbags.

Front: These deploy toward the front occupants and are now standard in all vehicles.

Head: These deploy from above the doors and are often called curtain airbags. They can reduce head injuries, shield from spraying glass, and provide protection in rollovers. Some form of these are in all vehicles.

Side: These deploy from the side of the seat or door and protect both the front and rear passengers in a side impact. Bags mounted in seats offer protection in a wider range of seating positions. Not all vehicles have these.

Rollover Protection: These head curtain airbags remain inflated for five seconds to protect in a sustained rollover. Not all vehicles have these.

Knee Bolster: These fill space between the front occupant's knees and instrument panel protecting the knees and legs. Not all vehicles have these.

deploy across the side windows. We've identified three additional types of airbags that the vehicle may have. The Side Airbags have historically been two separate bag systems. Recently, most manufacturers have been combining torso and pelvis protection into one bag. When the two are combined, we list *Front Pelvis/Torso from Seat* after each airbag type. Otherwise we identify specific bag type (or not) that comes with the vehicle.

Torso Side Airbag: This airbag protects the chest from serious injury in a side impact crash.

Pelvis Side Airbag: Provides extra protection around the pelvis and hip area, the portion of the body is usually closest to the vehicles exterior.

Rollover Sensing Airbags: This is a special side airbag system which keeps the side airbags inflated longer in the event of a rollover. These are standard in many 2017 models.

Knee Bolster Airbag: This airbag fills the space between the front passenger's knees and the dashboard.

Crash Avoidance

Collision Avoidance: Great new technology is available that can react faster than you in the event of a frontal collision. There are three basic systems available: Crash Imminent Braking (CIB), Dynamic Brake Support (DBS), and Frontal Collision Warning (FCW). All of these systems use radar or laser sensors to either alert the driver (FCW) or actively intervene to apply the brakes prior to a crash. CIB will actually apply the brakes if you are about to experience a frontal crash. DBS will increase your braking force if the sen-

sors determine that you are not applying enough force to stop in time. FCW will merely sound an alarm in the event of an imminent frontal collision. Whenever a vehicle has CIB or DBS, it will also have a Frontal Crash Warning. We believe that Crash Imminent Braking and Dynamic Brake Support are more useful than just a Frontal Collision Warning (and thus rated higher), however FCW is still a useful safety feature. The government has set standards for FCW and we've used a ^ to indicate which systems DON'T meet the FCW requirements.

Blind Spot Detection: This is a blind spot monitor that uses radar or other technologies to detect objects in the driver's blind spot. When switching lanes a visible, audible, or

vibrating alert warns if a vehicle has entered your blind spot.

Lane Keeping Assist: Going one step beyond a Lane Departure Warning, cars with Lane Keeping Assist will actually apply pressure to the brakes or adjust the steering when it senses that a car is drifting out of its lane. Lane Departure Warning (LDW) will simply alert the driver. If the vehicle has Land Keeping Assist, it will also have LDW. We have combined the two since the technology for Lane Departure Warning is required for Lane Keeping Assist, which we believe to be a better technology. The government has set standards for LDW and we've used an ^ to indicate which systems DON'T meet the low requirements.

THE BEST SAFETY FEATURES

The good news: automatic crash avoidance features are becoming more available. The bad news: it is hard to determine which ones work the best. Currently, the National Highway Traffic Safety Administration has standards for three important safety features: Back up cameras, Lane Depature Warning, and Frontal Collision Warning. Compliance to these standards is voluntary. In the tradition of *The Car Book*, exposing differences to stimulate market changes, in 2016 we published for the first time which of these three safety features meets the government standards and we continue to do so this year. However, it is important to note that having one of these features that doesn't meet government standards is better than not having it at all. Unfortunately, in order to get some of these features you often have to buy expensive "option packages" or a more expensive model which may include things you don't necessarily need or want.

Backup Camera: This camera allows the driver to see what is behind them on a dashboard screen. This is a critically important safety feature if you have children or drive near or around children. It's also a great parking assist. For a backup camera system to meet NHTSA's voluntary standards it must meet requirements regarding image size, linger time, response time, durability and deactivation. On the safety check list we've indicated which back up cameras DON'T meet federal standards with an asterisk (*).

Pedestrian Crash Avoidance: These systems utilize a variety of technologies (infrared, camera, radar) to detect pedestrians and adjust the car's course to avoid a collision.

General

Automatic Crash Notification: Using cellular technology and global positioning systems, some vehicles have the ability to send a call for help in the event of airbag deployment or accident. Often free initially, you'll have to pay extra later for this feature. There are several different types of ACN systems. Some simply dial 911 in the event of a crash while others connect your car to a call center which can determine the severity of the crash and dispatch emergency services. Some systems even send information about the crash to the call center.

Daytime Running Lights: Some cars offer daytime running lights that can reduce your chances of being in a crash by up to 40 percent by increasing the visibility of your vehicle. We indicate whether daytime running lights are standard, optional, or not available.

Safety Belts/Restraints

Dynamic Head Restraints: Many people position their seat and head restraint according to their own body and comfort requirements. This may not be the best position to protect you in a crash. These adjustors, sensing a crash, will automatically move the seat and headrest to the optimal position to help reduce injury during a rear-end crash. The IIHS has rated the performance of many headrests.

Adjustable Belts: Proper positioning of the safety belt across your chest is critical to obtaining the benefits of buckling up. Some systems allow you to adjust the height of the belt so it crosses your chest properly.

Specifications

Drive: This indicates the type of drive the manufacturer offers. This could be two wheel drive in the front (FWD) or rear (RWD) or all or four wheel drive (AWD/4WD).

Engine: This is the engine size (liters) and type that is expected to be the most popular. The engine types specify V6 or V8 for six or eight cylinders and I3, I4 or I6 for engines with cylinders in-line. For electric vehicles, we indicate the type of auxiliary power offered.

Transmission: This is the type of transmission expected to be the most popular. Most drivers today prefer automatic transmissions. The number listed with the transmission (5-sp.) is the number of gears or speeds. Then we list whether it's automatic or manual and if the transmission is a continuously variable transmission (CVT). CVT changes smoothly and efficiently between ratios of engine to car speeds and can provide better fuel economy.

Tow Rating: Ratings of very low, low, average, high, and very high indicate the vehicle's relative ability to tow trailers or other loads. Some manufacturers do not provide a tow rating.

Head/Leg Room: This tells how roomy the front seat is. The values are given in inches and rated in comparison to all other vehicles.

Interior Space: This tells how roomy the car's passenger area should feel. This value is given in cubic feet and rated in comparison to all other vehicles. Many SUVs do not provide interior space specifications.

Cargo Space: This gives you the cubic feet available for cargo. For minivans, the volume is behind the last row of seats. In cars, it's the trunk space. We rate the roominess of the cargo space compared to all trucks, SUVs, and cars.

Wheelbase/Length: The distance between the centers of the front and rear wheels is the wheelbase and the length is the distance from front bumper to rear bumper. Wheelbase can affect the ride and length affects how big the car "feels."

Ratings—10 Best, 1 Worst

Combo Crash Tests	5
Safety Features	8
Rollover	7
Preventive Maintenance	9
Repair Costs	6
Warranty	6
Fuel Economy	6
Complaints	3
Insurance Costs	10
OVERALL RATING	**8**

Acura ILX

Acura ILX

At-a-Glance

Status/Year Series Started. Unchanged/2013
Twins . . . .–
Body Styles . . . . .Sedan
Seating. 5
Anti-Theft Device . . . . . . Std. Pass. Immobil. & Alarm
Parking Index Rating . . . . Easy
Where Made. .Greensburg, IN
Fuel Factor:. . . . .
    MPG Rating (city/hwy) Poor-24/35
    Driving Range (mi.) . . . . .Very Short-369
    Fuel Type. . . . . .Premium
    Annual Fuel Cost . . . . .Average-$1438
    Gas Guzzler Tax . . . . .No
    Greenhouse Gas Emissions (tons/yr.). . Average-6.4
    Barrels of Oil Used per year Average-11.8

How the Competition Rates

Competitors	Rating	Pg.
Audi A3	7	85
BMW 3 Series	7	93
Cadillac ATS	8	108

Price Range

	Retail	Markup
Base	$27,990	6%
Premium Package	$29,990	6%
Technology Package	$32,990	6%
Technology Package w/A-SPEC	$34,980	6%

Safety Checklist

Crash Tests:
    Frontal. . . . . .Poor
    Side. . . . . Good
Airbags:
    Torso . . .Standard Front Pelvis/Torso from Seat
    Roll Sensing. . . . . .Yes
    Knee Bolster . . . . None
Crash Avoidance:
    Collision Avoidance . . . . . . Optional CIB & DBS
    Blind Spot Detection . . . . Optional
    Lane Keeping Assist . . . . Optional
    Backup Camera . . . . Standard
    Pedestrian Crash Avoidance . . . . Optional
General:
    Auto. Crash Notification . . . Operator Assist.-Fee
    Day Running Lamps . . . . Standard
Safety Belt/Restraint:
    Dynamic Head Restraints . . . . None
    Adjustable Belt. . . . . .Standard Front

^Warning feature does not meet government standards.
*Backup camera does not meet government standards.

Acura ILX

Specifications

Drive. . . . . .FWD
Engine 2.0-liter I4
Transmission . . . . 5-sp. Automatic
Tow Rating (lbs.) . . . .–
Head/Leg Room (in.) Cramped-38/42.3
Interior Space (cu. ft.). . . . . Very Cramped-89.3
Cargo Space (cu. ft.) . . . . Very Cramped-12.3
Wheelbase/Length (in.) 105.1/179.1

Ratings—10 Best, 1 Worst

Combo Crash Tests	9
Safety Features	10
Rollover	3
Preventive Maintenance	5
Repair Costs	6
Warranty	6
Fuel Economy	2
Complaints	2
Insurance Costs	10
OVERALL RATING	**8**

Acura MDX

Acura MDX

At-a-Glance

Status/Year Series Started........ Unchanged/2014
Twins . . . . –
Body Styles . . . . SUV
Seating 7
Anti-Theft Device . . . . . . Std. Pass. Immobil. & Alarm
Parking Index Rating . . . . Hard
Where Made. . . . . Lincoln, AL
Fuel Factor:. . . . .
MPG Rating (city/hwy) . . . . Very Poor-18/27
Driving Range (mi.) Average-413
Fuel Type . . . . Premium
Annual Fuel Cost . . . . Very High-$1898
Gas Guzzler Tax . . . . No
Greenhouse Gas Emissions (tons/yr.) High-8.6
Barrels of Oil Used per year High-15.7

How the Competition Rates

Competitors	Rating	Pg.
Audi Q5	3	90
BMW X5	6	100
Cadillac XT5	5	110

Price Range

	Retail	Markup
Base	$43,015	7%
SH-AWD w/Tech. Package	$45,015	7%
Advance w/RES	$55,230	8%
SH-AWD Advance w/RES	$57,230	8%

Safety Checklist

Crash Tests:
Frontal. . . . . Very Good
Side. . . . . Average
Airbags:
Torso . . . Standard Front Pelvis/Torso from Seat
Roll Sensing. . . . . Yes
Knee Bolster . . . . Standard Driver
Crash Avoidance:
Collision Avoidance . . . . . . Standard CIB & DBS
Blind Spot Detection . . . . Optional
Lane Keeping Assist . . . . Standard
Backup Camera . . . . Standard*
Pedestrian Crash Avoidance . . . . Optional
General:
Auto. Crash Notification . . . Operator Assist.-Fee
Day Running Lamps . . . . Standard
Safety Belt/Restraint:
Dynamic Head Restraints . . . . None
Adjustable Belt . . . . Standard Front

^Warning feature does not meet government standards.
*Backup camera does not meet government standards.

Acura MDX

Specifications

Drive. . . . . AWD
Engine 3.5-liter V6
Transmission . . . . 6-sp. Automatic
Tow Rating (lbs.) Low-3500
Head/Leg Room (in.) . . . . Very Cramped-38.1/41.4
Interior Space (cu. ft.). . . . . Very Roomy-132.3
Cargo Space (cu. ft.) Cramped-14.8
Wheelbase/Length (in.) 111/193.6

Acura RDX

Ratings—10 Best, 1 Worst	
Combo Crash Tests	10
Safety Features	8
Rollover	3
Preventive Maintenance	5
Repair Costs	6
Warranty	6
Fuel Economy	3
Complaints	5
Insurance Costs	10
OVERALL RATING	**9**

Acura RDX

At-a-Glance

Status/Year Series Started	Unchanged/2013
Twins	–
Body Styles	SUV
Seating	5
Anti-Theft Device	Std. Pass. Immobil. & Alarm
Parking Index Rating	Hard
Where Made	East Liberty, OH

Fuel Factor:

MPG Rating (city/hwy)	Very Poor-19/27
Driving Range (mi.)	Very Short-351
Fuel Type	Premium
Annual Fuel Cost	Very High-$1834
Gas Guzzler Tax	No
Greenhouse Gas Emissions (tons/yr.)	High-8.2
Barrels of Oil Used per year	High-15.0

How the Competition Rates

Competitors	Rating	Pg.
Buick Encore	10	104
Lexus NX	6	194
Lincoln MKC	5	198

Price Range	Retail	Markup
FWD	$35,370	6%
AWD	$36,870	6%
FWD w/Tech. Package	$39,070	6%
AWD w/Tech. Package	$40,570	6%

Safety Checklist

Crash Tests:

Frontal	Very Good
Side	Good

Airbags:

Torso	Standard Front Pelvis/Torso from Seat
Roll Sensing	Yes
Knee Bolster	None

Crash Avoidance:

Collision Avoidance	Optional CIB & DBS
Blind Spot Detection	Optional
Lane Keeping Assist	Optional
Backup Camera	Standard
Pedestrian Crash Avoidance	Optional

General:

Auto. Crash Notification	Operator Assist.-Fee
Day Running Lamps	Standard

Safety Belt/Restraint:

Dynamic Head Restraints	None
Adjustable Belt	Standard Front

^Warning feature does not meet government standards.
*Backup camera does not meet government standards.

Acura RDX

Specifications

Drive	AWD
Engine	3.5-liter V6
Transmission	6-sp. Automatic
Tow Rating (lbs.)	Very Low-1500
Head/Leg Room (in.)	Cramped-38.7/42
Interior Space (cu. ft.)	Average-103.5
Cargo Space (cu. ft.)	Roomy-26.1
Wheelbase/Length (in.)	105.7/183.5

Ratings—10 Best, 1 Worst

Combo Crash Tests	10
Safety Features	9
Rollover	8
Preventive Maintenance	5
Repair Costs	6
Warranty	6
Fuel Economy	4
Complaints	1
Insurance Costs	10
OVERALL RATING	**9**

Acura TLX

Acura TLX

At-a-Glance

Status/Year Series Started Unchanged/2015
Twins . . . . –
Body Styles . . . . Sedan
Seating 5
Anti-Theft Device . . . . . . Std. Pass. Immobil. & Alarm
Parking Index Rating . . . . Hard
Where Made. . . . . Marysville, OH
Fuel Factor: . . . .
  MPG Rating (city/hwy) . . . . .Very Poor-20/31
  Driving Range (mi.) Average-409
  Fuel Type . . . . .Premium
  Annual Fuel Cost . . . . .High-$1689
  Gas Guzzler Tax . . . . .No
  Greenhouse Gas Emissions (tons/yr.) . . Average-6.4
  Barrels of Oil Used per year Average-11.8

How the Competition Rates

Competitors	Rating	Pg.
Audi A6	6	88
Cadillac CTS	9	109
Lexus ES	7	190

Price Range

Price Range	Retail	Markup
Base 2.4L	$31,695	6%
Base 3.5L	$35,320	6%
3.5L w/Tech. Package	$39,375	6%
SH-AWD w/Advance Package	$44,800	6%

Safety Checklist

Crash Tests:
  Frontal. . . . . Very Good
  Side. . . . . Very Good
Airbags:
  Torso . . . Standard Front Pelvis/Torso from Seat
  Roll Sensing. . . . . .Yes
  Knee Bolster . . . . Standard Driver
Crash Avoidance:
  Collision Avoidance . . . . . . Optional CIB & DBS
  Blind Spot Detection . . . . Optional
  Lane Keeping Assist . . . . Optional
  Backup Camera . . . . Standard
  Pedestrian Crash Avoidance . . . . Optional
General:
  Auto. Crash Notification . . . Operator Assist.-Fee
  Day Running Lamps . . . . Standard
Safety Belt/Restraint:
  Dynamic Head Restraints . . . . None
  Adjustable Belt. . . . . .Standard Front

^Warning feature does not meet government standards.
*Backup camera does not meet government standards.

Acura TLX

Specifications

Drive. . . . . .FWD
Engine 2.0-liter I4
Transmission . . . . 8-sp. Automatic
Tow Rating (lbs.) . . . . –
Head/Leg Room (in.) Cramped-37.2/42.6
Interior Space (cu. ft.). Cramped-93.3
Cargo Space (cu. ft.) Cramped-13.2
Wheelbase/Length (in.) 109.3/190.3

Ratings—10 Best, 1 Worst

Combo Crash Tests	6
Safety Features	8
Rollover	7
Preventive Maintenance	1
Repair Costs	5
Warranty	7
Fuel Economy	6
Complaints	7
Insurance Costs	8
OVERALL RATING	**7**

Audi A3

Audi A3

At-a-Glance

Status/Year Series Started	Unchanged/2015
Twins	–
Body Styles	Sedan, Wagon
Seating	5
Anti-Theft Device	Std. Pass. Immobil. & Alarm
Parking Index Rating	Easy
Where Made	Gyor, Hungary

Fuel Factor:
MPG Rating (city/hwy)	Poor-24/33
Driving Range (mi.)	Short-397
Fuel Type	Premium
Annual Fuel Cost	Average-$1469
Gas Guzzler Tax	No
Greenhouse Gas Emissions (tons/yr.)	Average-6.6
Barrels of Oil Used per year	Average-12.2

How the Competition Rates

Competitors	Rating	Pg.
Acura ILX	8	81
Buick Verano	10	107
Lexus IS	6	193

Price Range

	Retail	Markup
1.8T Premium Sedan	$30,900	8%
2.0 TDI Premium Sedan	$33,200	8%
2.0T Premium Plus Sedan Quattro	$36,900	8%
2.0T Prestige Cabriolet Quattro	$48,450	8%

Audi A3

Safety Checklist

Crash Tests:
Frontal	Average
Side	Average

Airbags:
Torso	Std. Fr. & Opt. Rr. Pelvis/Torso from Seat
Roll Sensing	Yes
Knee Bolster	Standard Front

Crash Avoidance:
Collision Avoidance	Optional CIB & DBS
Blind Spot Detection	Optional
Lane Keeping Assist	Optional
Backup Camera	Standard*
Pedestrian Crash Avoidance	None

General:
Auto. Crash Notification	None
Day Running Lamps	Standard

Safety Belt/Restraint:
Dynamic Head Restraints	None
Adjustable Belt	Standard Front

^Warning feature does not meet government standards.
*Backup camera does not meet government standards.

Audi A3

Specifications

Drive	AWD
Engine	2.0-liter I4
Transmission	6-sp. Automatic
Tow Rating (lbs.)	–
Head/Leg Room (in.)	Very Cramped-36.5/41.2
Interior Space (cu. ft.)	Very Cramped-86
Cargo Space (cu. ft.)	Very Cramped-10.03
Wheelbase/Length (in.)	103.8/175.4

Ratings—10 Best, 1 Worst	
Combo Crash Tests	—
Safety Features	6
Rollover	7
Preventive Maintenance	6
Repair Costs	3
Warranty	7
Fuel Economy	6
Complaints	—
Insurance Costs	8
OVERALL RATING	**—**

Audi A4

Audi A4

At-a-Glance

Status/Year Series Started	All New/2017
Twins	–
Body Styles	Sedan
Seating	5
Anti-Theft Device	Std. Pass. Immobil. & Alarm
Parking Index Rating	Hard
Where Made	Ingolstadt, Germany
Fuel Factor:	
MPG Rating (city/hwy)	Poor-25/33
Driving Range (mi.)	Long-429
Fuel Type	Premium
Annual Fuel Cost	Average-$1433
Gas Guzzler Tax	No
Greenhouse Gas Emissions (tons/yr.)	Low-5.2
Barrels of Oil Used per year	Average-11.8

How the Competition Rates

Competitors	Rating	Pg.
BMW 3 Series	7	93
Cadillac ATS	8	108
Mercedes-Benz C-Class	3	206

Price Range	Retail	Markup
2.0T Premium Sedan	$37,300	8%
2.0T Premium Sedan Quattro	$39,400	8%
2.0T Premium Plus Sedan Quattro	$43,200	8%
2.0T Prestige Sedan Quattro	$48,000	8%

Safety Checklist

Crash Tests:
Frontal .... –
Side .... –

Airbags:
Torso Std. Fr. & Opt. Rr. Pelvis/Torso from Seat
Roll Sensing .... No
Knee Bolster .... None

Crash Avoidance:
Collision Avoidance ...... Std. CIB & Opt. DBS
Blind Spot Detection .... Optional
Lane Keeping Assist .... Optional
Backup Camera .... Standard*
Pedestrian Crash Avoidance .... Standard

General:
Auto. Crash Notification .... Dial Assist-Fee
Day Running Lamps .... Standard

Safety Belt/Restraint:
Dynamic Head Restraints .... None
Adjustable Belt .... Standard Front

^Warning feature does not meet government standards.
*Backup camera does not meet government standards.

Audi A4

Specifications

Drive	AWD
Engine	2.0-liter I4
Transmission	8-sp. Automatic
Tow Rating (lbs.)	–
Head/Leg Room (in.)	Cramped-38.9/41.3
Interior Space (cu. ft.)	–
Cargo Space (cu. ft.)	Very Cramped-13
Wheelbase/Length (in.)	111/186.1

Audi A5 — Intermediate

Ratings—10 Best, 1 Worst

Combo Crash Tests	—
Safety Features	2
Rollover	10
Preventive Maintenance	4
Repair Costs	1
Warranty	7
Fuel Economy	5
Complaints	—
Insurance Costs	3
OVERALL RATING	—

Audi A5

Audi A5

At-a-Glance

Status/Year Series Started . . . . All New/2017
Twins . . . . –
Body Styles . . . . .Coupe
Seating 4
Anti-Theft Device . . . . . . Std. Pass. Immobil. & Alarm
Parking Index Rating . . . . Average
Where Made. . . . . .Ingolstadt, Germany
Fuel Factor:. . . . .
  MPG Rating (city/hwy) Poor-22/30
  Driving Range (mi.) Short-403
  Fuel Type. . . . . .Premium
  Annual Fuel Cost . . . . .High-$1608
  Gas Guzzler Tax . . . . .No
  Greenhouse Gas Emissions (tons/yr.) Low-5.9
  Barrels of Oil Used per year High-13.2

How the Competition Rates

Competitors	Rating	Pg.
Acura ILX	8	81
BMW 3 Series	7	93
Lexus IS	6	193

Price Range

Price Range	Retail	Markup
2.0T Premium Coupe Quattro	$41,500	8%
2.0T Premium Plus Coupe Quattro	$43,800	8%
2.0T Premium Cabrio Quattro	$47,900	8%
2.0T Premium Plus Cabrio Quattro	$50,200	8%

Safety Checklist

Crash Tests:
  Frontal. . . . . –
  Side. . . . . –
Airbags:
  Torso . . . Standard Front Pelvis/Torso from Seat
  Roll Sensing. . . . . No
  Knee Bolster . . . . .Standard Front
Crash Avoidance:
  Collision Avoidance . . . . None
  Blind Spot Detection . . . . Optional
  Lane Keeping Assist . . .Warning Only Optional^
  Backup Camera . . . . Optional*
  Pedestrian Crash Avoidance . . . . None
General:
  Auto. Crash Notification . . . . None
  Day Running Lamps . . . . Standard
Safety Belt/Restraint:
  Dynamic Head Restraints . . . . None
  Adjustable Belt. None

^Warning feature does not meet government standards.
*Backup camera does not meet government standards.

Audi A5

Specifications

Drive. . . . . .AWD
Engine 2.0-liter I4
Transmission . . . . 8-sp. Automatic
Tow Rating (lbs.) . . . . –
Head/Leg Room (in.) . . . . Very Cramped-37.5/41.3
Interior Space (cu. ft.). . . . . –
Cargo Space (cu. ft.) . . . . Very Cramped-12.2
Wheelbase/Length (in.) 108.3/182.1

Ratings—10 Best, 1 Worst

Combo Crash Tests	8
Safety Features	7
Rollover	9
Preventive Maintenance	4
Repair Costs	2
Warranty	7
Fuel Economy	4
Complaints	7
Insurance Costs	5
OVERALL RATING	**6**

Audi A6

Audi A6

At-a-Glance

Status/Year Series Started Unchanged/2012
Twins . . . . –
Body Styles . . . . Sedan
Seating 5
Anti-Theft Device . . . . . . Std. Pass. Immobil. & Alarm
Parking Index Rating . . . . Hard
Where Made. . . . . Neckarsulm, Germany
Fuel Factor: . . . .
  MPG Rating (city/hwy) . . . . Very Poor-20/30
  Driving Range (mi.) Long-466
  Fuel Type . . . . Premium
  Annual Fuel Cost . . . . High-$1708
  Gas Guzzler Tax . . . . No
  Greenhouse Gas Emissions (tons/yr.) Low-5.1
  Barrels of Oil Used per year Average-11.8

How the Competition Rates

Competitors	Rating	Pg.
BMW 5 Series	6	95
Cadillac CTS	9	109
Volvo S60	10	266

Price Range

Price Range	Retail	Markup
2.0T Premium	$46,200	8%
2.0T Premium Plus Quattro	$52,100	8%
3.0 Prestige Quattro	$61,600	8%
3.0 Prestige TDI	$63,700	8%

Safety Checklist

Crash Tests:
  Frontal . . . . Very Good
  Side . . . . Average
Airbags:
  Torso   Std. Fr. & Opt. Rr. Pelvis/Torso from Seat
  Roll Sensing . . . . Yes
  Knee Bolster . . . . Standard Front
Crash Avoidance:
  Collision Avoidance . . . . . . Optional CIB & DBS
  Blind Spot Detection . . . . Optional
  Lane Keeping Assist . . . . Optional^
  Backup Camera . . . . Standard*
  Pedestrian Crash Avoidance . . . . None
General:
  Auto. Crash Notification . . . . None
  Day Running Lamps . . . . Standard
Safety Belt/Restraint:
  Dynamic Head Restraints . . . . None
  Adjustable Belt . . . . Standard Front

^Warning feature does not meet government standards.
*Backup camera does not meet government standards.

Audi A6

Specifications

Drive . . . . AWD
Engine 3.0-liter V6
Transmission . . . . 8-sp. Automatic
Tow Rating (lbs.) . . . . –
Head/Leg Room (in.) . . . . Very Cramped-37.2/41.3
Interior Space (cu. ft.) Average-98
Cargo Space (cu. ft.) Cramped-14.1
Wheelbase/Length (in.) 114.7/194.2

Ratings—10 Best, 1 Worst

Combo Crash Tests	—
Safety Features	3
Rollover	5
Preventive Maintenance	4
Repair Costs	3
Warranty	7
Fuel Economy	3
Complaints	10
Insurance Costs	8
OVERALL RATING	**—**

Audi Q3

Audi Q3

At-a-Glance

Status/Year Series Started	Unchanged/2015
Twins	–
Body Styles	SUV
Seating	5
Anti-Theft Device	Std. Pass. Immobil. & Alarm
Parking Index Rating	Average
Where Made	Martorell, Spain

Fuel Factor:

MPG Rating (city/hwy)	Very Poor-20/28
Driving Range (mi.)	Short-388
Fuel Type	Premium
Annual Fuel Cost	Very High-$1752
Gas Guzzler Tax	No
Greenhouse Gas Emissions (tons/yr.)	High-7.8
Barrels of Oil Used per year	High-14.3

How the Competition Rates

Competitors	Rating	Pg.
Acura RDX	9	83
Buick Encore	10	104
Lexus NX	6	194

Price Range

Price Range	Retail	Markup
2.0T Premium Plus	$33,700	8%
2.0T Premium Plus Quattro	$35,800	8%
2.0T Prestige	$38,600	8%
2.0T Prestige Quattro	$40,700	8%

Safety Checklist

Crash Tests:
- Frontal . . . . –
- Side . . . . –

Airbags:
- Torso . . . Standard Front Pelvis/Torso from Seat
- Roll Sensing . . . . Yes
- Knee Bolster . . . . None

Crash Avoidance:
- Collision Avoidance . . . . None
- Blind Spot Detection . . . . Optional
- Lane Keeping Assist . . . . None
- Backup Camera . . . . Standard*
- Pedestrian Crash Avoidance . . . . None

General:
- Auto. Crash Notification . . . . None
- Day Running Lamps . . . . Standard

Safety Belt/Restraint:
- Dynamic Head Restraints . . . . None
- Adjustable Belt . . . . Standard Front

^Warning feature does not meet government standards.
*Backup camera does not meet government standards.

Audi Q3

Specifications

Drive	AWD
Engine	2.0-liter I4
Transmission	6-sp. Automatic
Tow Rating (lbs.)	–
Head/Leg Room (in.)	Very Cramped-37/40
Interior Space (cu. ft.)	Very Cramped-84
Cargo Space (cu. ft.)	Cramped-16.7
Wheelbase/Length (in.)	102.5/172.6

Ratings—10 Best, 1 Worst

Combo Crash Tests	3
Safety Features	4
Rollover	3
Preventive Maintenance	4
Repair Costs	3
Warranty	7
Fuel Economy	3
Complaints	7
Insurance Costs	8
OVERALL RATING	**3**

Audi Q5

Audi Q5

At-a-Glance

Status/Year Series Started. Unchanged/2009
Twins . . . . –
Body Styles . . . . SUV
Seating 5
Anti-Theft Device . . . . . . Std. Pass. Immobil. & Alarm
Parking Index Rating . . . . Average
Where Made. . . . . .Ingolstadt, Germany
Fuel Factor:. . . . .
 MPG Rating (city/hwy). . . . . .Very Poor-20/28
 Driving Range (mi.) Long-454
 Fuel Type. . . . . .Premium
 Annual Fuel Cost . . . . Very High-$1752
 Gas Guzzler Tax . . . . .No
 Greenhouse Gas Emissions (tons/yr.). . Average-6.5
 Barrels of Oil Used per year High-14.3

How the Competition Rates

Competitors	Rating	Pg.
BMW X3	7	99
Cadillac XT5	5	110
Lexus RX	5	196

Price Range

Price Range	Retail	Markup
2.0T Premium	$40,900	8%
3.0T Premium Plus	$46,000	8%
Prestige Hybird	$52,500	8%
3.0 Prestige TDI	$55,600	8%

Safety Checklist

Crash Tests:
 Frontal. . . . . .Very Poor
 Side. . . . . Poor
Airbags:
 Torso Std. Fr. & Opt. Rr. Pelvis/Torso from Seat
 Roll Sensing. . . . . .Yes
 Knee Bolster . . . . None
Crash Avoidance:
 Collision Avoidance . . . . . . Optional CIB & DBS
 Blind Spot Detection . . . . Optional
 Lane Keeping Assist . . .Warning Only Optional^
 Backup Camera . . . . Optional*
 Pedestrian Crash Avoidance . . . . None
General:
 Auto. Crash Notification . . . . None
 Day Running Lamps . . . . Standard
Safety Belt/Restraint:
 Dynamic Head Restraints . . . . None
 Adjustable Belt. . . . . .Standard Front

^Warning feature does not meet government standards.
*Backup camera does not meet government standards.

Audi Q5

Specifications

Drive. . . . . .AWD
Engine 2.0-liter I4
Transmission . . . . 8-sp. Automatic
Tow Rating (lbs.) . . . . –
Head/Leg Room (in.) . . . . .Very Cramped-38.1/41
Interior Space (cu. ft.). –
Cargo Space (cu. ft.) Roomy-29.1
Wheelbase/Length (in.) 110.5/182.6

Ratings—10 Best, 1 Worst

Combo Crash Tests	—
Safety Features	9
Rollover	4
Preventive Maintenance	3
Repair Costs	1
Warranty	7
Fuel Economy	2
Complaints	10
Insurance Costs	8
OVERALL RATING	**—**

Audi Q7

Audi Q7

At-a-Glance

Status/Year Series Started	Unchanged/2016
Twins	—
Body Styles	SUV
Seating	7
Anti-Theft Device	Std. Pass. Immobil. & Alarm
Parking Index Rating	Very Hard
Where Made	Bratislava, Slovakia

Fuel Factor:

MPG Rating (city/hwy)	Very Poor-19/25
Driving Range (mi.)	Very Long-479
Fuel Type	Premium
Annual Fuel Cost	Very High-$1887
Gas Guzzler Tax	No
Greenhouse Gas Emissions (tons/yr.)	Average-6.9
Barrels of Oil Used per year	High-15.7

How the Competition Rates

Competitors	Rating	Pg.
BMW X5	6	100
Cadillac XT5	5	110
Lexus RX	5	196

Price Range	Retail	Markup
3.0 Premium	$54,800	8%
3.0 Premium Plus	$58,800	8%
3.0 Prestige	$64,300	8%

Audi Q7

Safety Checklist

Crash Tests:

Frontal	–
Side	–

Airbags:

Torso Std. Fr. & Opt. Rr. Pelvis/Torso from Seat

Roll Sensing	Yes
Knee Bolster	None

Crash Avoidance:

Collision Avoidance	Std. CIB & Opt. DBS
Blind Spot Detection	Optional
Lane Keeping Assist	Optional
Backup Camera	Standard*
Pedestrian Crash Avoidance	Standard

General:

Auto. Crash Notification	Dial Assist-Fee
Day Running Lamps	Standard

Safety Belt/Restraint:

Dynamic Head Restraints	None
Adjustable Belt	Standard Front

^Warning feature does not meet government standards.
*Backup camera does not meet government standards.

Specifications

Drive	AWD
Engine	3.0-liter V6
Transmission	8-sp. Automatic
Tow Rating (lbs.)	High-7700
Head/Leg Room (in.)	Cramped-38.4/41.7
Interior Space (cu. ft.)	–
Cargo Space (cu. ft.)	Cramped-14.8
Wheelbase/Length (in.)	117.9/199.6

Ratings—10 Best, 1 Worst

Combo Crash Tests	—
Safety Features	7
Rollover	7
Preventive Maintenance	4
Repair Costs	2
Warranty	9
Fuel Economy	6
Complaints	9
Insurance Costs	5
OVERALL RATING	**—**

BMW 2 Series

BMW 2 Series

At-a-Glance

Status/Year Series Started........ Unchanged/2016
Twins . . . .—
Body Styles . . . . .Coupe
Seating 4
Anti-Theft Device . . . . Std. Passive Alarm Only
Parking Index Rating . . . . Easy
Where Made. . . . . .Leipzig, Germany
Fuel Factor:. . . . .
  MPG Rating (city/hwy) Poor-23/35
  Driving Range (mi.) . . . . .Very Short-373
  Fuel Type. . . . . .Premium
  Annual Fuel Cost . . . . .Average-$1478
  Gas Guzzler Tax . . . . .No
  Greenhouse Gas Emissions (tons/yr.). . Average-6.4
  Barrels of Oil Used per year Average-12.2

How the Competition Rates

Competitors	Rating	Pg.
Acura ILX	8	81
Audi A3	7	85
Lexus IS	6	193

Price Range	Retail	Markup
228i AT	$32,850	7%
228xi Coupe	$34,850	7%
M235i Coupe	$44,150	7%
M235xi Coup	$46,150	7%

Safety Checklist

Crash Tests:
  Frontal. . . . .—
  Side. . . . .—
Airbags:
  Torso . . . . Standard Front Torso from Seat
  Roll Sensing. . . . . .Yes
  Knee Bolster . . . . .Standard Front
Crash Avoidance:
  Collision Avoidance . . . . . .Optional CIB & DBS^
  Blind Spot Detection . . . . None
  Lane Keeping Assist . . .Warning Only Optional^
  Backup Camera. . . . . Optional*
  Pedestrian Crash Avoidance . . . . Optional
General:
  Auto. Crash Notif. . . .Oper. Assist. & Crash Info-Free
  Day Running Lamps . . . . Standard
Safety Belt/Restraint:
  Dynamic Head Restraints . . . . None
  Adjustable Belt. . . . . None

^Warning feature does not meet government standards.
*Backup camera does not meet government standards.

BMW 2 Series

Specifications

Drive. . . . . .RWD
Engine 2.0-liter I4
Transmission . . . . 8-sp. Automatic
Tow Rating (lbs.) . . . . —
Head/Leg Room (in.) Cramped-40.1/41.5
Interior Space (cu. ft.). . . . . .Very Cramped-90
Cargo Space (cu. ft.) Cramped-13.8
Wheelbase/Length (in.) 105.9/174.7

Ratings—10 Best, 1 Worst	
Combo Crash Tests	7
Safety Features	7
Rollover	8
Preventive Maintenance	5
Repair Costs	2
Warranty	9
Fuel Economy	6
Complaints	7
Insurance Costs	5
OVERALL RATING	**7**

BMW 3 Series

BMW 3 Series

At-a-Glance

Status/Year Series Started	Unchanged/2013
Twins	–
Body Styles	Sedan, Wagon, Convertible
Seating	5
Anti-Theft Device	Std. Passive Alarm Only
Parking Index Rating	Average
Where Made	Munich, Germany
Fuel Factor:	
MPG Rating (city/hwy)	Poor-23/36
Driving Range (mi.)	Long-434
Fuel Type	Premium
Annual Fuel Cost	Average-$1464
Gas Guzzler Tax	No
Greenhouse Gas Emissions (tons/yr.)	Low-5.3
Barrels of Oil Used per year	Average-11.8

How the Competition Rates

Competitors	Rating	Pg.
Audi A3	7	85
Lexus IS	6	193
Mercedes-Benz C-Class	3	206

Price Range	Retail	Markup
320i	$33,150	7%
328d	$39,850	7%
335xi	$40,350	7%
340i	$45,800	7%

Safety Checklist

Crash Tests:
Frontal	Average
Side	Good

Airbags:
Torso	Standard Front Torso from Seat
Roll Sensing	Yes
Knee Bolster	Standard Front

Crash Avoidance:
Collision Avoidance	Optional CIB & DBS^
Blind Spot Detection	Optional
Lane Keeping Assist	Warning Only Optional^
Backup Camera	Optional*
Pedestrian Crash Avoidance	Optional

General:
Auto. Crash Notif.	Oper. Assist. & Crash Info-Free
Day Running Lamps	Standard

Safety Belt/Restraint:
Dynamic Head Restraints	None
Adjustable Belt	None

^Warning feature does not meet government standards.
*Backup camera does not meet government standards.

BMW 3 Series

Specifications

Drive	RWD
Engine	2.0-liter I4
Transmission	8-sp. Automatic
Tow Rating (lbs.)	–
Head/Leg Room (in.)	Roomy-40.3/42
Interior Space (cu. ft.)	Cramped-96
Cargo Space (cu. ft.)	Average-17
Wheelbase/Length (in.)	110.6/182.4

Ratings—10 Best, 1 Worst

Combo Crash Tests	—
Safety Features	7
Rollover	9
Preventive Maintenance	5
Repair Costs	2
Warranty	9
Fuel Economy	6
Complaints	8
Insurance Costs	5
OVERALL RATING	**—**

BMW 4 Series

BMW 4 Series

At-a-Glance

Status/Year Series Started........ Unchanged/2014
Twins . . . .—
Body Styles . . . . Coupe, Convertible
Seating 4
Anti-Theft Device . . . . Std. Passive Alarm Only
Parking Index Rating . . . . Average
Where Made. . . . . .Munich, Germany
Fuel Factor:. . . . .
  MPG Rating (city/hwy) Poor-23/35
  Driving Range (mi.) Long-430
  Fuel Type . . . . .Premium
  Annual Fuel Cost . . . . .Average-$1478
  Gas Guzzler Tax . . . . .No
  Greenhouse Gas Emissions (tons/yr.) . . Average-6.7
  Barrels of Oil Used per year Average-12.2

How the Competition Rates

Competitors	Rating	Pg.
Infiniti Q50	6	167
Lexus IS	6	193
Mercedes-Benz C-Class	3	206

Price Range

Price Range	Retail	Markup
430i Coupe	$41,850	7%
430xi Gran Coupe	$48,150	7%
435i Convertible	$56,950	8%
435xi Convertible	$58,950	8%

Safety Checklist

Crash Tests:
  Frontal. . . . .−
  Side. . . . .−
Airbags:
  Torso . . . . Standard Front Torso from Seat
  Roll Sensing. . . . . .Yes
  Knee Bolster . . . . .Standard Front
Crash Avoidance:
  Collision Avoidance . . . . . .Optional CIB & DBS^
  Blind Spot Detection . . . . Optional
  Lane Keeping Assist . . .Warning Only Optional^
  Backup Camera . . . . Optional*
  Pedestrian Crash Avoidance . . . . Optional
General:
  Auto. Crash Notif. . . .Oper. Assist. & Crash Info-Free
  Day Running Lamps . . . . Standard
Safety Belt/Restraint:
  Dynamic Head Restraints . . . . None
  Adjustable Belt. None

^Warning feature does not meet government standards.
*Backup camera does not meet government standards.

BMW 4 Series

Specifications

Drive. . . . . .RWD
Engine 2.0-liter I4
Transmission . . . . 8-sp. Automatic
Tow Rating (lbs.) . . . .−
Head/Leg Room (in.) Cramped-39.8/42.2
Interior Space (cu. ft.) . . . . Very Cramped-90
Cargo Space (cu. ft.) Cramped-15.7
Wheelbase/Length (in.) 110.6/182.6

Ratings—10 Best, 1 Worst

Combo Crash Tests	4
Safety Features	7
Rollover	9
Preventive Maintenance	9
Repair Costs	2
Warranty	9
Fuel Economy	6
Complaints	5
Insurance Costs	5
OVERALL RATING	**6**

BMW 5 Series

BMW 5 Series

At-a-Glance

Status/Year Series Started	Unchanged/2011
Twins	–
Body Styles	Sedan, Wagon
Seating	5
Anti-Theft Device	Std. Passive Alarm Only
Parking Index Rating	Very Hard
Where Made	Dingolfing, Germany
Fuel Factor:	
MPG Rating (city/hwy)	Poor-23/34
Driving Range (mi.)	Very Long-498
Fuel Type	Premium
Annual Fuel Cost	High-$1493
Gas Guzzler Tax	No
Greenhouse Gas Emissions (tons/yr.)	Average-6.6
Barrels of Oil Used per year	Average-12.2

How the Competition Rates

Competitors	Rating	Pg.
Infiniti Q50	6	167
Lincoln MKZ	5	199
Volvo S60	10	266

Price Range	Retail	Markup
528i	$50,200	8%
535i	$55,850	8%
550xi	$58,150	8%
535i Hybrid	$62,100	8%

Safety Checklist

Crash Tests:
- Frontal .... Very Poor
- Side .... Good

Airbags:
- Torso .... Standard Front Torso from Seat
- Roll Sensing .... Yes
- Knee Bolster .... None

Crash Avoidance:
- Collision Avoidance ...... Optional CIB & DBS^
- Blind Spot Detection .... Optional
- Lane Keeping Assist ...Warning Only Optional^
- Backup Camera .... Optional*
- Pedestrian Crash Avoidance .... Optional

General:
- Auto. Crash Notif. ...Oper. Assist. & Crash Info-Free
- Day Running Lamps .... Standard

Safety Belt/Restraint:
- Dynamic Head Restraints ......Standard Front
- Adjustable Belt .... None

^Warning feature does not meet government standards.
*Backup camera does not meet government standards.

BMW 5 Series

Specifications

Drive	RWD
Engine	2.0-liter I4
Transmission	8-sp. Automatic
Tow Rating (lbs.)	–
Head/Leg Room (in.)	Cramped-40.5/41.4
Interior Space (cu. ft.)	Average-102
Cargo Space (cu. ft.)	Average-18.4
Wheelbase/Length (in.)	116.9/193.4

Ratings—10 Best, 1 Worst

Combo Crash Tests	—
Safety Features	10
Rollover	7
Preventive Maintenance	9
Repair Costs	1
Warranty	9
Fuel Economy	4
Complaints	7
Insurance Costs	3

OVERALL RATING   —

BMW 7 Series

BMW 7 Series

At-a-Glance

Status/Year Series Started	Unchanged/2016
Twins	—
Body Styles	Sedan
Seating	5
Anti-Theft Device	Std. Passive Alarm Only
Parking Index Rating	Very Hard
Where Made	Dingolfing, Germany

Fuel Factor:

MPG Rating (city/hwy)	Very Poor-21/29
Driving Range (mi.)	Very Long-494
Fuel Type	Premium
Annual Fuel Cost	High-$1677
Gas Guzzler Tax	No
Greenhouse Gas Emissions (tons/yr.)	Average-6.1
Barrels of Oil Used per year	High-13.7

How the Competition Rates

Competitors	Rating	Pg.
Cadillac XTS	9	111
Infiniti Q50	6	167
Tesla Model S	10	242

Price Range

	Retail	Markup
740i	$81,500	8
740i xDrive	$84,500	8
750i	$94,600	8
750i xDrive	$97,600	8

Safety Checklist

Crash Tests:

Frontal	—
Side	—

Airbags:

Torso	Standard Front Torso from Seat
Roll Sensing	Yes
Knee Bolster	Standard Front

Crash Avoidance:

Collision Avoidance	Optional CIB & DBS^
Blind Spot Detection	Optional
Lane Keeping Assist	Optional^
Backup Camera	Standard
Pedestrian Crash Avoidance	Optional

General:

Auto. Crash Notif.	Oper. Assist. & Crash Info-Free
Day Running Lamps	Standard

Safety Belt/Restraint:

Dynamic Head Restraints	Standard Front
Adjustable Belt	None

^Warning feature does not meet government standards.
*Backup camera does not meet government standards.

BMW 7 Series

Specifications

Drive	RWD
Engine	6.0-liter V8
Transmission	8-sp. Automatic
Tow Rating (lbs.)	—
Head/Leg Room (in.)	Cramped-39.9/41.4
Interior Space (cu. ft.)	Roomy-107
Cargo Space (cu. ft.)	Average-18.2
Wheelbase/Length (in.)	126.4/206.6

Ratings—10 Best, 1 Worst

Combo Crash Tests	—
Safety Features	6
Rollover	5
Preventive Maintenance	4
Repair Costs	10
Warranty	9
Fuel Economy	10
Complaints	9
Insurance Costs	8
OVERALL RATING	**—**

BMW i3

BMW i3

At-a-Glance

Status/Year Series Started	Unchanged/2016
Twins	—
Body Styles	Coupe
Seating	4
Anti-Theft Device	Std. Passive Alarm Only
Parking Index Rating	Very Easy
Where Made	Leipzig, Germany
Fuel Factor:	
MPG Rating (city/hwy)	Average-137/111
Driving Range (mi.)	Very Short-114
Fuel Type	Premium
Annual Fuel Cost	Very Low-$324
Gas Guzzler Tax	No
Greenhouse Gas Emissions (tons/yr.)	Very Low-0.2
Barrels of Oil Used per year	Very Low-0.0

How the Competition Rates

Competitors	Rating	Pg.
Mercedes-Benz B-Class	—	205
Nissan Leaf	4	225
Toyota Prius C	7	252

Price Range

Price Range	Retail	Markup
Hatchback	$43,600	6%
Hbk w/Range Ext	$47,450	6%

Safety Checklist

Crash Tests:
- Frontal . . . . –
- Side . . . . –

Airbags:
- Torso . . . . Standard Front Torso from Seat
- Roll Sensing . . . . Yes
- Knee Bolster . . . . Standard Front

Crash Avoidance:
- Collision Avoidance . . . . . . Optional CIB & DBS^
- Blind Spot Detection . . . . None
- Lane Keeping Assist . . . Warning Only Optional^
- Backup Camera . . . . Optional*
- Pedestrian Crash Avoidance . . . . Optional

General:
- Auto. Crash Notif. . . . Oper. Assist. & Crash Info-Free
- Day Running Lamps . . . . Standard

Safety Belt/Restraint:
- Dynamic Head Restraints . . . . None
- Adjustable Belt . . . . None

^Warning feature does not meet government standards.
*Backup camera does not meet government standards.

BMW i3

Specifications

Drive	RWD
Engine	Electric
Transmission	CVT
Tow Rating (lbs.)	—
Head/Leg Room (in.)	Cramped-39.6/40.5
Interior Space (cu. ft.)	Very Cramped-83.1
Cargo Space (cu. ft.)	Very Cramped-11.8
Wheelbase/Length (in.)	101/157

Ratings—10 Best, 1 Worst	
Combo Crash Tests	—
Safety Features	6
Rollover	4
Preventive Maintenance	7
Repair Costs	2
Warranty	9
Fuel Economy	5
Complaints	8
Insurance Costs	5
OVERALL RATING	**—**

BMW X1

BMW X1

At-a-Glance

Status/Year Series Started	Unchanged/2016
Twins	—
Body Styles	SUV
Seating	5
Anti-Theft Device	Std. Passive Alarm Only
Parking Index Rating	Easy
Where Made	Leipzig, Germany
Fuel Factor:	
MPG Rating (city/hwy)	Poor-22/32
Driving Range (mi.)	Average-412
Fuel Type	Premium
Annual Fuel Cost	High-$1570
Gas Guzzler Tax	No
Greenhouse Gas Emissions (tons/yr.)	Low-5.7
Barrels of Oil Used per year	Average-12.7

How the Competition Rates

Competitors	Rating	Pg.
Buick Encore	10	104
Lexus NX	6	194
Volkswagen Tiguan	1	265

Price Range	Retail	Markup
sDrive28i	$32,800	6%
XDrive28i	$34,800	6%

Safety Checklist

Crash Tests:
Frontal . . . . –
Side . . . . –

Airbags:
Torso . . . . Standard Front Torso from Seat
Roll Sensing . . . . Yes
Knee Bolster . . . . Standard Front

Crash Avoidance:
Collision Avoidance . . . . . . Optional CIB & DBS
Blind Spot Detection . . . . None
Lane Keeping Assist . . . Warning Only Optional^
Backup Camera . . . . Optional*
Pedestrian Crash Avoidance . . . . Optional

General:
Auto. Crash Notif. . . . Oper. Assist. & Crash Info-Free
Day Running Lamps . . . . Standard

Safety Belt/Restraint:
Dynamic Head Restraints . . . . None
Adjustable Belt . . . . None

^Warning feature does not meet government standards.
*Backup camera does not meet government standards.

BMW X1

Specifications

Drive	RWD
Engine	2.0-liter I4
Transmission	8-sp. Automatic
Tow Rating (lbs.)	—
Head/Leg Room (in.)	Roomy-41.9/40.4
Interior Space (cu. ft.)	—
Cargo Space (cu. ft.)	Roomy-27.1
Wheelbase/Length (in.)	105.1/174.8

BMW X3

Ratings—10 Best, 1 Worst

Combo Crash Tests	6
Safety Features	8
Rollover	3
Preventive Maintenance	2
Repair Costs	5
Warranty	9
Fuel Economy	4
Complaints	8
Insurance Costs	8
OVERALL RATING	**7**

BMW X3

BMW X3

At-a-Glance

Status/Year Series Started	Unchanged/2011
Twins	–
Body Styles	SUV
Seating	5
Anti-Theft Device	Std. Passive Alarm Only
Parking Index Rating	Hard
Where Made	Spartanburg, SC
Fuel Factor:	
MPG Rating (city/hwy)	Very Poor-21/28
Driving Range (mi.)	Average-419
Fuel Type	Premium
Annual Fuel Cost	High-$1699
Gas Guzzler Tax	No
Greenhouse Gas Emissions (tons/yr.)	High-7.5
Barrels of Oil Used per year	High-13.7

How the Competition Rates

Competitors	Rating	Pg.
Audi Q5	3	90
Cadillac XT5	5	110
Lexus RX	5	196

Price Range	Retail	Markup
sDrive28i	$38,950	6%
XDrive28i	$40,950	6%
XDrive28d	$42,450	6%
XDrive35i	$47,650	6%

Safety Checklist

Crash Tests:
Frontal	Good
Side	Poor

Airbags:
Torso	Standard Front Torso from Seat
Roll Sensing	Yes
Knee Bolster	Standard Driver

Crash Avoidance:
Collision Avoidance	Optional CIB & DBS^
Blind Spot Detection	Optional
Lane Keeping Assist	Warning Only Optional^
Backup Camera	Optional
Pedestrian Crash Avoidance	Optional

General:
Auto. Crash Notif.	Oper. Assist. & Crash Info-Free
Day Running Lamps	Standard

Safety Belt/Restraint:
Dynamic Head Restraints	Standard Front
Adjustable Belt	None

^Warning feature does not meet government standards.
*Backup camera does not meet government standards.

BMW X3

Specifications

Drive	AWD
Engine	3.0-liter I6
Transmission	8-sp. Automatic
Tow Rating (lbs.)	–
Head/Leg Room (in.)	Cramped-40.7/39.9
Interior Space (cu. ft.)	Very Cramped-90.1
Cargo Space (cu. ft.)	Roomy-27.6
Wheelbase/Length (in.)	110.6/183.8

Ratings—10 Best, 1 Worst

Combo Crash Tests	8
Safety Features	9
Rollover	2
Preventive Maintenance	3
Repair Costs	1
Warranty	9
Fuel Economy	2
Complaints	10
Insurance Costs	3
OVERALL RATING	**6**

BMW X5

BMW X5

At-a-Glance

Status/Year Series Started	Unchanged/2014
Twins	–
Body Styles	SUV
Seating	5
Anti-Theft Device	Std. Passive Alarm Only
Parking Index Rating	Very Hard
Where Made	Spartanburg, SC
Fuel Factor:	
MPG Rating (city/hwy)	Very Poor-18/27
Driving Range (mi.)	Very Long-474
Fuel Type	Premium
Annual Fuel Cost	Very High-$1898
Gas Guzzler Tax	No
Greenhouse Gas Emissions (tons/yr.)	High-8.5
Barrels of Oil Used per year	High-15.7

How the Competition Rates

Competitors	Rating	Pg.
Audi Q5	3	90
Cadillac XT5	5	110
Lexus RX	5	196

Price Range	Retail	Markup
sDrive35i	$55,500	6%
XDrive35i	$57,800	7%
XDrive35d	$59,300	7%
XDrive50i	$72,300	7%

Safety Checklist

Crash Tests:
Frontal .... Good
Side .... Good

Airbags:
Torso .... Standard Front Torso from Seat
Roll Sensing .... Yes
Knee Bolster .... Standard Front

Crash Avoidance:
Collision Avoidance ...... Optional CIB & DBS^
Blind Spot Detection .... Optional
Lane Keeping Assist ...Warning Only Optional^
Backup Camera .... Optional*
Pedestrian Crash Avoidance .... Optional

General:
Auto. Crash Notif. ...Oper. Assist. & Crash Info-Free
Day Running Lamps .... Standard

Safety Belt/Restraint:
Dynamic Head Restraints ..... Standard Front
Adjustable Belt .... None

^Warning feature does not meet government standards.
*Backup camera does not meet government standards.

BMW X5

Specifications

Drive	AWD
Engine	3.0-liter V6
Transmission	8-sp. Automatic
Tow Rating (lbs.)	–
Head/Leg Room (in.)	Cramped-40.5/40.4
Interior Space (cu. ft.)	–
Cargo Space (cu. ft.)	Average-23
Wheelbase/Length (in.)	115.5/193.2

Ratings—10 Best, 1 Worst

Combo Crash Tests	—
Safety Features	9
Rollover	3
Preventive Maintenance	3
Repair Costs	1
Warranty	9
Fuel Economy	2
Complaints	4
Insurance Costs	3
OVERALL RATING	**—**

BMW X6

BMW X6

At-a-Glance

Status/Year Series Started	Unchanged/2010
Twins	—
Body Styles	SUV
Seating	5
Anti-Theft Device	Std. Passive Alarm Only
Parking Index Rating	Very Hard
Where Made	Spartanburg, SC
Fuel Factor:	
MPG Rating (city/hwy)	Very Poor-18/24
Driving Range (mi.)	Long-454
Fuel Type	Premium
Annual Fuel Cost	Very High-$1982
Gas Guzzler Tax	No
Greenhouse Gas Emissions (tons/yr.)	Average-7.0
Barrels of Oil Used per year	High-15.7

How the Competition Rates

Competitors	Rating	Pg.
Buick Enclave	6	103
Chevrolet Suburban	4	122
Toyota 4Runner	2	244

Price Range	Retail	Markup
sDrive35i	$61,400	7%
XDrive35i	$63,700	7%
XDrive50i	$76,100	7%
M	$102,200	7%

Safety Checklist

Crash Tests:
Frontal................................–
Side..................................–

Airbags:
Torso........Standard Front Torso from Seat
Roll Sensing...........................Yes
Knee Bolster................Standard Front

Crash Avoidance:
Collision Avoidance......Optional CIB & DBS^
Blind Spot Detection................Optional
Lane Keeping Assist...Warning Only Optional^
Backup Camera....................Optional*
Pedestrian Crash Avoidance.........Optional

General:
Auto. Crash Notif....Oper. Assist. & Crash Info-Free
Day Running Lamps..............Standard

Safety Belt/Restraint:
Dynamic Head Restraints......Standard Front
Adjustable Belt......................None

^Warning feature does not meet government standards.
*Backup camera does not meet government standards.

BMW X6

Specifications

Drive	AWD
Engine	3.0-liter V6
Transmission	8- sp. Automatic
Tow Rating (lbs.)	Average-6000
Head/Leg Room (in.)	Cramped-39.9/40.3
Interior Space (cu. ft.)	Average-101.4
Cargo Space (cu. ft.)	Roomy-26.6
Wheelbase/Length (in.)	115/193.8

Ratings—10 Best, 1 Worst

Combo Crash Tests	—
Safety Features	2
Rollover	7
Preventive Maintenance	2
Repair Costs	4
Warranty	8
Fuel Economy	3
Complaints	—
Insurance Costs	8
OVERALL RATING	**—**

Buick Cascada

Buick Cascada

At-a-Glance

Status/Year Series Started	All New/2017
Twins	—
Body Styles	Convertible
Seating	4
Anti-Theft Device	Std. Pass. Immobil. & Alarm
Parking Index Rating	Hard
Where Made	Gliwice, Poland
Fuel Factor:	
MPG Rating (city/hwy)	Very Poor-20/27
Driving Range (mi.)	Very Short-324
Fuel Type	Regular
Annual Fuel Cost	Average-$1424
Gas Guzzler Tax	No
Greenhouse Gas Emissions (tons/yr.)	Average-6.5
Barrels of Oil Used per year	High-14.3

How the Competition Rates

Competitors	Rating	Pg.
BMW 3 Series	7	93
Cadillac ATS	8	108
Lexus IS	6	193

Price Range	Retail	Markup
Convertible	$33,065	1%
Convertible Premium	$36,065	4%
Convertible Sport Touring	$37,065	4%

Safety Checklist

Crash Tests:
Frontal . . . . —
Side . . . . —

Airbags:
Torso . . . . Standard Front Torso from Seat
Roll Sensing . . . . No
Knee Bolster . . . . Standard Front

Crash Avoidance:
Collision Avoidance . . . . Warning Only Optional^
Blind Spot Detection . . . . None
Lane Keeping Assist . . . Warning Only Optional^
Backup Camera . . . . Standard*
Pedestrian Crash Avoidance . . . . None

General:
Auto. Crash Notif. . . . . Oper. Assist. & Crash Info-Free
Day Running Lamps . . . . Standard

Safety Belt/Restraint:
Dynamic Head Restraints . . . . None
Adjustable Belt . . . . Optional Rear

^Warning feature does not meet government standards.
*Backup camera does not meet government standards.

Buick Cascada

Specifications

Drive	FWD
Engine	1.6-liter I4
Transmission	6-sp. Automatic
Tow Rating (lbs.)	—
Head/Leg Room (in.)	Cramped-37.8/42.2
Interior Space (cu. ft.)	Very Cramped-82
Cargo Space (cu. ft.)	Cramped-13.4
Wheelbase/Length (in.)	106.1/184.9

Ratings—10 Best, 1 Worst

Combo Crash Tests	9
Safety Features	4
Rollover	3
Preventive Maintenance	2
Repair Costs	3
Warranty	8
Fuel Economy	2
Complaints	4
Insurance Costs	10
OVERALL RATING	**6**

Buick Enclave

Buick Enclave

At-a-Glance

Status/Year Series Started	Unchanged/2008
Twins	–
Body Styles	SUV
Seating	7/8
Anti-Theft Device	Std. Pass. Immobil. & Active Alarm
Parking Index Rating	Very Hard
Where Made	Lansing, MI
Fuel Factor:	
MPG Rating (city/hwy)	Very Poor-17/24
Driving Range (mi.)	Long-431
Fuel Type	Regular
Annual Fuel Cost	High-$1648
Gas Guzzler Tax	No
Greenhouse Gas Emissions (tons/yr.)	Very High-9.5
Barrels of Oil Used per year	Very High-17.3

How the Competition Rates

Competitors	Rating	Pg.
Chevrolet Traverse	6	124
Ford Expedition	7	139
Toyota 4Runner	2	244

Price Range

	Retail	Markup
Convenience FWD	$39,065	5%
Leather FWD	$43,660	5%
Leather AWD	$45,660	5%
Premium AWD	$49,515	5%

Safety Checklist

Crash Tests:
Frontal..............................Good
Side..................................Good

Airbags:
Torso . . . Standard Front Pelvis/Torso from Seat
Roll Sensing.........................Yes
Knee Bolster.......................None

Crash Avoidance:
Collision Avoidance.....Warning Only Optional
Blind Spot Detection................Optional
Lane Keeping Assist....Warning Only Optional
Backup Camera...................Standard*
Pedestrian Crash Avoidance...........None

General:
Auto. Crash Notif....Oper. Assist. & Crash Info-Free
Day Running Lamps...............Standard

Safety Belt/Restraint:
Dynamic Head Restraints..............None
Adjustable Belt.........Optional Front & Rear

^Warning feature does not meet government standards.
*Backup camera does not meet government standards.

Buick Enclave

Specifications

Drive	FWD
Engine	3.6-liter V6
Transmission	6-sp. Automatic
Tow Rating (lbs.)	Low-4500
Head/Leg Room (in.)	Cramped-40.4/41.3
Interior Space (cu. ft.)	Very Roomy-151.1
Cargo Space (cu. ft.)	Average-23.3
Wheelbase/Length (in.)	119/201.9

Ratings—10 Best, 1 Worst

Combo Crash Tests	9
Safety Features	8
Rollover	2
Preventive Maintenance	8
Repair Costs	8
Warranty	8
Fuel Economy	5
Complaints	9
Insurance Costs	8
OVERALL RATING	**10**

Buick Encore

Buick Encore

At-a-Glance

Status/Year Series Started Unchanged/2013
Twins . . . . –
Body Styles . . . . SUV
Seating 5
Anti-Theft Device . . . . . . Std. Pass. Immobil. & Alarm
Parking Index Rating . . . . Easy
Where Made . . . . .Bupyeong, South Korea
Fuel Factor: . . . .
  MPG Rating (city/hwy) Poor-23/30
  Driving Range (mi.) . . . . .Very Short-360
  Fuel Type . . . . .Regular
  Annual Fuel Cost . . . . Low-$1255
  Gas Guzzler Tax . . . . .No
  Greenhouse Gas Emissions (tons/yr.) . . Average-6.9
  Barrels of Oil Used per year Average-12.7

How the Competition Rates

Competitors	Rating	Pg.
Acura RDX	9	83
Ford Escape	7	138
Lincoln MKC	5	198

Price Range

Price Range	Retail	Markup
Preferred FWD	$24,365	4%
Sport Touring FWD	$25,565	4%
Essence AWD	$30,565	4%
Premium AWD	$31,965	4%

Safety Checklist

Crash Tests:
  Frontal . . . . Very Good
  Side . . . . Average
Airbags:
  Torso . . . Std. Fr. & Rear Pelvis/Torso from Seat
  Roll Sensing . . . . .Yes
  Knee Bolster . . . . .Standard Front
Crash Avoidance:
  Collision Avoidance . . . . .Warning Only Optional
  Blind Spot Detection . . . . Optional
  Lane Keeping Assist . . . .Warning Only Optional
  Backup Camera . . . . .Standard*
  Pedestrian Crash Avoidance . . . . None
General:
  Auto. Crash Notif. . . . .Oper. Assist. & Crash Info-Free
  Day Running Lamps . . . . Standard
Safety Belt/Restraint:
  Dynamic Head Restraints . . . . None
  Adjustable Belt . . . . Optional Front & Rear

^Warning feature does not meet government standards.
*Backup camera does not meet government standards.

Buick Encore

Specifications

Drive . . . . .AWD
Engine 1.4-liter I4
Transmission . . . . 6-sp. Automatic
Tow Rating (lbs.) . . . . –
Head/Leg Room (in.) Cramped-39.6/40.8
Interior Space (cu. ft.) Cramped-92.8
Cargo Space (cu. ft.) Average-18.8
Wheelbase/Length (in.) 100.6/168.4

Ratings—10 Best, 1 Worst

Combo Crash Tests	5
Safety Features	9
Rollover	7
Preventive Maintenance	2
Repair Costs	3
Warranty	8
Fuel Economy	4
Complaints	—
Insurance Costs	8
OVERALL RATING	**6**

BuickLaCrosse

BuickLaCrosse

At-a-Glance

Status/Year Series Started	All New/2017
Twins	—
Body Styles	Sedan
Seating	5
Anti-Theft Device	Std. Pass. Immobil. & Active Alarm
Parking Index Rating	Hard
Where Made	Fairfax, KS
Fuel Factor:	
MPG Rating (city/hwy)	Poor-21/31
Driving Range (mi.)	Short-388
Fuel Type	Regular
Annual Fuel Cost	Average-$1313
Gas Guzzler Tax	No
Greenhouse Gas Emissions (tons/yr.)	Low-6.0
Barrels of Oil Used per year	High-13.2

How the Competition Rates

Competitors	Rating	Pg.
Cadillac XTS	9	111
Chevrolet Impala	7	117
Toyota Avalon	7	246

Price Range	Retail	Markup
1SV	$32,065	1%
Preferred	$36,065	4%
Essence	$38,665	4%
Premium	$41,065	4%

Safety Checklist

Crash Tests:
Frontal	−^
Side	−^

Airbags:
Torso Std. Fr. & Opt. Rr. Pelvis/Torso from Seat
Roll Sensing . . . . Yes
Knee Bolster . . . . Standard Front

Crash Avoidance:
Collision Avoidance . . . . . . Optional CIB & DBS
Blind Spot Detection . . . . Optional
Lane Keeping Assist . . . . Optional
Backup Camera . . . . Standard*
Pedestrian Crash Avoidance . . . . Optional

General:
Auto. Crash Notif. . . . Oper. Assist. & Crash Info-Free
Day Running Lamps . . . . Standard

Safety Belt/Restraint:
Dynamic Head Restraints . . . . None
Adjustable Belt . . . . Optional Front & Rear

^Warning feature does not meet government standards.
*Backup camera does not meet government standards.

BuickLaCrosse

Specifications

Drive	FWD
Engine	3.6-liter V6
Transmission	8-sp. Automatic
Tow Rating (lbs.)	−
Head/Leg Room (in.)	Cramped-38.4/42
Interior Space (cu. ft.)	Average-100
Cargo Space (cu. ft.)	Cramped-15
Wheelbase/Length (in.)	114.4/197.5

Buick Regal

Ratings—10 Best, 1 Worst

Combo Crash Tests	5
Safety Features	5
Rollover	7
Preventive Maintenance	2
Repair Costs	4
Warranty	8
Fuel Economy	3
Complaints	6
Insurance Costs	5
OVERALL RATING	**4**

Buick Regal

At-a-Glance

Status/Year Series Started........ Unchanged/2011
Twins . . . .–
Body Styles . . . . .Sedan
Seating 5
Anti-Theft Device . Std. Pass. Immobil. & Active Alarm
Parking Index Rating . . . . Hard
Where Made. . . . . Oshawa, Ontario
Fuel Factor:. . . . .
  MPG Rating (city/hwy) . . . . . .Very Poor-19/31
  Driving Range (mi.) . . . . .Very Short-364
  Fuel Type. . . . . .Regular
  Annual Fuel Cost . . . . .Average-$1402
  Gas Guzzler Tax . . . . .No
  Greenhouse Gas Emissions (tons/yr.). High-7.9
  Barrels of Oil Used per year High-14.3

How the Competition Rates

Competitors	Rating	Pg.
Acura TLX	9	84
Cadillac CTS	9	109
Lincoln MKZ	5	199

Price Range

	Retail	Markup
1SV FWD	$27,065	1%
Leather AWD	$31,465	4%
Premium II FWD	$31,615	4%
GS AWD	$36,540	4%

Safety Checklist

Crash Tests:
  Frontal. . . . . Average
  Side. . . . . Average
Airbags:
  Torso Std. Fr. & Opt. Rr. Pelvis/Torso from Seat
  Roll Sensing. . . . . .Yes
  Knee Bolster . . . . None
Crash Avoidance:
  Collision Avoidance . . . . Optional CIB
  Blind Spot Detection . . . . Optional
  Lane Keeping Assist . . . .Warning Only Optional
  Backup Camera . . . . .Standard*
  Pedestrian Crash Avoidance . . . . None
General:
  Auto. Crash Notif. . . . .Oper. Assist. & Crash Info-Free
  Day Running Lamps . . . . Standard
Safety Belt/Restraint:
  Dynamic Head Restraints . . . . None
  Adjustable Belt. . . . . Optional Front & Rear

^Warning feature does not meet government standards.
*Backup camera does not meet government standards.

Buick Regal

Specifications

Drive. . . . . .FWD
Engine 2.4-liter I4
Transmission . . . . 6-sp. Automatic
Tow Rating (lbs.) . . . .–
Head/Leg Room (in.) Cramped-38.8/42.1
Interior Space (cu. ft.). Average-96.8
Cargo Space (cu. ft.) . . . . Very Cramped-11.1
Wheelbase/Length (in.) 107.8/190.2

Ratings—10 Best, 1 Worst

Combo Crash Tests	10
Safety Features	8
Rollover	6
Preventive Maintenance	8
Repair Costs	7
Warranty	8
Fuel Economy	5
Complaints	6
Insurance Costs	8
OVERALL RATING	**10**

Buick Verano

Buick Verano

At-a-Glance

Status/Year Series Started	Unchanged/2016
Twins	–
Body Styles	Sedan
Seating	5
Anti-Theft Device	Std. Pass. Immobil. & Alarm
Parking Index Rating	Easy
Where Made	Orion Township, MI
Fuel Factor:	
MPG Rating (city/hwy)	Poor-21/32
Driving Range (mi.)	Short-388
Fuel Type	Regular
Annual Fuel Cost	Average-$1298
Gas Guzzler Tax	No
Greenhouse Gas Emissions (tons/yr.)	Low-6.0
Barrels of Oil Used per year	High-13.2

How the Competition Rates

Competitors	Rating	Pg.
Acura ILX	8	81
Audi A3	7	85
Lexus IS	6	193

Price Range	Retail	Markup
1SV	$21,065	1%
Sport Touring	$24,115	4%
Leather	$26,555	4%

Safety Checklist

Crash Tests:
Frontal	Very Good
Side	Very Good

Airbags:
Torso	Std. Fr. & Rear Pelvis/Torso from Seat
Roll Sensing	Yes
Knee Bolster	Standard Front

Crash Avoidance:
Collision Avoidance	Warning Only Optional
Blind Spot Detection	Optional
Lane Keeping Assist	Warning Only Optional
Backup Camera	Standard*
Pedestrian Crash Avoidance	None

General:
Auto. Crash Notif.	Oper. Assist. & Crash Info-Free
Day Running Lamps	Standard

Safety Belt/Restraint:
Dynamic Head Restraints	None
Adjustable Belt	Optional Front & Rear

^Warning feature does not meet government standards.
*Backup camera does not meet government standards.

Buick Verano

Specifications

Drive	FWD
Engine	2.4-liter I4
Transmission	6-sp. Automatic
Tow Rating (lbs.)	Very Low-1000
Head/Leg Room (in.)	Cramped-38.3/42
Interior Space (cu. ft.)	Cramped-95
Cargo Space (cu. ft.)	Cramped-14.3
Wheelbase/Length (in.)	105.7/183.9

Ratings—10 Best, 1 Worst

Combo Crash Tests	8
Safety Features	9
Rollover	8
Preventive Maintenance	3
Repair Costs	5
Warranty	9
Fuel Economy	5
Complaints	3
Insurance Costs	8
OVERALL RATING	**8**

Cadillac ATS

Cadillac ATS

Cadillac ATS

At-a-Glance

Status/Year Series Started........ Unchanged/2013
Twins .... –
Body Styles .... Sedan, Coupe
Seating 5
Anti-Theft Device ..... Std. Pass. Immobil. & Alarm
Parking Index Rating .... Easy
Where Made......................... Lansing, MI
Fuel Factor:..
MPG Rating (city/hwy).............. Poor-21/33
Driving Range (mi.) Short-402
Fuel Type .... Regular
Annual Fuel Cost .... Low-$1284
Gas Guzzler Tax .... No
Greenhouse Gas Emissions (tons/yr.).. Average-7.2
Barrels of Oil Used per year High-13.2

How the Competition Rates

Competitors	Rating	Pg.
Acura ILX	8	81
Infiniti Q50	6	167
Mercedes-Benz C-Class	3	206

Price Range

Price Range	Retail	Markup
Base 2.0L Sedan RWD	$34,595	6%
Luxury 2.0L Sedan AWD	$40,395	6%
Performance 3.6L Sedan RWD	$46,995	7%
Premium 3.6L Coupe AWD	$48,995	7%

Safety Checklist

Crash Tests:
Frontal......................... Very Good
Side............................... Poor
Airbags:
Torso Std. Fr. & Opt. Rr. Pelvis/Torso from Seat
Roll Sensing........................... Yes
Knee Bolster .... Standard Front
Crash Avoidance:
Collision Avoidance ...... Optional CIB & DBS
Blind Spot Detection .... Optional
Lane Keeping Assist .... Optional
Backup Camera.................. Standard*
Pedestrian Crash Avoidance .... None
General:
Auto. Crash Notif. ....Oper. Assist. & Crash Info-Free
Day Running Lamps .... Standard
Safety Belt/Restraint:
Dynamic Head Restraints .... None
Adjustable Belt................. Optional Rear

^Warning feature does not meet government standards.
*Backup camera does not meet government standards.

Cadillac ATS

Specifications

Drive.................................RWD
Engine 2.5-liter I4
Transmission .... 6-sp. Automatic
Tow Rating (lbs.) .... –
Head/Leg Room (in.) Cramped-38.6/42.5
Interior Space (cu. ft.)............ Cramped-90.9
Cargo Space (cu. ft.) ...... Very Cramped-10.4
Wheelbase/Length (in.) 109.3/182.8

Ratings—10 Best, 1 Worst

Combo Crash Tests	8
Safety Features	8
Rollover	8
Preventive Maintenance	3
Repair Costs	3
Warranty	9
Fuel Economy	3
Complaints	8
Insurance Costs	10
OVERALL RATING	**9**

Cadillac CTS

Cadillac CTS

At-a-Glance

Status/Year Series Started........ Unchanged/2014
Twins ....–
Body Styles ....Sedan, Coupe, Wagon
Seating 5
Anti-Theft Device ...... Std. Pass. Immobil. & Alarm
Parking Index Rating .... Hard
Where Made......................... Lansing, MI
Fuel Factor:...
  MPG Rating (city/hwy) ....Very Poor-18/29
  Driving Range (mi.) Average-412
  Fuel Type ....Regular
  Annual Fuel Cost ....High-$1486
  Gas Guzzler Tax ....No
  Greenhouse Gas Emissions (tons/yr.) High-8.2
  Barrels of Oil Used per year High-15.0

How the Competition Rates

Competitors	Rating	Pg.
Acura TLX	9	84
Lexus ES	7	190
Tesla Model S	10	242

Price Range

	Retail	Markup
Base 2.0L RWD	$45,995	6%
Luxury 3.6 L AWD	$55,695	6%
Premium 3.6L AWD	$61,195	7%
Vsport Premium AWD	$70,795	7%

Cadillac CTS

Safety Checklist

Crash Tests:
  Frontal............................. Good
  Side................................. Good
Airbags:
  Torso Std. Fr. & Opt. Rr. Pelvis/Torso from Seat
  Roll Sensing..............................Yes
  Knee Bolster ....Standard Front
Crash Avoidance:
  Collision Avoidance ...... Optional CIB & DBS
  Blind Spot Detection .... Optional
  Lane Keeping Assist .... Optional
  Backup Camera .... Optional*
  Pedestrian Crash Avoidance .... None
General:
  Auto. Crash Notif. ...Oper. Assist. & Crash Info-Free
  Day Running Lamps .... Standard
Safety Belt/Restraint:
  Dynamic Head Restraints .... None
  Adjustable Belt........ Optional Front & Rear

^Warning feature does not meet government standards.
*Backup camera does not meet government standards.

Cadillac CTS

Specifications

Drive.......................................RWD
Engine 3.6-liter V6
Transmission .... 6-sp. Automatic
Tow Rating (lbs.) .... Very Low-1000
Head/Leg Room (in.) Cramped-42.6/39.2
Interior Space (cu. ft.)...................Average-97
Cargo Space (cu. ft.)...............Cramped-13.7
Wheelbase/Length (in.) 114.6/195.5

Cadillac XT5

Ratings—10 Best, 1 Worst

Combo Crash Tests	4
Safety Features	8
Rollover	3
Preventive Maintenance	2
Repair Costs	5
Warranty	9
Fuel Economy	2
Complaints	—
Insurance Costs	10
OVERALL RATING	**5**

Cadillac XT5

At-a-Glance

Status/Year Series Started. . . . . All New/2017
Twins . . . . —
Body Styles . . . . SUV
Seating 5
Anti-Theft Device . Std. Pass. Immobil. & Active Alarm
Parking Index Rating . . . . Very Easy
Where Made. . . . . Spring Hill, TN
Fuel Factor:. . . . .
  MPG Rating (city/hwy) . . . . Very Poor-19/25
  Driving Range (mi.) Average-405
  Fuel Type . . . . .Regular
  Annual Fuel Cost . . . . .High-$1514
  Gas Guzzler Tax . . . . .No
  Greenhouse Gas Emissions (tons/yr.). . Average-6.5
  Barrels of Oil Used per year High-15.0

How the Competition Rates

Competitors	Rating	Pg.
Acura RDX	9	83
Audi Q5	3	90
Lexus RX	5	196

Price Range

Price Range	Retail	Markup
Base FWD	$38,995	6%
Luxury FWD	$47,390	6%
Premium Luxury AWD	$54,390	7%
Platinum AWD	$62,500	7%

Safety Checklist

Crash Tests:
  Frontal. . . . . Average
  Side. . . . . .Very Poor
Airbags:
  Torso . . . Standard Front Pelvis/Torso from Seat
  Roll Sensing. . . . . .Yes
  Knee Bolster . . . . Standard Driver
Crash Avoidance:
  Collision Avoidance . . . . . . Optional CIB & DBS
  Blind Spot Detection . . . . Optional
  Lane Keeping Assist . . . . Optional
  Backup Camera . . . . .Standard*
  Pedestrian Crash Avoidance . . . . Optional
General:
  Auto. Crash Notif. . . .Oper. Assist. & Crash Info-Free
  Day Running Lamps . . . . Standard
Safety Belt/Restraint:
  Dynamic Head Restraints . . . . None
  Adjustable Belt . . . . .Standard Front

^Warning feature does not meet government standards.
*Backup camera does not meet government standards.

Cadillac XT5

Specifications

Drive. . . . . .FWD
Engine 3.6-liter V6
Transmission . . . . 8-sp. Automatic
Tow Rating (lbs.) . . . . —
Head/Leg Room (in.) . . . . Very Cramped-38.4/41.2
Interior Space (cu. ft.). . . . . —
Cargo Space (cu. ft.) Roomy-30
Wheelbase/Length (in.) 112.5/189.5

Ratings—10 Best, 1 Worst

Combo Crash Tests	10
Safety Features	8
Rollover	5
Preventive Maintenance	2
Repair Costs	4
Warranty	9
Fuel Economy	3
Complaints	7
Insurance Costs	8
OVERALL RATING	**9**

Cadillac XTS

Cadillac XTS

At-a-Glance

Status/Year Series Started	Unchanged/2013
Twins	–
Body Styles	Sedan
Seating	5
Anti-Theft Device	Std. Pass. Immobil. & Active Alarm
Parking Index Rating	Very Hard
Where Made	Oshawa, Ontario

Fuel Factor:

MPG Rating (city/hwy)	Very Poor-18/28
Driving Range (mi.)	Average-407
Fuel Type	Regular
Annual Fuel Cost	High-$1504
Gas Guzzler Tax	No
Greenhouse Gas Emissions (tons/yr.)	High-8.6
Barrels of Oil Used per year	High-15.7

How the Competition Rates

Competitors	Rating	Pg.
Buick LaCrosse	6	105
Chrysler 300	2	128
Ford Taurus	4	148

Price Range

	Retail	Markup
Base	$45,295	6%
Luxury AWD	$51,295	6%
Platinum	$64,595	7%
Platinum Vsport AWD	$72,395	7%

Safety Checklist

Crash Tests:
Frontal . . . . Very Good
Side . . . . Good

Airbags:
Torso Std. Fr. & Opt. Rr. Pelvis/Torso from Seat
Roll Sensing . . . . Yes
Knee Bolster . . . . Standard Front

Crash Avoidance:
Collision Avoidance . . . . . . Optional CIB & DBS
Blind Spot Detection . . . . Optional
Lane Keeping Assist . . . . Optional
Backup Camera . . . . Optional*
Pedestrian Crash Avoidance . . . . None

General:
Auto. Crash Notif. . . . Oper. Assist. & Crash Info-Free
Day Running Lamps . . . . Standard

Safety Belt/Restraint:
Dynamic Head Restraints . . . . None
Adjustable Belt . . . . Optional Front & Rear

^Warning feature does not meet government standards.
*Backup camera does not meet government standards.

Cadillac XTS

Specifications

Drive	FWD
Engine	3.6-liter V6
Transmission	6-sp. Automatic
Tow Rating (lbs.)	Very Low-1000
Head/Leg Room (in.)	Very Roomy-39/45.8
Interior Space (cu. ft.)	Roomy-104.2
Cargo Space (cu. ft.)	Average-18
Wheelbase/Length (in.)	111.7/202

Ratings—10 Best, 1 Worst

Combo Crash Tests	7
Safety Features	5
Rollover	10
Preventive Maintenance	2
Repair Costs	6
Warranty	6
Fuel Economy	3
Complaints	8
Insurance Costs	1
OVERALL RATING	**5**

Chevrolet Camaro

Chevrolet Camaro

At-a-Glance

Status/Year Series Started	Unchanged/2016
Twins	–
Body Styles	Coupe, Convertible
Seating	4
Anti-Theft Device	Std. Pass. Immobil. & Active Alarm
Parking Index Rating	–'
Where Made	Lansing, MI
Fuel Factor:	
MPG Rating (city/hwy)	Very Poor-19/28
Driving Range (mi.)	Average-422
Fuel Type	Premium
Annual Fuel Cost	Very High-$1810
Gas Guzzler Tax	No
Greenhouse Gas Emissions (tons/yr.)	Average-6.5
Barrels of Oil Used per year	High-14.3

How the Competition Rates

Competitors	Rating	Pg.
Chevrolet Corvette	–	114
Dodge Challenger	5	130
Ford Mustang	7	147

Price Range

Price Range	Retail	Markup
1LT Coupe	$26,305	4%
2LT Coupe	$30,405	4%
1SS Coupe	$36,905	4%
2SS Coupe	$41,908	4%

Safety Checklist

Crash Tests:
- Frontal . . . . –
- Side . . . . –

Airbags:
- Torso . . . Standard Front Pelvis/Torso from Seat
- Roll Sensing . . . . Yes
- Knee Bolster . . . . Standard Front

Crash Avoidance:
- Collision Avoidance . . . . None
- Blind Spot Detection . . . . Optional
- Lane Keeping Assist . . . . None
- Backup Camera . . . . Standard*
- Pedestrian Crash Avoidance . . . . None

General:
- Auto. Crash Notif. . . . Oper. Assist. & Crash Info-Free
- Day Running Lamps . . . . Standard

Safety Belt/Restraint:
- Dynamic Head Restraints . . . . None
- Adjustable Belt . . . . Optional Rear

^Warning feature does not meet government standards.
*Backup camera does not meet government standards.

Chevrolet Camaro

Specifications

Drive	RWD
Engine	3.6-liter V6
Transmission	8-sp. Automatic
Tow Rating (lbs.)	–
Head/Leg Room (in.)	Very Cramped-36.6/42.6
Interior Space (cu. ft.)	–
Cargo Space (cu. ft.)	Very Cramped-9.1
Wheelbase/Length (in.)	110.7/188.3

Ratings—10 Best, 1 Worst	Colorado	Canyon
Combo Crash Tests	4	—
Safety Features	4	4
Rollover	1	1
Preventive Maintenance	2	2
Repair Costs	5	5
Warranty	6	4
Fuel Economy	3	3
Complaints	3	2
Insurance Costs	10	8
OVERALL RATING		**3**

Chevrolet Colorado

GMC Canyon

At-a-Glance

Status/Year Series Started	Unchanged/2015
Twins	–
Body Styles	Pickup
Seating	5
Anti-Theft Device	Std. Pass. Immob. & Opt. Pass. Alarm
Parking Index Rating	Very Hard
Where Made	Wentzville, MO

Fuel Factor:

MPG Rating (city/hwy)	Very Poor-20/27
Driving Range (mi.)	Very Long-475
Fuel Type	Regular
Annual Fuel Cost	Average-$1424
Gas Guzzler Tax	No
Greenhouse Gas Emissions (tons/yr.)	High-8.2
Barrels of Oil Used per year	High-15.0

How the Competition Rates

Competitors	Rating	Pg.
Nissan Frontier	–	223
Toyota Tacoma	2	257
	–	

Price Range

	Retail	Markup
Base Ext. Cab 2WD	$20,100	0%
W/T Crew Cab 4WD	$30,005	5%
LT Crew Cab 4WD	$32,535	5%
Z71 Crew Cab 4WD	$34,640	5%

Safety Checklist

Crash Tests:
Frontal	Poor
Side	Average

Airbags:
Torso	Standard Front Pelvis/Torso from Seat
Roll Sensing	Yes
Knee Bolster	None

Crash Avoidance:
Collision Avoidance	Warning Only Optional
Blind Spot Detection	None
Lane Keeping Assist	Warning Only Optional
Backup Camera	Standard*
Pedestrian Crash Avoidance	None

General:
Auto. Crash Notif.	Oper. Assist. & Crash Info-Free
Day Running Lamps	Standard

Safety Belt/Restraint:
Dynamic Head Restraints	None
Adjustable Belt	Optional Front & Rear

^Warning feature does not meet government standards.
*Backup camera does not meet government standards.

Chevrolet Colorado

Specifications

Drive	RWD
Engine	2.5-liter I4
Transmission	6-sp. Automatic
Tow Rating (lbs.)	Low-3500
Head/Leg Room (in.)	Very Roomy-41.4/45
Interior Space (cu. ft.)	–
Cargo Space (cu. ft.)	Very Roomy-49.9
Wheelbase/Length (in.)	128.3/212.7

Ratings—10 Best, 1 Worst	
Combo Crash Tests	—
Safety Features	1
Rollover	10
Preventive Maintenance	3
Repair Costs	1
Warranty	6
Fuel Economy	2
Complaints	7
Insurance Costs	10
OVERALL RATING	**—**

Chevrolet Corvette

Chevrolet Corvette

At-a-Glance

Status/Year Series Started	Unchanged/2014
Twins	—
Body Styles	Coupe, Convertible
Seating	2
Anti-Theft Device	Std. Pass. Immobil. & Active Alarm
Parking Index Rating	Average
Where Made	Bowling Green, KY
Fuel Factor:	
MPG Rating (city/hwy)	Very Poor-16/29
Driving Range (mi.)	Very Short-371
Fuel Type	Premium
Annual Fuel Cost	Very High-$2006
Gas Guzzler Tax	No
Greenhouse Gas Emissions (tons/yr.)	High-9.0
Barrels of Oil Used per year	High-16.5

How the Competition Rates

Competitors	Rating	Pg.
Chevrolet Camaro	5	112
Dodge Challenger	5	130
Ford Mustang	7	147

Price Range	Retail	Markup
Base Coupe	$55,450	8%
Z51 Convertible	$64,450	8%
Grand Sport Coupe	$65,450	8%
Z06 Convertible	$83,450	8%

Safety Checklist

Crash Tests:
Frontal . . . . —
Side . . . . —

Airbags:
Torso . . . . Standard Front Torso from Seat
Roll Sensing . . . . No
Knee Bolster . . . . None

Crash Avoidance:
Collision Avoidance . . . . None
Blind Spot Detection . . . . None
Lane Keeping Assist . . . . None
Backup Camera . . . . Standard*
Pedestrian Crash Avoidance . . . . None

General:
Auto. Crash Notif. . . . Oper. Assist. & Crash Info-Free
Day Running Lamps . . . . Standard

Safety Belt/Restraint:
Dynamic Head Restraints . . . . None
Adjustable Belt . . . . None

^Warning feature does not meet government standards.
*Backup camera does not meet government standards.

Chevrolet Corvette

Specifications

Drive	RWD
Engine	6.2-liter V8
Transmission	8-sp. Automatic
Tow Rating (lbs.)	—
Head/Leg Room (in.)	Cramped-38/43
Interior Space (cu. ft.)	Very Cramped-52
Cargo Space (cu. ft.)	Cramped-15
Wheelbase/Length (in.)	106.7/176.9

Ratings—10 Best, 1 Worst

Combo Crash Tests	—
Safety Features	9
Rollover	6
Preventive Maintenance	5
Repair Costs	8
Warranty	6
Fuel Economy	8
Complaints	8
Insurance Costs	1

OVERALL RATING — —

Chevrolet Cruze

Chevrolet Cruze

At-a-Glance

Status/Year Series Started. Unchanged/2016
Twins . . . . —
Body Styles . . . . .Sedan
Seating. 5
Anti-Theft Device .Std. Pass. Immobil. & Active Alarm
Parking Index Rating . . . . Easy
Where Made. . . . . Lordstown, OH
Fuel Factor:. . . . .
 MPG Rating (city/hwy) Poor-26/38
 Driving Range (mi.) . . . . Very Long-473
 Fuel Type. . . . . .Regular
 Annual Fuel Cost . . . . Low-$1064
 Gas Guzzler Tax . . . . .No
 Greenhouse Gas Emissions (tons/yr.). Low-4.9
 Barrels of Oil Used per year Average-11.0

How the Competition Rates

Competitors	Rating	Pg.
Ford Focus	6	144
Honda Civic	8	153
Toyota Corolla	8	248

Price Range	Retail	Markup
L MT	$16,975	1%
LS AT	$19,525	4%
LT AT	$21,920	4%
Premier Sedan AT	$23,475	4%

Safety Checklist

Crash Tests:
 Frontal. . . . . —
 Side. . . . . —
Airbags:
 Torso . . .Std. Fr. & Rear Pelvis/Torso from Seat
 Roll Sensing. . . . . .Yes
 Knee Bolster . . . . .Standard Front
Crash Avoidance:
 Collision Avoidance . . . . .Warning Only Optional
 Blind Spot Detection . . . . Optional
 Lane Keeping Assist . . . . Optional
 Backup Camera. . . . . .Standard*
 Pedestrian Crash Avoidance . . . . None
General:
 Auto. Crash Notif. . . .Oper. Assist. & Crash Info-Free
 Day Running Lamps . . . . Standard
Safety Belt/Restraint:
 Dynamic Head Restraints . . . . None
 Adjustable Belt. . . . . .Optional Rear

^Warning feature does not meet government standards.
*Backup camera does not meet government standards.

Chevrolet Cruze

Specifications

Drive. . . . . .FWD
Engine 1.8-liter I4
Transmission . . . . .6-sp. Autonatic
Tow Rating (lbs.) . . . . —
Head/Leg Room (in.) Cramped-39.3/42.28
Interior Space (cu. ft.). Cramped-94.6
Cargo Space (cu. ft.) Cramped-15
Wheelbase/Length (in.) 105.7/181

Ratings—10 Best, 1 Worst	Equinox	Terrain
Combo Crash Tests	2	2
Safety Features	4	4
Rollover	2	2
Preventive Maintenance	2	2
Repair Costs	6	6
Warranty	6	4
Fuel Economy	5	5
Complaints	4	7
Insurance Costs	5	8
OVERALL RATING		**2**

Chevrolet Equinox

GMC Terrain

At-a-Glance

Status/Year Series Started	Unchanged/2005
Twins	–
Body Styles	SUV
Seating	5
Anti-Theft Device	Std. Pass. Immobil. & Active Alarm
Parking Index Rating	Very Hard
Where Made	Oshawa, Ontario / Spring Hill, TN

Fuel Factor:
MPG Rating (city/hwy)	Poor-22/32
Driving Range (mi.)	Very Long-481
Fuel Type	Regular
Annual Fuel Cost	Low-$1260
Gas Guzzler Tax	No
Greenhouse Gas Emissions (tons/yr.)	Average-6.9
Barrels of Oil Used per year	Average-12.7

How the Competition Rates

Competitors	Rating	Pg.
Dodge Journey	1	133
Ford Explorer	3	140
Honda Pilot	8	158

Price Range

Price Range	Retail	Markup
L FWD	$23,100	1%
LS FWD	$25,510	5%
LT AWD	$28,500	5%
Premier AWD	$31,790	5%

Safety Checklist

Crash Tests:
Frontal................................Poor
Side............................Very Poor

Airbags:
Torso . . . Standard Front Pelvis/Torso from Seat
Roll Sensing...........................Yes
Knee Bolster .... None

Crash Avoidance:
Collision Avoidance . . . . .Warning Only Optional
Blind Spot Detection .... Optional
Lane Keeping Assist . . . .Warning Only Optional
Backup Camera...................Standard*
Pedestrian Crash Avoidance .... None

General:
Auto. Crash Notif. . . .Oper. Assist. & Crash Info-Free
Day Running Lamps .... Standard

Safety Belt/Restraint:
Dynamic Head Restraints .... None
Adjustable Belt......... Optional Front & Rear

^Warning feature does not meet government standards.
*Backup camera does not meet government standards.

Chevrolet Equinox

Specifications

Drive	FWD
Engine	2.4-liter I4
Transmission	6-sp. Automatic
Tow Rating (lbs.)	Very Low-1500
Head/Leg Room (in.)	Cramped-40.9/41.2
Interior Space (cu. ft.)	Average-99.7
Cargo Space (cu. ft.)	Roomy-31.5
Wheelbase/Length (in.)	112.5/187.8

Chevrolet Impala

Ratings—10 Best, 1 Worst

Combo Crash Tests	7
Safety Features	7
Rollover	5
Preventive Maintenance	2
Repair Costs	7
Warranty	6
Fuel Economy	3
Complaints	7
Insurance Costs	8
OVERALL RATING	**7**

Chevrolet Impala

Chevrolet Impala

At-a-Glance

Status/Year Series Started	Unchanged/2014
Twins	–
Body Styles	Sedan
Seating	5
Anti-Theft Device	Std. Pass. Immobil. & Active Alarm
Parking Index Rating	Very Hard
Where Made	Detroit, MI / Oshawa, Ontario

Fuel Factor:

MPG Rating (city/hwy)	Very Poor-18/28
Driving Range (mi.)	Short-397
Fuel Type	Regular
Annual Fuel Cost	High-$1504
Gas Guzzler Tax	No
Greenhouse Gas Emissions (tons/yr.)	High-8.6
Barrels of Oil Used per year	High-15.7

How the Competition Rates

Competitors	Rating	Pg.
Buick LaCrosse	6	105
Ford Taurus	4	148
Toyota Avalon	7	246

Price Range	Retail	Markup
LS	$27,300	4%
LT	$29,565	5%
Premier	$35,645	6%
3LT	$40,915	5%

Safety Checklist

Crash Tests:

Frontal	Very Good
Side	Poor

Airbags:

Torso	Std. Fr. & Opt. Rr. Pelvis/Torso from Seat
Roll Sensing	Yes
Knee Bolster	Standard Front

Crash Avoidance:

Collision Avoidance	Optional CIB
Blind Spot Detection	Optional
Lane Keeping Assist	Warning Only Optional
Backup Camera	Optional*
Pedestrian Crash Avoidance	None

General:

Auto. Crash Notif.	Oper. Assist. & Crash Info-Free
Day Running Lamps	Standard

Safety Belt/Restraint:

Dynamic Head Restraints	None
Adjustable Belt	Optional Front & Rear

^Warning feature does not meet government standards.
*Backup camera does not meet government standards.

Chevrolet Impala

Specifications

Drive	FWD
Engine	3.6-liter V6
Transmission	6-sp. Automatic
Tow Rating (lbs.)	Very Low-1000
Head/Leg Room (in.)	Very Roomy-39.9/45.8
Interior Space (cu. ft.)	Roomy-105
Cargo Space (cu. ft.)	Average-18.8
Wheelbase/Length (in.)	111.7/201.3

Chevrolet Malibu

Ratings—10 Best, 1 Worst

Combo Crash Tests	6
Safety Features	10
Rollover	7
Preventive Maintenance	8
Repair Costs	7
Warranty	6
Fuel Economy	8
Complaints	10
Insurance Costs	3
OVERALL RATING	**10**

Chevrolet Malibu

Chevrolet Malibu

At-a-Glance

Status/Year Series Started........ Unchanged/2016
Twins .... –
Body Styles .... Sedan
Seating 5
Anti-Theft Device ...... Std. Pass. Immobil. & Alarm
Parking Index Rating .... Average
Where Made........................ Fairfax, KS
Fuel Factor:............................
  MPG Rating (city/hwy)............ Poor-27/37
  Driving Range (mi.) Short-400
  Fuel Type .... Regular
  Annual Fuel Cost .... Very Low-$1049
  Gas Guzzler Tax .... No
  Greenhouse Gas Emissions (tons/yr.)..... Low-4.8
  Barrels of Oil Used per year Average-10.6

How the Competition Rates

Competitors	Rating	Pg.
Ford Fusion	6	145
Honda Accord	9	152
Toyota Camry	8	247

Price Range	Retail	Markup
L	$21,680	1%
LS	$23,225	4%
LT	$25,125	4%
Hybrid	$27,875	4%

Safety Checklist

Crash Tests:
  Frontal............................... Poor
  Side............................. Very Good
Airbags:
  Torso ...Std. Fr. & Rear Pelvis/Torso from Seat
  Roll Sensing.......................... Yes
  Knee Bolster .... Standard Front
Crash Avoidance:
  Collision Avoidance ...... Optional CIB & DBS
  Blind Spot Detection .... Optional
  Lane Keeping Assist .... Optional
  Backup Camera................... Optional*
  Pedestrian Crash Avoidance .... Optional
General:
  Auto. Crash Notif. ...Oper. Assist. & Crash Info-Free
  Day Running Lamps .... Standard
Safety Belt/Restraint:
  Dynamic Head Restraints .... None
  Adjustable Belt................ Optional Rear

^Warning feature does not meet government standards.
*Backup camera does not meet government standards.

Chevrolet Malibu

Specifications

Drive.. FWD
Engine 1.5-liter I4
Transmission .... 8-sp. Auto
Tow Rating (lbs.) .... –
Head/Leg Room (in.) Cramped-39.1/42
Interior Space (cu. ft.)......... Average-102.9
Cargo Space (cu. ft.) Cramped-15.8
Wheelbase/Length (in.) 111.4/193.8

Ratings—10 Best, 1 Worst

Combo Crash Tests	8
Safety Features	4
Rollover	2
Preventive Maintenance	2
Repair Costs	5
Warranty	6
Fuel Economy	1
Complaints	8
Insurance Costs	8
OVERALL RATING	**5**

Chevrolet Silverado

At-a-Glance

Status/Year Series Started Appearance Change/2014
Twins . . . . –
Body Styles . . . . Pickup
Seating 5/6
Anti-Theft Device Std. Pass. Immobil. & Opt. Pass. Alarm
Parking Index Rating . . . . Very Hard
Where Made. Fort Wayne, IN
Fuel Factor:. . . . .
  MPG Rating (city/hwy) . . . . Very Poor-16/22
  Driving Range (mi.) . . . . Very Long-474
  Fuel Type. . . . . .Regular
  Annual Fuel Cost . . . . Very High-$1768
  Gas Guzzler Tax . . . . .No
  Greenhouse Gas Emissions (tons/yr.)Very High-10.0
  Barrels of Oil Used per year . . . . Very High-18.3

How the Competition Rates

Competitors	Rating	Pg.
Ford F-150	8	141
Ram 1500	4	235
Toyota Tundra	–	258

Price Range

	Retail	Markup
W/T Reg. Cab 2WD	$27,485	5%
LT Dbl. Cab 4WD	$39,865	7%
LTZ Crew Cab 4WD	$47,025	7%
High Country Crew Cab 4WD	$54,475	7%

Chevrolet Silverado

Safety Checklist

Crash Tests:
  Frontal. . . . . Very Good
  Side. . . . . .Poor
Airbags:
  Torso . . .Standard Front Pelvis/Torso from Seat
  Roll Sensing. . . . . .Yes
  Knee Bolster . . . . None
Crash Avoidance:
  Collision Avoidance . . . . Optional CIB
  Blind Spot Detection . . . . None
  Lane Keeping Assist . . . . Optional^
  Backup Camera . . . . Optional*
  Pedestrian Crash Avoidance . . . . None
General:
  Auto. Crash Notif. . . .Oper. Assist. & Crash Info-Free
  Day Running Lamps . . . . Standard
Safety Belt/Restraint:
  Dynamic Head Restraints . . . . None
  Adjustable Belt. . . . . . . Optional Front and Rear

^Warning feature does not meet government standards.
*Backup camera does not meet government standards.

Chevrolet Silverado

Specifications

Drive. 4WD
Engine 5.3-liter V8
Transmission . . . . 6-sp. Automatic
Tow Rating (lbs.) . . . . Very High-9200
Head/Leg Room (in.) . . . . Very Roomy-42.8/45.2
Interior Space (cu. ft.). . . . . –
Cargo Space (cu. ft.) . . . . Very Roomy-61
Wheelbase/Length (in.) 143.5/230

Chevrolet Sonic

Ratings—10 Best, 1 Worst

Combo Crash Tests	9
Safety Features	7
Rollover	5
Preventive Maintenance	10
Repair Costs	9
Warranty	6
Fuel Economy	7
Complaints	5
Insurance Costs	1
OVERALL RATING	**9**

Chevrolet Sonic

At-a-Glance

Status/Year Series Started Appearance Change/2012
Twins . . . . –
Body Styles . . . . Sedan, Hatchback
Seating 5
Anti-Theft Device . . . . . . Std. Pass. Immobil. & Alarm
Parking Index Rating . . . . .Very Easy
Where Made. . . . . Orion Township, MI
Fuel Factor:. . . . .
  MPG Rating (city/hwy) Poor-25/35
  Driving Range (mi.) . . . . .Very Short-350
  Fuel Type. . . . . .Regular
  Annual Fuel Cost . . . . Low-$1124
  Gas Guzzler Tax . . . . .No
  Greenhouse Gas Emissions (tons/yr.) . . Average-6.5
  Barrels of Oil Used per year Average-11.8

How the Competition Rates

Competitors	Rating	Pg.
Ford Fiesta	3	142
Nissan Versa	2	233
Toyota Yaris	5	259

Price Range	Retail	Markup
LS Sedan MT	$15,145	4%
LT Sedan MT	$17,530	4%
LT Hatchback AT	$18,970	4%
Premier Hatchback AT	$21,215	4%

Safety Checklist

Crash Tests:
  Frontal. . . . . Very Good
  Side. . . . . Average
Airbags:
  Torso . . .Std. Fr. & Rear Pelvis/Torso from Seat
  Roll Sensing. . . . . .Yes
  Knee Bolster . . . . .Standard Front
Crash Avoidance:
  Collision Avoidance . . . . .Warning Only Optional
  Blind Spot Detection . . . . None
  Lane Keeping Assist . . . .Warning Only Optional
  Backup Camera . . . . .Standard*
  Pedestrian Crash Avoidance . . . . None
General:
  Auto. Crash Notif. . . . .Oper. Assist. & Crash Info-Free
  Day Running Lamps . . . . Standard
Safety Belt/Restraint:
  Dynamic Head Restraints . . . . None
  Adjustable Belt. . . . . Optional Front & Rear

^Warning feature does not meet government standards.
*Backup camera does not meet government standards.

Chevrolet Sonic

Specifications

Drive. . . . . .FWD
Engine 1.8-liter I4
Transmission . . . . 6-sp. Automatic
Tow Rating (lbs.) . . . . –
Head/Leg Room (in.) Cramped-38.7/41.8
Interior Space (cu. ft.). Cramped-90.6
Cargo Space (cu. ft.) Average-19
Wheelbase/Length (in.) 99.4/159

Ratings—10 Best, 1 Worst

Combo Crash Tests	2
Safety Features	7
Rollover	2
Preventive Maintenance	9
Repair Costs	9
Warranty	6
Fuel Economy	9
Complaints	9
Insurance Costs	1
OVERALL RATING	**6**

Chevrolet Spark

Chevrolet Spark

At-a-Glance

Status/Year Series Started Unchanged/2016
Twins . . . . –
Body Styles . . . . Hatchback
Seating 4
Anti-Theft Device . . . . Std. Passive Immobil. Only
Parking Index Rating . . . . .Very Easy
Where Made. . . . . Changwon, South Korea
Fuel Factor:. . . . .
MPG Rating (city/hwy) Average-31/41
Driving Range (mi.) . . . . .Very Short-313
Fuel Type . . . . .Regular
Annual Fuel Cost . . . . .Very Low-$926
Gas Guzzler Tax . . . . .No
Greenhouse Gas Emissions (tons/yr.). Very Low-4.2
Barrels of Oil Used per year Low-9.4

How the Competition Rates

Competitors	Rating	Pg.
Fiat 500	2	134
Honda Fit	8	155
Kia Rio	5	181

Price Range

Price Range	Retail	Markup
LS MT	$13,000	3%
1LT MT	$14,825	4%
1LT AT	$15,925	4%
2LT AT	$17,425	4%

Safety Checklist

Crash Tests:
Frontal . . . . .Very Poor
Side . . . . Poor
Airbags:
Torso . . .Std. Fr. & Rear Pelvis/Torso from Seat
Roll Sensing . . . . .Yes
Knee Bolster . . . . .Standard Front
Crash Avoidance:
Collision Avoidance . . . . .Warning Only Optional
Blind Spot Detection . . . . None
Lane Keeping Assist . . . .Warning Only Optional
Backup Camera . . . . .Standard*
Pedestrian Crash Avoidance . . . . None
General:
Auto. Crash Notif. . . .Oper. Assist. & Crash Info-Free
Day Running Lamps . . . . Standard
Safety Belt/Restraint:
Dynamic Head Restraints . . . . None
Adjustable Belt . . . . .Optional Rear

^Warning feature does not meet government standards.
*Backup camera does not meet government standards.

Chevrolet Spark

Specifications

Drive . . . . .FWD
Engine 1.4-liter I4
Transmission . . . . CVT
Tow Rating (lbs.) . . . . –
Head/Leg Room (in.) Cramped-39/41.7
Interior Space (cu. ft.). . . . . .Very Cramped-83
Cargo Space (cu. ft.) . . . . Very Cramped-11.1
Wheelbase/Length (in.) 93.9/143.1

Ratings—10 Best, 1 Worst	Suburban	Yukon XL	Escalade ESV
Combo Crash Tests	6	6	—
Safety Features	5	5	7
Rollover	1	1	2
Preventive Maintenance	2	2	2
Repair Costs	6	6	2
Warranty	6	4	8
Fuel Economy	1	1	1
Complaints	3	8	5
Insurance Costs	10	10	8
OVERALL RATING			**4**

Chevrolet Suburban

GMC Yukon XL

At-a-Glance

Status/Year Series Started Appearance Change/2015
Twins . . . . –
Body Styles . . . . SUV
Seating 6/9
Anti-Theft Device . . . . . . Std. Pass. Immobil. & Alarm
Parking Index Rating . . . . Very Hard
Where Made. . . . . Arlington, TX
Fuel Factor: . . . .
MPG Rating (city/hwy) . . . . .Very Poor-15/22
Driving Range (mi.) . . . . Very Long-543
Fuel Type . . . . .Regular
Annual Fuel Cost . . . . Very High-$1842
Gas Guzzler Tax . . . . .No
Greenhouse Gas Emissions (tons/yr.)Very High-10.0
Barrels of Oil Used per year . . . . . . .Very High-18.3

How the Competition Rates

Competitors	Rating	Pg.
Buick Encore	10	104
Ford Expedition	7	139
Toyota 4Runner	2	244

Price Range	Retail	Markup
1500 LS RWD	$49,915	6%
1500 LT RWD	$55,045	6%
1500 LT 4WD	$58,045	6%
1500 Premier 4WD	$67,730	6%

Safety Checklist

Crash Tests:
Frontal. . . . . Average
Side. . . . . Average
Airbags:
Torso . . . Standard Front Pelvis/Torso from Seat
Roll Sensing. . . . . .Yes
Knee Bolster . . . . None
Crash Avoidance:
Collision Avoidance . . . . Optional CIB
Blind Spot Detection . . . . Optional
Lane Keeping Assist . . . . Optional
Backup Camera . . . . .Standard*
Pedestrian Crash Avoidance . . . . None
General:
Auto. Crash Notif. . . .Oper. Assist. & Crash Info-Free
Day Running Lamps . . . . Standard
Safety Belt/Restraint:
Dynamic Head Restraints . . . . None
Adjustable Belt. . . . . . . Optional Front and Rear

^Warning feature does not meet government standards.
*Backup camera does not meet government standards.

Cadillac Escalade ESV

Specifications

Drive. 4WD
Engine 5.3-liter V8
Transmission . . . . 6-sp. Automatic
Tow Rating (lbs.) High-8000
Head/Leg Room (in.) . . . . . . Very Roomy-42.8/45.3
Interior Space (cu. ft.). . . . . Very Roomy-122.4
Cargo Space (cu. ft.) . . . . Very Roomy-39.3
Wheelbase/Length (in.) 130/224.4

Ratings—10 Best, 1 Worst

	Tahoe	Yukon	Escalade
Combo Crash Tests	9	9	—
Safety Features	5	5	7
Rollover	1	1	2
Preventive Maintenance	2	2	2
Repair Costs	5	5	2
Warranty	6	4	8
Fuel Economy	1	1	1
Complaints	4	7	6
Insurance Costs	10	10	8
OVERALL RATING			**5**

Chevrolet Tahoe

Safety Checklist

Crash Tests:
Frontal............................ Good
Side........................... Very Good

Airbags:
Torso . . . Standard Front Pelvis/Torso from Seat
Roll Sensing.........................Yes
Knee Bolster .... None

Crash Avoidance:
Collision Avoidance .... Optional CIB
Blind Spot Detection .... Optional
Lane Keeping Assist .... Optional
Backup Camera ....Standard*
Pedestrian Crash Avoidance .... None

General:
Auto. Crash Notif. . . .Oper. Assist. & Crash Info-Free
Day Running Lamps .... Standard

Safety Belt/Restraint:
Dynamic Head Restraints .... None
Adjustable Belt......... Optional Front & Rear

^Warning feature does not meet government standards.
*Backup camera does not meet government standards.

GMC Yukon

At-a-Glance

Status/Year Series Started Appearance Change/2015
Twins ....–
Body Styles .... SUV
Seating...................................... 6/9
Anti-Theft Device ...... Std. Pass. Immobil. & Alarm
Parking Index Rating ....Very Hard
Where Made....................... Arlington, TX
Fuel Factor:..............................
MPG Rating (city/hwy)...........Very Poor-16/22
Driving Range (mi.) .... Very Long-474
Fuel Type.........................Regular
Annual Fuel Cost .... Very High-$1768
Gas Guzzler Tax ....No
Greenhouse Gas Emissions (tons/yr.)Very High-10.0
Barrels of Oil Used per year .... Very High-18.3

How the Competition Rates

Competitors	Rating	Pg.
Buick Enclave	6	103
Ford Expedition	7	139
Toyota 4Runner	2	244

Price Range	Retail	Markup
LS RWD	$47,215	6%
LT RWD	$52,345	6%
LT4WD	$55,345	6%
Premier 4WD	$65,030	6%

Cadillac Escalade

Specifications

Drive...................................4WD
Engine 5.3-liter V8
Transmission .... 6-sp. Automatic
Tow Rating (lbs.) .... Very High-8400
Head/Leg Room (in.) .... Very Roomy-42.8/45.3
Interior Space (cu. ft.)............... Roomy-120.8
Cargo Space (cu. ft.) Cramped-15.3
Wheelbase/Length (in.) 116/204

Ratings—10 Best, 1 Worst

Combo Crash Tests	9
Safety Features	4
Rollover	3
Preventive Maintenance	2
Repair Costs	5
Warranty	6
Fuel Economy	2
Complaints	4
Insurance Costs	10
OVERALL RATING	**6**

Chevrolet Traverse

Chevrolet Traverse

At-a-Glance

Status/Year Series Started Appearance Change/2009
Twins . . . . –
Body Styles . . . . SUV
Seating 7/8
Anti-Theft Device . Std. Pass. Immobil. & Active Alarm
Parking Index Rating . . . . Very Hard
Where Made. . . . . Lansing, MI
Fuel Factor:. . . . .
  MPG Rating (city/hwy) . . . . Very Poor-17/24
  Driving Range (mi.) Long-431
  Fuel Type. . . . . .Regular
  Annual Fuel Cost . . . . .High-$1648
  Gas Guzzler Tax . . . . .No
  Greenhouse Gas Emissions (tons/yr.) Very High-9.5
  Barrels of Oil Used per year . . . . . . .Very High-17.3

How the Competition Rates

Competitors	Rating	Pg.
Buick Enclave	6	103
Ford Expedition	7	139
Toyota Highlander	7	250

Price Range	Retail	Markup
LS FWD	$31,300	4%
LT FWD	$34,100	5%
2LT AWD	$38,650	5%
Permier AWD	$44,045	6%

Safety Checklist

Crash Tests:
  Frontal. . . . . Good
  Side. . . . . Good
Airbags:
  Torso . . . Standard Front Pelvis/Torso from Seat
  Roll Sensing. . . . . .Yes
  Knee Bolster . . . . None
Crash Avoidance:
  Collision Avoidance . . . . .Warning Only Optional
  Blind Spot Detection . . . . Optional
  Lane Keeping Assist . . . .Warning Only Optional
  Backup Camera . . . . .Standard*
  Pedestrian Crash Avoidance . . . . None
General:
  Auto. Crash Notif. . . . .Oper. Assist. & Crash Info-Free
  Day Running Lamps . . . . Standard
Safety Belt/Restraint:
  Dynamic Head Restraints . . . . None
  Adjustable Belt. . . . . Optional Front & Rear

^Warning feature does not meet government standards.
*Backup camera does not meet government standards.

Chevrolet Traverse

Specifications

Drive. . . . . .FWD
Engine 3.6-liter V6
Transmission . . . . 6-sp. Automatic
Tow Rating (lbs.) Low-5200
Head/Leg Room (in.) Cramped-40.4/41.3
Interior Space (cu. ft.). . . . . Very Roomy-150.8
Cargo Space (cu. ft.) Roomy-24.4
Wheelbase/Length (in.) 118.9/203.7

Ratings—10 Best, 1 Worst

Combo Crash Tests	9
Safety Features	8
Rollover	2
Preventive Maintenance	4
Repair Costs	5
Warranty	6
Fuel Economy	5
Complaints	9
Insurance Costs	8
OVERALL RATING	**8**

Chevrolet Trax

Chevrolet Trax

Chevrolet Trax

At-a-Glance

Status/Year Series Started Appearance Change/2015
Twins . . . . –
Body Styles . . . . SUV
Seating 5
Anti-Theft Device . . . . . . Std. Pass. Immobil. & Alarm
Parking Index Rating . . . . Easy
Where Made. . . . . .South Korea/Mexico
Fuel Factor:. . . . .
  MPG Rating (city/hwy) Poor-24/31
  Driving Range (mi.) . . . . Very Short-374
  Fuel Type . . . . .Regular
  Annual Fuel Cost . . . . Low-$1207
  Gas Guzzler Tax . . . . .No
  Greenhouse Gas Emissions (tons/yr.). . Average-6.7
  Barrels of Oil Used per year Average-12.2

How the Competition Rates

Competitors	Rating	Pg.
Ford Escape	7	138
Honda HR-V	5	156
Jeep Compass	3	173

Price Range

	Retail	Markup
LS FWD	$21,000	4%
LT FWD	$22,900	4%
LT AWD	$24,400	4%
Premier AWD	$27,600	4%

Safety Checklist

Crash Tests:
  Frontal. . . . . Very Good
  Side. . . . . Average
Airbags:
  Torso . . .Std. Fr. & Rear Pelvis/Torso from Seat
  Roll Sensing. . . . . .Yes
  Knee Bolster . . . . .Standard Front
Crash Avoidance:
  Collision Avoidance . . . . .Warning Only Optional
  Blind Spot Detection . . . . Optional
  Lane Keeping Assist . . . .Warning Only Optional
  Backup Camera. . . . . .Standard*
  Pedestrian Crash Avoidance . . . . None
General:
  Auto. Crash Notif. . . .Oper. Assist. & Crash Info-Free
  Day Running Lamps . . . . Standard
Safety Belt/Restraint:
  Dynamic Head Restraints . . . . None
  Adjustable Belt. . . . . Optional Front & Rear

^Warning feature does not meet government standards.
*Backup camera does not meet government standards.

Chevrolet Trax

Specifications

Drive. . . . . .AWD
Engine 1.4-liter I4
Transmission . . . . 6-sp. Automatic
Tow Rating (lbs.) . . . . –
Head/Leg Room (in.) Cramped-39.6/40.8
Interior Space (cu. ft.). Cramped-92.8
Cargo Space (cu. ft.) Average-18.7
Wheelbase/Length (in.) 100.6/168.5

Ratings—10 Best, 1 Worst

Combo Crash Tests	—
Safety Features	9
Rollover	7
Preventive Maintenance	3
Repair Costs	7
Warranty	6
Fuel Economy	10
Complaints	3
Insurance Costs	10

OVERALL RATING   —

Chevrolet Volt

Chevrolet Volt

At-a-Glance

Status/Year Series Started. Unchanged/2016
Twins . . . .—
Body Styles . . . . .Sedan
Seating. 5
Anti-Theft Device . Std. Pass. Immobil. & Active Alarm
Parking Index Rating . . . . Easy
Where Made. . . . . .Detroit, MI
Fuel Factor:. . . . .
  MPG Rating (city/hwy) Average-43/42
  Driving Range (mi.) Short-379
  Fuel Type . . . . .Regular
  Annual Fuel Cost . . . . Very Low-$758
  Gas Guzzler Tax . . . . .No
  Greenhouse Gas Emissions (tons/yr.). Very Low-0.8
  Barrels of Oil Used per year . . . . Very Low-2.0

How the Competition Rates

Competitors	Rating	Pg.
Ford Fusion Energi	9	146
Mercedes-Benz B-Class	—	205
Toyota Prius	7	251

Price Range

Price Range	Retail	Markup
LT	$33,120	4%
Premier	$37,470	4%

Chevrolet Volt

Safety Checklist

Crash Tests:
  Frontal. . . . .−
  Side. . . . .−
Airbags:
  Torso Std. Fr. & Opt. Rr. Pelvis/Torso from Seat
  Roll Sensing. . . . . .Yes
  Knee Bolster . . . . .Standard Front
Crash Avoidance:
  Collision Avoidance . . . . . . Optional CIB & DBS
  Blind Spot Detection . . . . Optional
  Lane Keeping Assist . . . . Optional
  Backup Camera. . . . . .Standard*
  Pedestrian Crash Avoidance . . . . None
General:
  Auto. Crash Notif. . . .Oper. Assist. & Crash Info-Free
  Day Running Lamps . . . . Standard
Safety Belt/Restraint:
  Dynamic Head Restraints . . . . None
  Adjustable Belt. . . . . Standard Front & Rear

^Warning feature does not meet government standards.
*Backup camera does not meet government standards.

Specifications

Drive. . . . . .FWD
Engine 1.5-liter I4
Transmission . . . . CVT
Tow Rating (lbs.) . . . . −
Head/Leg Room (in.) Cramped-37.8/42.1
Interior Space (cu. ft.). . . . . Very Cramped-90
Cargo Space (cu. ft.) . . . . Very Cramped-10.6
Wheelbase/Length (in.) 106.1/180.4

Ratings—10 Best, 1 Worst	
Combo Crash Tests	8
Safety Features	9
Rollover	7
Preventive Maintenance	9
Repair Costs	8
Warranty	4
Fuel Economy	6
Complaints	1
Insurance Costs	8
OVERALL RATING	**9**

Chrysler 200

Chrysler 200

At-a-Glance

Status/Year Series Started. Unchanged/2015
Twins . . . . –
Body Styles . . . . Sedan
Seating 5
Anti-Theft Device . . . . . . Std. Pass. Immobil. & Alarm
Parking Index Rating . . . . Very Hard
Where Made. . . . . Sterling Heights, MI
Fuel Factor:. . . . .
  MPG Rating (city/hwy). Poor-23/36
  Driving Range (mi.) Long-434
  Fuel Type. . . . . .Regular
  Annual Fuel Cost . . . . Low-$1174
  Gas Guzzler Tax . . . . .No
  Greenhouse Gas Emissions (tons/yr.). . Average-6.4
  Barrels of Oil Used per year Average-11.8

How the Competition Rates

Competitors	Rating	Pg.
Chevrolet Malibu	10	118
Ford Fusion	6	145
Kia Optima	9	180

Price Range	Retail	Markup
LX	$21,995	0%
Limited	$24,490	2%
S AWD	$29,905	3%
C AWD	$31,785	3%

Safety Checklist

Crash Tests:
  Frontal. . . . . Very Good
  Side. . . . . Average
Airbags:
  Torso . . .Standard Front Pelvis/Torso from Seat
  Roll Sensing. . . . . .Yes
  Knee Bolster . . . . .Standard Front
Crash Avoidance:
  Collision Avoidance . . . . Optional CIB & DBS
  Blind Spot Detection . . . . Optional
  Lane Keeping Assist . . . . Optional
  Backup Camera . . . . Optional
  Pedestrian Crash Avoidance . . . . None
General:
  Auto. Crash Notification . . . . None
  Day Running Lamps . . . . Optional
Safety Belt/Restraint:
  Dynamic Head Restraints . . . . . .Standard Front
  Adjustable Belt. . . . . .Standard Front

^Warning feature does not meet government standards.
*Backup camera does not meet government standards.

Chrysler 200

Specifications

Drive. . . . . .FWD
Engine 2.4-liter I4
Transmission . . . . 9-sp. Automatic
Tow Rating (lbs.) . . . . .Very Low-0
Head/Leg Room (in.) Cramped-37.7/42.2
Interior Space (cu. ft.). Average-101.4
Cargo Space (cu. ft.) Cramped-16
Wheelbase/Length (in.) 108/192.3

Ratings—10 Best, 1 Worst

Combo Crash Tests	3
Safety Features	6
Rollover	6
Preventive Maintenance	8
Repair Costs	6
Warranty	4
Fuel Economy	3
Complaints	2
Insurance Costs	1
OVERALL RATING	**2**

Chrysler 300

Chrysler 300

At-a-Glance

Status/Year Series Started Unchanged/2011
Twins . Dodge Charger, Ford Mustang, Mercury Capri
Body Styles . . . . Sedan
Seating 5
Anti-Theft Device . . . . . . Std. Pass. Immobil. & Alarm
Parking Index Rating . . . . Very Hard
Where Made . . . . Brampton, Ontario
Fuel Factor: . . . .
  MPG Rating (city/hwy) . . . . .Very Poor-19/31
  Driving Range (mi.) Average-426
  Fuel Type . . . . .Regular
  Annual Fuel Cost . . . . .Average-$1402
  Gas Guzzler Tax . . . . .No
  Greenhouse Gas Emissions (tons/yr.) High-7.8
  Barrels of Oil Used per year High-14.3

How the Competition Rates

Competitors	Rating	Pg.
Buick LaCrosse	6	105
Cadillac XTS	9	111
Toyota Avalon	7	246

Price Range

	Retail	Markup
Limited I4 RWD	$32,340	2%
S V6 AWD	$38,175	4%
C V8	$41,635	4%
C Platinum V8	$45,770	5%

Safety Checklist

Crash Tests:
  Frontal . . . . .Very Poor
  Side . . . . Poor
Airbags:
  Torso . . .Standard Front Pelvis/Torso from Seat
  Roll Sensing . . . . .Yes
  Knee Bolster . . . . Standard Driver
Crash Avoidance:
  Collision Avoidance . . . . . . Optional CIB & DBS
  Blind Spot Detection . . . . Optional
  Lane Keeping Assist . . . . Optional^
  Backup Camera . . . . Optional
  Pedestrian Crash Avoidance . . . . None
General:
  Auto. Crash Notification . . . . None
  Day Running Lamps . . . . Standard
Safety Belt/Restraint:
  Dynamic Head Restraints . . . . None
  Adjustable Belt . . . . Standard Front

^Warning feature does not meet government standards.
*Backup camera does not meet government standards.

Chrysler 300

Specifications

Drive . . . . .RWD
Engine 3.6-liter V6
Transmission . . . . 8-sp. Automatic
Tow Rating (lbs.) . . . . –
Head/Leg Room (in.) Cramped-38.6/41.8
Interior Space (cu. ft.) Roomy-106.3
Cargo Space (cu. ft.) Cramped-16.3
Wheelbase/Length (in.) 120.2/198.6

Chrysler Pacifica   Minivan

Ratings—10 Best, 1 Worst

Combo Crash Tests	8
Safety Features	8
Rollover	6
Preventive Maintenance	10
Repair Costs	7
Warranty	4
Fuel Economy	3
Complaints	—
Insurance Costs	8
OVERALL RATING	**9**

Chrysler Pacifica

Chrysler Pacifica

At-a-Glance

Status/Year Series Started	All New/2017
Twins	—
Body Styles	Minivan
Seating	7/8
Anti-Theft Device	Std. Pass. Immobil. & Opt. Pass. Alarm
Parking Index Rating	Very Hard
Where Made	Windsor, Ontario
Fuel Factor:	
MPG Rating (city/hwy)	Very Poor-18/28
Driving Range (mi.)	Average-407
Fuel Type	Regular
Annual Fuel Cost	High-$1504
Gas Guzzler Tax	No
Greenhouse Gas Emissions (tons/yr.)	Average-6.9
Barrels of Oil Used per year	High-15.0

How the Competition Rates

Competitors	Rating	Pg.
Honda Odyssey	8	157
Nissan Quest	–	229
Toyota Sienna	2	256

Price Range

	Retail	Markup
LX	$28,595	0%
Touring	$30,495	3%
Touring L Plus	$37,895	4%
Limited	$42,495	4%

Safety Checklist

Crash Tests:
Frontal . . . . Very Good
Side . . . . Poor
Airbags:
Torso . . . Standard Front Pelvis/Torso from Seat
Roll Sensing . . . . Yes
Knee Bolster . . . . Standard Front
Crash Avoidance:
Collision Avoidance . . . . . . Optional CIB & DBS
Blind Spot Detection . . . . Optional
Lane Keeping Assist . . . . Optional
Backup Camera . . . . Standard
Pedestrian Crash Avoidance . . . . None
General:
Auto. Crash Notification . . . . None
Day Running Lamps . . . . Standard
Safety Belt/Restraint:
Dynamic Head Restraints . . . . None
Adjustable Belt . . . . Standard Front & Rear

^Warning feature does not meet government standards.
*Backup camera does not meet government standards.

Chrysler Pacifica

Specifications

Drive	FWD
Engine	3.6-liter V6
Transmission	9-sp. Automatic
Tow Rating (lbs.)	Low-3600
Head/Leg Room (in.)	Cramped-40.1/41.1
Interior Space (cu. ft.)	Very Cramped-32.3
Cargo Space (cu. ft.)	Very Roomy-165
Wheelbase/Length (in.)	121.6/203.8

Ratings—10 Best, 1 Worst

Combo Crash Tests	8
Safety Features	3
Rollover	6
Preventive Maintenance	8
Repair Costs	8
Warranty	4
Fuel Economy	3
Complaints	6
Insurance Costs	1
OVERALL RATING	**5**

Dodge Challenger

Dodge Challenger

At-a-Glance

Status/Year Series Started. Unchanged/2015
Twins . . . . –
Body Styles . . . . .Coupe
Seating 5
Anti-Theft Device . . . . . . Std. Pass. Immobil. & Alarm
Parking Index Rating . . . . Hard
Where Made. . . . . Brampton, Ontario
Fuel Factor:. . . . .
  MPG Rating (city/hwy) . . . . .Very Poor-19/30
  Driving Range (mi.) Average-421
  Fuel Type. . . . . .Regular
  Annual Fuel Cost . . . . .Average-$1417
  Gas Guzzler Tax . . . . .No
  Greenhouse Gas Emissions (tons/yr.). High-7.8
  Barrels of Oil Used per year High-14.3

How the Competition Rates

Competitors	Rating	Pg.
Chevrolet Camaro	5	112
Chevrolet Corvette	–	114
Ford Mustang	7	147

Price Range

Price Range	Retail	Markup
SXT	$26,995	1%
R/T	$31,995	2%
SCAT PACK	$37,995	4%
SRT Hellcat	$62,495	4%

Safety Checklist

Crash Tests:
  Frontal. . . . . Average
  Side. . . . . Very Good
Airbags:
  Torso . . . Standard Front Pelvis/Torso from Seat
  Roll Sensing. . . . . .Yes
  Knee Bolster . . . . None
Crash Avoidance:
  Collision Avoidance . . . . .Warning Only Optional
  Blind Spot Detection . . . . Optional
  Lane Keeping Assist . . . . None
  Backup Camera . . . . Optional
  Pedestrian Crash Avoidance . . . . None
General:
  Auto. Crash Notification. . . . . None
  Day Running Lamps . . . . Standard
Safety Belt/Restraint:
  Dynamic Head Restraints . . . . None
  Adjustable Belt. None

^Warning feature does not meet government standards.
*Backup camera does not meet government standards.

Dodge Challenger

Specifications

Drive. . . . . .RWD
Engine 3.6-liter V6
Transmission . . . . 8-sp. Automatic
Tow Rating (lbs.) . . . . .Very Low-1000
Head/Leg Room (in.) Cramped-39.3/42
Interior Space (cu. ft.). Cramped-93.9
Cargo Space (cu. ft.) Cramped-16.2
Wheelbase/Length (in.) 116.2/197.9

Ratings—10 Best, 1 Worst

Combo Crash Tests	3
Safety Features	6
Rollover	8
Preventive Maintenance	8
Repair Costs	8
Warranty	4
Fuel Economy	3
Complaints	2
Insurance Costs	1
OVERALL RATING	**3**

Dodge Charger

Dodge Charger

At-a-Glance

Status/Year Series Started........ Unchanged/2011
Twins . . . Chrysler 300, Ford Mustang, Mercury Capri
Body Styles ....Sedan
Seating 5
Anti-Theft Device Std. Pass. Immobil. & Opt. Pass. Alarm
Parking Index Rating .... Hard
Where Made................... Brampton, Ontario
Fuel Factor:..................................
 MPG Rating (city/hwy) ....Very Poor-19/31
 Driving Range (mi.) Average-426
 Fuel Type ....Regular
 Annual Fuel Cost ....Average-$1402
 Gas Guzzler Tax ....No
 Greenhouse Gas Emissions (tons/yr.)..... High-7.8
 Barrels of Oil Used per year High-14.3

How the Competition Rates

Competitors	Rating	Pg.
Buick LaCrosse	6	105
Chevrolet Impala	7	117
Ford Taurus	4	148

Price Range	Retail	Markup
SE	$27,995	2%
SXT	$29,995	2%
R/T	$33,895	3%
SRT Hellcat	$65,945	4%

Safety Checklist

Crash Tests:
 Frontal............................Very Poor
 Side............................... Good
Airbags:
 Torso . . .Standard Front Pelvis/Torso from Seat
 Roll Sensing.........................Yes
 Knee Bolster .... Standard Driver
Crash Avoidance:
 Collision Avoidance ...... Optional CIB & DBS
 Blind Spot Detection .... Optional
 Lane Keeping Assist .... Optional
 Backup Camera.................. Optional
 Pedestrian Crash Avoidance .... None
General:
 Auto. Crash Notification .... None
 Day Running Lamps .... Standard
Safety Belt/Restraint:
 Dynamic Head Restraints .... None
 Adjustable Belt...............Standard Front

^Warning feature does not meet government standards.
*Backup camera does not meet government standards.

Dodge Charger

Specifications

Drive......................................RWD
Engine 3.6-liter V6
Transmission .... 8-sp. Automatic
Tow Rating (lbs.) .... Very Low-1000
Head/Leg Room (in.) Cramped-38.6/41.8
Interior Space (cu. ft.). Roomy-104.7
Cargo Space (cu. ft.) Cramped-16.1
Wheelbase/Length (in.) 120.2/198.4

Ratings—10 Best, 1 Worst

Combo Crash Tests	9
Safety Features	1
Rollover	7
Preventive Maintenance	8
Repair Costs	6
Warranty	4
Fuel Economy	6
Complaints	1
Insurance Costs	1
OVERALL RATING	**4**

Dodge Dart

Dodge Dart

At-a-Glance

Status/Year Series Started........ Unchanged/2013
Twins . . . . –
Body Styles . . . . .Sedan
Seating 5
Anti-Theft Device . . . . . . Std. Pass. Immobil. & Alarm
Parking Index Rating . . . . Easy
Where Made. Belvedere, IL
Fuel Factor:. . . . .
  MPG Rating (city/hwy) Poor-24/34
  Driving Range (mi.) Short-393
  Fuel Type. . . . . .Regular
  Annual Fuel Cost . . . . Low-$1166
  Gas Guzzler Tax . . . . .No
  Greenhouse Gas Emissions (tons/yr.). . Average-6.7
  Barrels of Oil Used per year Average-12.2

How the Competition Rates

Competitors	Rating	Pg.
Acura ILX	8	81
Ford Focus	6	144
Honda Civic	8	153

Price Range	Retail	Markup
SE	$16,995	1%
SXT	$19,395	1%
GT	$22,095	1%
Limited	$24,395	2%

Safety Checklist

Crash Tests:
  Frontal. . . . . Good
  Side. . . . . Very Good
Airbags:
  Torso . . . Standard Front Pelvis/Torso from Seat
  Roll Sensing. . . . . No
  Knee Bolster . . . . .Standard Front
Crash Avoidance:
  Collision Avoidance . . . . None
  Blind Spot Detection . . . . Optional
  Lane Keeping Assist . . . . None
  Backup Camera . . . . Optional*
  Pedestrian Crash Avoidance . . . . None
General:
  Auto. Crash Notification . . . . None
  Day Running Lamps . . . . None
Safety Belt/Restraint:
  Dynamic Head Restraints . . . . None
  Adjustable Belt. . . . . .Standard Front

^Warning feature does not meet government standards.
*Backup camera does not meet government standards.

Dodge Dart

Specifications

Drive. . . . . .FWD
Engine 2.0-liter I4
Transmission . . . . 6-sp. Automatic
Tow Rating (lbs.) . . . . .Very Low-1000
Head/Leg Room (in.) Cramped-38.6/42.2
Interior Space (cu. ft.). Average-97.2
Cargo Space (cu. ft.) Cramped-13.1
Wheelbase/Length (in.) 106.4/183.9

Ratings—10 Best, 1 Worst

Combo Crash Tests	2
Safety Features	4
Rollover	2
Preventive Maintenance	10
Repair Costs	4
Warranty	4
Fuel Economy	2
Complaints	1
Insurance Costs	5
OVERALL RATING	**1**

Dodge Journey

Dodge Journey

At-a-Glance

Status/Year Series Started	Unchanged/2009
Twins	–
Body Styles	SUV
Seating	5/7
Anti-Theft Device	Std. Pass. Immobil. & Alarm
Parking Index Rating	Hard
Where Made	Toluca, Mexico
Fuel Factor:	
MPG Rating (city/hwy)	Very Poor-17/25
Driving Range (mi.)	Average-407
Fuel Type	Regular
Annual Fuel Cost	High-$1624
Gas Guzzler Tax	No
Greenhouse Gas Emissions (tons/yr.)	Very High-9.4
Barrels of Oil Used per year	Very High-17.3

How the Competition Rates

Competitors	Rating	Pg.
Chevrolet Equinox	2	116
Ford Edge	8	137
Nissan Murano	4	227

Price Range

	Retail	Markup
SE FWD	$20,995	0%
SXT FWD	$24,895	3%
Crossroad AWD	$29,795	4%
R/T AWD	$33,695	4%

Safety Checklist

Crash Tests:
- Frontal .... Poor
- Side .... Very Poor

Airbags:
- Torso . . . Standard Front Pelvis/Torso from Seat
- Roll Sensing .... Yes
- Knee Bolster .... Standard Driver

Crash Avoidance:
- Collision Avoidance .... None
- Blind Spot Detection .... None
- Lane Keeping Assist .... None
- Backup Camera .... Optional
- Pedestrian Crash Avoidance .... None

General:
- Auto. Crash Notification .... None
- Day Running Lamps .... Standard

Safety Belt/Restraint:
- Dynamic Head Restraints ...... Standard Front
- Adjustable Belt .... Standard Front

^Warning feature does not meet government standards.
*Backup camera does not meet government standards.

Dodge Journey

Specifications

Drive	FWD
Engine	3.6-liter V6
Transmission	6-sp. Automatic
Tow Rating (lbs.)	Very Low-2500
Head/Leg Room (in.)	Cramped-40.8/40.8
Interior Space (cu. ft.)	Very Roomy-123.7
Cargo Space (cu. ft.)	Very Cramped-10.7
Wheelbase/Length (in.)	113.8/192.4

Fiat 500

Ratings—10 Best, 1 Worst

Combo Crash Tests	1
Safety Features	1
Rollover	4
Preventive Maintenance	8
Repair Costs	9
Warranty	5
Fuel Economy	7
Complaints	1
Insurance Costs	5
OVERALL RATING	**2**

Fiat 500

At-a-Glance

Status/Year Series Started. Unchanged/2012
Twins . . . . –
Body Styles . . . . Hatchback
Seating. 4
Anti-Theft Device Std. Pass. Immobil. & Opt. Pass. Alarm
Parking Index Rating . . . . .Very Easy
Where Made. . . . . .Toluca, Mexico
Fuel Factor:. . . . .
  MPG Rating (city/hwy). Poor-27/34
  Driving Range (mi.) . . . . .Very Short-312
  Fuel Type. . . . . .Regular
  Annual Fuel Cost . . . . Low-$1084
  Gas Guzzler Tax . . . . .No
  Greenhouse Gas Emissions (tons/yr.). Low-6.0
  Barrels of Oil Used per year Average-11.0

How the Competition Rates

Competitors	Rating	Pg.
Chevrolet Sonic	9	120
Mini Cooper	5	214
Volkswagen Beetle	1	261

Price Range

Price Range	Retail	Markup
Pop Hatchback	$14,995	1%
Lounge Hatchback	$18,395	2%
Abarth Cabriolet	$19,995	2%

Safety Checklist

Crash Tests:
  Frontal. . . . . .Very Poor
  Side. . . . . Poor
Airbags:
  Torso . . . Standard Front Pelvis/Torso from Seat
  Roll Sensing. . . . . No
  Knee Bolster . . . . Standard Driver
Crash Avoidance:
  Collision Avoidance . . . . None
  Blind Spot Detection . . . . None
  Lane Keeping Assist . . . . None
  Backup Camera . . . . None
  Pedestrian Crash Avoidance . . . . None
General:
  Auto. Crash Notification . . . . None
  Day Running Lamps . . . . Standard
Safety Belt/Restraint:
  Dynamic Head Restraints . . . . . .Standard Front
  Adjustable Belt. None

^Warning feature does not meet government standards.
*Backup camera does not meet government standards.

Fiat 500

Specifications

Drive. . . . . .FWD
Engine 1.4-liter I4
Transmission . . . . 6-sp. Automatic
Tow Rating (lbs.) . . . . .Very Low-0
Head/Leg Room (in.) . . . . Very Cramped-38.9/40.7
Interior Space (cu. ft.). . . . . Very Cramped-75.5
Cargo Space (cu. ft.) . . . . Very Cramped-9.5
Wheelbase/Length (in.) 90.6/139.6

Ratings—10 Best, 1 Worst

Combo Crash Tests	—
Safety Features	5
Rollover	4
Preventive Maintenance	8
Repair Costs	9
Warranty	5
Fuel Economy	5
Complaints	—
Insurance Costs	5
OVERALL RATING	—

Fiat 500X

Fiat 500X

At-a-Glance

Status/Year Series Started	Unchanged/2015
Twins	—
Body Styles	.
Seating	5
Anti-Theft Device	—
Parking Index Rating	Easy
Where Made	Melfi, Italy
Fuel Factor:	
MPG Rating (city/hwy)	Poor-22/31
Driving Range (mi.)	Very Short-321
Fuel Type	Regular
Annual Fuel Cost	Low-$1274
Gas Guzzler Tax	No
Greenhouse Gas Emissions (tons/yr.)	Low-5.8
Barrels of Oil Used per year	High-13.2

How the Competition Rates

Competitors	Rating	Pg.
Honda HR-V	5	156
Jeep Compass	3	173
Mazda CX-5	3	200

Price Range

	Retail	Markup
Pop FWD	$19,995	1%
Trekking AWD	$23,335	3%
Lounge AWD	$25,135	2%

Fiat 500X

Safety Checklist

Crash Tests:
  Frontal . . . . –
  Side . . . . –

Airbags:
  Torso . . . Standard Front Pelvis/Torso from Seat
  Roll Sensing . . . . Yes
  Knee Bolster . . . . Standard Driver

Crash Avoidance:
  Collision Avoidance . . . . . . Optional CIB & DBS^
  Blind Spot Detection . . . . Optional
  Lane Keeping Assist . . . . Optional^
  Backup Camera . . . . Optional*
  Pedestrian Crash Avoidance . . . . None

General:
  Auto. Crash Notification . . . . None
  Day Running Lamps . . . . Standard

Safety Belt/Restraint:
  Dynamic Head Restraints . . . . None
  Adjustable Belt . . . . Standard Front

^Warning feature does not meet government standards.
*Backup camera does not meet government standards.

Fiat 500X

Specifications

Drive	FWD
Engine	2.4-liter I4
Transmission	9-sp. Automatic
Tow Rating (lbs.)	Very Low-1000
Head/Leg Room (in.)	Cramped-39.1/41.4
Interior Space (cu. ft.)	Cramped-91.7
Cargo Space (cu. ft.)	Very Cramped-12.2
Wheelbase/Length (in.)	101.2/167.2

Ratings—10 Best, 1 Worst

Combo Crash Tests	4
Safety Features	5
Rollover	4
Preventive Maintenance	9
Repair Costs	10
Warranty	4
Fuel Economy	9
Complaints	2
Insurance Costs	3
OVERALL RATING	**5**

Ford C-MAX

Ford C-MAX

At-a-Glance

Status/Year Series Started	Unchanged/2013
Twins	–
Body Styles	Hatchback
Seating	5
Anti-Theft Device	Std. Passive Immobil. Only
Parking Index Rating	Average
Where Made	Wayne, MI

Fuel Factor:

MPG Rating (city/hwy)	Average-42/37
Driving Range (mi.)	Very Long-534
Fuel Type	Regular
Annual Fuel Cost	Very Low-$815
Gas Guzzler Tax	No
Greenhouse Gas Emissions (tons/yr.)	Very Low-4.5
Barrels of Oil Used per year	Low-8.2

How the Competition Rates

Competitors	Rating	Pg.
Chevrolet Volt	–	126
Nissan Leaf	4	225
Toyota Prius	7	251

Price Range	Retail	Markup
SE Hybrid	$24,120	5%
Titanium Hybrid	$27,120	5%
SE Energi	$27,120	5%
Titanium Energi	$30,120	5%

Safety Checklist

Crash Tests:

Frontal	Poor
Side	Poor

Airbags:

Torso	Standard Front Pelvis/Torso from Seat
Roll Sensing	Yes
Knee Bolster	Standard Driver

Crash Avoidance:

Collision Avoidance	None
Blind Spot Detection	Standard
Lane Keeping Assist	None
Backup Camera	Optional
Pedestrian Crash Avoidance	None

General:

Auto. Crash Notification	Dial Assist.-Free
Day Running Lamps	Standard

Safety Belt/Restraint:

Dynamic Head Restraints	None
Adjustable Belt	Standard Front

^Warning feature does not meet government standards.
*Backup camera does not meet government standards.

Ford C-MAX

Specifications

Drive	FWD
Engine	2.0-liter I4
Transmission	CVT
Tow Rating (lbs.)	Very Low-0
Head/Leg Room (in.)	Cramped-41/40.4
Interior Space (cu. ft.)	Average-99.7
Cargo Space (cu. ft.)	Roomy-24.5
Wheelbase/Length (in.)	104.3/173.6

Ratings—10 Best, 1 Worst

Combo Crash Tests	10
Safety Features	9
Rollover	3
Preventive Maintenance	7
Repair Costs	5
Warranty	4
Fuel Economy	4
Complaints	4
Insurance Costs	8
OVERALL RATING	**8**

Ford Edge

Ford Edge

At-a-Glance

Status/Year Series Started	Unchanged/2015
Twins	–
Body Styles	SUV
Seating	5
Anti-Theft Device	Std. Pass. Immobil. & Alarm
Parking Index Rating	Very Easy
Where Made	Oakville, Ontario

Fuel Factor:

MPG Rating (city/hwy)	Very Poor-20/30
Driving Range (mi.)	Long-431
Fuel Type	Regular
Annual Fuel Cost	Average-$1371
Gas Guzzler Tax	No
Greenhouse Gas Emissions (tons/yr.)	Average-7.1
Barrels of Oil Used per year	High-15.7

How the Competition Rates

Competitors	Rating	Pg.
Chevrolet Equinox	2	116
Dodge Journey	1	133
Nissan Murano	4	227

Price Range

	Retail	Markup
SE FWD	$28,950	4%
SEL FWD	$31,790	5%
Titanium AWD	$37,595	5%
Sport AWD	$40,900	5%

Safety Checklist

Crash Tests:

Frontal	Very Good
Side	Very Good

Airbags:

Torso	Standard Front Pelvis/Torso from Seat
Roll Sensing	Yes
Knee Bolster	Standard Front

Crash Avoidance:

Collision Avoidance	Optional CIB & DBS
Blind Spot Detection	Optional
Lane Keeping Assist	Optional
Backup Camera	Standard
Pedestrian Crash Avoidance	None

General:

Auto. Crash Notification	Dial Assist.-Free
Day Running Lamps	Standard

Safety Belt/Restraint:

Dynamic Head Restraints	None
Adjustable Belt	Standard Front

^Warning feature does not meet government standards.
*Backup camera does not meet government standards.

Ford Edge

Specifications

Drive	FWD
Engine	3.5-liter V6
Transmission	6-sp. Automatic
Tow Rating (lbs.)	Very Low-1500
Head/Leg Room (in.)	Roomy-40.2/42.6
Interior Space (cu. ft.)	Roomy-113.9
Cargo Space (cu. ft.)	Very Roomy-39.2
Wheelbase/Length (in.)	112.2/188.1

Ratings—10 Best, 1 Worst

Combo Crash Tests	8
Safety Features	7
Rollover	2
Preventive Maintenance	6
Repair Costs	9
Warranty	4
Fuel Economy	5
Complaints	5
Insurance Costs	5
OVERALL RATING	**7**

Ford Escape

At-a-Glance

Status/Year Series Started Unchanged/2013
Twins . . . . —
Body Styles . . . . SUV
Seating 5
Anti-Theft Device . . . . Std. Passive Immobil. Only
Parking Index Rating . . . . Average
Where Made. . . . . Louisville, Kentucky
Fuel Factor: . . . .
  MPG Rating (city/hwy) Poor-22/31
  Driving Range (mi.) Short-390
  Fuel Type . . . . .Regular
  Annual Fuel Cost . . . . Low-$1274
  Gas Guzzler Tax . . . . .No
  Greenhouse Gas Emissions (tons/yr.). . Average-7.2
  Barrels of Oil Used per year High-13.2

How the Competition Rates

Competitors	Rating	Pg.
Honda HR-V	5	156
Jeep Cherokee	5	172
Toyota RAV4	6	254

Price Range	Retail	Markup
S FWD	$23,600	6%
SE FWD	$25,100	7%
SE 4WD	$26,850	7%
Titanium 4WD	$30,850	7%

Ford Escape

Safety Checklist

Crash Tests:
  Frontal. . . . . Good
  Side . . . . Good
Airbags:
  Torso . . . Standard Front Pelvis/Torso from Seat
  Roll Sensing. . . . . .Yes
  Knee Bolster . . . . Standard Driver
Crash Avoidance:
  Collision Avoidance . . . . .Warning Only Optional
  Blind Spot Detection . . . . Optional
  Lane Keeping Assist . . . . Optional
  Backup Camera . . . . Standard
  Pedestrian Crash Avoidance . . . . None
General:
  Auto. Crash Notification . . . . . . Dial Assist.-Free
  Day Running Lamps . . . . Standard
Safety Belt/Restraint:
  Dynamic Head Restraints . . . . None
  Adjustable Belt. . . . . .Standard Front

^Warning feature does not meet government standards.
*Backup camera does not meet government standards.

Ford Escape

Specifications

Drive . . . . .FWD
Engine 2.5-liter I4
Transmission . . . . 6-sp. Automatic
Tow Rating (lbs.) . . . . Very Low-1500
Head/Leg Room (in.) Roomy-39.9/43.1
Interior Space (cu. ft.). Average-98.1
Cargo Space (cu. ft.) . . . . Very Roomy-34.3
Wheelbase/Length (in.) 105.9/178.1

Ratings—10 Best, 1 Worst	Expedition	Navigator
Combo Crash Tests	10	—
Safety Features	3	4
Rollover	1	1
Preventive Maintenance	3	4
Repair Costs	8	8
Warranty	4	4
Fuel Economy	1	1
Complaints	7	10
Insurance Costs	10	8
OVERALL RATING		**7**

Ford Expedition

Safety Checklist

Crash Tests:
Frontal . . . . Very Good
Side . . . . Very Good

Airbags:
Torso . . . . Standard Front Torso from Seat
Roll Sensing . . . . Yes
Knee Bolster . . . . None

Crash Avoidance:
Collision Avoidance . . . . None
Blind Spot Detection . . . . Optional
Lane Keeping Assist . . . . None
Backup Camera . . . . Standard
Pedestrian Crash Avoidance . . . . None

General:
Auto. Crash Notification . . . . . . Dial Assist.-Free
Day Running Lamps . . . . None

Safety Belt/Restraint:
Dynamic Head Restraints . . . . None
Adjustable Belt . . . . Standard Front

^Warning feature does not meet government standards.
*Backup camera does not meet government standards.

Lincoln Navigator

At-a-Glance

Status/Year Series Started Unchanged/2003
Twins . . . . –
Body Styles . . . . SUV
Seating 7/8
Anti-Theft Device . . . . . . Std. Pass. Immobil. & Alarm
Parking Index Rating . . . . Very Hard
Where Made . . . . Louisville, Kentucky
Fuel Factor: . . . .
MPG Rating (city/hwy) . . . . Very Poor-15/20
Driving Range (mi.) . . . . Very Long-473
Fuel Type . . . . Regular
Annual Fuel Cost . . . . Very High-$1908
Gas Guzzler Tax . . . . No
Greenhouse Gas Emissions (tons/yr.) Very High-10.6
Barrels of Oil Used per year . . . . Very High-19.4

Ford Expedition

How the Competition Rates

Competitors	Rating	Pg.
Buick Encore	10	104
Chevrolet Suburban	4	122
Toyota 4Runner	2	244

Price Range	Retail	Markup
XL 2WD	$41,700	7%
XLT 2WD	$46,226	7%
King Ranch 4WD	$62,860	7%
Platinum 4WD	$66,347	7%

Specifications

Drive 4WD
Engine 3.5-liter V6
Transmission . . . . 6-sp. Automatic
Tow Rating (lbs.) . . . . Very High-9200
Head/Leg Room (in.) Roomy-39.63/43
Interior Space (cu. ft.) . . . . Very Roomy-160.3
Cargo Space (cu. ft.) Average-18.6
Wheelbase/Length (in.) 119/206

Ratings—10 Best, 1 Worst

Combo Crash Tests	6
Safety Features	7
Rollover	2
Preventive Maintenance	5
Repair Costs	2
Warranty	4
Fuel Economy	2
Complaints	2
Insurance Costs	8
OVERALL RATING	**3**

Ford Explorer

Ford Explorer

At-a-Glance

Status/Year Series Started........ Unchanged/2011
Twins .... –
Body Styles .... SUV
Seating 6/7
Anti-Theft Device ...... Std. Pass. Immobil. & Alarm
Parking Index Rating .... Hard
Where Made......................... Chicago, IL
Fuel Factor:...............................
  MPG Rating (city/hwy) .... Very Poor-17/23
  Driving Range (mi.) .... Very Short-358
  Fuel Type....................... Regular
  Annual Fuel Cost .... High-$1674
  Gas Guzzler Tax .... No
  Greenhouse Gas Emissions (tons/yr.) Very High-9.5
  Barrels of Oil Used per year .... Very High-17.3

How the Competition Rates

Competitors	Rating	Pg.
Dodge Journey	1	133
Honda Pilot	8	158
Toyota Highlander	7	250

Price Range	Retail	Markup
Base FWD	$31,660	4%
XLT FWD	$33,775	5%
Limited 4WD	$43,825	5%
Platinum 4WD	$53,235	5%

Safety Checklist

Crash Tests:
  Frontal............................... Good
  Side.................................. Poor
Airbags:
  Torso ...Standard Front Pelvis/Torso from Seat
  Roll Sensing..........................Yes
  Knee Bolster .... Standard Passenger
Crash Avoidance:
  Collision Avoidance .....Warning Only Optional
  Blind Spot Detection .... Optional
  Lane Keeping Assist .... Optional
  Backup Camera .... Standard
  Pedestrian Crash Avoidance .... None
General:
  Auto. Crash Notification...... Dial Assist.-Free
  Day Running Lamps .... Standard
Safety Belt/Restraint:
  Dynamic Head Restraints .... None
  Adjustable Belt..............Standard Front

^Warning feature does not meet government standards.
*Backup camera does not meet government standards.

Ford Explorer

Specifications

Drive.......................................AWD
Engine 3.5-liter V6
Transmission .... 6-sp. Automatic
Tow Rating (lbs.) Low-5000
Head/Leg Room (in.) Cramped-41.4/40.6
Interior Space (cu. ft.)............. Very Roomy-151.7
Cargo Space (cu. ft.)................Average-21
Wheelbase/Length (in.) 112.6/197.1

Ratings—10 Best, 1 Worst

Combo Crash Tests	10
Safety Features	5
Rollover	2
Preventive Maintenance	8
Repair Costs	7
Warranty	4
Fuel Economy	2
Complaints	8
Insurance Costs	8
OVERALL RATING	**8**

Ford F-150

Ford F-150

Ford F-150

At-a-Glance

Status/Year Series Started Appearance Change/2015
Twins . . . . –
Body Styles . . . . Pickup
Seating 5/6
Anti-Theft Device . . . . . . Std. Pass. Immobil. & Alarm
Parking Index Rating . . . . .Very Hard
Where Made. . . . . Dearborn, MI
Fuel Factor:. . . . .
  MPG Rating (city/hwy) . . . . .Very Poor-17/23
  Driving Range (mi.) . . . . Very Long-693
  Fuel Type. . . . . .Regular
  Annual Fuel Cost . . . . .High-$1674
  Gas Guzzler Tax . . . . .No
  Greenhouse Gas Emissions (tons/yr.) Very High-9.5
  Barrels of Oil Used per year . . . . Very High-17.3

How the Competition Rates

Competitors	Rating	Pg.
Chevrolet Silverado	5	119
Ram 1500	4	235
Toyota Tundra	–	258

Price Range	Retail	Markup
XL Reg. Cab 2WD	$26,540	5%
XLT Supercab 2WD	$35,895	8%
Lariat Supercrew 4WD	$45,845	8%
Platinum Supercrew 4WD	$56,235	8%

Safety Checklist

Crash Tests:
  Frontal. . . . . Very Good
  Side. . . . . Very Good
Airbags:
  Torso . . . Standard Front Pelvis/Torso from Seat
  Roll Sensing. . . . . .Yes
  Knee Bolster . . . . None
Crash Avoidance:
  Collision Avoidance . . . . .Warning Only Optional
  Blind Spot Detection . . . . Optional
  Lane Keeping Assist . . . . Optional
  Backup Camera . . . . Optional
  Pedestrian Crash Avoidance . . . . None
General:
  Auto. Crash Notification. . . . . . Dial Assist.-Free
  Day Running Lamps . . . . Standard
Safety Belt/Restraint:
  Dynamic Head Restraints . . . . None
  Adjustable Belt. . . . . .Standard Front

^Warning feature does not meet government standards.
*Backup camera does not meet government standards.

Ford F-150

Specifications

Drive. 4WD
Engine 3.5-liter V6
Transmission . . . . 6-sp. Automatic
Tow Rating (lbs.) . . . . Very High-10700
Head/Leg Room (in.) . . . . Very Roomy-40.8/43.9
Interior Space (cu. ft.). Roomy-116
Cargo Space (cu. ft.) . . . . Very Roomy-49.4
Wheelbase/Length (in.) 145/231.9

Ratings—10 Best, 1 Worst

Combo Crash Tests	4
Safety Features	3
Rollover	4
Preventive Maintenance	6
Repair Costs	9
Warranty	4
Fuel Economy	8
Complaints	1
Insurance Costs	1
OVERALL RATING	**3**

Ford Fiesta

Ford Fiesta

At-a-Glance

Status/Year Series Started	Unchanged/2011
Twins	–
Body Styles	Sedan, Hatchback
Seating	5
Anti-Theft Device	Std. Passive Immobil. Only
Parking Index Rating	Very Easy
Where Made	Cuautitlán, Mexico

Fuel Factor:

MPG Rating (city/hwy)	Poor-27/37
Driving Range (mi.)	Short-381
Fuel Type	Regular
Annual Fuel Cost	Very Low-$1049
Gas Guzzler Tax	No
Greenhouse Gas Emissions (tons/yr.)	Low-5.8
Barrels of Oil Used per year	Average-10.6

How the Competition Rates

Competitors	Rating	Pg.
Chevrolet Sonic	9	120
Hyundai Accent	6	159
Toyota Yaris	5	259

Price Range

Price Range	Retail	Markup
S Sedan	$14,580	4%
SE Hatchback	$16,110	4%
Titanium Sedan	$18,530	4%
ST Hatchback	$21,460	4%

Safety Checklist

Crash Tests:
- Frontal . . . . Average
- Side . . . . Poor

Airbags:
- Torso . . . Standard Front Pelvis/Torso from Seat
- Roll Sensing . . . . Yes
- Knee Bolster . . . . Standard Driver

Crash Avoidance:
- Collision Avoidance . . . . None
- Blind Spot Detection . . . . None
- Lane Keeping Assist . . . . None
- Backup Camera . . . . Optional
- Pedestrian Crash Avoidance . . . . None

General:
- Auto. Crash Notification . . . . . . Dial Assist.-Free
- Day Running Lamps . . . . None

Safety Belt/Restraint:
- Dynamic Head Restraints . . . . None
- Adjustable Belt . . . . Standard Front

^Warning feature does not meet government standards.
*Backup camera does not meet government standards.

Ford Fiesta

Specifications

Drive	FWD
Engine	1.6-liter I4
Transmission	6-sp. Automatic
Tow Rating (lbs.)	Very Low-0
Head/Leg Room (in.)	Cramped-39.1/42.2
Interior Space (cu. ft.)	Very Cramped-85.1
Cargo Space (cu. ft.)	Cramped-14.9
Wheelbase/Length (in.)	98/159.7

Ford Flex

Ratings—10 Best, 1 Worst

Combo Crash Tests	—
Safety Features	4
Rollover	3
Preventive Maintenance	7
Repair Costs	3
Warranty	4
Fuel Economy	2
Complaints	2
Insurance Costs	5
OVERALL RATING	**—**

Ford Flex

Ford Flex

At-a-Glance

Status/Year Series Started	Unchanged/2009
Twins	—
Body Styles	SUV
Seating	6/7
Anti-Theft Device	Std. Active Immobil. & Pass. Alarm
Parking Index Rating	Very Hard
Where Made	Oakville, Ontario

Fuel Factor:

MPG Rating (city/hwy)	Very Poor-18/25
Driving Range (mi.)	Short-383
Fuel Type	Regular
Annual Fuel Cost	High-$1566
Gas Guzzler Tax	No
Greenhouse Gas Emissions (tons/yr.)	High-9.0
Barrels of Oil Used per year	High-16.5

How the Competition Rates

Competitors	Rating	Pg.
Chevrolet Traverse	6	124
Dodge Journey	1	133
Honda Pilot	8	158

Price Range	Retail	Markup
SE FWD	$30,025	4%
SEL AWD	$34,680	5%
Limited FWD	$38,230	5%
Limited Ecoboost AWD	$43,030	5%

Safety Checklist

Crash Tests:
Frontal	—
Side	—

Airbags:
Torso	Standard Front Torso from Seat
Roll Sensing	Yes
Knee Bolster	None

Crash Avoidance:
Collision Avoidance	Warning Only Optional
Blind Spot Detection	Optional
Lane Keeping Assist	None
Backup Camera	Standard
Pedestrian Crash Avoidance	None

General:
Auto. Crash Notification	Dial Assist.-Free
Day Running Lamps	None

Safety Belt/Restraint:
Dynamic Head Restraints	None
Adjustable Belt	Standard Front

^Warning feature does not meet government standards.
*Backup camera does not meet government standards.

Ford Flex

Specifications

Drive	FWD
Engine	3.5-liter V6
Transmission	6-sp. Automatic
Tow Rating (lbs.)	Low-4500
Head/Leg Room (in.)	Roomy-41.8/40.8
Interior Space (cu. ft.)	Very Roomy-155.8
Cargo Space (cu. ft.)	Average-20
Wheelbase/Length (in.)	117.9/201.8

Ratings—10 Best, 1 Worst

Combo Crash Tests	9
Safety Features	4
Rollover	6
Preventive Maintenance	6
Repair Costs	9
Warranty	4
Fuel Economy	8
Complaints	1
Insurance Costs	1
OVERALL RATING	**6**

Ford Focus

Ford Focus

At-a-Glance

Status/Year Series Started Unchanged/2012
Twins . . . . –
Body Styles . . . . Sedan, Hatchback
Seating 5
Anti-Theft Device . . . . Std. Passive Immobil. Only
Parking Index Rating . . . . Easy
Where Made . . . . Wayne, MI
Fuel Factor: . . . .
MPG Rating (city/hwy) Poor-27/40
Driving Range (mi.) Short-392
Fuel Type . . . . Regular
Annual Fuel Cost . . . . Very Low-$1020
Gas Guzzler Tax . . . . No
Greenhouse Gas Emissions (tons/yr.) Low-5.8
Barrels of Oil Used per year Average-10.6

How the Competition Rates

Competitors	Rating	Pg.
Honda Civic	8	153
Kia Forte	6	179
Mazda Mazda3	8	202

Price Range

Price Range	Retail	Markup
S Sedan	$16,775	4%
Titanum Sedan	$23,575	5%
ST Hatchback	$24,775	5%
Electric Hatchback	$29,120	5%

Safety Checklist

Crash Tests:
Frontal . . . . Good
Side . . . . Good
Airbags:
Torso . . . Standard Front Pelvis/Torso from Seat
Roll Sensing . . . . Yes
Knee Bolster . . . . Standard Driver
Crash Avoidance:
Collision Avoidance . . . . None
Blind Spot Detection . . . . None
Lane Keeping Assist . . . . Optional
Backup Camera . . . . Standard
Pedestrian Crash Avoidance . . . . None
General:
Auto. Crash Notification . . . . . . Dial Assist.-Free
Day Running Lamps . . . . None
Safety Belt/Restraint:
Dynamic Head Restraints . . . . None
Adjustable Belt . . . . Standard Front

^Warning feature does not meet government standards.
*Backup camera does not meet government standards.

Ford Focus

Specifications

Drive . . . . FWD
Engine 2.0-liter I4
Transmission . . . . 6-sp. Automatic
Tow Rating (lbs.) . . . . Very Low-0
Head/Leg Room (in.) Cramped-38.3/43.7
Interior Space (cu. ft.) Cramped-90.7
Cargo Space (cu. ft.) Cramped-13.2
Wheelbase/Length (in.) 104.3/178.5

Ratings—10 Best, 1 Worst	
Combo Crash Tests	3
Safety Features	9
Rollover	7
Preventive Maintenance	8
Repair Costs	10
Warranty	4
Fuel Economy	5
Complaints	5
Insurance Costs	5
OVERALL RATING	**6**

Ford Fusion

Ford Fusion

At-a-Glance

Status/Year Series Started Appearance Change/2013
Twins . . . . –
Body Styles . . . . Sedan
Seating 5
Anti-Theft Device . . . . . . Std. Pass. Immobil. & Alarm
Parking Index Rating . . . . Hard
Where Made. . . . . Flat Rock, MI / Hermosillo, Mexico
Fuel Factor:. . . . .
 MPG Rating (city/hwy) Poor-22/34
 Driving Range (mi.) Long-432
 Fuel Type. . . . . Regular
 Annual Fuel Cost . . . . Low-$1233
 Gas Guzzler Tax . . . . .No
 Greenhouse Gas Emissions (tons/yr.). . Average-6.9
 Barrels of Oil Used per year Average-12.7

How the Competition Rates

Competitors	Rating	Pg.
Chevrolet Malibu	10	118
Hyundai Sonata	10	164
Toyota Camry	8	247

Price Range	Retail	Markup
S	$22,610	7%
SE AWD	$27,405	8%
Titanium Energi	$34,120	8%
Platinum	$36,620	8%

Safety Checklist

Crash Tests:
 Frontal . . . . .Very Poor
 Side . . . . Poor
Airbags:
 Torso . . . Standard Front Pelvis/Torso from Seat
 Roll Sensing. . . . . .Yes
 Knee Bolster . . . . .Standard Front
Crash Avoidance:
 Collision Avoidance . . . . . . Optional CIB & DBS
 Blind Spot Detection . . . . Optional
 Lane Keeping Assist . . . . Optional
 Backup Camera . . . . Standard
 Pedestrian Crash Avoidance . . . . None
General:
 Auto. Crash Notification . . . . . . Dial Assist.-Free
 Day Running Lamps . . . . Standard
Safety Belt/Restraint:
 Dynamic Head Restraints . . . . None
 Adjustable Belt. . . . . .Standard Front

^Warning feature does not meet government standards.
*Backup camera does not meet government standards.

Ford Fusion

Specifications

Drive. . . . . .FWD
Engine 2.5-liter I4
Transmission . . . . 6-sp. Automatic
Tow Rating (lbs.) . . . . –
Head/Leg Room (in.) Roomy-39.2/44.3
Interior Space (cu. ft.). Roomy-118.8
Cargo Space (cu. ft.) Cramped-16
Wheelbase/Length (in.) 112.2/191.7

Ratings—10 Best, 1 Worst

Combo Crash Tests	7
Safety Features	9
Rollover	7
Preventive Maintenance	6
Repair Costs	10
Warranty	4
Fuel Economy	9
Complaints	6
Insurance Costs	5
OVERALL RATING	**9**

Ford Fusion Energi

Ford Fusion Energi

At-a-Glance

Status/Year Series Started Appearance Change/2016
Twins . . . . –
Body Styles . . . . .Sedan
Seating 5
Anti-Theft Device . . . . . . Std. Pass. Immobil. & Alarm
Parking Index Rating . . . . Hard
Where Made. . . . . .Hermosillo, Mexico
Fuel Factor:. . . . . :
  MPG Rating (city/hwy) Average-40/36
  Driving Range (mi.) . . . . Very Long-533
  Fuel Type . . . . .Regular
  Annual Fuel Cost . . . . .Very Low-$847
  Gas Guzzler Tax . . . . .No
  Greenhouse Gas Emissions (tons/yr.). Very Low-2.1
  Barrels of Oil Used per year . . . . Very Low-4.9

How the Competition Rates

Competitors	Rating	Pg.
Honda Accord	9	152
Hyundai Sonata	10	164
Subaru Legacy	6	239

Price Range

	Retail	Markup
SE Luxury Energi	$33,120	8%
Titanium Energi	$34,120	8%
Platinum Energi	$41,120	8%

Safety Checklist

Crash Tests:
  Frontal . . . . Very Good
  Side . . . . Poor
Airbags:
  Torso . . . Standard Front Pelvis/Torso from Seat
  Roll Sensing. . . . . .Yes
  Knee Bolster . . . . .Standard Front
Crash Avoidance:
  Collision Avoidance . . . . . . Optional CIB & DBS
  Blind Spot Detection . . . . Optional
  Lane Keeping Assist . . . . Optional
  Backup Camera . . . . Standard
  Pedestrian Crash Avoidance . . . . None
General:
  Auto. Crash Notification . . . . . . Dial Assist.-Free
  Day Running Lamps . . . . Standard
Safety Belt/Restraint:
  Dynamic Head Restraints . . . . None
  Adjustable Belt. . . . . .Standard Front

^Warning feature does not meet government standards.
*Backup camera does not meet government standards.

Ford Fusion Energi

Specifications

Drive. . . . . .FWD
Engine 2.0-liter I4
Transmission . . . . CVT
Tow Rating (lbs.) . . . . –
Head/Leg Room (in.) Roomy-39.2/44.3
Interior Space (cu. ft.). Roomy-111
Cargo Space (cu. ft.) . . . . Very Cramped-8.2
Wheelbase/Length (in.) 112.2/191.8

Ratings—10 Best, 1 Worst

Combo Crash Tests	8
Safety Features	3
Rollover	10
Preventive Maintenance	9
Repair Costs	9
Warranty	4
Fuel Economy	3
Complaints	5
Insurance Costs	5
OVERALL RATING	**7**

Ford Mustang

Ford Mustang

At-a-Glance

Status/Year Series Started Appearance Change/2015
Twins . . . . –
Body Styles . . . . Coupe, Convertible
Seating 4
Anti-Theft Device . . . . . Std. Pass. Immobil. & Alarm
Parking Index Rating . . . . Average
Where Made. . . . . Flat Rock, MI
Fuel Factor:. . . . .
  MPG Rating (city/hwy) . . . . .Very Poor-19/28
  Driving Range (mi.) . . . . .Very Short-355
  Fuel Type. . . . . .Regular
  Annual Fuel Cost . . . . .Average-$1452
  Gas Guzzler Tax . . . . .No
  Greenhouse Gas Emissions (tons/yr.). High-8.1
  Barrels of Oil Used per year High-15.0

How the Competition Rates

Competitors	Rating	Pg.
Chevrolet Camaro	5	112
Chevrolet Corvette	–	114
Dodge Challenger	5	130

Price Range

	Retail	Markup
Base Coupe	$24,645	4%
Eco Premium Coupe	$29,645	6%
GT Premium Convertible	$42,145	6%
Shelby GT350	$54,295	6%

Safety Checklist

Crash Tests:
  Frontal . . . . Very Good
  Side . . . . .Poor
Airbags:
  Torso . . .Standard Front Pelvis/Torso from Seat
  Roll Sensing. . . . . No
  Knee Bolster . . . . .Standard Front
Crash Avoidance:
  Collision Avoidance . . . . .Warning Only Optional
  Blind Spot Detection . . . . Optional
  Lane Keeping Assist . . . . None
  Backup Camera . . . . Standard
  Pedestrian Crash Avoidance . . . . None
General:
  Auto. Crash Notification . . . . . . Dial Assist.-Free
  Day Running Lamps . . . . None
Safety Belt/Restraint:
  Dynamic Head Restraints . . . . None
  Adjustable Belt. . . . . None

^Warning feature does not meet government standards.
*Backup camera does not meet government standards.

Ford Mustang

Specifications

Drive. . . . . .RWD
Engine 3.7-liter V6
Transmission . . . . 6-sp. Automatic
Tow Rating (lbs.) . . . . –
Head/Leg Room (in.) Cramped-37.6/44.5
Interior Space (cu. ft.). . . . . Very Cramped-84.5
Cargo Space (cu. ft.) Cramped-13.5
Wheelbase/Length (in.) 107.1/188.3

Ratings—10 Best, 1 Worst

Combo Crash Tests	7
Safety Features	5
Rollover	6
Preventive Maintenance	5
Repair Costs	4
Warranty	4
Fuel Economy	3
Complaints	6
Insurance Costs	1
OVERALL RATING	**4**

Ford Taurus

Ford Taurus

At-a-Glance

Status/Year Series Started	Unchanged/2010
Twins	–
Body Styles	Sedan
Seating	5
Anti-Theft Device	Std. Pass. Immobil. & Alarm
Parking Index Rating	Very Hard
Where Made	Chicago, IL
Fuel Factor:	
MPG Rating (city/hwy)	Very Poor-19/29
Driving Range (mi.)	Average-427
Fuel Type	Regular
Annual Fuel Cost	Average-$1434
Gas Guzzler Tax	No
Greenhouse Gas Emissions (tons/yr.)	High-7.8
Barrels of Oil Used per year	High-14.3

How the Competition Rates

Competitors	Rating	Pg.
Buick LaCrosse	6	105
Chevrolet Impala	7	117
Toyota Avalon	7	246

Price Range	Retail	Markup
SE	$27,345	6%
SEL	$29,775	6%
Limited AWD	$38,705	6%
SHO AWD	$42,520	6%

Safety Checklist

Crash Tests:
Frontal . . . . Very Good
Side . . . . Poor

Airbags:
Torso . . . . Standard Front Torso from Seat
Roll Sensing. . . . . Yes
Knee Bolster . . . . None

Crash Avoidance:
Collision Avoidance . . . . . Warning Only Optional
Blind Spot Detection . . . . Optional
Lane Keeping Assist . . . . Optional
Backup Camera . . . . Standard
Pedestrian Crash Avoidance . . . . None

General:
Auto. Crash Notification . . . . . . Dial Assist.-Free
Day Running Lamps . . . . None

Safety Belt/Restraint:
Dynamic Head Restraints . . . . None
Adjustable Belt. . . . . Standard Front

^Warning feature does not meet government standards.
*Backup camera does not meet government standards.

Ford Taurus

Specifications

Drive	FWD
Engine	3.5-liter V6
Transmission	6-sp. Automatic
Tow Rating (lbs.)	Very Low-1000
Head/Leg Room (in.)	Cramped-39/41.9
Interior Space (cu. ft.)	Average-102.2
Cargo Space (cu. ft.)	Average-20.1
Wheelbase/Length (in.)	112.9/202.9

Genesis G80 — Large

Ratings—10 Best, 1 Worst

Combo Crash Tests	—
Safety Features	10
Rollover	6
Preventive Maintenance	4
Repair Costs	4
Warranty	10
Fuel Economy	3
Complaints	—
Insurance Costs	1
OVERALL RATING	**—**

Genesis G80

Genesis G80

At-a-Glance

Status/Year Series Started . . . . All New/2017
Twins . . . . –
Body Styles . . . . Sedan
Seating 5
Anti-Theft Device . Std. Pass. Immobil. & Active Alarm
Parking Index Rating . . . . Very Easy
Where Made . . . . Ulsan, South Korea
Fuel Factor: . . . .
  MPG Rating (city/hwy) . . . . Very Poor-18/28
  Driving Range (mi.) Long-435
  Fuel Type . . . . Regular
  Annual Fuel Cost . . . . High-$1504
  Gas Guzzler Tax . . . . No
  Greenhouse Gas Emissions (tons/yr.) . . Average-6.8
  Barrels of Oil Used per year High-15.0

How the Competition Rates

Competitors	Rating	Pg.
Acura TLX	9	84
Cadillac XTS	9	111
Lexus ES	7	190

Price Range	Retail	Markup
3.8L V6	$41,400	5%
3.8L V6 AWD	$43,900	6%
5.0L V8	$54,550	7%

Safety Checklist

Crash Tests:
  Frontal . . . . –
  Side . . . . –
Airbags:
  Torso Std. Fr. & Opt. Rr. Pelvis/Torso from Seat
  Roll Sensing . . . . Yes
  Knee Bolster . . . . Standard Driver
Crash Avoidance:
  Collision Avoidance . . . . . . Standard CIB & DBS
  Blind Spot Detection . . . . Standard
  Lane Keeping Assist . . . . Standard
  Backup Camera . . . . Standard*
  Pedestrian Crash Avoidance . . . . None
General:
  Auto. Crash Notification . . . Operator Assist.-Fee
  Day Running Lamps . . . . Standard
Safety Belt/Restraint:
  Dynamic Head Restraints . . . . None
  Adjustable Belt . . . . Standard Front

^Warning feature does not meet government standards.
*Backup camera does not meet government standards.

Genesis G80

Specifications

Drive . . . . RWD
Engine 3.8-liter V6
Transmission . . . . 8-sp. Automatic
Tow Rating (lbs.) . . . . –
Head/Leg Room (in.) . . . . Very Roomy-39.4/45.7
Interior Space (cu. ft.) Roomy-107.7
Cargo Space (cu. ft.) Cramped-15.3
Wheelbase/Length (in.) 118.5/196.5

Ratings—10 Best, 1 Worst

Combo Crash Tests	—
Safety Features	8
Rollover	3
Preventive Maintenance	2
Repair Costs	4
Warranty	5
Fuel Economy	2
Complaints	—
Insurance Costs	10

OVERALL RATING — —

GMC Acadia

At-a-Glance

Status/Year Series Started. . . . . All New/2017
Twins . . . . —
Body Styles . . . . SUV
Seating 5/6/7
Anti-Theft Device . Std. Pass. Immobil. & Active Alarm
Parking Index Rating . . . . Hard
Where Made. . . . . Lansing, MI
Fuel Factor:. . . . .
  MPG Rating (city/hwy) . . . . Very Poor-18/25
  Driving Range (mi.) Short-391
  Fuel Type. . . . . Regular
  Annual Fuel Cost . . . . High-$1566
  Gas Guzzler Tax . . . . No
  Greenhouse Gas Emissions (tons/yr.) . . Average-7.0
  Barrels of Oil Used per year High-15.7

How the Competition Rates

Competitors	Rating	Pg.
Buick Enclave	6	103
Chevrolet Traverse	6	124
Toyota Highlander	7	250

Price Range	Retail	Markup
SLE1 FWD	$32,450	5%
SLT1 FWD	$38,350	5%
SLT2 AWD	$43,750	5%
Denali AWD	$46,920	5%

GMC Acadia

Safety Checklist

Crash Tests:
  Frontal . . . . —
  Side . . . . —
Airbags:
  Torso . . . Standard Front Pelvis/Torso from Seat
  Roll Sensing. . . . . Yes
  Knee Bolster . . . . Standard Driver
Crash Avoidance:
  Collision Avoidance . . . . . . Optional CIB & DBS
  Blind Spot Detection . . . . Optional
  Lane Keeping Assist . . . . Optional
  Backup Camera . . . . Standard*
  Pedestrian Crash Avoidance . . . . Optional
General:
  Auto. Crash Notif. . . . . Oper. Assist. & Crash Info-Free
  Day Running Lamps . . . . Standard
Safety Belt/Restraint:
  Dynamic Head Restraints . . . . None
  Adjustable Belt. None

^Warning feature does not meet government standards.
*Backup camera does not meet government standards.

GMC Acadia

Specifications

Drive. . . . . FWD
Engine 3.6-liter V6
Transmission . . . . 6-sp. Automatic
Tow Rating (lbs.) . . . . —
Head/Leg Room (in.) Cramped-40/41
Interior Space (cu. ft.). . . . . —
Cargo Space (cu. ft.) . . . . Very Cramped-12.8
Wheelbase/Length (in.) 112.5/193.6

Ratings—10 Best, 1 Worst

Combo Crash Tests	8
Safety Features	4
Rollover	2
Preventive Maintenance	2
Repair Costs	6
Warranty	5
Fuel Economy	1
Complaints	5
Insurance Costs	10
OVERALL RATING	**5**

GMC Sierra

GMC Sierra

At-a-Glance

Status/Year Series Started Appearance Change/2014
Twins . . . .–
Body Styles . . . .
Seating. 5/6
Anti-Theft Device Std. Pass. Immobil. & Opt. Pass. Alarm
Parking Index Rating . . . . .Very Hard
Where Made. . . . . .Fort Wayne, IN
Fuel Factor:. . . . .
 MPG Rating (city/hwy) . . . . .Very Poor-16/22
 Driving Range (mi.) . . . . Very Long-474
 Fuel Type. . . . . .Regular
 Annual Fuel Cost . . . . Very High-$1768
 Gas Guzzler Tax . . . . .No
 Greenhouse Gas Emissions (tons/yr.)Very High-10.0
 Barrels of Oil Used per year . . . . . . .Very High-18.3

How the Competition Rates

Competitors	Rating	Pg.
Ford F-150	8	141
Ram 1500	4	235
Toyota Tundra	–	258

Price Range

	Retail	Markup
Base Reg. Cab 2WD	$28,105	5%
SLE Dbl. Cab 2WD	$37,460	7%
SLT Dbl. Cab 4WD	$45,180	7%
Denali Crew Cab 4WD	$55,155	7%

Safety Checklist

Crash Tests:
 Frontal . . . . Very Good
 Side . . . . .Poor
Airbags:
 Torso . . . Standard Front Pelvis/Torso from Seat
 Roll Sensing. . . . . .Yes
 Knee Bolster . . . . None
Crash Avoidance:
 Collision Avoidance . . . . Optional CIB
 Blind Spot Detection . . . . None
 Lane Keeping Assist . . . . Optional
 Backup Camera . . . . Optional*
 Pedestrian Crash Avoidance . . . . None
General:
 Auto. Crash Notif. . . . . Oper. Assist. & Crash Info-Free
 Day Running Lamps . . . . Standard
Safety Belt/Restraint:
 Dynamic Head Restraints . . . . None
 Adjustable Belt. . . . . .Standard Front

^Warning feature does not meet government standards.
*Backup camera does not meet government standards.

GMC Sierra

Specifications

Drive. 4WD
Engine 5.3-liter V8
Transmission . . . . 6-sp. Automatic
Tow Rating (lbs.) . . . . Very High-9200
Head/Leg Room (in.) . . . . .Very Roomy-42.8/45.2
Interior Space (cu. ft.). . . . .–
Cargo Space (cu. ft.) . . . . Very Roomy-61
Wheelbase/Length (in.) 143.5/230

Ratings—10 Best, 1 Worst

Combo Crash Tests	9
Safety Features	7
Rollover	8
Preventive Maintenance	10
Repair Costs	7
Warranty	2
Fuel Economy	8
Complaints	6
Insurance Costs	5
OVERALL RATING	**9**

Honda Accord

Honda Accord

At-a-Glance

Status/Year Series Started. Unchanged/2013
Twins . . . . –
Body Styles . . . . Sedan, Coupe
Seating 5
Anti-Theft Device . . . . . . Std. Pass. Immobil. & Alarm
Parking Index Rating . . . . Hard
Where Made. . . . . Marysville, OH
Fuel Factor:. . . . .
  MPG Rating (city/hwy). Poor-27/36
  Driving Range (mi.) . . . . Very Long-523
  Fuel Type. . . . . .Regular
  Annual Fuel Cost . . . . Low-$1060
  Gas Guzzler Tax . . . . .No
  Greenhouse Gas Emissions (tons/yr.). Low-5.8
  Barrels of Oil Used per year Average-10.6

How the Competition Rates

Competitors	Rating	Pg.
Ford Fusion	6	145
Nissan Altima	5	221
Toyota Camry	8	247

Price Range	Retail	Markup
LX Sedan MT	$22,355	9%
EX Sedan AT	$26,530	9%
EX-L Coupe V6 AT	$31,175	9%
Touring Sedan V6 AT	$34,830	9%

Safety Checklist

Crash Tests:
  Frontal . . . . Very Good
  Side . . . . Good
Airbags:
  Torso . . . Standard Front Pelvis/Torso from Seat
  Roll Sensing. . . . . .Yes
  Knee Bolster . . . . None
Crash Avoidance:
  Collision Avoidance . . . . . . Optional CIB & DBS
  Blind Spot Detection . . . . None
  Lane Keeping Assist . . . . Optional
  Backup Camera. . . . . Standard
  Pedestrian Crash Avoidance . . . . Optional
General:
  Auto. Crash Notification . . . . . . Dial Assist.-Free
  Day Running Lamps . . . . Standard
Safety Belt/Restraint:
  Dynamic Head Restraints . . . . None
  Adjustable Belt. None

^Warning feature does not meet government standards.
*Backup camera does not meet government standards.

Honda Accord

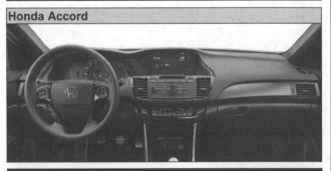

Specifications

Drive. . . . . .FWD
Engine 2.4-liter I4
Transmission . . . . CVT
Tow Rating (lbs.) . . . . –
Head/Leg Room (in.) Cramped-39.1/42.5
Interior Space (cu. ft.). Average-103.2
Cargo Space (cu. ft.) Cramped-15.8
Wheelbase/Length (in.) 109.3/191.4

Honda Civic

Compact

Honda Civic

Ratings—10 Best, 1 Worst	
Combo Crash Tests	5
Safety Features	7
Rollover	9
Preventive Maintenance	10
Repair Costs	8
Warranty	2
Fuel Economy	9
Complaints	3
Insurance Costs	8
OVERALL RATING	**8**

Honda Civic

At-a-Glance

Status/Year Series Started........ Unchanged/2016
Twins .... –
Body Styles .... Coupe
Seating 5
Anti-Theft Device ...... Std. Pass. Immobil. & Alarm
Parking Index Rating .... Easy
Where Made...... Greensburg, IN / Alliston, Ontario
Fuel Factor:.................................
  MPG Rating (city/hwy) Average-31/41
  Driving Range (mi.) Long-432
  Fuel Type ....Regular
  Annual Fuel Cost .... Very Low-$926
  Gas Guzzler Tax ....No
  Greenhouse Gas Emissions (tons/yr.). Very Low-4.2
  Barrels of Oil Used per year Low-9.4

How the Competition Rates

Competitors	Rating	Pg.
Nissan Sentra	5	231
Toyota Corolla	8	248
Volkswagen Jetta	5	263

Price Range	Retail	Markup
LX Coupe MT	$19,050	8%
EX Sedan AT	$21,040	8%
EX-L Sedan w/Sensing	$24,700	8%
Touring Sedan	$26,500	8%

Safety Checklist

Crash Tests:
  Frontal .... Average
  Side .... Poor
Airbags:
  Torso . . .Standard Front Pelvis/Torso from Seat
  Roll Sensing...........................Yes
  Knee Bolster .... None
Crash Avoidance:
  Collision Avoidance ...... Optional CIB & DBS
  Blind Spot Detection .... None
  Lane Keeping Assist .... Optional
  Backup Camera .... Standard
  Pedestrian Crash Avoidance .... Optional
General:
  Auto. Crash Notification ...... Dial Assist.-Free
  Day Running Lamps .... Standard
Safety Belt/Restraint:
  Dynamic Head Restraints .... None
  Adjustable Belt...............Standard Front

^Warning feature does not meet government standards.
*Backup camera does not meet government standards.

Honda Civic

Specifications

Drive..FWD
Engine 1.8-liter I4
Transmission .... CVT
Tow Rating (lbs.) .... –
Head/Leg Room (in.) Cramped-39.3/42.3
Interior Space (cu. ft.)............. Cramped-94.8
Cargo Space (cu. ft.) Cramped-15.1
Wheelbase/Length (in.) 106.3/179.4

Ratings—10 Best, 1 Worst

Combo Crash Tests	—
Safety Features	8
Rollover	3
Preventive Maintenance	10
Repair Costs	8
Warranty	2
Fuel Economy	7
Complaints	—
Insurance Costs	10

OVERALL RATING   —

Honda CR-V

At-a-Glance

Status/Year Series Started. . . . . All New/2017
Twins . . . .—
Body Styles . . . .
Seating 5
Anti-Theft Device .Std. Pass. Immob. & Opt. Pass. Alarm
Parking Index Rating . . . . Average
Where Made. . . . . .East Liberty, OH
Fuel Factor:. . . . .
  MPG Rating (city/hwy) Poor-26/32
  Driving Range (mi.) Short-398
  Fuel Type. . . . . .Regular
  Annual Fuel Cost . . . . Low-$1136
  Gas Guzzler Tax . . . . .No
  Greenhouse Gas Emissions (tons/yr.). Low-5.2
  Barrels of Oil Used per year Average-11.8

How the Competition Rates

Competitors	Rating	Pg.
Ford Escape	7	138
Jeep Cherokee	5	172
Toyota RAV4	6	254

Price Range	Retail	Markup
LX 2WD	$23,595	6%
EX 2WD	$25,845	6%
EX-L AWD	$29,595	7%
Touring AWD	$33,245	7%

Honda CR-V

Safety Checklist

Crash Tests:
  Frontal . . . .‾
  Side . . . .‾
Airbags:
  Torso . . . Standard Front Pelvis/Torso from Seat
  Roll Sensing. . . . . .Yes
  Knee Bolster . . . . None
Crash Avoidance:
  Collision Avoidance . . . . . . Optional CIB & DBS
  Blind Spot Detection . . . . Optional
  Lane Keeping Assist . . . . Optional
  Backup Camera . . . . Standard
  Pedestrian Crash Avoidance . . . . Optional
General:
  Auto. Crash Notification . . . . . . Dial Assist.-Free
  Day Running Lamps . . . . Standard
Safety Belt/Restraint:
  Dynamic Head Restraints . . . . None
  Adjustable Belt. . . . . .Standard Front

^Warning feature does not meet government standards.
*Backup camera does not meet government standards.

Honda CR-V

Specifications

Drive. . . . . .FWD
Engine 2.4-liter I4
Transmission . . . . CVT
Tow Rating (lbs.) . . . . .Very Low-1500
Head/Leg Room (in.) . . . . .Very Cramped-38/41.3
Interior Space (cu. ft.). Average-102.9
Cargo Space (cu. ft.) . . . . .Very Roomy-39.2
Wheelbase/Length (in.) 104.7/180.6

Honda Fit

Ratings—10 Best, 1 Worst

Combo Crash Tests	9
Safety Features	3
Rollover	4
Preventive Maintenance	10
Repair Costs	8
Warranty	2
Fuel Economy	9
Complaints	5
Insurance Costs	5
OVERALL RATING	**8**

Honda Fit

At-a-Glance

Status/Year Series Started Appearance Change/2015
Twins . . . . –
Body Styles . . . . Sedan, Hatchback
Seating 5
Anti-Theft Device . . . . . . Std. Pass. Immobil. & Alarm
Parking Index Rating . . . . Very Easy
Where Made. . . . . .Celaya, Mexico
Fuel Factor: . . . .
MPG Rating (city/hwy) Average-33/41
Driving Range (mi.) Short-383
Fuel Type . . . . .Regular
Annual Fuel Cost . . . . .Very Low-$891
Gas Guzzler Tax . . . . .No
Greenhouse Gas Emissions (tons/yr.) Low-5.0
Barrels of Oil Used per year Low-9.1

How the Competition Rates

Competitors	Rating	Pg.
Chevrolet Silverado	5	119
Nissan Versa	2	233
Toyota Yaris	5	259

Price Range

	Retail	Markup
LX MT	$15,990	8%
EX MT	$17,900	8%
EX AT	$18,700	8%
EX-L AT w/Nav	$21,265	8%

Safety Checklist

Crash Tests:
Frontal . . . . Good
Side . . . . Good
Airbags:
Torso . . .Standard Front Pelvis/Torso from Seat
Roll Sensing. . . . . .Yes
Knee Bolster . . . . None
Crash Avoidance:
Collision Avoidance . . . . None
Blind Spot Detection . . . . None
Lane Keeping Assist . . . . None
Backup Camera . . . . Standard
Pedestrian Crash Avoidance . . . . None
General:
Auto. Crash Notification . . . . . . Dial Assist.-Free
Day Running Lamps . . . . Standard
Safety Belt/Restraint:
Dynamic Head Restraints . . . . None
Adjustable Belt . . . . .Standard Front

^Warning feature does not meet government standards.
*Backup camera does not meet government standards.

Honda Fit

Specifications

Drive. . . . . .FWD
Engine 1.5-liter I4
Transmission . . . . CVT
Tow Rating (lbs.) . . . . –
Head/Leg Room (in.) Cramped-39.5/41.4
Interior Space (cu. ft.). Cramped-95.7
Cargo Space (cu. ft.) Cramped-16.6
Wheelbase/Length (in.) 99.6/160

Honda HR-V
Small SUV

Ratings—10 Best, 1 Worst

Combo Crash Tests	4
Safety Features	3
Rollover	5
Preventive Maintenance	7
Repair Costs	8
Warranty	2
Fuel Economy	8
Complaints	3
Insurance Costs	8
OVERALL RATING	**5**

Honda HR-V

At-a-Glance

Status/Year Series Started........ Unchanged/2016
Twins .... –
Body Styles .... SUV
Seating 5
Anti-Theft Device ...... Std. Pass. Immobil. & Alarm
Parking Index Rating .... Easy
Where Made..................... Celaya, Mexico
Fuel Factor:................................
  MPG Rating (city/hwy)............... Poor-28/35
  Driving Range (mi.) Average-406
  Fuel Type............................ Regular
  Annual Fuel Cost .... Very Low-$1048
  Gas Guzzler Tax .... No
  Greenhouse Gas Emissions (tons/yr.)..... Low-4.7
  Barrels of Oil Used per year Average-10.6

How the Competition Rates

Competitors	Rating	Pg.
Chevrolet Traverse	6	124
Jeep Renegade	2	176
Nissan Juke	2	224

Price Range	Retail	Markup
LX FWD MT	$19,365	3%
LX AWD AT	$21,415	3%
EX FWD AT	$22,215	3%
EX-L AWD w/Nav	$26,140	3%

Honda HR-V

Safety Checklist

Crash Tests:
  Frontal .... Poor
  Side .... Average
Airbags:
  Torso ... Standard Front Pelvis/Torso from Seat
  Roll Sensing......................... Yes
  Knee Bolster .... None
Crash Avoidance:
  Collision Avoidance .... None
  Blind Spot Detection .... None
  Lane Keeping Assist .... None
  Backup Camera .... Standard
  Pedestrian Crash Avoidance .... None
General:
  Auto. Crash Notification...... Dial Assist.-Free
  Day Running Lamps .... Standard
Safety Belt/Restraint:
  Dynamic Head Restraints .... None
  Adjustable Belt.............. Standard Front

^Warning feature does not meet government standards.
*Backup camera does not meet government standards.

Honda HR-V

Specifications

Drive.......................... 2WD
Engine 1.8-liter I4
Transmission .... CVT
Tow Rating (lbs.) .... –
Head/Leg Room (in.) Cramped-39.5/41.2
Interior Space (cu. ft.)....... Average-100.1
Cargo Space (cu. ft.) Roomy-24.3
Wheelbase/Length (in.) 102.8/169.1

Ratings—10 Best, 1 Worst	
Combo Crash Tests	8
Safety Features	7
Rollover	5
Preventive Maintenance	9
Repair Costs	8
Warranty	2
Fuel Economy	3
Complaints	5
Insurance Costs	10
OVERALL RATING	**8**

Honda Odyssey

Honda Odyssey

At-a-Glance

Status/Year Series Started	Unchanged/2005
Twins	–
Body Styles	Minivan
Seating	7/8
Anti-Theft Device	Std. Pass. Immobil. & Alarm
Parking Index Rating	Hard
Where Made	–

Fuel Factor:

MPG Rating (city/hwy)	Very Poor-19/28
Driving Range (mi.)	Long-466
Fuel Type	Regular
Annual Fuel Cost	Average-$1452
Gas Guzzler Tax	No
Greenhouse Gas Emissions (tons/yr.)	Average-7.1
Barrels of Oil Used per year	High-15.0

How the Competition Rates

Competitors	Rating	Pg.
Chrysler Pacifica	9	129
Nissan Quest	–	229
Toyota Sienna	2	256

Price Range	Retail	Markup
LX	$29,275	9%
EX	$32,425	9%
EX-L w/Nav	$37,925	9%
Touring Elite	$42,180	9%

Safety Checklist

Crash Tests:

Frontal	Good
Side	Good

Airbags:

Torso	Standard Front Pelvis/Torso from Seat
Roll Sensing	Yes
Knee Bolster	None

Crash Avoidance:

Collision Avoidance	Warning Only Optional
Blind Spot Detection	Optional
Lane Keeping Assist	Warning Only Optional
Backup Camera	Standard
Pedestrian Crash Avoidance	None

General:

Auto. Crash Notification	Dial Assist.-Free
Day Running Lamps	Standard

Safety Belt/Restraint:

Dynamic Head Restraints	Standard Front
Adjustable Belt	Standard Front & Rear

^Warning feature does not meet government standards.
*Backup camera does not meet government standards.

Honda Odyssey

Specifications

Drive	FWD
Engine	3.5-liter V6
Transmission	5-sp. Automatic
Tow Rating (lbs.)	Low-3500
Head/Leg Room (in.)	Cramped-39.7/40.9
Interior Space (cu. ft.)	Very Roomy-172.6
Cargo Space (cu. ft.)	Very Roomy-38.4
Wheelbase/Length (in.)	118.1/202.9

Ratings—10 Best, 1 Worst	
Combo Crash Tests	9
Safety Features	7
Rollover	3
Preventive Maintenance	10
Repair Costs	7
Warranty	2
Fuel Economy	3
Complaints	2
Insurance Costs	10
OVERALL RATING	**8**

Honda Pilot

Honda Pilot

At-a-Glance

Status/Year Series Started.	Unchanged/2016
Twins	—
Body Styles	SUV
Seating	8
Anti-Theft Device	Std. Pass. Immobil. & Alarm
Parking Index Rating	Very Hard
Where Made	Lincoln, AL
Fuel Factor:	
MPG Rating (city/hwy)	Very Poor-19/27
Driving Range (mi.)	Average-428
Fuel Type	Regular
Annual Fuel Cost	Average-$1471
Gas Guzzler Tax	No
Greenhouse Gas Emissions (tons/yr.)	Average-6.4
Barrels of Oil Used per year	High-14.3

How the Competition Rates

Competitors	Rating	Pg.
Ford Expedition	7	139
Ford Explorer	3	140
Toyota 4Runner	2	244

Price Range	Retail	Markup
LX 2WD	$29,995	9%
EX AWD	$34,230	9%
EX-L AWD	$37,705	9%
Touring AWD	$42,820	9%

Safety Checklist

Crash Tests:
Frontal . . . . Good
Side . . . . Very Good

Airbags:
Torso . . . Standard Front Pelvis/Torso from Seat
Roll Sensing . . . . Yes
Knee Bolster . . . . None

Crash Avoidance:
Collision Avoidance . . . . . . Optional CIB & DBS
Blind Spot Detection . . . . Optional
Lane Keeping Assist . . . . Optional
Backup Camera . . . . Standard*
Pedestrian Crash Avoidance . . . . Optional

General:
Auto. Crash Notification . . . . . . Dial Assist.-Free
Day Running Lamps . . . . Standard

Safety Belt/Restraint:
Dynamic Head Restraints . . . . None
Adjustable Belt . . . . Standard Front

^Warning feature does not meet government standards.
*Backup camera does not meet government standards.

Honda Pilot

Specifications

Drive	AWD
Engine	3.5-liter V6
Transmission	6-sp. Automatic
Tow Rating (lbs.)	Low-3500
Head/Leg Room (in.)	Cramped-40.1/40.9
Interior Space (cu. ft.)	Very Roomy-152.9
Cargo Space (cu. ft.)	Cramped-16.5
Wheelbase/Length (in.)	111/194.5

Hyundai Accent | Subcompact

Hyundai Accent

Ratings—10 Best, 1 Worst

Combo Crash Tests	3
Safety Features	2
Rollover	5
Preventive Maintenance	6
Repair Costs	10
Warranty	10
Fuel Economy	7
Complaints	9
Insurance Costs	1
OVERALL RATING	**6**

Hyundai Accent

At-a-Glance

Status/Year Series Started........ Unchanged/2012
Twins . . . . –
Body Styles . . . . Sedan, Hatchback
Seating 5
Anti-Theft Device .None
Parking Index Rating . . . . .Very Easy
Where Made. . . . . Ulsan, South Korea
Fuel Factor:. . . . .
 MPG Rating (city/hwy) Poor-26/37
 Driving Range (mi.) . . . . .Very Short-342
 Fuel Type . . . . .Regular
 Annual Fuel Cost . . . . Low-$1074
 Gas Guzzler Tax . . . . .No
 Greenhouse Gas Emissions (tons/yr.) Low-6.0
 Barrels of Oil Used per year Average-11.0

How the Competition Rates

Competitors	Rating	Pg.
Ford Fiesta	3	142
Nissan Versa	2	233
Toyota Yaris	5	259

Price Range

	Retail	Markup
SE Sedan MT	$14,745	3%
SE Hatchback AT	$16,195	3%
Sport Hatchback MT	$16,495	3%
Sport Hatchback AT	$17,495	3%

Safety Checklist

Crash Tests:
 Frontal . . . . Poor
 Side . . . . .Very Poor
Airbags:
 Torso . . .Standard Front Pelvis/Torso from Seat
 Roll Sensing. . . . . .Yes
 Knee Bolster . . . . None
Crash Avoidance:
 Collision Avoidance . . . . None
 Blind Spot Detection . . . . None
 Lane Keeping Assist . . . . None
 Backup Camera . . . . Optional*
 Pedestrian Crash Avoidance . . . . None
General:
 Auto. Crash Notification . . . Operator Assist.-Fee
 Day Running Lamps . . . . None
Safety Belt/Restraint:
 Dynamic Head Restraints . . . . None
 Adjustable Belt. . . . . .Standard Front

^Warning feature does not meet government standards.
*Backup camera does not meet government standards.

Hyundai Accent

Specifications

Drive. . . . . .FWD
Engine 1.6-liter I4
Transmission . . . . 6-sp. Automatic
Tow Rating (lbs.) . . . . –
Head/Leg Room (in.) Cramped-39.9/41.8
Interior Space (cu. ft.). . . . . Very Cramped-90.1
Cargo Space (cu. ft.) Average-21.2
Wheelbase/Length (in.) 101.2/162

Ratings—10 Best, 1 Worst

Combo Crash Tests	—
Safety Features	6
Rollover	7
Preventive Maintenance	4
Repair Costs	10
Warranty	10
Fuel Economy	4
Complaints	4
Insurance Costs	5
OVERALL RATING	**—**

Hyundai Azera

Hyundai Azera

At-a-Glance

Status/Year Series Started........ Unchanged/2012
Twins . . . . –
Body Styles . . . . .Sedan
Seating 5
Anti-Theft Device . Std. Pass. Immobil. & Active Alarm
Parking Index Rating . . . . Average
Where Made. . . . . .Asan, South Korea
Fuel Factor:. . . . .
  MPG Rating (city/hwy) . . . . .Very Poor-20/29
  Driving Range (mi.) Long-430
  Fuel Type . . . . .Regular
  Annual Fuel Cost . . . . .Average-$1387
  Gas Guzzler Tax . . . . .No
  Greenhouse Gas Emissions (tons/yr.). High-7.8
  Barrels of Oil Used per year High-14.3

How the Competition Rates

Competitors	Rating	Pg.
Chevrolet Impala	7	117
Ford Fusion	6	145
Nissan Maxima	4	226

Price Range

Price Range	Retail	Markup
Sedan	$34,100	7%
Sedan Limited	$39,300	7%

Safety Checklist

Crash Tests:
  Frontal . . . .–
  Side . . . .–
Airbags:
  Torso Std. Fr. & Opt. Rr. Pelvis/Torso from Seat
  Roll Sensing. . . . . .Yes
  Knee Bolster . . . . Standard Driver
Crash Avoidance:
  Collision Avoidance . . . . .Warning Only Optional
  Blind Spot Detection . . . . Standard
  Lane Keeping Assist . . . .Warning Only Optional
  Backup Camera . . . . Optional*
  Pedestrian Crash Avoidance . . . . None
General:
  Auto. Crash Notification . . . Operator Assist.-Fee
  Day Running Lamps . . . . Standard
Safety Belt/Restraint:
  Dynamic Head Restraints . . . . None
  Adjustable Belt. . . . . .Standard Front

^Warning feature does not meet government standards.
*Backup camera does not meet government standards.

Hyundai Azera

Specifications

Drive. . . . . .FWD
Engine 3.3-liter V6
Transmission . . . . 6-sp. Automatic
Tow Rating (lbs.) . . . .—
Head/Leg Room (in.) . . . . Very Roomy-40.3/45.5
Interior Space (cu. ft.). Roomy-107
Cargo Space (cu. ft.) Cramped-16.3
Wheelbase/Length (in.) 112/193.3

Ratings—10 Best, 1 Worst	
Combo Crash Tests	3
Safety Features	8
Rollover	7
Preventive Maintenance	4
Repair Costs	10
Warranty	10
Fuel Economy	8
Complaints	—
Insurance Costs	1
OVERALL RATING	6

Hyundai Elantra

Hyundai Elantra

At-a-Glance

Status/Year Series Started	All New/2017
Twins	—
Body Styles	Sedan, Coupe, Hatchback
Seating	5
Anti-Theft Device	Std. Pass. Immobil. & Active Alarm
Parking Index Rating	Easy
Where Made	Montgomery, AL

Fuel Factor:

MPG Rating (city/hwy)	Poor-28/37
Driving Range (mi.)	Long-440
Fuel Type	Regular
Annual Fuel Cost	Very Low-$1026
Gas Guzzler Tax	No
Greenhouse Gas Emissions (tons/yr.)	Low-4.7
Barrels of Oil Used per year	Low-10.3

How the Competition Rates

Competitors	Rating	Pg.
Honda Civic	8	153
Nissan Sentra	5	231
Toyota Corolla	8	248

Price Range	Retail	Markup
SE MT	$17,150	3%
GT AT	$19,800	4%
Eco AT	$20,650	4%
Limited AT	$22,350	5%

Safety Checklist

Crash Tests:
Frontal . . . . Poor
Side . . . . Poor

Airbags:
Torso . . . Standard Front Pelvis/Torso from Seat
Roll Sensing . . . . Yes
Knee Bolster . . . . Standard Driver

Crash Avoidance:
Collision Avoidance . . . . . . Optional CIB & DBS
Blind Spot Detection . . . . Optional
Lane Keeping Assist . . . . Optional
Backup Camera . . . . Optional
Pedestrian Crash Avoidance . . . . Optional

General:
Auto. Crash Notification . . . Operator Assist.-Fee
Day Running Lamps . . . . Standard

Safety Belt/Restraint:
Dynamic Head Restraints . . . . None
Adjustable Belt . . . . Standard Front

^Warning feature does not meet government standards.
*Backup camera does not meet government standards.

Hyundai Elantra

Specifications

Drive	FWD
Engine	2.0-liter I4
Transmission	6-sp. Automatic
Tow Rating (lbs.)	—
Head/Leg Room (in.)	Cramped-38.8/42.2
Interior Space (cu. ft.)	Cramped-95.8
Cargo Space (cu. ft.)	Cramped-14.4
Wheelbase/Length (in.)	106.3/179.9

Ratings—10 Best, 1 Worst

Combo Crash Tests	—
Safety Features	8
Rollover	4
Preventive Maintenance	4
Repair Costs	8
Warranty	10
Fuel Economy	2
Complaints	4
Insurance Costs	5
OVERALL RATING	**—**

Hyundai Santa Fe

Hyundai Santa Fe

At-a-Glance

Status/Year Series Started Unchanged/2013
Twins . . . .—
Body Styles . . . . SUV
Seating 6/7
Anti-Theft Device . Std. Pass. Immobil. & Active Alarm
Parking Index Rating . . . . Average
Where Made . . . . West Point, GA
Fuel Factor: . . . .
  MPG Rating (city/hwy) . . . . . Very Poor-18/25
  Driving Range (mi.) Short-387
  Fuel Type . . . . .Regular
  Annual Fuel Cost . . . . .High-$1566
  Gas Guzzler Tax . . . . .No
  Greenhouse Gas Emissions (tons/yr.) High-8.5
  Barrels of Oil Used per year High-15.7

How the Competition Rates

Competitors	Rating	Pg.
Acura MDX	8	82
Mitsubishi Outlander	4	218
Nissan Pathfinder	2	228

Price Range	Retail	Markup
SE FWD	$30,800	5%
Limited FWD	$34,950	6%
SE Limited AWD	$40,450	5%
Limited Ultimate AWD	$41,150	6%

Safety Checklist

Crash Tests:
  Frontal . . . .–
  Side . . . .–
Airbags:
  Torso . . . Standard Front Pelvis/Torso from Seat
  Roll Sensing . . . . .Yes
  Knee Bolster . . . . Standard Driver
Crash Avoidance:
  Collision Avoidance . . . . . . Optional CIB & DBS
  Blind Spot Detection . . . . Optional
  Lane Keeping Assist . . . .Warning Only Optional
  Backup Camera . . . . Standard
  Pedestrian Crash Avoidance . . . . Optional
General:
  Auto. Crash Notification . . . Operator Assist.-Fee
  Day Running Lamps . . . . Standard
Safety Belt/Restraint:
  Dynamic Head Restraints . . . . None
  Adjustable Belt . . . . .Standard Front

^Warning feature does not meet government standards.
*Backup camera does not meet government standards.

Hyundai Santa Fe

Specifications

Drive . . . . .FWD
Engine 3.3-liter V6
Transmission . . . . 6-sp. Automatic
Tow Rating (lbs.) Low-5000
Head/Leg Room (in.) Cramped-39.6/41.3
Interior Space (cu. ft.) . . . . .Very Roomy-146.6
Cargo Space (cu. ft.) Cramped-13.5
Wheelbase/Length (in.) 110.2/193.1

Hyundai Santa Fe Sport

Ratings—10 Best, 1 Worst

Combo Crash Tests	7
Safety Features	7
Rollover	3
Preventive Maintenance	4
Repair Costs	8
Warranty	10
Fuel Economy	3
Complaints	5
Insurance Costs	5
OVERALL RATING	**7**

Hyundai Santa Fe Sport

At-a-Glance

Status/Year Series Started. Unchanged/2014
Twins . . . . –
Body Styles . . . . SUV
Seating 5
Anti-Theft Device . Std. Pass. Immobil. & Active Alarm
Parking Index Rating . . . . Easy
Where Made. . . . . West Point, GA
Fuel Factor:. . . . .
  MPG Rating (city/hwy) . . . . Very Poor-20/27
  Driving Range (mi.) Short-394
  Fuel Type . . . . Regular
  Annual Fuel Cost . . . . .Average-$1424
  Gas Guzzler Tax . . . . .No
  Greenhouse Gas Emissions (tons/yr.) High-7.9
  Barrels of Oil Used per year High-14.3

How the Competition Rates

Competitors	Rating	Pg.
Kia Sorento	6	183
Mazda CX-5	3	200
Mitsubishi Outlander Sport	4	219

Price Range	Retail	Markup
Base 2.4L FWD	$25,350	4%
Base 2.4L AWD	$27,100	4%
Ultimate 2.0T Turbo FWD	$36,500	6%
Ultimate 2.0T Turbo AWD	$38,250	6%

Safety Checklist

Crash Tests:
  Frontal . . . . Good
  Side . . . . Average
Airbags:
  Torso . . .Standard Front Pelvis/Torso from Seat
  Roll Sensing. . . . . .Yes
  Knee Bolster . . . . Standard Driver
Crash Avoidance:
  Collision Avoidance . . . . . . Optional CIB & DBS
  Blind Spot Detection . . . . Optional
  Lane Keeping Assist . . . .Warning Only Optional
  Backup Camera . . . . .Standard*
  Pedestrian Crash Avoidance . . . . Optional
General:
  Auto. Crash Notification . . . Operator Assist.-Fee
  Day Running Lamps . . . . Standard
Safety Belt/Restraint:
  Dynamic Head Restraints . . . . None
  Adjustable Belt. . . . . .Standard Front

^Warning feature does not meet government standards.
*Backup camera does not meet government standards.

Hyundai Santa Fe Sport

Specifications

Drive. . . . . .FWD
Engine 2.4-liter I4
Transmission . . . . 6-sp. Automatic
Tow Rating (lbs.) . . . . .Very Low-2000
Head/Leg Room (in.) Cramped-39.6/41.3
Interior Space (cu. ft.). Roomy-108
Cargo Space (cu. ft.) . . . . Very Roomy-35.4
Wheelbase/Length (in.) 106.3/184.6

Ratings—10 Best, 1 Worst

Combo Crash Tests	9
Safety Features	7
Rollover	7
Preventive Maintenance	6
Repair Costs	9
Warranty	10
Fuel Economy	7
Complaints	5
Insurance Costs	3
OVERALL RATING	**10**

Hyundai Sonata

Hyundai Sonata

At-a-Glance

Status/Year Series Started Appearance Change/2015
Twins . . . .–
Body Styles . . . . .Sedan
Seating 5
Anti-Theft Device . Std. Pass. Immobil. & Active Alarm
Parking Index Rating . . . . Average
Where Made . . . . .Montgomery, AL
Fuel Factor: . . . .
  MPG Rating (city/hwy) Poor-25/37
  Driving Range (mi.) . . . . Very Long-542
  Fuel Type . . . . .Regular
  Annual Fuel Cost . . . . Low-$1102
  Gas Guzzler Tax . . . . .No
  Greenhouse Gas Emissions (tons/yr.) . . Average-6.2
  Barrels of Oil Used per year Average-11.4

How the Competition Rates

Competitors	Rating	Pg.
Mazda Mazda3	8	202
Toyota Camry	8	247
Volkswagen Passat	3	264

Price Range	Retail	Markup
SE 2.4L	$21,950	4%
Sport 2.4L	$23,400	5%
Sport 2.0L Turbo	$26,600	6%
Sedan Plug-in Hybrid	$34,600	5%

Safety Checklist

Crash Tests:
  Frontal . . . . Very Good
  Side . . . . Average
Airbags:
  Torso . . . Standard Front Pelvis/Torso from Seat
  Roll Sensing . . . . .Yes
  Knee Bolster . . . . Standard Driver
Crash Avoidance:
  Collision Avoidance . . . . . . Optional CIB & DBS
  Blind Spot Detection . . . . Optional
  Lane Keeping Assist . . . .Warning Only Optional
  Backup Camera . . . . Optional*
  Pedestrian Crash Avoidance . . . . Optional
General:
  Auto. Crash Notification . . . Operator Assist.-Fee
  Day Running Lamps . . . . Standard
Safety Belt/Restraint:
  Dynamic Head Restraints . . . . None
  Adjustable Belt . . . . .Standard Front

^Warning feature does not meet government standards.
*Backup camera does not meet government standards.

Hyundai Sonata

Specifications

Drive . . . . .FWD
Engine 2.4-liter I4
Transmission . . . . 6-sp. Automatic
Tow Rating (lbs.) . . . . .Very Low-0
Head/Leg Room (in.) . . . . Very Roomy-40.4/45.5
Interior Space (cu. ft.) Roomy-106.1
Cargo Space (cu. ft.) Cramped-16.3
Wheelbase/Length (in.) 110.4/191.1

Ratings—10 Best, 1 Worst

Combo Crash Tests	4
Safety Features	9
Rollover	3
Preventive Maintenance	4
Repair Costs	9
Warranty	10
Fuel Economy	5
Complaints	1
Insurance Costs	8
OVERALL RATING	**6**

Hyundai Tucson

Hyundai Tucson

At-a-Glance

Status/Year Series Started Unchanged/2016
Twins . . . . –
Body Styles . . . . SUV
Seating 5
Anti-Theft Device . Std. Pass. Immobil. & Active Alarm
Parking Index Rating . . . . .Very Easy
Where Made. . . . . Ulsan, South Korea
Fuel Factor:. . . . .
  MPG Rating (city/hwy) Poor-24/28
  Driving Range (mi.) Average-421
  Fuel Type . . . . .Regular
  Annual Fuel Cost . . . . Low-$1257
  Gas Guzzler Tax . . . . .No
  Greenhouse Gas Emissions (tons/yr.) Low-5.8
  Barrels of Oil Used per year Average-12.7

How the Competition Rates

Competitors	Rating	Pg.
Ford Escape	7	138
Honda HR-V	5	156
Toyota RAV4	6	254

Price Range

	Retail	Markup
SE FWD	$22,700	4%
SE AWD	$24,100	4%
Sport AWD	$27,300	5%
Limited AWD	$31,175	5%

Safety Checklist

Crash Tests:
  Frontal . . . . .Poor
  Side . . . . Average
Airbags:
  Torso . . . Standard Front Pelvis/Torso from Seat
  Roll Sensing. . . . . .Yes
  Knee Bolster . . . . None
Crash Avoidance:
  Collision Avoidance . . . . Optional CIB & DBS
  Blind Spot Detection . . . . Optional
  Lane Keeping Assist . . . .Warning Only Optional
  Backup Camera . . . . Standard
  Pedestrian Crash Avoidance . . . . Optional
General:
  Auto. Crash Notification . . . Operator Assist.-Fee
  Day Running Lamps . . . . Optional
Safety Belt/Restraint:
  Dynamic Head Restraints . . . . . .Standard Front
  Adjustable Belt. . . . . .Standard Front

^Warning feature does not meet government standards.
*Backup camera does not meet government standards.

Hyundai Tucson

Specifications

Drive. . . . . .FWD
Engine 2.0-liter I4
Transmission . . . . 6-sp. Automatic
Tow Rating (lbs.) . . . . –
Head/Leg Room (in.) Cramped-39.6/41.5
Interior Space (cu. ft.). Average-102.2
Cargo Space (cu. ft.) Roomy-31
Wheelbase/Length (in.) 105.1/176.2

Ratings—10 Best, 1 Worst	
Combo Crash Tests	4
Safety Features	3
Rollover	7
Preventive Maintenance	6
Repair Costs	9
Warranty	10
Fuel Economy	8
Complaints	2
Insurance Costs	1
OVERALL RATING	**5**

Hyundai Veloster

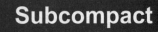

Hyundai Veloster

Hyundai Veloster

At-a-Glance

Status/Year Series Started Unchanged/2016
Twins . . . .–
Body Styles . . . . .Coupe
Seating 5
Anti-Theft Device . Std. Pass. Immobil. & Active Alarm
Parking Index Rating . . . . .Very Easy
Where Made. . . . . Ulsan, South Korea
Fuel Factor:. . . . .
  MPG Rating (city/hwy) Poor-28/36
  Driving Range (mi.) Average-411
  Fuel Type. . . . . .Regular
  Annual Fuel Cost . . . . .Very Low-$1037
  Gas Guzzler Tax . . . . .No
  Greenhouse Gas Emissions (tons/yr.)Very High-10.6
  Barrels of Oil Used per year . . . . Very Low-4.7

How the Competition Rates

Competitors	Rating	Pg.
Chevrolet Sonic	9	120
Mini Cooper	5	214
Toyota Yaris	5	259

Price Range	Retail	Markup
Base MT	$18,000	4%
Base AT	$19,100	4%
Turbo MT	$22,600	5%
Turbo AT	$23,800	5%

Safety Checklist

Crash Tests:
  Frontal . . . . .Poor
  Side . . . . .Poor
Airbags:
  Torso . . . Standard Front Pelvis/Torso from Seat
  Roll Sensing. . . . . .Yes
  Knee Bolster . . . . None
Crash Avoidance:
  Collision Avoidance . . . . None
  Blind Spot Detection . . . . None
  Lane Keeping Assist . . . . None
  Backup Camera . . . . .Standard*
  Pedestrian Crash Avoidance . . . . None
General:
  Auto. Crash Notification . . . Operator Assist.-Fee
  Day Running Lamps . . . . Standard
Safety Belt/Restraint:
  Dynamic Head Restraints . . . . . .Standard Front
  Adjustable Belt. None

^Warning feature does not meet government standards.
*Backup camera does not meet government standards.

Hyundai Veloster

Specifications

Drive. . . . . .FWD
Engine 1.6-liter I4
Transmission . . . . 6-dp. Automatic
Tow Rating (lbs.) . . . .–
Head/Leg Room (in.) Roomy-39/43.9
Interior Space (cu. ft.). . . . . Very Cramped-89.8
Cargo Space (cu. ft.) Cramped-15.5
Wheelbase/Length (in.) 104.3/166.1

Ratings—10 Best, 1 Worst

Combo Crash Tests	5
Safety Features	6
Rollover	8
Preventive Maintenance	6
Repair Costs	2
Warranty	8
Fuel Economy	4
Complaints	10
Insurance Costs	5
OVERALL RATING	**6**

Infiniti Q50

Infiniti Q50

At-a-Glance

Status/Year Series Started Appearance Change/2014
Twins . . . . –
Body Styles . . . . .Sedan
Seating 5
Anti-Theft Device . . . . . . Std. Pass. Immobil. & Alarm
Parking Index Rating . . . . Average
Where Made . . . . Tochigi, Japan
Fuel Factor: . . . .
  MPG Rating (city/hwy) . . . . .Very Poor-20/29
  Driving Range (mi.) Long-465
  Fuel Type . . . . .Premium
  Annual Fuel Cost . . . . .High-$1729
  Gas Guzzler Tax . . . . .No
  Greenhouse Gas Emissions (tons/yr.) High-7.8
  Barrels of Oil Used per year High-14.3

How the Competition Rates

Competitors	Rating	Pg.
BMW 3 Series	7	93
Lexus IS	6	193
Lincoln MKZ	5	199

Price Range

	Retail	Markup
Base RWD	$33,950	8%
Premium RWD	$37,650	8%
Sport AWD	$45,900	8%
Hybrid Premium AWD	$49,050	8%

Safety Checklist

Crash Tests:
  Frontal . . . . .Very Poor
  Side . . . . Very Good
Airbags:
  Torso Std. Fr. & Opt. Rr. Pelvis/Torso from Seat
  Roll Sensing . . . . .Yes
  Knee Bolster . . . . None
Crash Avoidance:
  Collision Avoidance . . . . . . Optional CIB & DBS
  Blind Spot Detection . . . . Optional
  Lane Keeping Assist . . . .Warning Only Optional
  Backup Camera . . . . .Standard*
  Pedestrian Crash Avoidance . . . . None
General:
  Auto. Crash Notification . . . Operator Assist.-Fee
  Day Running Lamps . . . . Standard
Safety Belt/Restraint:
  Dynamic Head Restraints . . . . None
  Adjustable Belt . . . . .Standard Front

^Warning feature does not meet government standards.
*Backup camera does not meet government standards.

Infiniti Q50

Specifications

Drive . . . . .RWD
Engine 3.7-liter V6
Transmission . . . . 7-sp. Automatic
Tow Rating (lbs.) . . . . –
Head/Leg Room (in.) . . . . Very Roomy-39.5/44.5
Interior Space (cu. ft.) Average-100
Cargo Space (cu. ft.) Cramped-13.5
Wheelbase/Length (in.) 112.2/188.3

Ratings—10 Best, 1 Worst

Combo Crash Tests	—
Safety Features	7
Rollover	5
Preventive Maintenance	8
Repair Costs	2
Warranty	8
Fuel Economy	2
Complaints	3
Insurance Costs	5
OVERALL RATING	**—**

Infiniti Q70

Infiniti Q70

At-a-Glance

Status/Year Series Started. Unchanged/2011
Twins . . . .—
Body Styles . . . . .Sedan
Seating. 5
Anti-Theft Device . . . . . . Std. Pass. Immobil. & Alarm
Parking Index Rating . . . . Hard
Where Made. . . . . Tochigi, Japan
Fuel Factor:. . . . .
  MPG Rating (city/hwy) . . . . .Very Poor-18/24
  Driving Range (mi.) Average-406
  Fuel Type. . . . . .Premium
  Annual Fuel Cost . . . . Very High-$1982
  Gas Guzzler Tax . . . . .No
  Greenhouse Gas Emissions (tons/yr.). High-9.0
  Barrels of Oil Used per year High-16.5

How the Competition Rates

Competitors	Rating	Pg.
Audi A6	6	88
BMW 5 Series	6	95
Lexus ES	7	190

Price Range	Retail	Markup
3.7L	$49,850	8%
3.7L AWD	$52,000	8%
Hybrid	$55,900	8%
5.6L AWD	$65,350	8%

Safety Checklist

Crash Tests:
  Frontal . . . .—
  Side . . . .—
Airbags:
  Torso . . . Standard Front Pelvis/Torso from Seat
  Roll Sensing. . . . . .Yes
  Knee Bolster . . . . None
Crash Avoidance:
  Collision Avoidance . . . . . . Optional CIB & DBS
  Blind Spot Detection . . . . Optional
  Lane Keeping Assist . . . .Warning Only Optional
  Backup Camera . . . . .Standard*
  Pedestrian Crash Avoidance . . . . None
General:
  Auto. Crash Notification . . . Operator Assist.-Fee
  Day Running Lamps . . . . Standard
Safety Belt/Restraint:
  Dynamic Head Restraints . . . . . .Standard Front
  Adjustable Belt. . . . . .Standard Front

^Warning feature does not meet government standards.
*Backup camera does not meet government standards.

Infiniti Q70

Specifications

Drive. . . . . .AWD
Engine 3.7-liter V6
Transmission . . . . 7-sp. Automatic
Tow Rating (lbs.) . . . .—
Head/Leg Room (in.) Roomy-39.1/44.4
Interior Space (cu. ft.). Average-103.6
Cargo Space (cu. ft.) Cramped-14.9
Wheelbase/Length (in.) 114.2/196.1

Ratings—10 Best, 1 Worst

Combo Crash Tests	—
Safety Features	4
Rollover	4
Preventive Maintenance	9
Repair Costs	1
Warranty	8
Fuel Economy	2
Complaints	1
Insurance Costs	8
OVERALL RATING	**—**

Infiniti QX50

Infiniti QX50

At-a-Glance

Status/Year Series Started	Unchanged/2008
Twins	—
Body Styles	SUV
Seating	5
Anti-Theft Device	Std. Pass. Immobil. & Alarm
Parking Index Rating	Average
Where Made	Tochigi, Japan
Fuel Factor:	
MPG Rating (city/hwy)	Very Poor-17/24
Driving Range (mi.)	Short-391
Fuel Type	Premium
Annual Fuel Cost	Very High-$2054
Gas Guzzler Tax	No
Greenhouse Gas Emissions (tons/yr.)	High-7.4
Barrels of Oil Used per year	High-16.5

How the Competition Rates

Competitors	Rating	Pg.
Buick Encore	10	104
Lincoln MKC	5	198
Mazda CX-5	3	200

Price Range

Price Range	Retail	Markup
RWD	$34,450	8%
AWD	$35,850	8%

Infiniti QX50

Safety Checklist

Crash Tests:
Frontal . . . . –
Side . . . . –
Airbags:
Torso . . . Standard Front Pelvis/Torso from Seat
Roll Sensing . . . . No
Knee Bolster . . . . None
Crash Avoidance:
Collision Avoidance . . . . Optional CIB
Blind Spot Detection . . . . Optional
Lane Keeping Assist . . . .Warning Only Optional
Backup Camera . . . . .Standard*
Pedestrian Crash Avoidance . . . . None
General:
Auto. Crash Notification . . . Operator Assist.-Fee
Day Running Lamps . . . . Standard
Safety Belt/Restraint:
Dynamic Head Restraints . . . . . .Standard Front
Adjustable Belt . . . . .Standard Front

^Warning feature does not meet government standards.
*Backup camera does not meet government standards.

Specifications

Drive	RWD
Engine	3.7-liter V6
Transmission	7-sp. Automatic
Tow Rating (lbs.)	—
Head/Leg Room (in.)	Roomy-38.7/44.3
Interior Space (cu. ft.)	Roomy-115.4
Cargo Space (cu. ft.)	Average-18.6
Wheelbase/Length (in.)	113.4/186.8

Ratings—10 Best, 1 Worst

Combo Crash Tests	6
Safety Features	7
Rollover	2
Preventive Maintenance	1
Repair Costs	1
Warranty	8
Fuel Economy	3
Complaints	3
Insurance Costs	8
OVERALL RATING	**3**

Infiniti QX60

Infiniti QX60

At-a-Glance

Status/Year Series Started	Appearance Change/2013
Twins	–
Body Styles	SUV
Seating	7
Anti-Theft Device	Std. Pass. Immobil. & Alarm
Parking Index Rating	Hard
Where Made	Smyrna, TN

Fuel Factor:

MPG Rating (city/hwy)	Very Poor-19/26
Driving Range (mi.)	Average-422
Fuel Type	Premium
Annual Fuel Cost	Very High-$1859
Gas Guzzler Tax	No
Greenhouse Gas Emissions (tons/yr.)	High-8.2
Barrels of Oil Used per year	High-15.0

How the Competition Rates

Competitors	Rating	Pg.
Acura MDX	8	82
Cadillac XT5	5	110
Lexus RX	5	196

Price Range	Retail	Markup
Base FWD	$42,600	8%
Base FWD	$44,400	8%
Hybrid FWD	$52,050	8%
Hybrid AWD	$53,450	8%

Safety Checklist

Crash Tests:

Frontal	Average
Side	Average

Airbags:

Torso	Standard Front Pelvis/Torso from Seat
Roll Sensing	Yes
Knee Bolster	None

Crash Avoidance:

Collision Avoidance	Optional CIB & DBS
Blind Spot Detection	Optional
Lane Keeping Assist	Warning Only Optional
Backup Camera	Standard*
Pedestrian Crash Avoidance	Optional

General:

Auto. Crash Notification	Operator Assist.-Fee
Day Running Lamps	Standard

Safety Belt/Restraint:

Dynamic Head Restraints	Standard Front
Adjustable Belt	Standard Front & Rear

^Warning feature does not meet government standards.
*Backup camera does not meet government standards.

Infiniti QX60

Specifications

Drive	AWD
Engine	3.5-liter V6
Transmission	7-sp. Automatic
Tow Rating (lbs.)	Low-5000
Head/Leg Room (in.)	Roomy-40.7/42.3
Interior Space (cu. ft.)	Very Roomy-149.8
Cargo Space (cu. ft.)	Cramped-15.8
Wheelbase/Length (in.)	114.2/196.4

Ratings—10 Best, 1 Worst

Combo Crash Tests	—
Safety Features	8
Rollover	2
Preventive Maintenance	3
Repair Costs	3
Warranty	8
Fuel Economy	1
Complaints	6
Insurance Costs	8

OVERALL RATING — —

Infiniti QX80

Infiniti QX80

Infiniti QX80

At-a-Glance

Status/Year Series Started. Unchanged/2011
Twins . . . . —
Body Styles . . . . SUV
Seating. 7/8
Anti-Theft Device . . . . . . Std. Pass. Immobil. & Alarm
Parking Index Rating . . . . Very Hard
Where Made. Kyushu, Japan
Fuel Factor:. . . . .
  MPG Rating (city/hwy) . . . . .Very Poor-14/20
  Driving Range (mi.) Average-421
  Fuel Type. . . . . .Premium
  Annual Fuel Cost . . . . Very High-$2484
  Gas Guzzler Tax . . . . .No
  Greenhouse Gas Emissions (tons/yr.)Very High-11.2
  Barrels of Oil Used per year . . . . Very High-20.6

How the Competition Rates

Competitors	Rating	Pg.
Buick Enclave	6	103
Chevrolet Suburban	4	122
Ford Expedition	7	139

Price Range

	Retail	Markup
Base RWD	$63,250	8%
Base AWD	$66,350	8%
Limited AWD	$88,850	8%

Safety Checklist

Crash Tests:
  Frontal . . . .—
  Side . . . .—
Airbags:
  Torso . . . Standard Front Pelvis/Torso from Seat
  Roll Sensing. . . . . .Yes
  Knee Bolster . . . . None
Crash Avoidance:
  Collision Avoidance . . . . . . Optional CIB & DBS
  Blind Spot Detection . . . . Optional
  Lane Keeping Assist . . . .Warning Only Optional
  Backup Camera. . . . . .Standard*
  Pedestrian Crash Avoidance . . . . Optional
General:
  Auto. Crash Notification . . . Operator Assist.-Fee
  Day Running Lamps . . . . Standard
Safety Belt/Restraint:
  Dynamic Head Restraints . . . . . .Standard Front
  Adjustable Belt. . . . . Standard Front & Rear

^Warning feature does not meet government standards.
*Backup camera does not meet government standards.

Infiniti QX80

Specifications

Drive. . . . . .AWD
Engine 5.6-liter V8
Transmission . . . . 7-sp. Automatic
Tow Rating (lbs.) . . . . Very High-8500
Head/Leg Room (in.) . . . . Very Cramped-39.9/39.6
Interior Space (cu. ft.). . . . . Very Roomy-151.3
Cargo Space (cu. ft.) Cramped-16.6
Wheelbase/Length (in.) 121.1/208.9

Ratings—10 Best, 1 Worst

Combo Crash Tests	5
Safety Features	7
Rollover	2
Preventive Maintenance	10
Repair Costs	6
Warranty	3
Fuel Economy	4
Complaints	1
Insurance Costs	8
OVERALL RATING	**5**

Jeep Cherokee

Jeep Cherokee

Jeep Cherokee

At-a-Glance

Status/Year Series Started Appearance Change/2014
Twins . . . . –
Body Styles . . . . SUV
Seating 5
Anti-Theft Device .Std. Pass. Immobil. & Opt. Pass. Alarm
Parking Index Rating . . . . Average
Where Made. . . . . Toldeo, OH
Fuel Factor:. . . . .
  MPG Rating (city/hwy) . . . . Very Poor-21/28
  Driving Range (mi.) . . . . Very Short-376
  Fuel Type. . . . . Regular
  Annual Fuel Cost . . . . Average-$1363
  Gas Guzzler Tax . . . . No
  Greenhouse Gas Emissions (tons/yr.) High-7.5
  Barrels of Oil Used per year High-13.7

How the Competition Rates

Competitors	Rating	Pg.
Ford Escape	7	138
Mazda CX-5	3	200
Toyota RAV4	6	254

Price Range

Price Range	Retail	Markup
Sport FWD	$23,595	1%
Latitude FWD	$25,545	2%
Trailhawk 4WD	$31,195	2%
Limited 4WD	$31,495	2%

Safety Checklist

Crash Tests:
  Frontal . . . . Very Poor
  Side . . . . Very Good
Airbags:
  Torso Std. Fr. & Opt. Rr. Pelvis/Torso from Seat
  Roll Sensing. . . . . Yes
  Knee Bolster . . . . Standard Front
Crash Avoidance:
  Collision Avoidance . . . . . . Optional CIB & DBS
  Blind Spot Detection . . . . Optional
  Lane Keeping Assist . . . . Optional^
  Backup Camera . . . . Optional
  Pedestrian Crash Avoidance . . . . None
General:
  Auto. Crash Notification . . . . None
  Day Running Lamps . . . . Standard
Safety Belt/Restraint:
  Dynamic Head Restraints . . . . None
  Adjustable Belt . . . . Standard Front

^Warning feature does not meet government standards.
*Backup camera does not meet government standards.

Jeep Cherokee

Specifications

Drive. . . . . AWD
Engine 2.4-liter I4
Transmission . . . . 9-sp. Automatic
Tow Rating (lbs.) . . . . Very Low-2000
Head/Leg Room (in.) Cramped-39.4/41.1
Interior Space (cu. ft.). Average-103.4
Cargo Space (cu. ft.) Roomy-24.6
Wheelbase/Length (in.) 106.3/182

Ratings—10 Best, 1 Worst

Combo Crash Tests	1
Safety Features	3
Rollover	2
Preventive Maintenance	10
Repair Costs	8
Warranty	3
Fuel Economy	2
Complaints	4
Insurance Costs	8
OVERALL RATING	**3**

Jeep Compass

Jeep Compass

At-a-Glance

Status/Year Series Started........ Unchanged/2007
Twins . . . . –
Body Styles . . . . SUV
Seating 5
Anti-Theft Device .Std. Pass. Immobil. & Opt. Pass. Alarm
Parking Index Rating . . . . Easy
Where Made. Toluca, Mexico
Fuel Factor:. . . . .
  MPG Rating (city/hwy) . . . . . .Very Poor-20/23
  Driving Range (mi.) . . . . .Very Short-287
  Fuel Type. . . . . .Regular
  Annual Fuel Cost . . . . .High-$1518
  Gas Guzzler Tax . . . . .No
  Greenhouse Gas Emissions (tons/yr.). High-8.6
  Barrels of Oil Used per year High-15.7

How the Competition Rates

Competitors	Rating	Pg.
Acura RDX	9	83
Ford Escape	7	138
Honda HR-V	5	156

Price Range

	Retail	Markup
Sport FWD	$19,795	1%
Sport AWD	$21,795	1%
Latitude FWD	$24,195	2%
Latitude 4WD	$26,195	2%

Jeep Compass

Safety Checklist

Crash Tests:
  Frontal . . . . .Very Poor
  Side . . . . .Very Poor
Airbags:
  Torso . . .Standard Front Pelvis/Torso from Seat
  Roll Sensing. . . . . .Yes
  Knee Bolster . . . . None
Crash Avoidance:
  Collision Avoidance . . . . None
  Blind Spot Detection . . . . None
  Lane Keeping Assist . . . . None
  Backup Camera . . . . Optional*
  Pedestrian Crash Avoidance . . . . None
General:
  Auto. Crash Notification . . . . None
  Day Running Lamps . . . . Optional
Safety Belt/Restraint:
  Dynamic Head Restraints . . . . . .Standard Front
  Adjustable Belt. . . . . .Standard Front

^Warning feature does not meet government standards.
*Backup camera does not meet government standards.

Jeep Compass

Specifications

Drive. 4WD
Engine 2.4-liter I4
Transmission . . . . CVT
Tow Rating (lbs.) . . . . .Very Low-2000
Head/Leg Room (in.) Cramped-40.7/40.6
Interior Space (cu. ft.). Average-101.3
Cargo Space (cu. ft.) Average-22.7
Wheelbase/Length (in.) 103.7/175.1

Ratings—10 Best, 1 Worst

Combo Crash Tests	6
Safety Features	8
Rollover	1
Preventive Maintenance	8
Repair Costs	6
Warranty	3
Fuel Economy	1
Complaints	1
Insurance Costs	8
OVERALL RATING	**4**

Jeep Grand Cherokee

Jeep Grand Cherokee

At-a-Glance

Status/Year Series Started........ Unchanged/2011
Twins .... –
Body Styles .... SUV
Seating 5
Anti-Theft Device .Std. Pass. Immobil. & Opt. Pass. Alarm
Parking Index Rating .... Average
Where Made........................ .Detroit, MI
Fuel Factor:..............................
  MPG Rating (city/hwy) .... Very Poor-14/20
  Driving Range (mi.) Short-398
  Fuel Type............................ .Regular
  Annual Fuel Cost .... Very High-$1993
  Gas Guzzler Tax ....No
  Greenhouse Gas Emissions (tons/yr.)Very High-11.3
  Barrels of Oil Used per year .... Very High-20.6

How the Competition Rates

Competitors	Rating	Pg.
Chevrolet Equinox	2	116
Ford Explorer	3	140
Honda Pilot	8	158

Price Range

	Retail	Markup
Laredo RWD	$30,295	1%
Limited RWD	$37,895	3%
Trailhawk 4WD	$42,995	4%
Overland 4WD	$47,695	4%

Safety Checklist

Crash Tests:
  Frontal .... Good
  Side .... .Poor
Airbags:
  Torso . . . Standard Front Pelvis/Torso from Seat
  Roll Sensing........................ .Yes
  Knee Bolster .... Standard Driver
Crash Avoidance:
  Collision Avoidance ...... Optional CIB & DBS
  Blind Spot Detection .... Optional
  Lane Keeping Assist .... Optional^
  Backup Camera .... Optional
  Pedestrian Crash Avoidance .... None
General:
  Auto. Crash Notification .... None
  Day Running Lamps .... Standard
Safety Belt/Restraint:
  Dynamic Head Restraints ......Standard Front
  Adjustable Belt...............Standard Front

^Warning feature does not meet government standards.
*Backup camera does not meet government standards.

Jeep Grand Cherokee

Specifications

Drive.. .4WD
Engine 5.7-liter V8
Transmission .... 8-sp. Automatic
Tow Rating (lbs.) Average-7200
Head/Leg Room (in.) Cramped-39.9/40.3
Interior Space (cu. ft.)................ Roomy-103.9
Cargo Space (cu. ft.) .... Very Roomy-36.3
Wheelbase/Length (in.) 114.8/189.8

Ratings—10 Best, 1 Worst

Combo Crash Tests	1
Safety Features	3
Rollover	1
Preventive Maintenance	10
Repair Costs	10
Warranty	3
Fuel Economy	2
Complaints	3
Insurance Costs	5
OVERALL RATING	**2**

Jeep Patriot

Jeep Patriot

At-a-Glance

Status/Year Series Started Unchanged/2007
Twins . . . . –
Body Styles . . . . SUV
Seating 5
Anti-Theft Device .Std. Pass. Immobil. & Opt. Pass. Alarm
Parking Index Rating . . . . Easy
Where Made . . . . Belvedere, IL
Fuel Factor:
  MPG Rating (city/hwy) . . . . .Very Poor-20/23
  Driving Range (mi.) . . . . .Very Short-287
  Fuel Type . . . . .Regular
  Annual Fuel Cost . . . . .High-$1518
  Gas Guzzler Tax . . . . .No
  Greenhouse Gas Emissions (tons/yr.) High-8.6
  Barrels of Oil Used per year High-15.7

How the Competition Rates

Competitors	Rating	Pg.
Ford Escape	7	138
Mitsubishi Outlander Sport	4	219
Toyota RAV4	6	254

Price Range	Retail	Markup
Sport FWD	$17,895	1%
Sport AWD	$19,895	1%
Latitude FWD	$22,395	2%
Latitude 4WD	$25,695	3%

Safety Checklist

Crash Tests:
  Frontal . . . . .Very Poor
  Side . . . . .Very Poor
Airbags:
  Torso . . .Standard Front Pelvis/Torso from Seat
  Roll Sensing. . . . . .Yes
  Knee Bolster . . . . None
Crash Avoidance:
  Collision Avoidance . . . . None
  Blind Spot Detection . . . . None
  Lane Keeping Assist . . . . None
  Backup Camera . . . . Optional
  Pedestrian Crash Avoidance . . . . None
General:
  Auto. Crash Notification . . . . None
  Day Running Lamps . . . . None
Safety Belt/Restraint:
  Dynamic Head Restraints . . . . None
  Adjustable Belt . . . . .Standard Front

^Warning feature does not meet government standards.
*Backup camera does not meet government standards.

Jeep Patriot

Specifications

Drive 4WD
Engine 2.4-liter I4
Transmission . . . . CVT
Tow Rating (lbs.) . . . . .Very Low-2000
Head/Leg Room (in.) Cramped-41/40.6
Interior Space (cu. ft.) Roomy-104.4
Cargo Space (cu. ft.) Average-23
Wheelbase/Length (in.) 103.7/173.8

Jeep Renegade   Small SUV

Ratings—10 Best, 1 Worst

Combo Crash Tests	3
Safety Features	5
Rollover	2
Preventive Maintenance	2
Repair Costs	10
Warranty	3
Fuel Economy	4
Complaints	1
Insurance Costs	5
OVERALL RATING	**2**

Jeep Renegade

At-a-Glance

Status/Year Series Started Appearance Change/2015
Twins . . . . –
Body Styles . . . . SUV
Seating 5
Anti-Theft Device . . . . . . Std. Pass. Immobil. & Alarm
Parking Index Rating . . . . Easy
Where Made . . . . Melfi, Italy
Fuel Factor: . . . .
  MPG Rating (city/hwy) . . . . Very Poor-21/29
  Driving Range (mi.) . . . . Very Short-304
  Fuel Type . . . . Premium
  Annual Fuel Cost . . . . High-$1677
  Gas Guzzler Tax . . . . No
  Greenhouse Gas Emissions (tons/yr.) . . Average-6.1
  Barrels of Oil Used per year . . . . Very Low-0.0

How the Competition Rates

Competitors	Rating	Pg.
Chevrolet Traverse	6	124
Ford Edge	8	137
Nissan Juke	2	224

Price Range

	Retail	Markup
Sport FWD	$17,995	1%
Latitude FWD	$21,495	2%
Trailhawk 4WD	$26,645	2%
Limited 4WD	$27,195	2%

Jeep Renegade

Safety Checklist

Crash Tests:
  Frontal . . . . Poor
  Side . . . . Very Poor
Airbags:
  Torso . . . Standard Front Pelvis/Torso from Seat
  Roll Sensing . . . . Yes
  Knee Bolster . . . . Standard Driver
Crash Avoidance:
  Collision Avoidance . . . . . . Optional CIB & DBS^
  Blind Spot Detection . . . . Optional
  Lane Keeping Assist . . . . Optional^
  Backup Camera . . . . Optional*
  Pedestrian Crash Avoidance . . . . None
General:
  Auto. Crash Notification . . . . None
  Day Running Lamps . . . . Optional
Safety Belt/Restraint:
  Dynamic Head Restraints . . . . None
  Adjustable Belt . . . . Standard Front

^Warning feature does not meet government standards.
*Backup camera does not meet government standards.

Jeep Renegade

Specifications

Drive . . . . FWD
Engine 1.4-liter I4
Transmission . . . . 6-sp. Automatic
Tow Rating (lbs.) . . . . Very Low-2000
Head/Leg Room (in.) Roomy-41.1/41.2
Interior Space (cu. ft.) Average-100.1
Cargo Space (cu. ft.) . . . . Very Roomy-50.8
Wheelbase/Length (in.) 101.2/166.6

Ratings—10 Best, 1 Worst

Combo Crash Tests	—
Safety Features	1
Rollover	1
Preventive Maintenance	10
Repair Costs	9
Warranty	3
Fuel Economy	1
Complaints	1
Insurance Costs	5

OVERALL RATING — —

Jeep Wrangler

At-a-Glance

Status/Year Series Started Unchanged/2007
Twins . . . . —
Body Styles . . . . SUV
Seating 4
Anti-Theft Device .Std. Pass. Immobil. & Opt. Pass. Alarm
Parking Index Rating . . . . .Very Easy
Where Made. .Toledo, OH
Fuel Factor:. . . . .
  MPG Rating (city/hwy) . . . . .Very Poor-17/21
  Driving Range (mi.) . . . . .Very Short-346
  Fuel Type. . . . . .Regular
  Annual Fuel Cost . . . . .High-$1734
  Gas Guzzler Tax . . . . .No
  Greenhouse Gas Emissions (tons/yr.)Very High-10.0
  Barrels of Oil Used per year . . . . . . .Very High-18.3

How the Competition Rates

Competitors	Rating	Pg.
Mazda CX-5	3	200
Mitsubishi Outlander Sport	4	219
Subaru Forester	4	237

Price Range

	Retail	Markup
Sport	$23,995	1%
Rubicon	$33,645	5%
Unlimited Sahara	$34,245	5%
Unlimited Rubicon	$37,445	5%

Jeep Wrangler

Safety Checklist

Crash Tests:
  Frontal . . . . –
  Side . . . . –
Airbags:
  Torso . . . . None
  Roll Sensing. . . . . No
  Knee Bolster . . . . None
Crash Avoidance:
  Collision Avoidance . . . . None
  Blind Spot Detection . . . . None
  Lane Keeping Assist . . . . None
  Backup Camera . . . . None
  Pedestrian Crash Avoidance . . . . None
General:
  Auto. Crash Notification . . . . None
  Day Running Lamps . . . . None
Safety Belt/Restraint:
  Dynamic Head Restraints . . . . None
  Adjustable Belt. . . . . .Standard Front

^Warning feature does not meet government standards.
*Backup camera does not meet government standards.

Jeep Wrangler

Specifications

Drive. 4WD
Engine 3.6-liter V6
Transmission . . . . 5-sp. Automatic
Tow Rating (lbs.) . . . . .Very Low-2000
Head/Leg Room (in.) Roomy-41.3/41
Interior Space (cu. ft.). . . . . Very Cramped-88.4
Cargo Space (cu. ft.) . . . . Very Cramped-12.8
Wheelbase/Length (in.) 95.4/152.8

Ratings—10 Best, 1 Worst

Combo Crash Tests	—
Safety Features	9
Rollover	6
Preventive Maintenance	4
Repair Costs	10
Warranty	10
Fuel Economy	3
Complaints	—
Insurance Costs	5
OVERALL RATING	**—**

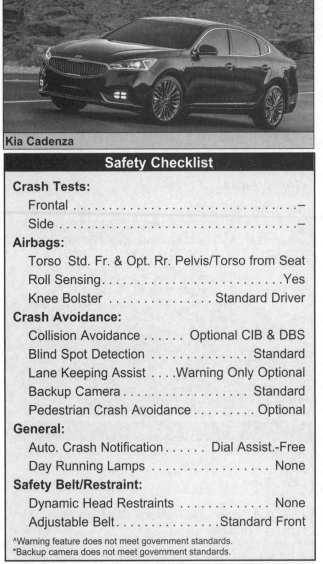
Kia Cadenza

Kia Cadenza

At-a-Glance

Status/Year Series Started . . . . All New/2017
Twins . . . .—
Body Styles . . . . .Sedan
Seating 5
Anti-Theft Device . Std. Pass. Immobil. & Active Alarm
Parking Index Rating . . . . Hard
Where Made. . . . . Hwasung, South Korea
Fuel Factor:. . . . .
  MPG Rating (city/hwy) . . . . .Very Poor-20/28
  Driving Range (mi.) Average-425
  Fuel Type . . . . .Regular
  Annual Fuel Cost . . . . .Average-$1405
  Gas Guzzler Tax . . . . .No
  Greenhouse Gas Emissions (tons/yr.) . . Average-6.3
  Barrels of Oil Used per year High-14.3

How the Competition Rates

Competitors	Rating	Pg.
Acura TLX	9	84
Honda Accord	9	152
Lexus ES	7	190

Price Range

Price Range	Retail	Markup
Base	$32,990	5%
Premium	$35,990	7%
Limited	$44,090	8%

Safety Checklist

Crash Tests:
  Frontal . . . .—
  Side . . . .—
Airbags:
  Torso Std. Fr. & Opt. Rr. Pelvis/Torso from Seat
  Roll Sensing. . . . . .Yes
  Knee Bolster . . . . Standard Driver
Crash Avoidance:
  Collision Avoidance . . . . . . Optional CIB & DBS
  Blind Spot Detection . . . . Standard
  Lane Keeping Assist . . . .Warning Only Optional
  Backup Camera . . . . Standard
  Pedestrian Crash Avoidance . . . . Optional
General:
  Auto. Crash Notification . . . . . . Dial Assist.-Free
  Day Running Lamps . . . . None
Safety Belt/Restraint:
  Dynamic Head Restraints . . . . None
  Adjustable Belt . . . . .Standard Front

^Warning feature does not meet government standards.
*Backup camera does not meet government standards.

Kia Cadenza

Specifications

Drive. . . . . .FWD
Engine 3.3-liter V6
Transmission . . . . 5-sp. Automatic
Tow Rating (lbs.) . . . .—
Head/Leg Room (in.) . . . . Very Roomy-40.2/45.5
Interior Space (cu. ft.). Roomy-107.8
Cargo Space (cu. ft.) Cramped-16
Wheelbase/Length (in.) 112.4/195.7

Ratings—10 Best, 1 Worst

Combo Crash Tests	3
Safety Features	3
Rollover	7
Preventive Maintenance	9
Repair Costs	10
Warranty	10
Fuel Economy	7
Complaints	3
Insurance Costs	1
OVERALL RATING	**6**

Kia Forte

Kia Forte

At-a-Glance

Status/Year Series Started Appearance Change/2014
Twins . . . . —
Body Styles . . . . Sedan, Hatchback
Seating 5
Anti-Theft Device . Std. Pass. Immobil. & Active Alarm
Parking Index Rating . . . . Easy
Where Made. . . . . Pesquería, Mexico
Fuel Factor:. . . . .
  MPG Rating (city/hwy) Poor-25/36
  Driving Range (mi.) Short-383
  Fuel Type . . . . Regular
  Annual Fuel Cost . . . . Low-$1113
  Gas Guzzler Tax . . . . No
  Greenhouse Gas Emissions (tons/yr.) . . Average-6.2
  Barrels of Oil Used per year Average-11.4

How the Competition Rates

Competitors	Rating	Pg.
Ford Focus	6	144
Honda Civic	8	153
Toyota Corolla	8	248

Price Range

Price Range	Retail	Markup
LX Sedan MT	$16,490	2%
LX Sedan AT	$17,500	4%
S Sedan	$19,200	5%
EX Hatchback AT	$21,200	6%

Safety Checklist

Crash Tests:
  Frontal . . . . Poor
  Side . . . . Poor
Airbags:
  Torso . . . Standard Front Pelvis/Torso from Seat
  Roll Sensing. . . . . Yes
  Knee Bolster . . . . None
Crash Avoidance:
  Collision Avoidance . . . . None
  Blind Spot Detection . . . . Optional
  Lane Keeping Assist . . . Warning Only Optional^
  Backup Camera . . . . Optional*
  Pedestrian Crash Avoidance . . . . Optional
General:
  Auto. Crash Notification . . . . . . Dial Assist.-Free
  Day Running Lamps . . . . None
Safety Belt/Restraint:
  Dynamic Head Restraints . . . . None
  Adjustable Belt . . . . Standard Front

^Warning feature does not meet government standards.
*Backup camera does not meet government standards.

Kia Forte

Specifications

Drive. . . . . FWD
Engine 2.0-liter I4
Transmission . . . . 6-sp. Automatic
Tow Rating (lbs.) . . . . —
Head/Leg Room (in.) Cramped-39.1/42.2
Interior Space (cu. ft.). Cramped-96.2
Cargo Space (cu. ft.) Cramped-14.9
Wheelbase/Length (in.) 106.3/179.5

Ratings—10 Best, 1 Worst

Combo Crash Tests	7
Safety Features	8
Rollover	8
Preventive Maintenance	6
Repair Costs	10
Warranty	10
Fuel Economy	6
Complaints	7
Insurance Costs	1
OVERALL RATING	**9**

Kia Optima

Kia Optima

At-a-Glance

Status/Year Series Started........ Unchanged/2011
Twins .... –
Body Styles .... Sedan
Seating.................................... 5
Anti-Theft Device . Std. Pass. Immobil. & Active Alarm
Parking Index Rating .... Easy
Where Made.................... West Point, GA
Fuel Factor:..............................
  MPG Rating (city/hwy)........... Poor-23/34
  Driving Range (mi.) .... Very Long-498
  Fuel Type............................Regular
  Annual Fuel Cost .... Low-$1198
  Gas Guzzler Tax ....No
  Greenhouse Gas Emissions (tons/yr.).. Average-6.7
  Barrels of Oil Used per year Average-12.2

How the Competition Rates

Competitors	Rating	Pg.
Honda Accord	9	152
Nissan Altima	5	221
Toyota Camry	8	247

Price Range	Retail	Markup
LX	$22,140	3%
Hybrid	$25,995	7%
EX Hybrid	$32,195	8%
SXL Turbo	$36,040	8%

Safety Checklist

Crash Tests:
  Frontal .... Good
  Side .... Poor
Airbags:
  Torso . . . Standard Front Pelvis/Torso from Seat
  Roll Sensing.........................Yes
  Knee Bolster .... Standard Driver
Crash Avoidance:
  Collision Avoidance ...... Optional CIB & DBS
  Blind Spot Detection .... Optional
  Lane Keeping Assist ....Warning Only Optional
  Backup Camera.................... Standard
  Pedestrian Crash Avoidance .... Optional
General:
  Auto. Crash Notification ...... Dial Assist.-Free
  Day Running Lamps .... Optional
Safety Belt/Restraint:
  Dynamic Head Restraints .... None
  Adjustable Belt................Standard Front

^Warning feature does not meet government standards.
*Backup camera does not meet government standards.

Kia Optima

Specifications

Drive...................................FWD
Engine 2.4-liter I4
Transmission .... 6-sp. Automatic
Tow Rating (lbs.) .... –
Head/Leg Room (in.) .... Very Roomy-40/45.5
Interior Space (cu. ft.)........... Roomy-117.6
Cargo Space (cu. ft.) Cramped-15.4
Wheelbase/Length (in.) 110/190.7

Ratings—10 Best, 1 Worst

Combo Crash Tests	2
Safety Features	1
Rollover	3
Preventive Maintenance	7
Repair Costs	10
Warranty	10
Fuel Economy	8
Complaints	8
Insurance Costs	1
OVERALL RATING	**5**

Kia Rio

Kia Rio

At-a-Glance

Status/Year Series Started. Unchanged/2012
Twins . . . . –
Body Styles . . . . Sedan, Hatchback
Seating 5
Anti-Theft Device . Std. Pass. Immobil. & Active Alarm
Parking Index Rating . . . . .Very Easy
Where Made. . . . . .Gwanmyeong, South Korea
Fuel Factor:. . . . .
  MPG Rating (city/hwy) Poor-27/37
  Driving Range (mi.) . . . . .Very Short-350
  Fuel Type . . . . .Regular
  Annual Fuel Cost . . . . .Very Low-$1049
  Gas Guzzler Tax . . . . .No
  Greenhouse Gas Emissions (tons/yr.) Low-5.8
  Barrels of Oil Used per year Average-10.6

How the Competition Rates

Competitors	Rating	Pg.
Chevrolet Sonic	9	120
Ford Focus	6	144
Nissan Versa	2	233

Price Range

Price Range	Retail	Markup
LX Sedan MT	$14,165	2%
LX Hatchback AT	$15,495	3%
EX Sedan AT	$17,755	5%
SX Hatchback AT	$20,905	6%

Safety Checklist

Crash Tests:
  Frontal . . . . .Very Poor
  Side . . . . .Very Poor
Airbags:
  Torso . . .Standard Front Pelvis/Torso from Seat
  Roll Sensing. . . . . No
  Knee Bolster . . . . None
Crash Avoidance:
  Collision Avoidance . . . . None
  Blind Spot Detection . . . . None
  Lane Keeping Assist . . . . None
  Backup Camera . . . . Optional*
  Pedestrian Crash Avoidance . . . . None
General:
  Auto. Crash Notification . . . . . . Dial Assist.-Free
  Day Running Lamps . . . . None
Safety Belt/Restraint:
  Dynamic Head Restraints . . . . None
  Adjustable Belt. . . . . .Standard Front

^Warning feature does not meet government standards.
*Backup camera does not meet government standards.

Kia Rio

Specifications

Drive. . . . . .FWD
Engine 1.6-liter I4
Transmission . . . . 6-sp. Automatic
Tow Rating (lbs.) . . . . –
Head/Leg Room (in.) Roomy-40/43.8
Interior Space (cu. ft.). . . . . Very Cramped-88.4
Cargo Space (cu. ft.) Cramped-13.7
Wheelbase/Length (in.) 101.2/171.9

Ratings—10 Best, 1 Worst

Combo Crash Tests	7
Safety Features	5
Rollover	5
Preventive Maintenance	4
Repair Costs	7
Warranty	10
Fuel Economy	2
Complaints	6
Insurance Costs	8
OVERALL RATING	**7**

Kia Sedona

Kia Sedona

At-a-Glance

Status/Year Series Started Unchanged/2015
Twins . . . . –
Body Styles . . . . Minivan
Seating 7/8
Anti-Theft Device . Std. Pass. Immobil. & Active Alarm
Parking Index Rating . . . . Hard
Where Made . . . . West Point, GA
Fuel Factor: . . . .
  MPG Rating (city/hwy) . . . . Very Poor-18/24
  Driving Range (mi.) Average-428
  Fuel Type . . . . .Regular
  Annual Fuel Cost . . . . .High-$1590
  Gas Guzzler Tax . . . . .No
  Greenhouse Gas Emissions (tons/yr.) High-9.0
  Barrels of Oil Used per year High-16.5

How the Competition Rates

Competitors	Rating	Pg.
Honda Odyssey	8	157
Nissan Rogue	2	230
Toyota Sienna	2	256

Price Range	Retail	Markup
L	$26,400	3%
EX	$32,700	6%
SX	$36,400	7%
SXL	$39,900	7%

Safety Checklist

Crash Tests:
  Frontal . . . . Very Good
  Side . . . . .Very Poor
Airbags:
  Torso . . . Standard Front Pelvis/Torso from Seat
  Roll Sensing . . . . .Yes
  Knee Bolster . . . . None
Crash Avoidance:
  Collision Avoidance . . . . . . Optional CIB & DBS
  Blind Spot Detection . . . . Optional
  Lane Keeping Assist . . . .Warning Only Optional
  Backup Camera . . . . Optional*
  Pedestrian Crash Avoidance . . . . Optional
General:
  Auto. Crash Notification . . . . . . Dial Assist.-Free
  Day Running Lamps . . . . None
Safety Belt/Restraint:
  Dynamic Head Restraints . . . . None
  Adjustable Belt . . . . Standard Front & Rear

^Warning feature does not meet government standards.
*Backup camera does not meet government standards.

Kia Sedona

Specifications

Drive . . . . .FWD
Engine 3.3-liter V6
Transmission . . . . 6-sp. Automatic
Tow Rating (lbs.) Low-3500
Head/Leg Room (in.) Roomy-39.8/43.1
Interior Space (cu. ft.) . . . . .Very Roomy-172.3
Cargo Space (cu. ft.) . . . . .Very Roomy-33.9
Wheelbase/Length (in.) 120.5/201.4

Ratings—10 Best, 1 Worst

Combo Crash Tests	7
Safety Features	5
Rollover	3
Preventive Maintenance	5
Repair Costs	4
Warranty	10
Fuel Economy	4
Complaints	4
Insurance Costs	5
OVERALL RATING	**6**

Kia Sorento

Kia Sorento

At-a-Glance

Status/Year Series Started	Unchanged/2016
Twins	–
Body Styles	SUV
Seating	5
Anti-Theft Device	Std. Pass. Immobil. & Active Alarm
Parking Index Rating	Very Easy
Where Made	West Point, GA
Fuel Factor:	
MPG Rating (city/hwy)	Very Poor-21/29
Driving Range (mi.)	Long-451
Fuel Type	Regular
Annual Fuel Cost	Average-$1345
Gas Guzzler Tax	No
Greenhouse Gas Emissions (tons/yr.)	Average-6.2
Barrels of Oil Used per year	High-13.7

How the Competition Rates

Competitors	Rating	Pg.
Ford Edge	8	137
Jeep Grand Cherokee	4	174
Nissan Rogue	2	230

Price Range	Retail	Markup
LX FWD	$26,700	4%
LX AWD V6	$30,790	4%
SX AWD	$40,400	6%
SXL AWD	$45,700	7%

Safety Checklist

Crash Tests:
- Frontal . . . . Good
- Side . . . . Poor

Airbags:
- Torso . . . Standard Front Pelvis/Torso from Seat
- Roll Sensing . . . . Yes
- Knee Bolster . . . . None

Crash Avoidance:
- Collision Avoidance . . . . . . Optional CIB & DBS
- Blind Spot Detection . . . . Optional
- Lane Keeping Assist . . . . Warning Only Optional
- Backup Camera . . . . Standard*
- Pedestrian Crash Avoidance . . . . Optional

General:
- Auto. Crash Notification . . . . . . Dial Assist.-Free
- Day Running Lamps . . . . None

Safety Belt/Restraint:
- Dynamic Head Restraints . . . . None
- Adjustable Belt . . . . Standard Front

^Warning feature does not meet government standards.
*Backup camera does not meet government standards.

Kia Sorento

Specifications

Drive	FWD
Engine	2.4-liter I4
Transmission	6-sp. Automatic
Tow Rating (lbs.)	Very Low-2000
Head/Leg Room (in.)	Roomy-39.5/44.1
Interior Space (cu. ft.)	Very Roomy-146.4
Cargo Space (cu. ft.)	Very Roomy-38.8
Wheelbase/Length (in.)	109.4/187.4

Ratings—10 Best, 1 Worst

Combo Crash Tests	9
Safety Features	5
Rollover	4
Preventive Maintenance	5
Repair Costs	9
Warranty	10
Fuel Economy	5
Complaints	5
Insurance Costs	1
OVERALL RATING	**8**

Kia Soul

Kia Soul

At-a-Glance

Status/Year Series Started Appearance Change/2014
Twins . . . . –
Body Styles . . . . Wagon
Seating 5
Anti-Theft Device . Std. Pass. Immobil. & Active Alarm
Parking Index Rating . . . . .Very Easy
Where Made. . . . . .Gwangju, South Korea
Fuel Factor:. . . . .
  MPG Rating (city/hwy) Poor-23/31
  Driving Range (mi.) . . . . .Very Short-370
  Fuel Type . . . . .Regular
  Annual Fuel Cost . . . . .Low-$1239
  Gas Guzzler Tax . . . . .No
  Greenhouse Gas Emissions (tons/yr.). . Average-6.9
  Barrels of Oil Used per year Average-12.7

How the Competition Rates

Competitors	Rating	Pg.
Chevrolet Spark	6	121
Mini Cooper	5	214
Toyota Yaris iA	–	260

Price Range

Price Range	Retail	Markup
Base MT	$15,900	2%
!	$21,300	6%
EV e	$31,950	7%
EV +	$35,950	8%

Safety Checklist

Crash Tests:
  Frontal . . . . Good
  Side . . . . Very Good
Airbags:
  Torso . . . Standard Front Pelvis/Torso from Seat
  Roll Sensing. . . . . .Yes
  Knee Bolster . . . . None
Crash Avoidance:
  Collision Avoidance . . . . . .Optional CIB & DBS#
  Blind Spot Detection . . . . Optional
  Lane Keeping Assist . . . . None
  Backup Camera. . . . . Optional
  Pedestrian Crash Avoidance . . . . Optional#
General:
  Auto. Crash Notification. . . . . . Dial Assist.-Free
  Day Running Lamps . . . . Optional
Safety Belt/Restraint:
  Dynamic Head Restraints . . . . None
  Adjustable Belt. . . . . .Standard Front

^Warning feature does not meet government standards.
*Backup camera does not meet government standards.

Kia Soul

Specifications

Drive. . . . . .FWD
Engine 2.0-liter I4
Transmission . . . . 6-sp. Automatic
Tow Rating (lbs.) . . . . –
Head/Leg Room (in.) Cramped-39.6/40.9
Interior Space (cu. ft.). Average-101
Cargo Space (cu. ft.) Roomy-24.2
Wheelbase/Length (in.) 101.2/163

#Caution: Models produced prior to March 2017 may not have these options.

Ratings—10 Best, 1 Worst

Combo Crash Tests	7
Safety Features	7
Rollover	4
Preventive Maintenance	5
Repair Costs	7
Warranty	10
Fuel Economy	4
Complaints	9
Insurance Costs	5
OVERALL RATING	**8**

Kia Sportage

Kia Sportage

At-a-Glance

Status/Year Series Started	Unchanged/2011
Twins	–
Body Styles	SUV
Seating	5
Anti-Theft Device	Std. Pass. Immobil. & Active Alarm
Parking Index Rating	Very Easy
Where Made	Gwangju, South Korea
Fuel Factor:	
MPG Rating (city/hwy)	Very Poor-21/28
Driving Range (mi.)	Very Short-343
Fuel Type	Regular
Annual Fuel Cost	Average-$1363
Gas Guzzler Tax	No
Greenhouse Gas Emissions (tons/yr.)	High-7.5
Barrels of Oil Used per year	High-13.7

How the Competition Rates

Competitors	Rating	Pg.
Ford Escape	7	138
Honda HR-V	5	156
Toyota RAV4	6	254

Price Range	Retail	Markup
LX FWD	$22,990	4%
EX FWD	$25,500	5%
EX AWD	$27,000	5%
SX AWD	$34,000	6%

Safety Checklist

Crash Tests:
Frontal . . . . Average
Side . . . . Good
Airbags:
Torso . . . Standard Front Pelvis/Torso from Seat
Roll Sensing . . . . Yes
Knee Bolster . . . . None
Crash Avoidance:
Collision Avoidance . . . . . . Optional CIB & DBS
Blind Spot Detection . . . . Optional
Lane Keeping Assist . . . .Warning Only Optional
Backup Camera . . . . Standard
Pedestrian Crash Avoidance . . . . Optional
General:
Auto. Crash Notification . . . . . . Dial Assist.-Free
Day Running Lamps . . . . Standard
Safety Belt/Restraint:
Dynamic Head Restraints . . . . None
Adjustable Belt . . . . .Standard Front

^Warning feature does not meet government standards.
*Backup camera does not meet government standards.

Kia Sportage

Specifications

Drive	FWD
Engine	2.4-liter I4
Transmission	6-sp. Automaitc
Tow Rating (lbs.)	Very Low-2000
Head/Leg Room (in.)	Cramped-39.1/41.4
Interior Space (cu. ft.)	Average-100
Cargo Space (cu. ft.)	Roomy-26.1
Wheelbase/Length (in.)	103.9/174.8

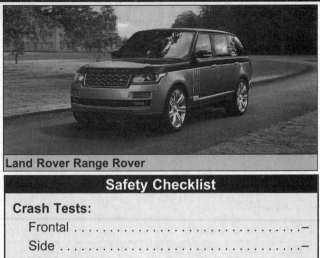

Land Rover Range Rover

Ratings—10 Best, 1 Worst

Rating	
Combo Crash Tests	—
Safety Features	6
Rollover	2
Preventive Maintenance	6
Repair Costs	2
Warranty	7
Fuel Economy	1
Complaints	5
Insurance Costs	8

OVERALL RATING   —

Land Rover Range Rover

At-a-Glance

Status/Year Series Started. Unchanged/2013
Twins . . . . —
Body Styles . . . . SUV
Seating 5
Anti-Theft Device . . . . . . Std. Pass. Immobil. & Alarm
Parking Index Rating . . . . Very Hard
Where Made. . . . . Solihull, England
Fuel Factor:. . . . .
  MPG Rating (city/hwy) . . . . . . .Very Poor-14/19
  Driving Range (mi.) Long-440
  Fuel Type. . . . . Premium
  Annual Fuel Cost . . . . Very High-$2531
  Gas Guzzler Tax . . . . .No
  Greenhouse Gas Emissions (tons/yr.)Very High-11.3
  Barrels of Oil Used per year . . . . . . .Very High-20.6

How the Competition Rates

Competitors	Rating	Pg.
Buick Enclave	6	103
Chevrolet Suburban	4	122
Toyota 4Runner	2	244

Price Range	Retail	Markup
Base	$84,950	10%
HSE	$91,950	10%
Supercharged	$103,195	10%
Autobiography	$139,995	10%

Safety Checklist

Crash Tests:
  Frontal . . . . −
  Side . . . . −
Airbags:
  Torso . . .Standard Front Pelvis/Torso from Seat
  Roll Sensing. . . . . .Yes
  Knee Bolster . . . . None
Crash Avoidance:
  Collision Avoidance . . . . . Std. CIB & Opt. DBS^
  Blind Spot Detection . . . . Optional
  Lane Keeping Assist . . . . Optional^
  Backup Camera . . . . .Standard*
  Pedestrian Crash Avoidance . . . . None
General:
  Auto. Crash Notification . . . Operator Assist.-Fee
  Day Running Lamps . . . . Standard
Safety Belt/Restraint:
  Dynamic Head Restraints . . . . None
  Adjustable Belt. . . . . .Standard Front

^Warning feature does not meet government standards.
*Backup camera does not meet government standards.

Land Rover Range Rover

Specifications

Drive. 4WD
Engine 5.0-liter V8
Transmission . . . . 6-sp. Automatic
Tow Rating (lbs.) High-7716
Head/Leg Room (in.) Cramped-42.5/39.1
Interior Space (cu. ft.). . . . . —
Cargo Space (cu. ft.) . . . . Very Roomy-32.1
Wheelbase/Length (in.) 115/196.8

Ratings—10 Best, 1 Worst

Combo Crash Tests	—
Safety Features	7
Rollover	5
Preventive Maintenance	7
Repair Costs	5
Warranty	7
Fuel Economy	4
Complaints	7
Insurance Costs	5
OVERALL RATING	—

Land Rover Range Rover Evoque

At-a-Glance

Status/Year Series Started. Unchanged/2012
Twins . . . .–
Body Styles . . . . SUV
Seating 5
Anti-Theft Device . . . . . . Std. Pass. Immobil. & Alarm
Parking Index Rating . . . . Easy
Where Made. . . . . Halewood, England
Fuel Factor:. . . . .
  MPG Rating (city/hwy) . . . . .Very Poor-21/30
  Driving Range (mi.) Long-449
  Fuel Type . . . . .Premium
  Annual Fuel Cost . . . . .High-$1656
  Gas Guzzler Tax . . . . .No
  Greenhouse Gas Emissions (tons/yr.) High-7.5
  Barrels of Oil Used per year High-13.7

How the Competition Rates

Competitors	Rating	Pg.
Lexus NX	6	194
Mazda CX-5	3	200
Subaru Crosstrek	6	241

Price Range	Retail	Markup
SE	$41,175	6%
SE Premium	$45,675	6%
HSE	$50,475	6%
HSE Dynamic	$53,775	6%

Land Rover Range Rover Evoque

Safety Checklist

Crash Tests:
  Frontal . . . . –
  Side . . . . –
Airbags:
  Torso . . . Standard Front Pelvis/Torso from Seat
  Roll Sensing. . . . . .Yes
  Knee Bolster . . . . Standard Driver
Crash Avoidance:
  Collision Avoidance . . . . . Std. CIB & Opt. DBS^
  Blind Spot Detection . . . . Optional
  Lane Keeping Assist . . . . Optional^
  Backup Camera . . . . .Standard*
  Pedestrian Crash Avoidance . . . . None
General:
  Auto. Crash Notification . . . Operator Assist.-Fee
  Day Running Lamps . . . . Standard
Safety Belt/Restraint:
  Dynamic Head Restraints . . . . None
  Adjustable Belt. None

^Warning feature does not meet government standards.
*Backup camera does not meet government standards.

Land Rover Range Rover Evoque

Specifications

Drive. 4WD
Engine 2.0-liter I4
Transmission . . . . 9-sp. Automatic
Tow Rating (lbs.) . . . . –
Head/Leg Room (in.) Cramped-40.3/40.1
Interior Space (cu. ft.). . . . . –
Cargo Space (cu. ft.) Average-20.3
Wheelbase/Length (in.) 104.8/171.5

Land Rover Range Rover Sport — Medium SUV

Ratings—10 Best, 1 Worst

Combo Crash Tests	—
Safety Features	6
Rollover	3
Preventive Maintenance	1
Repair Costs	2
Warranty	7
Fuel Economy	1
Complaints	8
Insurance Costs	3

OVERALL RATING — —

Land Rover Range Rover Sport

Land Rover Range Rover Sport

At-a-Glance

Status/Year Series Started	Unchanged/2014
Twins	—
Body Styles	SUV
Seating	5
Anti-Theft Device	Std. Pass. Immobil. & Alarm
Parking Index Rating	Very Hard
Where Made	Solihull, England
Fuel Factor:	
MPG Rating (city/hwy)	Very Poor-14/19
Driving Range (mi.)	Long-440
Fuel Type	Premium
Annual Fuel Cost	Very High-$2531
Gas Guzzler Tax	No
Greenhouse Gas Emissions (tons/yr.)	Very High-11.2
Barrels of Oil Used per year	Very High-20.6

How the Competition Rates

Competitors	Rating	Pg.
Acura MDX	8	82
Audi Q5	3	90
BMW X5	6	100

Price Range

Price Range	Retail	Markup
SE	$64,950	6%
HSE	$69,950	6%
Supercharged	$79,950	6%
Autobiography	$93,295	6%

Land Rover Range Rover Sport

Safety Checklist

Crash Tests:
Frontal . . . . —
Side . . . . —

Airbags:
Torso . . . Standard Front Pelvis/Torso from Seat
Roll Sensing . . . . Yes
Knee Bolster . . . . None

Crash Avoidance:
Collision Avoidance . . . . . Std. CIB & Opt. DBS^
Blind Spot Detection . . . . Optional
Lane Keeping Assist . . . . Optional^
Backup Camera . . . . Standard*
Pedestrian Crash Avoidance . . . . None

General:
Auto. Crash Notification . . . Operator Assist.-Fee
Day Running Lamps . . . . Standard

Safety Belt/Restraint:
Dynamic Head Restraints . . . . None
Adjustable Belt . . . . Standard Front

^Warning feature does not meet government standards.
*Backup camera does not meet government standards.

Land Rover Range Rover Sport

Specifications

Drive	4WD
Engine	5.0-liter V8
Transmission	8-sp. Automatic
Tow Rating (lbs.)	High-7716
Head/Leg Room (in.)	Cramped-39.4/42.2
Interior Space (cu. ft.)	—
Cargo Space (cu. ft.)	Roomy-27.7
Wheelbase/Length (in.)	115.1/191.8

Ratings—10 Best, 1 Worst

Combo Crash Tests	—
Safety Features	3
Rollover	6
Preventive Maintenance	9
Repair Costs	3
Warranty	7
Fuel Economy	9
Complaints	6
Insurance Costs	3
OVERALL RATING	**—**

Lexus CT

Lexus CT

At-a-Glance

Status/Year Series Started........ Unchanged/2011
Twins . . . . –
Body Styles . . . . Hatchback
Seating 5
Anti-Theft Device . . . . . . Std. Pass. Immobil. & Alarm
Parking Index Rating . . . . Easy
Where Made. . . . . Kyushu, Japan
Fuel Factor:. . . . .
  MPG Rating (city/hwy) Average-43/40
  Driving Range (mi.) . . . . Very Long-495
  Fuel Type . . . . .Regular
  Annual Fuel Cost . . . . .Very Low-$775
  Gas Guzzler Tax . . . . .No
  Greenhouse Gas Emissions (tons/yr.). Very Low-4.3
  Barrels of Oil Used per year . . . . Very Low-7.8

How the Competition Rates

Competitors	Rating	Pg.
Chevrolet Volt	–	126
Ford C-MAX	5	136
Toyota Prius	7	251

Price Range

	Retail	Markup
Hybrid	$31,250	5%

Safety Checklist

Crash Tests:
  Frontal . . . . –
  Side . . . . –
Airbags:
  Torso . . . Standard Front Pelvis/Torso from Seat
  Roll Sensing. . . . . No
  Knee Bolster . . . . .Standard Front
Crash Avoidance:
  Collision Avoidance . . . . . . Optional CIB & DBS
  Blind Spot Detection . . . . None
  Lane Keeping Assist . . . . None
  Backup Camera . . . . None
  Pedestrian Crash Avoidance . . . . None
General:
  Auto. Crash Notification . . . Operator Assist.-Fee
  Day Running Lamps . . . . Standard
Safety Belt/Restraint:
  Dynamic Head Restraints . . . . None
  Adjustable Belt. . . . . .Standard Front

^Warning feature does not meet government standards.
*Backup camera does not meet government standards.

Lexus CT

Specifications

Drive. . . . . .FWD
Engine 1.8-liter I4
Transmission . . . . CVT
Tow Rating (lbs.) . . . . –
Head/Leg Room (in.) Cramped-38.3/42.1
Interior Space (cu. ft.). . . . . Very Cramped-86.1
Cargo Space (cu. ft.) Cramped-14.3
Wheelbase/Length (in.) 102.4/171.2

Ratings—10 Best, 1 Worst

Combo Crash Tests	8
Safety Features	10
Rollover	6
Preventive Maintenance	6
Repair Costs	2
Warranty	7
Fuel Economy	4
Complaints	8
Insurance Costs	3
OVERALL RATING	**7**

Lexus ES

Lexus ES

At-a-Glance

Status/Year Series Started	Unchanged/2013
Twins	—
Body Styles	Sedan
Seating	5
Anti-Theft Device	Std. Pass. Immobil. & Alarm
Parking Index Rating	Average
Where Made	Kyushu, Japan
Fuel Factor:	
MPG Rating (city/hwy)	Poor-21/31
Driving Range (mi.)	Average-423
Fuel Type	Regular
Annual Fuel Cost	Average-$1313
Gas Guzzler Tax	No
Greenhouse Gas Emissions (tons/yr.)	High-7.5
Barrels of Oil Used per year	High-13.7

How the Competition Rates

Competitors	Rating	Pg.
Acura TLX	9	84
Audi A6	6	88
Volkswagen Passat	3	264

Price Range	Retail	Markup
Sedan	$38,900	7%
Hybrid	$41,820	7%

Safety Checklist

Crash Tests:
Frontal .... Good
Side .... Good

Airbags:
Torso ...Std. Fr. & Rear Pelvis/Torso from Seat
Roll Sensing .... Yes
Knee Bolster .... Standard Front

Crash Avoidance:
Collision Avoidance ...... Optional CIB & DBS
Blind Spot Detection .... Optional
Lane Keeping Assist .... Optional
Backup Camera .... Standard
Pedestrian Crash Avoidance .... None

General:
Auto. Crash Notification ... Operator Assist.-Fee
Day Running Lamps .... Standard

Safety Belt/Restraint:
Dynamic Head Restraints .... None
Adjustable Belt .... Standard Front

^Warning feature does not meet government standards.
*Backup camera does not meet government standards.

Lexus ES

Specifications

Drive	FWD
Engine	3.5-liter V6
Transmission	6-sp. Automatic
Tow Rating (lbs.)	—
Head/Leg Room (in.)	Very Cramped-37.5/41.9
Interior Space (cu. ft.)	Average-100.1
Cargo Space (cu. ft.)	Cramped-15.2
Wheelbase/Length (in.)	111/192.7

Ratings—10 Best, 1 Worst

Combo Crash Tests	—
Safety Features	10
Rollover	7
Preventive Maintenance	8
Repair Costs	1
Warranty	7
Fuel Economy	3
Complaints	10
Insurance Costs	1
OVERALL RATING	**—**

Lexus GS

Lexus GS

At-a-Glance

Status/Year Series Started Unchanged/2012
Twins . . . . –
Body Styles . . . . Sedan
Seating 5
Anti-Theft Device . . . . . . Std. Pass. Immobil. & Alarm
Parking Index Rating . . . . Average
Where Made . . . . Tahara, Japan
Fuel Factor: . . . .
  MPG Rating (city/hwy) . . . . Very Poor-19/29
  Driving Range (mi.) Short-391
  Fuel Type . . . . Premium
  Annual Fuel Cost . . . . Very High-$1787
  Gas Guzzler Tax . . . . No
  Greenhouse Gas Emissions (tons/yr.) High-7.8
  Barrels of Oil Used per year High-14.3

How the Competition Rates

Competitors	Rating	Pg.
Acura TLX	9	84
Audi A6	6	88
Cadillac XTS	9	111

Price Range	Retail	Markup
200T Sedan	$45,615	8%
350 Sedan AWD	$50,470	8%
450H Sedan	$63,080	8%

Safety Checklist

Crash Tests:
  Frontal . . . . –
  Side . . . . –
Airbags:
  Torso . . . Std. Fr. & Rear Pelvis/Torso from Seat
  Roll Sensing . . . . Yes
  Knee Bolster . . . . Standard Front
Crash Avoidance:
  Collision Avoidance . . . . . . Optional CIB & DBS
  Blind Spot Detection . . . . Optional
  Lane Keeping Assist . . . . Optional
  Backup Camera . . . . Standard
  Pedestrian Crash Avoidance . . . . None
General:
  Auto. Crash Notification . . . Operator Assist.-Fee
  Day Running Lamps . . . . Standard
Safety Belt/Restraint:
  Dynamic Head Restraints . . . . None
  Adjustable Belt . . . . Standard Front

^Warning feature does not meet government standards.
*Backup camera does not meet government standards.

Lexus GS

Specifications

Drive . . . . RWD
Engine 3.5-liter V6
Transmission . . . . 8-sp. Automatic
Tow Rating (lbs.) . . . . –
Head/Leg Room (in.) Cramped-38/42.3
Interior Space (cu. ft.) Average-99
Cargo Space (cu. ft.) Cramped-14.1
Wheelbase/Length (in.) 112.2/190.7

Ratings—10 Best, 1 Worst

Combo Crash Tests	—
Safety Features	9
Rollover	7
Preventive Maintenance	6
Repair Costs	3
Warranty	7
Fuel Economy	1
Complaints	9
Insurance Costs	10

OVERALL RATING   —

Lexus GX

Lexus GX

At-a-Glance

Status/Year Series Started.	Unchanged/2003
Twins	–
Body Styles	SUV
Seating	7
Anti-Theft Device	Std. Pass. Immobil. & Alarm
Parking Index Rating	Very Hard
Where Made.	Tahara, Japan

Fuel Factor:. . . . .
MPG Rating (city/hwy)	Very Poor-15/20
Driving Range (mi.)	Short-389
Fuel Type	Premium
Annual Fuel Cost	Very High-$2378
Gas Guzzler Tax	No
Greenhouse Gas Emissions (tons/yr.)	Very High-10.6
Barrels of Oil Used per year	Very High-19.4

How the Competition Rates

Competitors	Rating	Pg.
Buick Enclave	6	103
Chevrolet Suburban	4	122
Toyota 4Runner	2	244

Price Range	Retail	Markup
4WD	$51,280	9%
4WD Luxury	$62,980	9%

Safety Checklist

Crash Tests:
Frontal . . . . –
Side . . . . –

Airbags:
Torso Std. Fr. & Opt. Rr. Pelvis/Torso from Seat
Roll Sensing. . . . . .Yes
Knee Bolster . . . . Standard Front

Crash Avoidance:
Collision Avoidance . . . . . . Optional CIB & DBS
Blind Spot Detection . . . . Optional
Lane Keeping Assist . . . .Warning Only Optional
Backup Camera . . . . .Standard*
Pedestrian Crash Avoidance . . . . None

General:
Auto. Crash Notification . . . Operator Assist.-Fee
Day Running Lamps . . . . Standard

Safety Belt/Restraint:
Dynamic Head Restraints . . . . None
Adjustable Belt . . . . .Standard Front

^Warning feature does not meet government standards.
*Backup camera does not meet government standards.

Lexus GX

Specifications

Drive.	4WD
Engine	4.6-liter V8
Transmission	6-sp. Automatic
Tow Rating (lbs.)	Average-6500
Head/Leg Room (in.)	Cramped-38/41.7
Interior Space (cu. ft.).	Very Roomy-129.7
Cargo Space (cu. ft.)	Very Cramped-11.6
Wheelbase/Length (in.)	109.8/192.1

Lexus IS — Compact

Ratings—10 Best, 1 Worst

Combo Crash Tests	4
Safety Features	10
Rollover	8
Preventive Maintenance	7
Repair Costs	1
Warranty	7
Fuel Economy	4
Complaints	10
Insurance Costs	3
OVERALL RATING	**6**

Lexus IS

Lexus IS

At-a-Glance

Status/Year Series Started	Unchanged/2014
Twins	–
Body Styles	Sedan, Convertible
Seating	5
Anti-Theft Device	Std. Pass. Immobil. & Alarm
Parking Index Rating	Easy
Where Made	Kyushu, Japan / Tahara, Japan
Fuel Factor:	
MPG Rating (city/hwy)	Very Poor-21/30
Driving Range (mi.)	Average-422
Fuel Type	Premium
Annual Fuel Cost	High-$1656
Gas Guzzler Tax	No
Greenhouse Gas Emissions (tons/yr.)	High-7.5
Barrels of Oil Used per year	High-13.7

How the Competition Rates

Competitors	Rating	Pg.
Acura ILX	8	81
BMW 3 Series	7	93
Infiniti Q50	6	167

Price Range

	Retail	Markup
200T Sedan	$37,325	8%
300 Sedan AWD	$39,700	8%
350 Sedan	$40,870	8%
350 Sedan AWD	$43,035	8%

Safety Checklist

Crash Tests:
- Frontal .... Very Poor
- Side .... Good

Airbags:
- Torso . . . Std. Fr. & Rear Pelvis/Torso from Seat
- Roll Sensing .... Yes
- Knee Bolster .... Standard Front

Crash Avoidance:
- Collision Avoidance ...... Optional CIB & DBS^
- Blind Spot Detection .... Optional
- Lane Keeping Assist .... Standard
- Backup Camera .... Optional
- Pedestrian Crash Avoidance .... None

General:
- Auto. Crash Notification . . . Operator Assist.-Fee
- Day Running Lamps .... Standard

Safety Belt/Restraint:
- Dynamic Head Restraints .... None
- Adjustable Belt .... Standard Front

^Warning feature does not meet government standards.
*Backup camera does not meet government standards.

Lexus IS

Specifications

Drive	RWD
Engine	2.5-liter V6
Transmission	6-sp. Automatic
Tow Rating (lbs.)	–
Head/Leg Room (in.)	Roomy-38.2/44.8
Interior Space (cu. ft.)	Very Cramped-90.2
Cargo Space (cu. ft.)	Cramped-13.8
Wheelbase/Length (in.)	110.2/183.7

Ratings—10 Best, 1 Worst

Combo Crash Tests	7
Safety Features	9
Rollover	3
Preventive Maintenance	1
Repair Costs	1
Warranty	7
Fuel Economy	4
Complaints	10
Insurance Costs	5
OVERALL RATING	**6**

Lexus NX

At-a-Glance

Status/Year Series Started. Unchanged/2015
Twins . . . .–
Body Styles . . . . SUV
Seating. 5
Anti-Theft Device . . . . . . Std. Pass. Immobil. & Alarm
Parking Index Rating . . . . .Very Easy
Where Made. Kyushu, Japan
Fuel Factor:. . . . .
  MPG Rating (city/hwy). . . . . .Very Poor-22/28
  Driving Range (mi.) Short-387
  Fuel Type. . . . . .Premium
  Annual Fuel Cost . . . . .High-$1651
  Gas Guzzler Tax . . . . .No
  Greenhouse Gas Emissions (tons/yr.). Very Low-3.5
  Barrels of Oil Used per year High-13.7

How the Competition Rates

Competitors	Rating	Pg.
Buick Encore	10	104
Lincoln MKC	5	198
Mazda CX-5	3	200

Price Range

Price Range	Retail	Markup
200T Base	$34,965	7%
200T F Sport	$37,065	7%
200T F Sport AWD	$38,465	7%
300H AWD	$41,310	6%

Lexus NX

Safety Checklist

Crash Tests:
  Frontal . . . . Very Good
  Side . . . . .Very Poor
Airbags:
  Torso . . . Standard Front Pelvis/Torso from Seat
  Roll Sensing. . . . . .Yes
  Knee Bolster . . . . .Standard Front
Crash Avoidance:
  Collision Avoidance . . . . . . Optional CIB & DBS
  Blind Spot Detection . . . . Optional
  Lane Keeping Assist . . . . Optional
  Backup Camera . . . . Standard
  Pedestrian Crash Avoidance . . . . None
General:
  Auto. Crash Notification . . . Operator Assist.-Fee
  Day Running Lamps . . . . Standard
Safety Belt/Restraint:
  Dynamic Head Restraints . . . . None
  Adjustable Belt . . . . .Standard Front

^Warning feature does not meet government standards.
*Backup camera does not meet government standards.

Lexus NX

Specifications

Drive. . . . . .AWD
Engine 2.0-liter I4
Transmission . . . . 6-sp. Automatic
Tow Rating (lbs.) .Very Low-2000
Head/Leg Room (in.) Cramped-38.2/42.8
Interior Space (cu. ft.). . . . . Very Cramped-71.6
Cargo Space (cu. ft.) Average-17.7
Wheelbase/Length (in.) 104.7/182.3

Ratings—10 Best, 1 Worst

Combo Crash Tests	—
Safety Features	9
Rollover	9
Preventive Maintenance	7
Repair Costs	1
Warranty	7
Fuel Economy	5
Complaints	—
Insurance Costs	8

OVERALL RATING —

Lexus RC

Lexus RC

At-a-Glance

Status/Year Series Started. Unchanged/2016
Twins . . . .–
Body Styles . . . . .Coupe
Seating 4
Anti-Theft Device . . . . . . Std. Pass. Immobil. & Alarm
Parking Index Rating . . . . Easy
Where Made. . . . . Tahara, Japan
Fuel Factor:. . . . .
MPG Rating (city/hwy). Poor-22/32
Driving Range (mi.) Long-445
Fuel Type . . . . .Premium
Annual Fuel Cost . . . . .High-$1570
Gas Guzzler Tax . . . . .No
Greenhouse Gas Emissions (tons/yr.). Low-5.7
Barrels of Oil Used per year Average-12.7

How the Competition Rates

Competitors	Rating	Pg.
Acura ILX	8	81
Audi A5	–	87
Mercedes-Benz C-Class	3	206

Price Range

Price Range	Retail	Markup
200T Coupe	$39,995	8%
300 Coupe AWD	$42,610	8%
350 Coupe AWD	$45,015	8%
F Coupe	$62,805	8%

Safety Checklist

Crash Tests:
Frontal . . . .–
Side . . . .–
Airbags:
Torso . . . Standard Front Pelvis/Torso from Seat
Roll Sensing. . . . . .Yes
Knee Bolster . . . . .Standard Front
Crash Avoidance:
Collision Avoidance . . . . . . Optional CIB & DBS
Blind Spot Detection . . . . Standard
Lane Keeping Assist . . . .Warning Only Optional
Backup Camera . . . . Standard
Pedestrian Crash Avoidance . . . . None
General:
Auto. Crash Notification . . . Operator Assist.-Fee
Day Running Lamps . . . . Standard
Safety Belt/Restraint:
Dynamic Head Restraints . . . . None
Adjustable Belt. . . . . .Standard Front

^Warning feature does not meet government standards.
*Backup camera does not meet government standards.

Lexus RC

Specifications

Drive. . . . . .RWD
Engine 2.0-liter I4
Transmission . . . . 8-sp. Automatic
Tow Rating (lbs.) . . . .–
Head/Leg Room (in.) Roomy-37.8/45.4
Interior Space (cu. ft.). . . . . .Very Cramped-82
Cargo Space (cu. ft.) . . . . Very Cramped-10.4
Wheelbase/Length (in.) 107.5/184.8

Ratings—10 Best, 1 Worst

Combo Crash Tests	5
Safety Features	9
Rollover	3
Preventive Maintenance	5
Repair Costs	1
Warranty	7
Fuel Economy	3
Complaints	7
Insurance Costs	8
OVERALL RATING	**5**

Lexus RX

Lexus RX

At-a-Glance

Status/Year Series Started. Unchanged/2016
Twins . . . . –
Body Styles . . . . SUV
Seating 5
Anti-Theft Device . . . . . . Std. Pass. Immobil. & Alarm
Parking Index Rating . . . . Hard
Where Made. . . . Kyushu, Japan / Cambridge, Ontario
Fuel Factor:. . . . .
MPG Rating (city/hwy) . . . . Very Poor-20/28
Driving Range (mi.) Long-441
Fuel Type. . . . . .Regular
Annual Fuel Cost . . . . .Average-$1405
Gas Guzzler Tax . . . . .No
Greenhouse Gas Emissions (tons/yr.) . . Average-6.4
Barrels of Oil Used per year High-14.3

How the Competition Rates

Competitors	Rating	Pg.
Audi Q5	3	90
BMW X3	7	99
Lincoln MKC	5	198

Price Range

Price Range	Retail	Markup
350 Base FWD	$41,900	7%
350 Base AWD	$43,300	7%
350 F Sport AWD	$49,125	7%
450 Hybrid AWD	$53,635	6%

Safety Checklist

Crash Tests:
Frontal . . . . .Very Poor
Side . . . . Very Good
Airbags:
Torso Std. Fr. & Opt. Rr. Pelvis/Torso from Seat
Roll Sensing. . . . . .Yes
Knee Bolster . . . . Standard Driver
Crash Avoidance:
Collision Avoidance . . . . . . Optional CIB & DBS
Blind Spot Detection . . . . Standard
Lane Keeping Assist . . . . Optional
Backup Camera . . . . Standard
Pedestrian Crash Avoidance . . . . None
General:
Auto. Crash Notification . . . Operator Assist.-Fee
Day Running Lamps . . . . Standard
Safety Belt/Restraint:
Dynamic Head Restraints . . . . None
Adjustable Belt. . . . . .Standard Front

^Warning feature does not meet government standards.
*Backup camera does not meet government standards.

Lexus RX

Specifications

Drive. . . . . .FWD
Engine 3.5-liter V6
Transmission . . . . 8-sp. Automatic
Tow Rating (lbs.) . . . . –
Head/Leg Room (in.) Roomy-39.4/44.4
Interior Space (cu. ft.). . . . . Very Roomy-139.7
Cargo Space (cu. ft.) Average-18.4
Wheelbase/Length (in.) 109.8/192.5

Lincoln Continental

Ratings—10 Best, 1 Worst

Combo Crash Tests	—
Safety Features	9
Rollover	7
Preventive Maintenance	5
Repair Costs	3
Warranty	9
Fuel Economy	2
Complaints	—
Insurance Costs	5
OVERALL RATING	**—**

Lincoln Continental

Lincoln Continental

At-a-Glance

Status/Year Series Started	All New/2017
Twins	—
Body Styles	Sedan
Seating	5
Anti-Theft Device	Std. Pass. Immobil. & Alarm
Parking Index Rating	Very Hard
Where Made	Chicago, IL
Fuel Factor:	
MPG Rating (city/hwy)	Very Poor-17/26
Driving Range (mi.)	Very Short-362
Fuel Type	Regular
Annual Fuel Cost	High-$1602
Gas Guzzler Tax	No
Greenhouse Gas Emissions (tons/yr.)	Average-7.3
Barrels of Oil Used per year	High-16.5

How the Competition Rates

Competitors	Rating	Pg.
Buick LaCrosse	6	105
Cadillac XTS	9	111
Dodge Charger	3	131

Price Range

Price Range	Retail	Markup
Premier FWD	$44,560	5%
Select FWD	$47,515	5%
Reserve AWD	$55,915	6%
Black Label AWD	$64,915	6%

Safety Checklist

Crash Tests:
- Frontal .... —
- Side .... —

Airbags:
- Torso . . . Standard Front Pelvis/Torso from Seat
- Roll Sensing .... Yes
- Knee Bolster .... Standard Front

Crash Avoidance:
- Collision Avoidance ...... Optional CIB & DBS
- Blind Spot Detection .... Optional
- Lane Keeping Assist .... Optional
- Backup Camera .... Standard
- Pedestrian Crash Avoidance .... None

General:
- Auto. Crash Notification ...... Dial Assist.-Free
- Day Running Lamps .... Standard

Safety Belt/Restraint:
- Dynamic Head Restraints .... None
- Adjustable Belt .... Standard Front

^Warning feature does not meet government standards.
*Backup camera does not meet government standards.

Lincoln Continental

Specifications

Drive	FWD
Engine	3.7-liter V6
Transmission	6-sp. Automatic
Tow Rating (lbs.)	—
Head/Leg Room (in.)	Roomy-39.3/44.4
Interior Space (cu. ft.)	Roomy-106.4
Cargo Space (cu. ft.)	—
Wheelbase/Length (in.)	117.9/201.4

Lincoln MKC

Ratings—10 Best, 1 Worst

Combo Crash Tests	3
Safety Features	6
Rollover	3
Preventive Maintenance	6
Repair Costs	3
Warranty	9
Fuel Economy	3
Complaints	8
Insurance Costs	8
OVERALL RATING	**5**

Lincoln MKC

Lincoln MKC

At-a-Glance

Status/Year Series Started Unchanged/2015
Twins . . . . –
Body Styles . . . . SUV
Seating 5
Anti-Theft Device . . . . . . Std. Pass. Immobil. & Alarm
Parking Index Rating . . . . Average
Where Made . . . . Louisville, Kentucky
Fuel Factor: . . . .
  MPG Rating (city/hwy) . . . . Very Poor-19/26
  Driving Range (mi.) . . . . Very Short-335
  Fuel Type . . . . Regular
  Annual Fuel Cost . . . . High-$1492
  Gas Guzzler Tax . . . . No
  Greenhouse Gas Emissions (tons/yr.) High-8.2
  Barrels of Oil Used per year High-15.0

How the Competition Rates

Competitors	Rating	Pg.
Buick Encore	10	104
Lexus NX	6	194
Mitsubishi Outlander Sport	4	219

Price Range

Price Range	Retail	Markup
Premiere FWD	$32,720	5%
Select FWD	$35,720	6%
Reserve AWD	$41,895	6%
Black Label AWD	$47,880	7%

Safety Checklist

Crash Tests:
  Frontal . . . . Poor
  Side . . . . Poor
Airbags:
  Torso . . . Standard Front Pelvis/Torso from Seat
  Roll Sensing . . . . Yes
  Knee Bolster . . . . Standard Driver
Crash Avoidance:
  Collision Avoidance . . . . . Warning Only Optional
  Blind Spot Detection . . . . Optional
  Lane Keeping Assist . . . . Optional
  Backup Camera . . . . Standard
  Pedestrian Crash Avoidance . . . . None
General:
  Auto. Crash Notification . . . . . . Dial Assist.-Free
  Day Running Lamps . . . . Optional
Safety Belt/Restraint:
  Dynamic Head Restraints . . . . None
  Adjustable Belt . . . . Standard Front

^Warning feature does not meet government standards.
*Backup camera does not meet government standards.

Lincoln MKC

Specifications

Drive . . . . AWD
Engine 2.0-liter I5
Transmission . . . . 6-sp. Automatic
Tow Rating (lbs.) . . . . Very Low-2000
Head/Leg Room (in.) Roomy-39.6/42.8
Interior Space (cu. ft.) Average-97.9
Cargo Space (cu. ft.) Roomy-25.2
Wheelbase/Length (in.) 105.9/179.2

Ratings—10 Best, 1 Worst

Combo Crash Tests	3
Safety Features	9
Rollover	7
Preventive Maintenance	8
Repair Costs	2
Warranty	9
Fuel Economy	2
Complaints	7
Insurance Costs	3
OVERALL RATING	**5**

Lincoln MKZ

Lincoln MKZ

At-a-Glance

Status/Year Series Started	Appearance Change/2013
Twins	–
Body Styles	Sedan
Seating	5
Anti-Theft Device	Std. Pass. Immobil. & Alarm
Parking Index Rating	Hard
Where Made	Hermosillo, Mexico

Fuel Factor:

MPG Rating (city/hwy)	Very Poor-18/27
Driving Range (mi.)	Very Short-349
Fuel Type	Regular
Annual Fuel Cost	High-$1523
Gas Guzzler Tax	No
Greenhouse Gas Emissions (tons/yr.)	High-8.1
Barrels of Oil Used per year	High-15.0

How the Competition Rates

Competitors	Rating	Pg.
BMW 3 Series	7	93
Buick Regal	4	106
Cadillac CTS	9	109

Price Range

	Retail	Markup
Hybrid Premier	$35,010	5%
Base FWD	$35,010	5%
Black Label Hybrid FWD	$47,670	6%
Black Label AWD	$49,560	6%

Safety Checklist

Crash Tests:

Frontal	Very Poor
Side	Poor

Airbags:

Torso	Standard Front Pelvis/Torso from Seat
Roll Sensing	Yes
Knee Bolster	Standard Front

Crash Avoidance:

Collision Avoidance	Optional CIB & DBS
Blind Spot Detection	Optional
Lane Keeping Assist	Optional
Backup Camera	Standard
Pedestrian Crash Avoidance	None

General:

Auto. Crash Notification	Dial Assist.-Free
Day Running Lamps	Standard

Safety Belt/Restraint:

Dynamic Head Restraints	None
Adjustable Belt	Standard Front

^Warning feature does not meet government standards.
*Backup camera does not meet government standards.

Lincoln MKZ

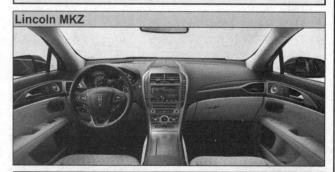

Specifications

Drive	FWD
Engine	3.7-liter V6
Transmission	6-sp. Automatic
Tow Rating (lbs.)	Very Low-1000
Head/Leg Room (in.)	Cramped-37.9/44.3
Interior Space (cu. ft.)	Cramped-96.5
Cargo Space (cu. ft.)	Cramped-15.4
Wheelbase/Length (in.)	112.2/194.1

Ratings—10 Best, 1 Worst

Combo Crash Tests	3
Safety Features	5
Rollover	2
Preventive Maintenance	7
Repair Costs	10
Warranty	1
Fuel Economy	7
Complaints	3
Insurance Costs	3
OVERALL RATING	**3**

Mazda CX-5

Mazda CX-5

At-a-Glance

Status/Year Series Started........ Unchanged/2013
Twins . . . . –
Body Styles . . . . SUV
Seating 5
Anti-Theft Device . . . . Std. Passive Immobil. Only
Parking Index Rating . . . . Average
Where Made. . . . . Hiroshima, Japan
Fuel Factor:. . . . .
   MPG Rating (city/hwy) Poor-26/32
   Driving Range (mi.) Average-420
   Fuel Type . . . . .Regular
   Annual Fuel Cost . . . . Low-$1136
   Gas Guzzler Tax . . . . .No
   Greenhouse Gas Emissions (tons/yr.). . Average-6.2
   Barrels of Oil Used per year Average-11.4

How the Competition Rates

Competitors	Rating	Pg.
Buick Encore	10	104
Honda HR-V	5	156
Mitsubishi Outlander Sport	4	219

Price Range	Retail	Markup
Sport FWD MT	$21,795	3%
Sport AWD AT	$24,445	3%
Touring AWD	$26,465	3%
Grand Touring AWD	$29,470	3%

Safety Checklist

Crash Tests:
   Frontal . . . . .Very Poor
   Side . . . . Average
Airbags:
   Torso . . . Standard Front Pelvis/Torso from Seat
   Roll Sensing. . . . . .Yes
   Knee Bolster . . . . None
Crash Avoidance:
   Collision Avoidance . . . . . .Optional CIB & DBS^
   Blind Spot Detection . . . . Optional
   Lane Keeping Assist . . . . Optional^
   Backup Camera . . . . .Standard*
   Pedestrian Crash Avoidance . . . . None
General:
   Auto. Crash Notification . . . . . . Dial Assist.-Free
   Day Running Lamps . . . . Standard
Safety Belt/Restraint:
   Dynamic Head Restraints . . . . None
   Adjustable Belt. . . . . .Standard Front

^Warning feature does not meet government standards.
*Backup camera does not meet government standards.

Mazda CX-5

Specifications

Drive. . . . . .FWD
Engine 2.0-liter I4
Transmission . . . . 6-sp. Automatic
Tow Rating (lbs.) . . . . .Very Low-2000
Head/Leg Room (in.) Cramped-40.1/41
Interior Space (cu. ft.). Roomy-103.8
Cargo Space (cu. ft.) . . . . .Very Roomy-34.1
Wheelbase/Length (in.) 106.3/178.7

Ratings—10 Best, 1 Worst

Combo Crash Tests	—
Safety Features	6
Rollover	3
Preventive Maintenance	7
Repair Costs	4
Warranty	1
Fuel Economy	4
Complaints	—
Insurance Costs	8
OVERALL RATING	**—**

Mazda CX-9

Mazda CX-9

At-a-Glance

Status/Year Series Started Unchanged/2017
Twins . . . . —
Body Styles . . . . SUV
Seating 7
Anti-Theft Device . . . . Std. Passive Immobil. Only
Parking Index Rating . . . . Very Hard
Where Made . . . . Hiroshima, Japan
Fuel Factor: . . . .
  MPG Rating (city/hwy) . . . . Very Poor-21/27
  Driving Range (mi.) Long-443
  Fuel Type . . . . Regular
  Annual Fuel Cost . . . . Average-$1382
  Gas Guzzler Tax . . . . No
  Greenhouse Gas Emissions (tons/yr.)Very High-10.0
  Barrels of Oil Used per year . . . . Very High-18.3

How the Competition Rates

Competitors	Rating	Pg.
Kia Sorento	6	183
Lexus RX	5	196
Nissan Murano	4	227

Price Range	Retail	Markup
Sport FWD	$31,520	6%
Touring FWD	$37,770	6%
Grand Touring AWD	$41,970	6%
Signature AWD	$44,015	6%

Safety Checklist

Crash Tests:
  Frontal . . . . —
  Side . . . . —
Airbags:
  Torso . . . Standard Front Pelvis/Torso from Seat
  Roll Sensing . . . . Yes
  Knee Bolster . . . . None
Crash Avoidance:
  Collision Avoidance . . . . . . Optional CIB & DBS^
  Blind Spot Detection . . . . Optional
  Lane Keeping Assist . . . . Optional^
  Backup Camera . . . . Standard
  Pedestrian Crash Avoidance . . . . None
General:
  Auto. Crash Notification . . . . . . Dial Assist.-Free
  Day Running Lamps . . . . Standard
Safety Belt/Restraint:
  Dynamic Head Restraints . . . . None
  Adjustable Belt . . . . Standard Front

^Warning feature does not meet government standards.
*Backup camera does not meet government standards.

Mazda CX-9

Specifications

Drive . . . . AWD
Engine 3.7-liter I4
Transmission . . . . 6-sp. Automatic
Tow Rating (lbs.) Low-3500
Head/Leg Room (in.) Cramped-39.3/40.9
Interior Space (cu. ft.) . . . . Very Roomy-135.1
Cargo Space (cu. ft.) Cramped-14.4
Wheelbase/Length (in.) 115.3/199.4

Ratings—10 Best, 1 Worst

Combo Crash Tests	6
Safety Features	7
Rollover	7
Preventive Maintenance	7
Repair Costs	9
Warranty	1
Fuel Economy	9
Complaints	9
Insurance Costs	3
OVERALL RATING	**8**

Mazda Mazda3

At-a-Glance

Status/Year Series Started Appearance Change/2014
Twins . . . . –
Body Styles . . . . Sedan, Hatchback
Seating 5
Anti-Theft Device . . . . Std. Passive Immobil. Only
Parking Index Rating . . . . Average
Where Made. . . . . Hofu, Japan
Fuel Factor: . . . .
  MPG Rating (city/hwy) Average-30/41
  Driving Range (mi.) Long-450
  Fuel Type . . . . Regular
  Annual Fuel Cost . . . . Very Low-$945
  Gas Guzzler Tax . . . . No
  Greenhouse Gas Emissions (tons/yr.) Low-5.3
  Barrels of Oil Used per year Low-9.7

How the Competition Rates

Competitors	Rating	Pg.
Ford Focus	6	144
Mitsubishi Lancer	4	216
Volkswagen Jetta	5	263

Price Range	Retail	Markup
i Sport MT	$17,845	4%
i Touring Sedan AT	$21,095	5%
s Touring Hatchback MT	$25,495	5%
s Grand Touring Hatchback AT	$26,495	5%

Mazda Mazda3

Safety Checklist

Crash Tests:
  Frontal . . . . Good
  Side . . . . Poor
Airbags:
  Torso . . . Standard Front Pelvis/Torso from Seat
  Roll Sensing. . . . . Yes
  Knee Bolster . . . . None
Crash Avoidance:
  Collision Avoidance . . . . . . Optional CIB & DBS^
  Blind Spot Detection . . . . Optional
  Lane Keeping Assist . . . . Optional
  Backup Camera . . . . Standard
  Pedestrian Crash Avoidance . . . . None
General:
  Auto. Crash Notification . . . . . . Dial Assist.-Free
  Day Running Lamps . . . . Standard
Safety Belt/Restraint:
  Dynamic Head Restraints . . . . None
  Adjustable Belt. . . . . Standard Front

^Warning feature does not meet government standards.
*Backup camera does not meet government standards.

Mazda Mazda3

Specifications

Drive. . . . . FWD
Engine 2.0-liter I4
Transmission . . . . 6-sp. Automatic
Tow Rating (lbs.) . . . . –
Head/Leg Room (in.) Cramped-38.6/42.2
Interior Space (cu. ft.). Cramped-96.3
Cargo Space (cu. ft.) . . . . . Very Cramped-12.4
Wheelbase/Length (in.) 106.3/180.3

Ratings—10 Best, 1 Worst

Combo Crash Tests	8
Safety Features	6
Rollover	7
Preventive Maintenance	7
Repair Costs	9
Warranty	1
Fuel Economy	8
Complaints	4
Insurance Costs	5
OVERALL RATING	**8**

Mazda Mazda6

Mazda Mazda6

At-a-Glance

Status/Year Series Started Appearance Change/2014
Twins . . . . –
Body Styles . . . . .Sedan
Seating. 5
Anti-Theft Device . . . . Std. Passive Immobil. Only
Parking Index Rating . . . . Average
Where Made. Flat Rock, MI
Fuel Factor:. . . . .
  MPG Rating (city/hwy) Poor-26/38
  Driving Range (mi.) . . . . Very Long-497
  Fuel Type. . . . . .Regular
  Annual Fuel Cost . . . . Low-$1064
  Gas Guzzler Tax . . . . .No
  Greenhouse Gas Emissions (tons/yr.) Low-6.0
  Barrels of Oil Used per year Average-11.0

How the Competition Rates

Competitors	Rating	Pg.
Kia Optima	9	180
Nissan Altima	5	221
Toyota Camry	8	247

Price Range	Retail	Markup
i Sport MT	$21,945	5%
i Sport AT	$22,995	5%
i Touring AT	$25,245	6%
i Grand Touring	$30,695	6%

Safety Checklist

Crash Tests:
  Frontal . . . . Good
  Side . . . . Good
Airbags:
  Torso . . .Standard Front Pelvis/Torso from Seat
  Roll Sensing. . . . . .Yes
  Knee Bolster . . . . None
Crash Avoidance:
  Collision Avoidance . . . . . . Optional CIB & DBS
  Blind Spot Detection . . . . Optional
  Lane Keeping Assist . . . .Warning Only Optional
  Backup Camera . . . . Standard
  Pedestrian Crash Avoidance . . . . None
General:
  Auto. Crash Notification . . . . . . Dial Assist.-Free
  Day Running Lamps . . . . Standard
Safety Belt/Restraint:
  Dynamic Head Restraints . . . . None
  Adjustable Belt . . . . .Standard Front

^Warning feature does not meet government standards.
*Backup camera does not meet government standards.

Mazda Mazda6

Specifications

Drive. . . . . .FWD
Engine 2.5-liter I4
Transmission . . . . 6-sp. Automatic
Tow Rating (lbs.) . . . . –
Head/Leg Room (in.) Cramped-38.4/42.2
Interior Space (cu. ft.). Average-99.7
Cargo Space (cu. ft.) Cramped-14.8
Wheelbase/Length (in.) 111.4/191.5

Ratings—10 Best, 1 Worst

Combo Crash Tests	—
Safety Features	1
Rollover	10
Preventive Maintenance	6
Repair Costs	6
Warranty	1
Fuel Economy	8
Complaints	4
Insurance Costs	5

OVERALL RATING —

Mazda MX-5 Miata

Mazda MX-5 Miata

At-a-Glance

Status/Year Series Started........ Unchanged/2016
Twins . . . . —
Body Styles . . . . Coupe, Convertible
Seating 2
Anti-Theft Device . . . . Std. Passive Immobil. Only
Parking Index Rating . . . . .Very Easy
Where Made . . . . Hiroshima, Japan
Fuel Factor: . . . .
　MPG Rating (city/hwy) Poor-27/36
　Driving Range (mi.) . . . . .Very Short-362
　Fuel Type . . . . .Premium
　Annual Fuel Cost . . . . .Average-$1321
　Gas Guzzler Tax . . . . .No
　Greenhouse Gas Emissions (tons/yr.) Low-4.9
　Barrels of Oil Used per year Average-11.0

How the Competition Rates

Competitors	Rating	Pg.
Buick Cascada	–	102
Toyota 86	–	245
	–	

Price Range	Retail	Markup
Sport MT	$24,915	6%
Sport AT	$26,395	6%
Club AT	$29,330	6%
Grand Touring AT	$31,270	6%

Safety Checklist

Crash Tests:
　Frontal . . . . –
　Side . . . . –
Airbags:
　Torso . . . Standard Front Pelvis/Torso from Seat
　Roll Sensing. . . . . No
　Knee Bolster . . . . None
Crash Avoidance:
　Collision Avoidance . . . . None
　Blind Spot Detection . . . . Optional
　Lane Keeping Assist . . . .Warning Only Optional
　Backup Camera . . . . None
　Pedestrian Crash Avoidance . . . . None
General:
　Auto. Crash Notification . . . . None
　Day Running Lamps . . . . Standard
Safety Belt/Restraint:
　Dynamic Head Restraints . . . . None
　Adjustable Belt . . . . None

^Warning feature does not meet government standards.
*Backup camera does not meet government standards.

Mazda MX-5 Miata

Specifications

Drive . . . . .RWD
Engine 2.0-liter I4
Transmission . . . . 6-sp. Manual
Tow Rating (lbs.) . . . . –
Head/Leg Room (in.) Cramped-37.4/43.1
Interior Space (cu. ft.) . . . . –
Cargo Space (cu. ft.) . . . . Very Cramped-4.6
Wheelbase/Length (in.) 90.9/154.1

Ratings—10 Best, 1 Worst

Combo Crash Tests	—
Safety Features	5
Rollover	4
Preventive Maintenance	6
Repair Costs	10
Warranty	3
Fuel Economy	10
Complaints	—
Insurance Costs	5
OVERALL RATING	**—**

Mercedes-Benz B-Class

Mercedes-Benz B-Class

At-a-Glance

Status/Year Series Started. Unchanged/2012
Twins . . . . –
Body Styles . . . . Hatchback
Seating. 5
Anti-Theft Device . Std. Active Immobil. & Pass. Alarm
Parking Index Rating . . . . Easy
Where Made Rastatt, Germany / Kecskemet, Hungary
Fuel Factor:. . . . .
  MPG Rating (city/hwy) Average-85/82
  Driving Range (mi.) . . . . Very Short-87
  Fuel Type. . . . . Electricity
  Annual Fuel Cost . . . . Very Low-$502
  Gas Guzzler Tax . . . . No
  Greenhouse Gas Emissions (tons/yr.). Very Low-0.2
  Barrels of Oil Used per year . . . . Very Low-0.0

How the Competition Rates

Competitors	Rating	Pg.
BMW i3	–	97
Nissan Leaf	4	225
Toyota Prius C	7	252

Price Range

	Retail	Markup
B250e	$39,900	8%

Safety Checklist

Crash Tests:
  Frontal . . . . –
  Side . . . . –
Airbags:
  Torso Std. Fr. & Opt. Rr. Pelvis/Torso from Seat
  Roll Sensing. . . . . No
  Knee Bolster . . . . Standard Driver
Crash Avoidance:
  Collision Avoidance . . . . . . Standard CIB & DBS
  Blind Spot Detection . . . . Optional
  Lane Keeping Assist . . . .Warning Only Optional
  Backup Camera . . . . Optional*
  Pedestrian Crash Avoidance . . . . None
General:
  Auto. Crash Notif. . . . . Oper. Assist. & Crash Info-Free
  Day Running Lamps . . . . None
Safety Belt/Restraint:
  Dynamic Head Restraints . . . . None
  Adjustable Belt. . . . . .Standard Front

^Warning feature does not meet government standards.
*Backup camera does not meet government standards.

Mercedes-Benz B-Class

Specifications

Drive. . . . . .FWD
Engine . . . . Electric
Transmission . . . . CVT
Tow Rating (lbs.) . . . . –
Head/Leg Room (in.) . . . . –
Interior Space (cu. ft.). Cramped-90.5
Cargo Space (cu. ft.) Average-21.6
Wheelbase/Length (in.) 106.3/171.5

Mercedes-Benz C-Class Compact

Ratings—10 Best, 1 Worst

Combo Crash Tests	4
Safety Features	9
Rollover	6
Preventive Maintenance	2
Repair Costs	2
Warranty	3
Fuel Economy	5
Complaints	6
Insurance Costs	5
OVERALL RATING	**3**

Mercedes-Benz C-Class

Mercedes-Benz C-Class

At-a-Glance

Status/Year Series Started. Unchanged/2015
Twins . . . . –
Body Styles . . . . Sedan, Coupe, Wagon
Seating 5
Anti-Theft Device . Std. Active Immobil. & Pass. Alarm
Parking Index Rating . . . . Average
Where Made. . . . . Tuscaloosa, AL
Fuel Factor:. . . . .
  MPG Rating (city/hwy) Poor-22/31
  Driving Range (mi.) Long-456
  Fuel Type. . . . . .Premium
  Annual Fuel Cost . . . . .High-$1589
  Gas Guzzler Tax . . . . .No
  Greenhouse Gas Emissions (tons/yr.). . Average-7.2
  Barrels of Oil Used per year High-13.2

How the Competition Rates

Competitors	Rating	Pg.
BMW 3 Series	7	93
Buick Verano	10	107
Lexus IS	6	193

Price Range

Price Range	Retail	Markup
C300 Sedan	$39,500	8%
C300 Coupe	$42,650	8%
C300 Coupe 4Matic	$44,650	8%
AMG C63 Coupe	$67,000	8%

Safety Checklist

Crash Tests:
  Frontal . . . . Average
  Side . . . . .Very Poor
Airbags:
  Torso Std. Fr. & Opt. Rr. Pelvis/Torso from Seat
  Roll Sensing. . . . . No
  Knee Bolster . . . . Standard Driver
Crash Avoidance:
  Collision Avoidance . . . . . . Standard CIB & DBS
  Blind Spot Detection . . . . Optional
  Lane Keeping Assist . . . . Optional
  Backup Camera . . . . Standard
  Pedestrian Crash Avoidance . . . . Optional
General:
  Auto. Crash Notif. . . . . . . Oper. Assist. & Crash Info-Free
  Day Running Lamps . . . . None
Safety Belt/Restraint:
  Dynamic Head Restraints . . . . . .Standard Front
  Adjustable Belt. . . . . None

^Warning feature does not meet government standards.
*Backup camera does not meet government standards.

Mercedes-Benz C-Class

Specifications

Drive. . . . . .RWD
Engine 2.0-liter I4
Transmission . . . . 7-sp. Automatic
Tow Rating (lbs.) . . . . –
Head/Leg Room (in.) . . . Very Cramped-37.1/41.7
Interior Space (cu. ft.). . . . . .Very Cramped-81
Cargo Space (cu. ft.) . . . . . . Very Cramped-12.8
Wheelbase/Length (in.) 111.8/184.5

Ratings—10 Best, 1 Worst

Combo Crash Tests	—
Safety Features	9
Rollover	7
Preventive Maintenance	2
Repair Costs	4
Warranty	3
Fuel Economy	8
Complaints	2
Insurance Costs	3
OVERALL RATING	**—**

Mercedes-Benz CLA-Class

Mercedes-Benz CLA-Class

At-a-Glance

Status/Year Series Started Unchanged/2014
Twins . . . . —
Body Styles . . . . .Coupe
Seating 5
Anti-Theft Device . Std. Active Immobil. & Pass. Alarm
Parking Index Rating . . . . .Easy
Where Made . . . . Kecskemet, Hungary
Fuel Factor: . . . .
  MPG Rating (city/hwy) Poor-26/38
  Driving Range (mi.) Short-400
  Fuel Type . . . . .Premium
  Annual Fuel Cost . . . . .Average-$1326
  Gas Guzzler Tax . . . . .No
  Greenhouse Gas Emissions (tons/yr.) . . Average-6.1
  Barrels of Oil Used per year Average-11.0

How the Competition Rates

Competitors	Rating	Pg.
Acura ILX	8	81
Cadillac ATS	8	108
Infiniti Q50	6	167

Price Range

	Retail	Markup
CLA250	$32,400	8%
CLA250 4Matic	$34,400	8%
CLA45 4Matic AMG	$49,950	8%

Safety Checklist

Crash Tests:
  Frontal . . . . —
  Side . . . . —
Airbags:
  Torso Std. Fr. & Opt. Rr. Pelvis/Torso from Seat
  Roll Sensing . . . . .Yes
  Knee Bolster . . . . .Standard Front
Crash Avoidance:
  Collision Avoidance . . . . . . Standard CIB & DBS
  Blind Spot Detection . . . . Optional
  Lane Keeping Assist . . . .Warning Only Optional
  Backup Camera . . . . Optional*
  Pedestrian Crash Avoidance . . . . None
General:
  Auto. Crash Notif. . . . . Oper. Assist. & Crash Info-Free
  Day Running Lamps . . . . None
Safety Belt/Restraint:
  Dynamic Head Restraints . . . . None
  Adjustable Belt . . . . .Standard Front

^Warning feature does not meet government standards.
*Backup camera does not meet government standards.

Mercedes-Benz CLA-Class

Specifications

Drive . . . . .FWD
Engine 2.0-liter I4
Transmission . . . . 7-sp. Automatic
Tow Rating (lbs.) . . . . —
Head/Leg Room (in.) . . . . Very Cramped-38.2/40.2
Interior Space (cu. ft.) . . . . .Very Cramped-88
Cargo Space (cu. ft.) . . . . .Very Cramped-13
Wheelbase/Length (in.) 106.3/182.3

Ratings—10 Best, 1 Worst

Combo Crash Tests	—
Safety Features	10
Rollover	7
Preventive Maintenance	4
Repair Costs	1
Warranty	3
Fuel Economy	4
Complaints	—
Insurance Costs	5

OVERALL RATING   —

Mercedes-Benz E-Class

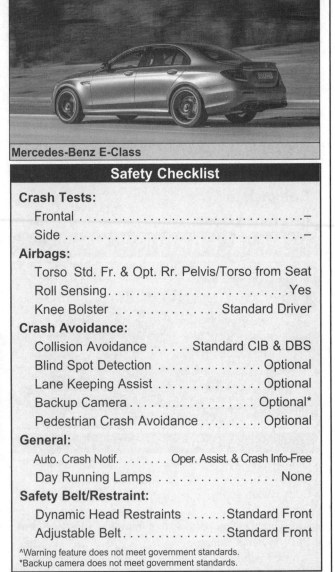

Mercedes-Benz E-Class

At-a-Glance

Status/Year Series Started. . . . . All New/2017
Twins . . . . –
Body Styles . . . . .Sedan
Seating 5
Anti-Theft Device . Std. Active Immobil. & Pass. Alarm
Parking Index Rating . . . . Average
Where Made. . . . . .Sindelfingen, Germany
Fuel Factor:. . . . .
  MPG Rating (city/hwy) . . . . .Very Poor-20/30
  Driving Range (mi.) . . . . Very Long-496
  Fuel Type. . . . . .Premium
  Annual Fuel Cost . . . . .High-$1708
  Gas Guzzler Tax . . . . .No
  Greenhouse Gas Emissions (tons/yr.). Low-5.8
  Barrels of Oil Used per year High-13.2

How the Competition Rates

Competitors	Rating	Pg.
Audi A6	6	88
BMW 5 Series	6	95
Tesla Model S	10	242

Price Range

Price Range	Retail	Markup
E300 Sedan	$52,150	8%
E400 Coupe	$54,550	8%
E400 Cabriolet	$62,600	8%
E550 Cabriolet	$69,100	8%

Safety Checklist

Crash Tests:
  Frontal . . . .–
  Side . . . .–
Airbags:
  Torso Std. Fr. & Opt. Rr. Pelvis/Torso from Seat
  Roll Sensing. . . . . .Yes
  Knee Bolster . . . . Standard Driver
Crash Avoidance:
  Collision Avoidance . . . . . . Standard CIB & DBS
  Blind Spot Detection . . . . Optional
  Lane Keeping Assist . . . . Optional
  Backup Camera . . . . Optional*
  Pedestrian Crash Avoidance . . . . Optional
General:
  Auto. Crash Notif. . . . . Oper. Assist. & Crash Info-Free
  Day Running Lamps . . . . None
Safety Belt/Restraint:
  Dynamic Head Restraints . . . . . .Standard Front
  Adjustable Belt. . . . . .Standard Front

^Warning feature does not meet government standards.
*Backup camera does not meet government standards.

Mercedes-Benz E-Class

Specifications

Drive. . . . . .RWD
Engine 3.5-liter V6
Transmission . . . . 7-sp. Automatic
Tow Rating (lbs.) . . . . –
Head/Leg Room (in.) . . . . Very Cramped-37.9/41.3
Interior Space (cu. ft.). . . . . –
Cargo Space (cu. ft.) . . . . Very Cramped-12.9
Wheelbase/Length (in.) 113.2/192.1

Ratings—10 Best, 1 Worst

Combo Crash Tests	—
Safety Features	9
Rollover	5
Preventive Maintenance	10
Repair Costs	2
Warranty	3
Fuel Economy	6
Complaints	7
Insurance Costs	8
OVERALL RATING	**—**

Mercedes-Benz GLA-Class

Mercedes-Benz GLA-Class

Mercedes-Benz GLA-Class

At-a-Glance

Status/Year Series Started Appearance Change/2015
Twins . . . . —
Body Styles . . . . SUV
Seating 5
Anti-Theft Device . Std. Active Immobil. & Pass. Alarm
Parking Index Rating . . . . Average
Where Made . . . . Rastatt, Germany
Fuel Factor: . . . .
　MPG Rating (city/hwy) Poor-24/32
　Driving Range (mi.) Short-400
　Fuel Type . . . . Premium
　Annual Fuel Cost . . . . High-$1487
　Gas Guzzler Tax . . . . No
　Greenhouse Gas Emissions (tons/yr.) . . Average-6.7
　Barrels of Oil Used per year Average-12.2

How the Competition Rates

Competitors	Rating	Pg.
Acura RDX	9	83
Buick Encore	10	104
Lexus RX	5	196

Price Range

Price Range	Retail	Markup
GLA250	$32,850	8%
GLA250 4Matic	$34,850	8%
AMG GLA45 4Matic	$49,900	8%

Safety Checklist

Crash Tests:
　Frontal . . . . –
　Side . . . . –
Airbags:
　Torso Std. Fr. & Opt. Rr. Pelvis/Torso from Seat
　Roll Sensing . . . . Yes
　Knee Bolster . . . . Standard Front
Crash Avoidance:
　Collision Avoidance . . . . . . Standard CIB & DBS
　Blind Spot Detection . . . . Optional
　Lane Keeping Assist . . . . Warning Only Optional
　Backup Camera . . . . Optional
　Pedestrian Crash Avoidance . . . . None
General:
　Auto. Crash Notif. . . . Oper. Assist. & Crash Info-Free
　Day Running Lamps . . . . None
Safety Belt/Restraint:
　Dynamic Head Restraints . . . . None
　Adjustable Belt . . . . None

^Warning feature does not meet government standards.
*Backup camera does not meet government standards.

Mercedes-Benz GLA-Class

Specifications

Drive . . . . AWD
Engine 2.0-liter I4
Transmission . . . . 7-sp. Automatic
Tow Rating (lbs.) . . . . –
Head/Leg Room (in.) Cramped-38.3/41.9
Interior Space (cu. ft.) Cramped-91
Cargo Space (cu. ft.) Average-17.2
Wheelbase/Length (in.) 106.3/173.9

Ratings—10 Best, 1 Worst

Combo Crash Tests	—
Safety Features	10
Rollover	3
Preventive Maintenance	3
Repair Costs	2
Warranty	3
Fuel Economy	2
Complaints	4
Insurance Costs	8

OVERALL RATING — —

Mercedes-Benz GLC-Class

Mercedes-Benz GLC-Class

At-a-Glance

Status/Year Series Started	Unchanged/2016
Twins	–
Body Styles	SUV
Seating	5
Anti-Theft Device	Std. Active Immobil. & Pass. Alarm
Parking Index Rating	Average
Where Made	Tuscaloosa, AL
Fuel Factor:	
MPG Rating (city/hwy)	Very Poor-18/25
Driving Range (mi.)	Very Short-358
Fuel Type	Premium
Annual Fuel Cost	Very High-$1952
Gas Guzzler Tax	No
Greenhouse Gas Emissions (tons/yr.)	High-8.6
Barrels of Oil Used per year	Very High-45.7

How the Competition Rates

Competitors	Rating	Pg.
Audi Q5	3	90
BMW X3	7	99
Lexus RX	5	196

Price Range

Price Range	Retail	Markup
GLC300	$39,150	8%
GLC300 4Matic	$41,150	8%
AMG GLC43	$54,900	8%

Safety Checklist

Crash Tests:
Frontal .... –
Side .... –

Airbags:
Torso Std. Fr. & Opt. Rr. Pelvis/Torso from Seat
Roll Sensing .... Yes
Knee Bolster .... Standard Driver

Crash Avoidance:
Collision Avoidance ...... Standard CIB & DBS
Blind Spot Detection .... Optional
Lane Keeping Assist .... Optional
Backup Camera .... Standard
Pedestrian Crash Avoidance .... Optional

General:
Auto. Crash Notif. ....Oper. Assist. & Crash Info-Free
Day Running Lamps .... None

Safety Belt/Restraint:
Dynamic Head Restraints ......Standard Front
Adjustable Belt ....Standard Front

^Warning feature does not meet government standards.
*Backup camera does not meet government standards.

Mercedes-Benz GLC-Class

Specifications

Drive	4WD
Engine	2.1-liter I4
Transmission	7-sp. Auto
Tow Rating (lbs.)	Low-3500
Head/Leg Room (in.)	Cramped-39/41.4
Interior Space (cu. ft.)	Very Cramped-79.5
Cargo Space (cu. ft.)	Cramped-16.5
Wheelbase/Length (in.)	108.5/178.3

Ratings—10 Best, 1 Worst

Combo Crash Tests	—
Safety Features	9
Rollover	2
Preventive Maintenance	3
Repair Costs	2
Warranty	3
Fuel Economy	3
Complaints	10
Insurance Costs	8
OVERALL RATING	**—**

Mercedes-Benz GL-Class

Mercedes-Benz GL-Class

Mercedes-Benz GL-Class

At-a-Glance

Status/Year Series Started Unchanged/2016
Twins . . . . —
Body Styles . . . . SUV
Seating 5
Anti-Theft Device . Std. Active Immobil. & Pass. Alarm
Parking Index Rating . . . . .Very Hard
Where Made. Tuscaloosa, AL
Fuel Factor:. . . . .
  MPG Rating (city/hwy) . . . . .Very Poor-19/26
  Driving Range (mi.) . . . . Very Long-571
  Fuel Type . . . . .Premium
  Annual Fuel Cost . . . . Very High-$1859
  Gas Guzzler Tax . . . . .No
  Greenhouse Gas Emissions (tons/yr.) Low-5.1
  Barrels of Oil Used per year . . . . Very Low-0.0

How the Competition Rates

Competitors	Rating	Pg.
Buick Enclave	6	103
Chevrolet Suburban	4	122
Ford Expedition	7	139

Price Range	Retail	Markup
GL350	$63,600	8%
GL450	$65,200	8%
GL550	$89,950	8%
GL63 AMG	$119,450	8%

Safety Checklist

Crash Tests:
  Frontal . . . .—
  Side . . . .—
Airbags:
  Torso Std. Fr. & Opt. Rr. Pelvis/Torso from Seat
  Roll Sensing. . . . . .Yes
  Knee Bolster . . . . Standard Driver
Crash Avoidance:
  Collision Avoidance . . . . . . Standard CIB & DBS
  Blind Spot Detection . . . . Optional
  Lane Keeping Assist . . . . Optional
  Backup Camera . . . . .Standard*
  Pedestrian Crash Avoidance . . . . Optional
General:
  Auto. Crash Notif. . . .Oper. Assist. & Crash Info-Free
  Day Running Lamps . . . . None
Safety Belt/Restraint:
  Dynamic Head Restraints . . . . None
  Adjustable Belt . . . . .Standard Front

^Warning feature does not meet government standards.
*Backup camera does not meet government standards.

Mercedes-Benz GL-Class

Specifications

Drive. 4WD
Engine 3.0-liter V6
Transmission . . . . 7-sp. Automatic
Tow Rating (lbs.) . . . . —
Head/Leg Room (in.) Cramped-41.2/40.3
Interior Space (cu. ft.). . . . . —
Cargo Space (cu. ft.) Cramped-16
Wheelbase/Length (in.) 121.1/201.6

Mercedes-Benz GLE-Class

Ratings—10 Best, 1 Worst

Combo Crash Tests	—
Safety Features	10
Rollover	3
Preventive Maintenance	3
Repair Costs	2
Warranty	3
Fuel Economy	2
Complaints	10
Insurance Costs	3
OVERALL RATING	**—**

Mercedes-Benz GLE-Class

Mercedes-Benz GLE-Class

At-a-Glance

Status/Year Series Started Unchanged/2012
Twins . . . . –
Body Styles . . . . SUV
Seating 5
Anti-Theft Device . Std. Active Immobil. & Pass. Alarm
Parking Index Rating . . . . Hard
Where Made . . . . Bremen, Germany
Fuel Factor: . . . .
  MPG Rating (city/hwy) . . . . .Very Poor-18/24
  Driving Range (mi.) . . . . Very Long-499
  Fuel Type . . . . .Premium
  Annual Fuel Cost . . . . Very High-$1982
  Gas Guzzler Tax . . . . .No
  Greenhouse Gas Emissions (tons/yr.) . . Average-7.3
  Barrels of Oil Used per year High-16.5

How the Competition Rates

Competitors	Rating	Pg.
Audi Q5	3	90
BMW X5	6	100
Lexus RX	5	196

Price Range

Price Range	Retail	Markup
GLE350	$52,000	8%
GLE350 4Matic	$54,500	8%
GLE400 4Matic	$65,650	8%
AMG GLE63	$101,690	8%

Safety Checklist

Crash Tests:
  Frontal . . . .–
  Side . . . .–
Airbags:
  Torso Std. Fr. & Opt. Rr. Pelvis/Torso from Seat
  Roll Sensing . . . . .Yes
  Knee Bolster . . . . Standard Driver
Crash Avoidance:
  Collision Avoidance . . . . . . Std. CIB & Opt. DBS
  Blind Spot Detection . . . . Optional
  Lane Keeping Assist . . . . Standard
  Backup Camera . . . . Standard
  Pedestrian Crash Avoidance . . . . Optional
General:
  Auto. Crash Notif. . . .Oper. Assist. & Crash Info-Free
  Day Running Lamps . . . . None
Safety Belt/Restraint:
  Dynamic Head Restraints . . . . None
  Adjustable Belt . . . . .Standard Front

^Warning feature does not meet government standards.
*Backup camera does not meet government standards.

Mercedes-Benz GLE-Class

Specifications

Drive . . . . .RWD
Engine 3.5-liter V6
Transmission . . . . 7-sp. Automatic
Tow Rating (lbs.) Average-6600
Head/Leg Room (in.) . . . . Very Cramped-38.9/40.3
Interior Space (cu. ft.) . . . . –
Cargo Space (cu. ft.) . . . . Very Roomy-38.2
Wheelbase/Length (in.) 114.8/189.1

Ratings—10 Best, 1 Worst

Combo Crash Tests	—
Safety Features	10
Rollover	7
Preventive Maintenance	4
Repair Costs	1
Warranty	3
Fuel Economy	2
Complaints	3
Insurance Costs	5
OVERALL RATING	—

Mercedes-Benz S-Class

At-a-Glance

Status/Year Series Started Appearance Change/2014
Twins . . . . –
Body Styles . . . . Sedan, Coupe
Seating 5
Anti-Theft Device . Std. Active Immobil. & Pass. Alarm
Parking Index Rating . . . . Very Hard
Where Made . . . . Sindelfingen, Germany
Fuel Factor: . . . .
  MPG Rating (city/hwy) . . . . Very Poor-17/26
  Driving Range (mi.) Average-425
  Fuel Type . . . . Premium
  Annual Fuel Cost . . . . Very High-$1996
  Gas Guzzler Tax . . . . No
  Greenhouse Gas Emissions (tons/yr.) High-9.0
  Barrels of Oil Used per year High-16.5

How the Competition Rates

Competitors	Rating	Pg.
Buick LaCrosse	6	105
Cadillac XTS	9	111
Infiniti Q50	6	167

Price Range	Retail	Markup
S550	$96,600	8%
S550 4Matic	$99,600	8%
AMG S63	$144,700	8%
S600	$170,750	8%

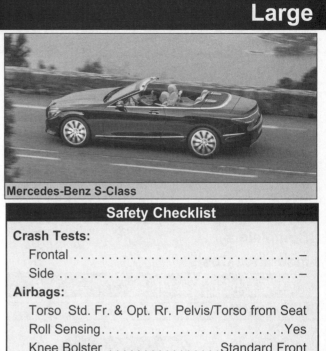

Mercedes-Benz S-Class

Safety Checklist

Crash Tests:
  Frontal . . . .–
  Side . . . .–
Airbags:
  Torso Std. Fr. & Opt. Rr. Pelvis/Torso from Seat
  Roll Sensing . . . . Yes
  Knee Bolster . . . . Standard Front
Crash Avoidance:
  Collision Avoidance . . . . . . Standard CIB & DBS
  Blind Spot Detection . . . . Optional
  Lane Keeping Assist . . . . Optional
  Backup Camera . . . . Standard*
  Pedestrian Crash Avoidance . . . . Optional
General:
  Auto. Crash Notif. . . . Oper. Assist. & Crash Info-Free
  Day Running Lamps . . . . None
Safety Belt/Restraint:
  Dynamic Head Restraints . . . . . . Standard Front
  Adjustable Belt . . . . None

^Warning feature does not meet government standards.
*Backup camera does not meet government standards.

Mercedes-Benz S-Class

Specifications

Drive . . . . RWD
Engine 4.7-liter V8
Transmission . . . . 7-sp. Automatic
Tow Rating (lbs.) . . . .–
Head/Leg Room (in.) Cramped-39.7/41.4
Interior Space (cu. ft.) Roomy-112
Cargo Space (cu. ft.) Cramped-16.5
Wheelbase/Length (in.) 124.6/206.5

Ratings—10 Best, 1 Worst

Combo Crash Tests	4
Safety Features	4
Rollover	6
Preventive Maintenance	3
Repair Costs	4
Warranty	9
Fuel Economy	7
Complaints	7
Insurance Costs	5
OVERALL RATING	**5**

Mini Cooper

At-a-Glance

Status/Year Series Started........ Unchanged/2016
Twins . . . . –
Body Styles . . . . Sedan
Seating 4
Anti-Theft Device . . . . Std. Passive Alarm Only
Parking Index Rating . . . . .Very Easy
Where Made. . . . . Oxford, England
Fuel Factor:. . . . .
  MPG Rating (city/hwy) Poor-27/32
  Driving Range (mi.) . . . . .Very Short-337
  Fuel Type. . . . . .Premium
  Annual Fuel Cost . . . . .Average-$1384
  Gas Guzzler Tax . . . . .No
  Greenhouse Gas Emissions (tons/yr.). Low-5.2
  Barrels of Oil Used per year Average-11.4

How the Competition Rates

Competitors	Rating	Pg.
Chevrolet Sonic	9	120
Kia Soul	8	184
Volkswagen Beetle	1	261

Price Range	Retail	Markup
Base Hatchback	$20,700	5%
S Coupe	$24,100	9%
S Hatchback	$25,100	9%
John Cooper Works Hatchback	$30,600	12%

Mini Cooper

Safety Checklist

Crash Tests:
  Frontal . . . . Average
  Side . . . . .Very Poor
Airbags:
  Torso . . . . Standard Front Torso from Seat
  Roll Sensing. . . . . .Yes
  Knee Bolster . . . . .Standard Front
Crash Avoidance:
  Collision Avoidance . . . . . .Optional CIB & DBS^
  Blind Spot Detection . . . . None
  Lane Keeping Assist . . . . None
  Backup Camera . . . . Optional*
  Pedestrian Crash Avoidance . . . . None
General:
  Auto. Crash Notification . . . . None
  Day Running Lamps . . . . Standard
Safety Belt/Restraint:
  Dynamic Head Restraints . . . . None
  Adjustable Belt. . . . . None

^Warning feature does not meet government standards.
*Backup camera does not meet government standards.

Mini Cooper

Specifications

Drive. . . . . .FWD
Engine 1.5-liter I3
Transmission . . . . 6-sp. Automatic
Tow Rating (lbs.) . . . . –
Head/Leg Room (in.) Cramped-39.9/41.4
Interior Space (cu. ft.). . . . . .Very Cramped-84
Cargo Space (cu. ft.) . . . . .Very Cramped-9
Wheelbase/Length (in.) 101.1/157.4

Ratings—10 Best, 1 Worst

Combo Crash Tests	—
Safety Features	4
Rollover	4
Preventive Maintenance	3
Repair Costs	6
Warranty	9
Fuel Economy	7
Complaints	10
Insurance Costs	5

OVERALL RATING —

Mini Countryman

At-a-Glance

Status/Year Series Started	Unchanged/2012
Twins	—
Body Styles	Hatchback
Seating	5
Anti-Theft Device	Std. Passive Alarm Only
Parking Index Rating	Easy
Where Made	Oxford, England

Fuel Factor:

MPG Rating (city/hwy)	Poor-27/34
Driving Range (mi.)	Very Short-369
Fuel Type	Premium
Annual Fuel Cost	Average-$1351
Gas Guzzler Tax	No
Greenhouse Gas Emissions (tons/yr.)	Low-6.0
Barrels of Oil Used per year	Average-11.0

How the Competition Rates

Competitors	Rating	Pg.
Kia Soul	8	184
Mitsubishi Mirage	3	217
Toyota Yaris	5	259

Price Range	Retail	Markup
Base	$22,750	5%
S	$26,100	9%
S ALL4	$27,850	9%
John Cooper Works ALL4	$35,350	12%

Mini Countryman

Safety Checklist

Crash Tests:

Frontal	—
Side	—

Airbags:

Torso	Standard Front Torso from Seat
Roll Sensing	Yes
Knee Bolster	Standard Front

Crash Avoidance:

Collision Avoidance	Optional CIB & DBS^
Blind Spot Detection	None
Lane Keeping Assist	None
Backup Camera	Optional*
Pedestrian Crash Avoidance	None

General:

Auto. Crash Notification	None
Day Running Lamps	Standard

Safety Belt/Restraint:

Dynamic Head Restraints	None
Adjustable Belt	None

^Warning feature does not meet government standards.
*Backup camera does not meet government standards.

Mini Countryman

Specifications

Drive	FWD
Engine	1.6-liter I4
Transmission	6-sp. Manual
Tow Rating (lbs.)	—
Head/Leg Room (in.)	Cramped-39.9/40.4
Interior Space (cu. ft.)	Very Cramped-87
Cargo Space (cu. ft.)	Average-17.5
Wheelbase/Length (in.)	102.2/162.2

Mitsubishi Lancer Compact

Ratings—10 Best, 1 Worst

Combo Crash Tests	2
Safety Features	2
Rollover	5
Preventive Maintenance	10
Repair Costs	4
Warranty	10
Fuel Economy	7
Complaints	5
Insurance Costs	1
OVERALL RATING	**4**

Mitsubishi Lancer

Mitsubishi Lancer

At-a-Glance

Status/Year Series Started. Unchanged/2008
Twins . . . . –
Body Styles . . . . .Sedan
Seating 5
Anti-Theft Device . . . . Std. Passive Alarm Only
Parking Index Rating . . . . .Very Easy
Where Made. . . . . Mizushima, Japan
Fuel Factor:. . . . .
  MPG Rating (city/hwy) Poor-26/34
  Driving Range (mi.) Long-451
  Fuel Type. . . . . .Regular
  Annual Fuel Cost . . . . Low-$1109
  Gas Guzzler Tax . . . . .No
  Greenhouse Gas Emissions (tons/yr.). . Average-6.2
  Barrels of Oil Used per year Average-11.4

How the Competition Rates

Competitors	Rating	Pg.
Honda Civic	8	153
Mazda Mazda3	8	202
Nissan Sentra	5	231

Price Range	Retail	Markup
ES MT	$17,595	3%
SE AWD	$20,995	3%
SEL AWD	$21,995	3%
GT AT	$23,495	3%

Safety Checklist

Crash Tests:
  Frontal . . . . .Poor
  Side . . . . .Very Poor
Airbags:
  Torso . . . Standard Front Pelvis/Torso from Seat
  Roll Sensing. . . . . .Yes
  Knee Bolster . . . . Standard Driver
Crash Avoidance:
  Collision Avoidance . . . . None
  Blind Spot Detection . . . . None
  Lane Keeping Assist . . . . None
  Backup Camera . . . . Optional*
  Pedestrian Crash Avoidance . . . . None
General:
  Auto. Crash Notification. . . . . None
  Day Running Lamps . . . . Optional
Safety Belt/Restraint:
  Dynamic Head Restraints . . . . None
  Adjustable Belt. . . . . .Standard Front

^Warning feature does not meet government standards.
*Backup camera does not meet government standards.

Mitsubishi Lancer

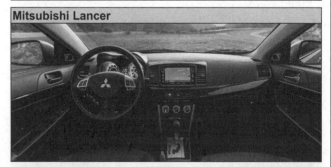

Specifications

Drive. . . . . .FWD
Engine 2.0-liter I4
Transmission . . . . .CVT
Tow Rating (lbs.) . . . . –
Head/Leg Room (in.) Cramped-39.6/42.3
Interior Space (cu. ft.). Cramped-93.5
Cargo Space (cu. ft.) . . . . Very Cramped-12.3
Wheelbase/Length (in.) 103.7/180

Ratings—10 Best, 1 Worst

Combo Crash Tests	2
Safety Features	2
Rollover	3
Preventive Maintenance	8
Repair Costs	5
Warranty	10
Fuel Economy	9
Complaints	2
Insurance Costs	1
OVERALL RATING	**3**

Mitsubishi Mirage

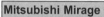
Mitsubishi Mirage

At-a-Glance

Status/Year Series Started........ Unchanged/2014
Twins ....–
Body Styles .... Hatchback
Seating..5
Anti-Theft Device ...... Std. Pass. Immobil. & Alarm
Parking Index Rating .... Very Easy
Where Made............. Laem Chabang, Thailand
Fuel Factor:.....................................
  MPG Rating (city/hwy) Average-37/44
  Driving Range (mi.) .... Very Short-367
  Fuel Type........................... Regular
  Annual Fuel Cost .... Very Low-$809
  Gas Guzzler Tax .... No
  Greenhouse Gas Emissions (tons/yr.). Very Low-4.5
  Barrels of Oil Used per year Low-8.2

How the Competition Rates

Competitors	Rating	Pg.
Ford Fiesta	3	142
Nissan Versa	2	233
Toyota Yaris	5	259

Price Range	Retail	Markup
ES MT	$12,995	2%
SE MT	$14,795	2%
SE AT	$15,995	2%
GT AT	$16,495	2%

Safety Checklist

Crash Tests:
  Frontal .... Poor
  Side .... Very Poor
Airbags:
  Torso . . . Standard Front Pelvis/Torso from Seat
  Roll Sensing.......................... Yes
  Knee Bolster .... Standard Driver
Crash Avoidance:
  Collision Avoidance .... None
  Blind Spot Detection .... None
  Lane Keeping Assist .... None
  Backup Camera .... None
  Pedestrian Crash Avoidance .... None
General:
  Auto. Crash Notification .... None
  Day Running Lamps .... None
Safety Belt/Restraint:
  Dynamic Head Restraints .... None
  Adjustable Belt............... Standard Front

^Warning feature does not meet government standards.
*Backup camera does not meet government standards.

Mitsubishi Mirage

Specifications

Drive... FWD
Engine 1.2-liter I3
Transmission .... CVT
Tow Rating (lbs.) .... –
Head/Leg Room (in.) Cramped-39.1/41.7
Interior Space (cu. ft.)............. Very Cramped-86.1
Cargo Space (cu. ft.) Average-17.2
Wheelbase/Length (in.) 96.5/148.8

Ratings—10 Best, 1 Worst

Combo Crash Tests	5
Safety Features	6
Rollover	3
Preventive Maintenance	4
Repair Costs	7
Warranty	10
Fuel Economy	5
Complaints	2
Insurance Costs	1
OVERALL RATING	**4**

Mitsubishi Outlander

At-a-Glance

Status/Year Series Started Unchanged/2014
Twins . . . . –
Body Styles . . . . SUV
Seating 7
Anti-Theft Device . . . . . . Std. Pass. Immobil. & Alarm
Parking Index Rating . . . . Easy
Where Made . . . . Okazaki, Japan
Fuel Factor: . . . .
  MPG Rating (city/hwy) Poor-24/29
  Driving Range (mi.) Average-411
  Fuel Type . . . . .Regular
  Annual Fuel Cost . . . . Low-$1239
  Gas Guzzler Tax . . . . .No
  Greenhouse Gas Emissions (tons/yr.) . . Average-6.9
  Barrels of Oil Used per year Average-12.7

How the Competition Rates

Competitors	Rating	Pg.
Hyundai Santa Fe	–	162
Nissan Pathfinder	2	228
Toyota Highlander	7	250

Price Range

Price Range	Retail	Markup
ES FWD	$23,495	3%
SE FWD	$24,495	3%
SEL AWD	$27,495	3%
GT AWD	$31,695	3%

Mitsubishi Outlander

Safety Checklist

Crash Tests:
  Frontal . . . . Average
  Side . . . . Poor
Airbags:
  Torso . . . Standard Front Pelvis/Torso from Seat
  Roll Sensing . . . . .Yes
  Knee Bolster . . . . Standard Driver
Crash Avoidance:
  Collision Avoidance . . . . . . Optional CIB & DBS
  Blind Spot Detection . . . . Optional
  Lane Keeping Assist . . . .Warning Only Optional
  Backup Camera . . . . Optional*
  Pedestrian Crash Avoidance . . . . Optional
General:
  Auto. Crash Notification . . . . None
  Day Running Lamps . . . . Standard
Safety Belt/Restraint:
  Dynamic Head Restraints . . . . None
  Adjustable Belt . . . . .Standard Front

^Warning feature does not meet government standards.
*Backup camera does not meet government standards.

Mitsubishi Outlander

Specifications

Drive 4WD
Engine 2.4-liter I4
Transmission . . . . CVT
Tow Rating (lbs.) . . . . .Very Low-1500
Head/Leg Room (in.) Cramped-40.6/40.9
Interior Space (cu. ft.) . . . . Very Roomy-128.2
Cargo Space (cu. ft.) . . . . Very Cramped-10.3
Wheelbase/Length (in.) 105.1/183.3

Ratings—10 Best, 1 Worst

Combo Crash Tests	4
Safety Features	2
Rollover	3
Preventive Maintenance	7
Repair Costs	3
Warranty	10
Fuel Economy	6
Complaints	6
Insurance Costs	3
OVERALL RATING	**4**

Mitsubishi Outlander Sport

Mitsubishi Outlander Sport

At-a-Glance

Status/Year Series Started	Unchanged/2013
Twins	–
Body Styles	SUV
Seating	5
Anti-Theft Device	Std. Pass. Immobil. & Alarm
Parking Index Rating	Very Easy
Where Made	Okazaki, Japan
Fuel Factor:	
MPG Rating (city/hwy)	Poor-25/32
Driving Range (mi.)	Average-424
Fuel Type	Regular
Annual Fuel Cost	Low-$1163
Gas Guzzler Tax	No
Greenhouse Gas Emissions (tons/yr.)	Average-6.4
Barrels of Oil Used per year	Average-11.8

How the Competition Rates

Competitors	Rating	Pg.
Acura RDX	9	83
Hyundai Santa Fe Sport	7	163
Jeep Cherokee	5	172

Price Range

	Retail	Markup
ES 2.0L FWD MT	$19,595	3%
ES 2.4L FWD AT	$21,295	3%
SEL 2.4L FWD AT	$23,995	3%
GT 2.4L 4WD	$27,395	3%

Safety Checklist

Crash Tests:
Frontal	Average
Side	Very Poor

Airbags:
Torso	Standard Front Pelvis/Torso from Seat
Roll Sensing	Yes
Knee Bolster	Standard Driver

Crash Avoidance:
Collision Avoidance	None
Blind Spot Detection	None
Lane Keeping Assist	None
Backup Camera	Optional*
Pedestrian Crash Avoidance	None

General:
Auto. Crash Notification	None
Day Running Lamps	None

Safety Belt/Restraint:
Dynamic Head Restraints	None
Adjustable Belt	Standard Front

^Warning feature does not meet government standards.
*Backup camera does not meet government standards.

Mitsubishi Outlander Sport

Specifications

Drive	FWD
Engine	2.0-liter I4
Transmission	CVT
Tow Rating (lbs.)	–
Head/Leg Room (in.)	Cramped-39.4/41.6
Interior Space (cu. ft.)	Average-97.5
Cargo Space (cu. ft.)	Average-21.7
Wheelbase/Length (in.)	105.1/169.1

Ratings—10 Best, 1 Worst

Combo Crash Tests	—
Safety Features	1
Rollover	10
Preventive Maintenance	9
Repair Costs	4
Warranty	1
Fuel Economy	3
Complaints	3
Insurance Costs	3

OVERALL RATING — —

Nissan 370Z

Nissan 370Z

At-a-Glance

Status/Year Series Started........ Unchanged/2010
Twins . . . .—
Body Styles . . . . Coupe, Convertible
Seating 2
Anti-Theft Device . . . . . . Std. Pass. Immobil. & Alarm
Parking Index Rating . . . . Very Easy
Where Made. . . . . Tochigi, Japan
Fuel Factor:. . . . .
  MPG Rating (city/hwy) . . . . .Very Poor-19/26
  Driving Range (mi.) Average-411
  Fuel Type . . . . .Premium
  Annual Fuel Cost . . . . Very High-$1859
  Gas Guzzler Tax . . . . .No
  Greenhouse Gas Emissions (tons/yr.). High-7.6
  Barrels of Oil Used per year High-15.7

How the Competition Rates

Competitors	Rating	Pg.
Honda Accord	9	152
Kia Optima	9	180
Toyota Camry	8	247

Price Range

Price Range	Retail	Markup
Base Coupe MT	$29,990	8%
Sport Coupe AT	$34,870	8%
Nismo Tech Coupe AT	$46,790	8%
Touring Sport Roadster AT	$49,400	8%

Safety Checklist

Crash Tests:
  Frontal . . . .–
  Side . . . .–
Airbags:
  Torso . . . Standard Front Pelvis/Torso from Seat
  Roll Sensing. . . . . No
  Knee Bolster . . . . None
Crash Avoidance:
  Collision Avoidance . . . . None
  Blind Spot Detection . . . . None
  Lane Keeping Assist . . . . None
  Backup Camera . . . . Optional*
  Pedestrian Crash Avoidance . . . . None
General:
  Auto. Crash Notification . . . . None
  Day Running Lamps . . . . Standard
Safety Belt/Restraint:
  Dynamic Head Restraints . . . . . .Standard Front
  Adjustable Belt. . . . . None

^Warning feature does not meet government standards.
*Backup camera does not meet government standards.

Nissan 370Z

Specifications

Drive. . . . . .RWD
Engine 3.7-liter V6
Transmission . . . . 7-sp. Automatic
Tow Rating (lbs.) . . . . .Very Low-0
Head/Leg Room (in.) Cramped-38.2/42.9
Interior Space (cu. ft.). . . . . Very Cramped-51.6
Cargo Space (cu. ft.) . . . . Very Cramped-6.9
Wheelbase/Length (in.) 100.4/167.5

Ratings—10 Best, 1 Worst

Combo Crash Tests	7
Safety Features	3
Rollover	7
Preventive Maintenance	5
Repair Costs	8
Warranty	1
Fuel Economy	8
Complaints	5
Insurance Costs	1
OVERALL RATING	**5**

Nissan Altima

Nissan Altima

At-a-Glance

Status/Year Series Started	Unchanged/2013
Twins	–
Body Styles	Sedan, Coupe
Seating	5
Anti-Theft Device	Std. Pass. Immobil. & Alarm
Parking Index Rating	Average
Where Made	Smyrna, TN / Canton, MS
Fuel Factor:	
MPG Rating (city/hwy)	Poor-27/38
Driving Range (mi.)	Very Long-559
Fuel Type	Regular
Annual Fuel Cost	Very Low-$1039
Gas Guzzler Tax	No
Greenhouse Gas Emissions (tons/yr.)	Low-5.8
Barrels of Oil Used per year	Average-10.6

How the Competition Rates

Competitors	Rating	Pg.
Chevrolet Malibu	10	118
Chevrolet Suburban	4	122
Ford Expedition	7	139

Price Range

Price Range	Retail	Markup
Base	$22,500	5%
S 2.5L	$22,900	7%
SV 3.5L	$25,460	7%
SL 3.5L	$32,690	7%

Safety Checklist

Crash Tests:
Frontal . . . . Very Good
Side . . . . .Very Poor

Airbags:
Torso . . . Standard Front Pelvis/Torso from Seat
Roll Sensing. . . . . .Yes
Knee Bolster . . . . None

Crash Avoidance:
Collision Avoidance . . . . . . Optional CIB & DBS
Blind Spot Detection . . . . Optional
Lane Keeping Assist . . . . None
Backup Camera . . . . Optional*
Pedestrian Crash Avoidance . . . . None

General:
Auto. Crash Notification . . . . None
Day Running Lamps . . . . Optional

Safety Belt/Restraint:
Dynamic Head Restraints . . . . None
Adjustable Belt. . . . . .Standard Front

^Warning feature does not meet government standards.
*Backup camera does not meet government standards.

Nissan Altima

Specifications

Drive	FWD
Engine	2.5-liter I4
Transmission	6-sp. Automatic
Tow Rating (lbs.)	–
Head/Leg Room (in.)	Very Roomy-40/45
Interior Space (cu. ft.)	Average-101.9
Cargo Space (cu. ft.)	Cramped-15.4
Wheelbase/Length (in.)	109.3/191.5

Ratings—10 Best, 1 Worst

Combo Crash Tests	—
Safety Features	7
Rollover	1
Preventive Maintenance	3
Repair Costs	4
Warranty	1
Fuel Economy	1
Complaints	—
Insurance Costs	10

OVERALL RATING   —

Nissan Armada

Nissan Armada

At-a-Glance

Status/Year Series Started. . . . . All New/2017
Twins . . . . –
Body Styles . . . . SUV
Seating 7/8
Anti-Theft Device . . . . . . Std. Pass. Immobil. & Alarm
Parking Index Rating . . . . .Very Hard
Where Made. . . . . Canton, MS
Fuel Factor:. . . . .
  MPG Rating (city/hwy) . . . . .Very Poor-14/19
  Driving Range (mi.) Average-413
  Fuel Type . . . . .Regular
  Annual Fuel Cost . . . . Very High-$2031
  Gas Guzzler Tax . . . . .No
  Greenhouse Gas Emissions (tons/yr.) Very High-9.2
  Barrels of Oil Used per year . . . . . . .Very High-20.6

How the Competition Rates

Competitors	Rating	Pg.
Chevrolet Suburban	4	122
Ford Expedition	7	139
Toyota 4Runner	2	244

Price Range

Price Range	Retail	Markup
SV 2WD	$44,400	7%
SL 2WD	$49,150	7%
SL 4WD	$52,050	7%
Platinum 4WD	$59,990	7%

Safety Checklist

Crash Tests:
  Frontal . . . .–
  Side . . . .–
Airbags:
  Torso . . .Standard Front Pelvis/Torso from Seat
  Roll Sensing. . . . . .Yes
  Knee Bolster . . . . None
Crash Avoidance:
  Collision Avoidance . . . . . . Optional CIB & DBS
  Blind Spot Detection . . . . .Optional
  Lane Keeping Assist . . . .Warning Only Optional
  Backup Camera . . . . .Standard*
  Pedestrian Crash Avoidance . . . . None
General:
  Auto. Crash Notification . . . . None
  Day Running Lamps . . . . Standard
Safety Belt/Restraint:
  Dynamic Head Restraints . . . . . .Standard Front
  Adjustable Belt. . . . . Standard Front & Rear

^Warning feature does not meet government standards.
*Backup camera does not meet government standards.

Nissan Armada

Specifications

Drive. . . . . .RWD
Engine 5.6-liter V8
Transmission . . . . 7-sp. Automatic
Tow Rating (lbs.) . . . . Very High-8500
Head/Leg Room (in.) Roomy-40.9/41.9
Interior Space (cu. ft.). . . . . Very Roomy-154.5
Cargo Space (cu. ft.) Cramped-16.2
Wheelbase/Length (in.) 121.1/208.9

Ratings—10 Best, 1 Worst

Combo Crash Tests	—
Safety Features	2
Rollover	1
Preventive Maintenance	3
Repair Costs	7
Warranty	1
Fuel Economy	1
Complaints	6
Insurance Costs	8
OVERALL RATING	**—**

Nissan Frontier

Nissan Frontier

At-a-Glance

Status/Year Series Started. Unchanged/2005
Twins . . . .—
Body Styles . . . . Pickup
Seating 5
Anti-Theft Device . . . . . . Std. Pass. Immobil. & Alarm
Parking Index Rating . . . . Very Hard
Where Made. . . . . Canton, MS
Fuel Factor:. . . . .
  MPG Rating (city/hwy) . . . . .Very Poor-15/21
  Driving Range (mi.) . . . . .Very Short-363
  Fuel Type. . . . . .Regular
  Annual Fuel Cost . . . . Very High-$1874
  Gas Guzzler Tax . . . . .No
  Greenhouse Gas Emissions (tons/yr.)Very High-10.5
  Barrels of Oil Used per year . . . . . . Very High-19.4

How the Competition Rates

Competitors	Rating	Pg.
Chevrolet Colorado	3	113
Toyota Tacoma	2	257

Price Range

	Retail	Markup
S King Cab I4 2WD MT	$18,290	3%
SV Crew Cab V6 2WD AT	$24,960	4%
PRO-4X Crew Cab 4WD AT	$32,890	6%
SL Crew Cab 4WD AT	$34,360	6%

Safety Checklist

Crash Tests:
  Frontal . . . .—
  Side . . . .—
Airbags:
  Torso . . . Standard Front Pelvis/Torso from Seat
  Roll Sensing. . . . . .Yes
  Knee Bolster . . . . None
Crash Avoidance:
  Collision Avoidance . . . . None
  Blind Spot Detection . . . . None
  Lane Keeping Assist . . . . None
  Backup Camera . . . . Optional*
  Pedestrian Crash Avoidance . . . . None
General:
  Auto. Crash Notification . . . . None
  Day Running Lamps . . . . None
Safety Belt/Restraint:
  Dynamic Head Restraints . . . . . .Standard Front
  Adjustable Belt . . . . .Standard Front

^Warning feature does not meet government standards.
*Backup camera does not meet government standards.

Nissan Frontier

Specifications

Drive. 4WD
Engine 4.0-liter V6
Transmission . . . . 5-sp. Automatic
Tow Rating (lbs.) Average-6300
Head/Leg Room (in.) Cramped-39.7/42.4
Interior Space (cu. ft.). . . . . Very Cramped-87.7
Cargo Space (cu. ft.) . . . . Very Roomy-33.5
Wheelbase/Length (in.) 125.9/205.5

Ratings—10 Best, 1 Worst

Combo Crash Tests	1
Safety Features	3
Rollover	3
Preventive Maintenance	5
Repair Costs	6
Warranty	1
Fuel Economy	6
Complaints	7
Insurance Costs	5
OVERALL RATING	**2**

Nissan Juke

Nissan Juke

At-a-Glance

Status/Year Series Started	Unchanged/2011
Twins	–
Body Styles	SUV
Seating	5
Anti-Theft Device	Std. Pass. Immobil. & Alarm
Parking Index Rating	Very Easy
Where Made	Oppama, Japan
Fuel Factor:	
MPG Rating (city/hwy)	Poor-26/31
Driving Range (mi.)	Very Short-331
Fuel Type	Premium
Annual Fuel Cost	Average-$1434
Gas Guzzler Tax	No
Greenhouse Gas Emissions (tons/yr.)	Average-6.5
Barrels of Oil Used per year	Average-11.8

How the Competition Rates

Competitors	Rating	Pg.
Ford Escape	7	138
Mitsubishi Outlander Sport	4	219
Subaru Forester	4	237

Price Range

Price Range	Retail	Markup
S FWD	$20,250	3%
SV FWD	$22,300	4%
SL AWD	$26,940	4%
NISMO RS AWD	$30,020	4%

Safety Checklist

Crash Tests:
- Frontal .... Very Poor
- Side .... Very Poor

Airbags:
- Torso . . . Standard Front Pelvis/Torso from Seat
- Roll Sensing........................Yes
- Knee Bolster .... None

Crash Avoidance:
- Collision Avoidance .... None
- Blind Spot Detection .... None
- Lane Keeping Assist .... None
- Backup Camera................... Standard*
- Pedestrian Crash Avoidance .... None

General:
- Auto. Crash Notification.............. None
- Day Running Lamps .... Optional

Safety Belt/Restraint:
- Dynamic Head Restraints ......Standard Front
- Adjustable Belt...............Standard Front

^Warning feature does not meet government standards.
*Backup camera does not meet government standards.

Nissan Juke

Specifications

Drive	AWD
Engine	1.6-liter I4
Transmission	CVT
Tow Rating (lbs.)	–
Head/Leg Room (in.)	Cramped-39.6/42.1
Interior Space (cu. ft.)	Very Cramped-87
Cargo Space (cu. ft.)	Very Cramped-10.5
Wheelbase/Length (in.)	99.6/162.4

Ratings—10 Best, 1 Worst

Combo Crash Tests	1
Safety Features	1
Rollover	7
Preventive Maintenance	8
Repair Costs	10
Warranty	1
Fuel Economy	10
Complaints	2
Insurance Costs	10
OVERALL RATING	**4**

Nissan Leaf

Nissan Leaf

At-a-Glance

Status/Year Series Started	Unchanged/2011
Twins	–
Body Styles	Hatchback
Seating	5
Anti-Theft Device	Std. Pass. Immobil. & Alarm
Parking Index Rating	Very Easy
Where Made	Smyrna, TN
Fuel Factor:	
MPG Rating (city/hwy)	Average-126/101
Driving Range (mi.)	Very Short-107
Fuel Type	Electricity
Annual Fuel Cost	Very Low-$370
Gas Guzzler Tax	No
Greenhouse Gas Emissions (tons/yr.)	Very Low-3.1
Barrels of Oil Used per year	Very Low-0.2

How the Competition Rates

Competitors	Rating	Pg.
BMW i3	–	97
Mercedes-Benz B-Class	–	205
Toyota Prius	7	251

Price Range	Retail	Markup
S	$29,010	6%
SV	$34,200	6%
SL	$36,790	6%

Safety Checklist

Crash Tests:
- Frontal . . . . Very Poor
- Side . . . . Very Poor

Airbags:
- Torso . . . Standard Front Pelvis/Torso from Seat
- Roll Sensing . . . . No
- Knee Bolster . . . . None

Crash Avoidance:
- Collision Avoidance . . . . None
- Blind Spot Detection . . . . None
- Lane Keeping Assist . . . . None
- Backup Camera . . . . Standard*
- Pedestrian Crash Avoidance . . . . None

General:
- Auto. Crash Notification . . . . None
- Day Running Lamps . . . . None

Safety Belt/Restraint:
- Dynamic Head Restraints . . . . None
- Adjustable Belt . . . . Standard Front

^Warning feature does not meet government standards.
*Backup camera does not meet government standards.

Nissan Leaf

Specifications

Drive	FWD
Engine	Electric
Transmission	CVT
Tow Rating (lbs.)	Very Low-0
Head/Leg Room (in.)	Roomy-41.2/42.1
Interior Space (cu. ft.)	Cramped-92.4
Cargo Space (cu. ft.)	Roomy-24
Wheelbase/Length (in.)	106.3/175

Ratings—10 Best, 1 Worst

Combo Crash Tests	7
Safety Features	4
Rollover	8
Preventive Maintenance	6
Repair Costs	6
Warranty	1
Fuel Economy	5
Complaints	4
Insurance Costs	3
OVERALL RATING	**4**

Nissan Maxima

At-a-Glance

Status/Year Series Started	Unchanged/2016
Twins	–
Body Styles	Sedan
Seating	5
Anti-Theft Device	Std. Pass. Immobil. & Alarm
Parking Index Rating	Hard
Where Made	Smyrna, TN

Fuel Factor:

MPG Rating (city/hwy)	Poor-22/30
Driving Range (mi.)	Long-450
Fuel Type	Premium
Annual Fuel Cost	High-$1608
Gas Guzzler Tax	No
Greenhouse Gas Emissions (tons/yr.)	Low-6.0
Barrels of Oil Used per year	High-13.2

How the Competition Rates

Competitors	Rating	Pg.
Chevrolet Malibu	10	118
Ford Fusion	6	145
Honda Accord	9	152

Price Range	Retail	Markup
S	$32,560	6%
SV	$34,540	6%
SR	$37,820	6%
Platinum	$39,990	6%

Nissan Maxima

Safety Checklist

Crash Tests:

Frontal	Good
Side	Average

Airbags:

Torso	Standard Front Pelvis/Torso from Seat
Roll Sensing	Yes
Knee Bolster	None

Crash Avoidance:

Collision Avoidance	Optional CIB & DBS
Blind Spot Detection	Optional
Lane Keeping Assist	None
Backup Camera	Standard*
Pedestrian Crash Avoidance	None

General:

Auto. Crash Notification	None
Day Running Lamps	Standard

Safety Belt/Restraint:

Dynamic Head Restraints	None
Adjustable Belt	Standard Front

^Warning feature does not meet government standards.
*Backup camera does not meet government standards.

Nissan Maxima

Specifications

Drive	FWD
Engine	3.5-liter V6
Transmission	CVT
Tow Rating (lbs.)	–
Head/Leg Room (in.)	Very Roomy-39.4/45
Interior Space (cu. ft.)	Average-98.6
Cargo Space (cu. ft.)	Cramped-14.3
Wheelbase/Length (in.)	109.3/192.8

Ratings—10 Best, 1 Worst

Combo Crash Tests	3
Safety Features	5
Rollover	3
Preventive Maintenance	8
Repair Costs	6
Warranty	1
Fuel Economy	4
Complaints	5
Insurance Costs	10
OVERALL RATING	**4**

Nissan Murano

Nissan Murano

At-a-Glance

Status/Year Series Started Unchanged/2015
Twins . . . . –
Body Styles . . . . SUV
Seating 5
Anti-Theft Device . . . . . . Std. Pass. Immobil. & Alarm
Parking Index Rating . . . . Hard
Where Made. . . . . Canton, MS
Fuel Factor:. . . . .
  MPG Rating (city/hwy) . . . . .Very Poor-21/28
  Driving Range (mi.) Long-450
  Fuel Type . . . . .Regular
  Annual Fuel Cost . . . . .Average-$1363
  Gas Guzzler Tax . . . . .No
  Greenhouse Gas Emissions (tons/yr.). High-7.5
  Barrels of Oil Used per year High-13.7

How the Competition Rates

Competitors	Rating	Pg.
Chevrolet Equinox	2	116
Ford Expedition	7	139
Honda Pilot	8	158

Price Range

	Retail	Markup
S FWD	$29,660	6%
SV FWD	$32,720	7%
SL AWD	$37,050	7%
Platinum AWD	$40,700	7%

Safety Checklist

Crash Tests:
  Frontal . . . . .Very Poor
  Side . . . . Average
Airbags:
  Torso . . . Standard Front Pelvis/Torso from Seat
  Roll Sensing. . . . . .Yes
  Knee Bolster . . . . Standard Driver
Crash Avoidance:
  Collision Avoidance . . . . . . Optional CIB & DBS
  Blind Spot Detection . . . . Optional
  Lane Keeping Assist . . . . None
  Backup Camera . . . . .Standard*
  Pedestrian Crash Avoidance . . . . None
General:
  Auto. Crash Notification . . . . None
  Day Running Lamps . . . . Standard
Safety Belt/Restraint:
  Dynamic Head Restraints . . . . None
  Adjustable Belt. . . . . .Standard Front

^Warning feature does not meet government standards.
*Backup camera does not meet government standards.

Nissan Murano

Specifications

Drive. . . . . .AWD
Engine 3.5-liter V6
Transmission . . . . CVT
Tow Rating (lbs.) . . . . .Very Low-1500
Head/Leg Room (in.) Cramped-39.9/40.5
Interior Space (cu. ft.). Roomy-108.1
Cargo Space (cu. ft.) . . . . .Very Roomy-39.6
Wheelbase/Length (in.) 111.2/192.4

Ratings—10 Best, 1 Worst

Combo Crash Tests	6
Safety Features	4
Rollover	2
Preventive Maintenance	1
Repair Costs	5
Warranty	1
Fuel Economy	3
Complaints	2
Insurance Costs	10
OVERALL RATING	**2**

Nissan Pathfinder

Nissan Pathfinder

At-a-Glance

Status/Year Series Started Appearance Change/2013
Twins . . . . –
Body Styles . . . . SUV
Seating 7
Anti-Theft Device . . . . . . Std. Pass. Immobil. & Alarm
Parking Index Rating . . . . Hard
Where Made. . . . . Smyrna, TN
Fuel Factor:. . . . .
  MPG Rating (city/hwy) . . . . .Very Poor-19/26
  Driving Range (mi.) Average-422
  Fuel Type. . . . . .Regular
  Annual Fuel Cost . . . . .High-$1492
  Gas Guzzler Tax . . . . .No
  Greenhouse Gas Emissions (tons/yr.). High-8.2
  Barrels of Oil Used per year High-15.0

How the Competition Rates

Competitors	Rating	Pg.
Buick Enclave	6	103
Chevrolet Traverse	6	124
Toyota Highlander	7	250

Price Range

Price Range	Retail	Markup
S FWD	$29,990	8%
SV FWD	$32,680	8%
SL 4WD	$37,390	8%
Platinum 4WD	$43,560	8%

Safety Checklist

Crash Tests:
  Frontal . . . . Average
  Side . . . . Average
Airbags:
  Torso . . . Standard Front Pelvis/Torso from Seat
  Roll Sensing. . . . . .Yes
  Knee Bolster . . . . None
Crash Avoidance:
  Collision Avoidance . . . . . . Optional CIB & DBS
  Blind Spot Detection . . . . Optional
  Lane Keeping Assist . . . . None
  Backup Camera . . . . Optional*
  Pedestrian Crash Avoidance . . . . None
General:
  Auto. Crash Notification. . . . . None
  Day Running Lamps . . . . Standard
Safety Belt/Restraint:
  Dynamic Head Restraints . . . . None
  Adjustable Belt. . . . . Standard Front & Rear

^Warning feature does not meet government standards.
*Backup camera does not meet government standards.

Nissan Pathfinder

Specifications

Drive. 4WD
Engine 3.5-liter V6
Transmission . . . . CVT
Tow Rating (lbs.) Low-5000
Head/Leg Room (in.) Roomy-41.1/42.3
Interior Space (cu. ft.). . . . . Very Roomy-157.8
Cargo Space (cu. ft.) Cramped-16
Wheelbase/Length (in.) 114.2/197.2

Ratings—10 Best, 1 Worst

Combo Crash Tests	—
Safety Features	2
Rollover	3
Preventive Maintenance	8
Repair Costs	6
Warranty	1
Fuel Economy	3
Complaints	6
Insurance Costs	8
OVERALL RATING	**—**

Nissan Quest

Nissan Quest

At-a-Glance

Status/Year Series Started. Unchanged/2011
Twins . . . . –
Body Styles . . . . .Minivan
Seating 7/8
Anti-Theft Device . . . . . . Std. Pass. Immobil. & Alarm
Parking Index Rating . . . . Average
Where Made. Kyushu, Japan
Fuel Factor:. . . . .
  MPG Rating (city/hwy) . . . . .Very Poor-20/27
  Driving Range (mi.) Long-453
  Fuel Type . . . . .Regular
  Annual Fuel Cost . . . . .Average-$1424
  Gas Guzzler Tax . . . . .No
  Greenhouse Gas Emissions (tons/yr.). High-8.2
  Barrels of Oil Used per year High-15.0

How the Competition Rates

Competitors	Rating	Pg.
Chrysler Pacifica	9	129
Honda Odyssey	8	157
Toyota Sienna	2	256

Price Range	Retail	Markup
S	$26,580	5%
SV	$30,540	6%
SL	$34,110	7%
Platinum	$43,230	7%

Nissan Quest

Safety Checklist

Crash Tests:
  Frontal . . . .–
  Side . . . .–
Airbags:
  Torso . . .Standard Front Pelvis/Torso from Seat
  Roll Sensing. . . . . No
  Knee Bolster . . . . None
Crash Avoidance:
  Collision Avoidance . . . . None
  Blind Spot Detection . . . . Optional
  Lane Keeping Assist . . . . None
  Backup Camera . . . . Optional*
  Pedestrian Crash Avoidance . . . . None
General:
  Auto. Crash Notification . . . . None
  Day Running Lamps . . . . None
Safety Belt/Restraint:
  Dynamic Head Restraints . . . . . .Standard Front
  Adjustable Belt . . . . Standard Front & Rear

^Warning feature does not meet government standards.
*Backup camera does not meet government standards.

Specifications

Drive. . . . . .FWD
Engine 3.5-liter V6
Transmission . . . . CVT
Tow Rating (lbs.) Low-3500
Head/Leg Room (in.) . . . . Very Roomy-42.1/43.8
Interior Space (cu. ft.). . . . . Very Roomy-177.8
Cargo Space (cu. ft.) . . . . Very Roomy-37.1
Wheelbase/Length (in.) 118.1/200.8

Ratings—10 Best, 1 Worst

Combo Crash Tests	1
Safety Features	5
Rollover	3
Preventive Maintenance	3
Repair Costs	3
Warranty	1
Fuel Economy	6
Complaints	8
Insurance Costs	8
OVERALL RATING	**2**

Nissan Rogue

At-a-Glance

```
Status/Year Series Started........ Unchanged/2014
Twins . . . . . . . . . . . . . . . . . . . . . . . . . . . . . . . . . . . . –
Body Styles . . . . . . . . . . . . . . . . . . . . . . . . . . . . . SUV
Seating . . . . . . . . . . . . . . . . . . . . . . . . . . . . . . . . 5/7
Anti-Theft Device . . . . . . Std. Pass. Immobil. & Alarm
Parking Index Rating . . . . . . . . . . . . . . . . . . Average
Where Made . . . . . . . . . . . . . . . . . . . . . . . Smyrna, TN
```

Fuel Factor: . . . .
```
  MPG Rating (city/hwy) . . . . . . . . . . . Poor-25/32
  Driving Range (mi.) . . . . . . . . . . . . . . . Short-402
  Fuel Type . . . . . . . . . . . . . . . . . . . . . . . . . . .Regular
  Annual Fuel Cost . . . . . . . . . . . . . . . . . . Low-$1163
  Gas Guzzler Tax . . . . . . . . . . . . . . . . . . . . . . . .No
  Greenhouse Gas Emissions (tons/yr.). . Average-6.4
  Barrels of Oil Used per year . . . . . . . . Average-11.8
```

How the Competition Rates

Competitors	Rating	Pg.
Kia Sorento	6	183
Mazda CX-5	3	200
Subaru Outback	7	240

Price Range

	Retail	Markup
S FWD	$23,290	6%
SV FWD	$24,740	6%
SV AWD	$26,090	6%
SL AWD	$30,040	6%

Nissan Rogue

Safety Checklist

Crash Tests:
```
  Frontal . . . . . . . . . . . . . . . . . . . . . . . . . .Very Poor
  Side . . . . . . . . . . . . . . . . . . . . . . . . . . . .Very Poor
```
Airbags:
```
  Torso . . . Standard Front Pelvis/Torso from Seat
  Roll Sensing. . . . . . . . . . . . . . . . . . . . . . . . .Yes
  Knee Bolster . . . . . . . . . . . . . . . . . . . . . . None
```
Crash Avoidance:
```
  Collision Avoidance . . . . . . Optional CIB & DBS
  Blind Spot Detection . . . . . . . . . . . . . . Optional
  Lane Keeping Assist . . . .Warning Only Optional
  Backup Camera . . . . . . . . . . . . . . . . . . .Standard*
  Pedestrian Crash Avoidance . . . . . . . . Optional
```
General:
```
  Auto. Crash Notification . . . . . . . . . . . . . None
  Day Running Lamps . . . . . . . . . . . . . Standard
```
Safety Belt/Restraint:
```
  Dynamic Head Restraints . . . . . . . . . . . None
  Adjustable Belt . . . . . . . . . . . . . .Standard Front
```
^Warning feature does not meet government standards.
*Backup camera does not meet government standards.

Nissan Rogue

Specifications

```
Drive . . . . . . . . . . . . . . . . . . . . . . . . . . . . . . . . . .AWD
Engine . . . . . . . . . . . . . . . . . . . . . . . . . . .2.5-liter I4
Transmission . . . . . . . . . . . . . . . . . . . . . . . . . . . CVT
Tow Rating (lbs.) . . . . . . . . . . . . . . . Very Low-1000
Head/Leg Room (in.) . . . . . . . . Very Roomy-41.6/43
Interior Space (cu. ft.). . . . . . . . . . . . . Roomy-105.8
Cargo Space (cu. ft.) . . . . . . . . . . . . Very Cramped-9.4
Wheelbase/Length (in.) . . . . . . . . . . 106.5/182.3
```

Ratings—10 Best, 1 Worst

Combo Crash Tests	3
Safety Features	3
Rollover	5
Preventive Maintenance	8
Repair Costs	9
Warranty	1
Fuel Economy	8
Complaints	8
Insurance Costs	5
OVERALL RATING	**5**

Nissan Sentra

Nissan Sentra

At-a-Glance

Status/Year Series Started........ Unchanged/2013
Twins . . . . –
Body Styles . . . . .Sedan
Seating 5
Anti-Theft Device . . . . . . Std. Pass. Immobil. & Alarm
Parking Index Rating . . . . Easy
Where Made Aguascalientes, Mexico / Kyushu, Japan
Fuel Factor:. . . . .
  MPG Rating (city/hwy) Average-30/39
  Driving Range (mi.) Long-442
  Fuel Type . . . . .Regular
  Annual Fuel Cost . . . . Very Low-$963
  Gas Guzzler Tax . . . . .No
  Greenhouse Gas Emissions (tons/yr.) Low-5.3
  Barrels of Oil Used per year Low-9.7

How the Competition Rates

Competitors	Rating	Pg.
Ford Focus	6	144
Honda Civic	8	153
Toyota Corolla	8	248

Price Range

	Retail	Markup
S MT	$16,990	6%
SV	$18,790	6%
SR	$19,990	6%
SL	$21,500	6%

Safety Checklist

Crash Tests:
  Frontal . . . . .Very Poor
  Side . . . . Poor
Airbags:
  Torso . . . Standard Front Pelvis/Torso from Seat
  Roll Sensing. . . . . .Yes
  Knee Bolster . . . . None
Crash Avoidance:
  Collision Avoidance . . . . . . Optional CIB & DBS
  Blind Spot Detection . . . . Optional
  Lane Keeping Assist . . . . None
  Backup Camera . . . . Optional*
  Pedestrian Crash Avoidance . . . . None
General:
  Auto. Crash Notification . . . . None
  Day Running Lamps . . . . None
Safety Belt/Restraint:
  Dynamic Head Restraints . . . . None
  Adjustable Belt. . . . . .Standard Front

^Warning feature does not meet government standards.
*Backup camera does not meet government standards.

Nissan Sentra

Specifications

Drive. . . . . .FWD
Engine 2.0-liter I4
Transmission . . . . CVT
Tow Rating (lbs.) . . . . –
Head/Leg Room (in.) Cramped-39.4/42.5
Interior Space (cu. ft.). Cramped-95.9
Cargo Space (cu. ft.) Cramped-15.1
Wheelbase/Length (in.) 106.3/182.1

Ratings—10 Best, 1 Worst

Combo Crash Tests	—
Safety Features	2
Rollover	1
Preventive Maintenance	1
Repair Costs	4
Warranty	1
Fuel Economy	1
Complaints	6
Insurance Costs	8
OVERALL RATING	**—**

Nissan Titan

Nissan Titan

At-a-Glance

Status/Year Series Started........ Unchanged/2016
Twins .... —
Body Styles .... Extended Cab
Seating.................................... 6
Anti-Theft Device ...... Std. Pass. Immobil. & Alarm
Parking Index Rating .... Very Hard
Where Made...................... Canton, MS
Fuel Factor:.....................................
　MPG Rating (city/hwy) .....Very Poor-15/21
　Driving Range (mi.) Long-448
　Fuel Type..........................Regular
　Annual Fuel Cost .... Very High-$1874
　Gas Guzzler Tax ....No
　Greenhouse Gas Emissions (tons/yr.)..... High-8.4
　Barrels of Oil Used per year ....Very High-18.3

How the Competition Rates

Competitors	Rating	Pg.
Chevrolet Silverado	5	119
Ford F-150	8	141
Toyota Tundra	—	258

Price Range

Price Range	Retail	Markup
S Crew Cab 2WD	$35,290	4%
SV Crew Cab 4WD	$42,010	7%
SL Crew Cab 4WD	$50,030	7%
Platinum Crew Cab 4WD	$55,520	7%

Safety Checklist

Crash Tests:
　Frontal .... —
　Side .... —
Airbags:
　Torso . . . Standard Front Pelvis/Torso from Seat
　Roll Sensing..........................Yes
　Knee Bolster .... None
Crash Avoidance:
　Collision Avoidance .... None
　Blind Spot Detection .... Optional
　Lane Keeping Assist .... None
　Backup Camera................... Optional*
　Pedestrian Crash Avoidance .... None
General:
　Auto. Crash Notification .... None
　Day Running Lamps .... Optional
Safety Belt/Restraint:
　Dynamic Head Restraints .... None
　Adjustable Belt................Standard Front

^Warning feature does not meet government standards.
*Backup camera does not meet government standards.

Nissan Titan

Specifications

Drive.....................................4WD
Engine 5.0-liter V8
Transmission .... 6-sp. Automatic
Tow Rating (lbs.) .... Very High-12038
Head/Leg Room (in.) Roomy-41/41.8
Interior Space (cu. ft.)...................... —
Cargo Space (cu. ft.) .... Very Roomy-58.1
Wheelbase/Length (in.) 151.6/242.7

Ratings—10 Best, 1 Worst

Combo Crash Tests	—
Safety Features	6
Rollover	3
Preventive Maintenance	7
Repair Costs	4
Warranty	1
Fuel Economy	4
Complaints	—
Insurance Costs	8
OVERALL RATING	**—**

Mazda CX-9

Mazda CX-9

At-a-Glance

Status/Year Series Started. Unchanged/2017
Twins . . . . —
Body Styles . . . . SUV
Seating 7
Anti-Theft Device . . . . Std. Passive Immobil. Only
Parking Index Rating . . . . .Very Hard
Where Made. . . . . Hiroshima, Japan
Fuel Factor:. . . . .
    MPG Rating (city/hwy) . . . . .Very Poor-21/27
    Driving Range (mi.) Long-443
    Fuel Type . . . . .Regular
    Annual Fuel Cost . . . . .Average-$1382
    Gas Guzzler Tax . . . . .No
    Greenhouse Gas Emissions (tons/yr.)Very High-10.0
    Barrels of Oil Used per year . . . . . . .Very High-18.3

How the Competition Rates

Competitors	Rating	Pg.
Kia Sorento	6	183
Lexus RX	5	196
Nissan Murano	4	227

Price Range	Retail	Markup
Sport FWD	$31,520	6%
Touring FWD	$37,770	6%
Grand Touring AWD	$41,970	6%
Signature AWD	$44,015	6%

Safety Checklist

Crash Tests:
    Frontal . . . .—
    Side . . . .—
Airbags:
    Torso . . .Standard Front Pelvis/Torso from Seat
    Roll Sensing. . . . . .Yes
    Knee Bolster . . . . None
Crash Avoidance:
    Collision Avoidance . . . . . .Optional CIB & DBS^
    Blind Spot Detection . . . . Optional
    Lane Keeping Assist . . . . Optional^
    Backup Camera . . . . Standard
    Pedestrian Crash Avoidance . . . . None
General:
    Auto. Crash Notification . . . . . . Dial Assist.-Free
    Day Running Lamps . . . . Standard
Safety Belt/Restraint:
    Dynamic Head Restraints . . . . None
    Adjustable Belt . . . . .Standard Front

^Warning feature does not meet government standards.
*Backup camera does not meet government standards.

Mazda CX-9

Specifications

Drive. . . . . .AWD
Engine 3.7-liter I4
Transmission . . . . 6-sp. Automatic
Tow Rating (lbs.) Low-3500
Head/Leg Room (in.) Cramped-39.3/40.9
Interior Space (cu. ft.). . . . . .Very Roomy-135.1
Cargo Space (cu. ft.) Cramped-14.4
Wheelbase/Length (in.) 115.3/199.4

Ratings—10 Best, 1 Worst

Combo Crash Tests	6
Safety Features	7
Rollover	7
Preventive Maintenance	7
Repair Costs	9
Warranty	1
Fuel Economy	9
Complaints	9
Insurance Costs	3
OVERALL RATING	**8**

Mazda Mazda3

Mazda Mazda3

At-a-Glance

Status/Year Series Started Appearance Change/2014
Twins . . . .—
Body Styles . . . . Sedan, Hatchback
Seating 5
Anti-Theft Device . . . . Std. Passive Immobil. Only
Parking Index Rating . . . . Average
Where Made. . . . . Hofu, Japan
Fuel Factor:. . . . .
  MPG Rating (city/hwy) Average-30/41
  Driving Range (mi.) Long-450
  Fuel Type. . . . . .Regular
  Annual Fuel Cost . . . . Very Low-$945
  Gas Guzzler Tax . . . . .No
  Greenhouse Gas Emissions (tons/yr.) Low-5.3
  Barrels of Oil Used per year Low-9.7

How the Competition Rates

Competitors	Rating	Pg.
Ford Focus	6	144
Mitsubishi Lancer	4	216
Volkswagen Jetta	5	263

Price Range

	Retail	Markup
i Sport MT	$17,845	4%
i Touring Sedan AT	$21,095	5%
s Touring Hatchback MT	$25,495	5%
s Grand Touring Hatchback AT	$26,495	5%

Safety Checklist

Crash Tests:
  Frontal . . . . Good
  Side . . . . .Poor
Airbags:
  Torso . . . Standard Front Pelvis/Torso from Seat
  Roll Sensing. . . . . .Yes
  Knee Bolster . . . . None
Crash Avoidance:
  Collision Avoidance . . . . . .Optional CIB & DBS^
  Blind Spot Detection . . . . Optional
  Lane Keeping Assist . . . . Optional
  Backup Camera . . . . Standard
  Pedestrian Crash Avoidance . . . . None
General:
  Auto. Crash Notification . . . . . . Dial Assist.-Free
  Day Running Lamps . . . . Standard
Safety Belt/Restraint:
  Dynamic Head Restraints . . . . None
  Adjustable Belt. . . . . .Standard Front

^Warning feature does not meet government standards.
*Backup camera does not meet government standards.

Mazda Mazda3

Specifications

Drive. . . . . .FWD
Engine 2.0-liter I4
Transmission . . . . 6-sp. Automatic
Tow Rating (lbs.) . . . .—
Head/Leg Room (in.) Cramped-38.6/42.2
Interior Space (cu. ft.). Cramped-96.3
Cargo Space (cu. ft.) . . . . Very Cramped-12.4
Wheelbase/Length (in.) 106.3/180.3

Nissan Versa

Ratings—10 Best, 1 Worst

Combo Crash Tests	1
Safety Features	1
Rollover	4
Preventive Maintenance	9
Repair Costs	9
Warranty	1
Fuel Economy	9
Complaints	6
Insurance Costs	1
OVERALL RATING	**2**

Nissan Versa

Safety Checklist

Crash Tests:
Frontal . . . . .Very Poor
Side . . . . .Very Poor
Airbags:
Torso . . . Standard Front Pelvis/Torso from Seat
Roll Sensing. . . . . .Yes
Knee Bolster . . . . None
Crash Avoidance:
Collision Avoidance . . . . None
Blind Spot Detection . . . . None
Lane Keeping Assist . . . . None
Backup Camera . . . . Optional*
Pedestrian Crash Avoidance . . . . None
General:
Auto. Crash Notification . . . . None
Day Running Lamps . . . . None
Safety Belt/Restraint:
Dynamic Head Restraints . . . . None
Adjustable Belt. . . . . .Standard Front

^Warning feature does not meet government standards.
*Backup camera does not meet government standards.

At-a-Glance

Status/Year Series Started. Unchanged/2006
Twins . . . . –
Body Styles . . . . Sedan, Hatchback
Seating 4
Anti-Theft Device . . . . Std. Passive Immobil. Only
Parking Index Rating . . . . .Very Easy
Where Made Aguascalientes, Mexico / Kyushu, Japan
Fuel Factor:. . . . .
MPG Rating (city/hwy) Average-31/40
Driving Range (mi.) . . . . .Very Short-373
Fuel Type . . . . .Regular
Annual Fuel Cost . . . . Very Low-$935
Gas Guzzler Tax . . . . .No
Greenhouse Gas Emissions (tons/yr.). Low-5.1
Barrels of Oil Used per year Low-9.4

Nissan Versa

How the Competition Rates

Competitors	Rating	Pg.
Hyundai Accent	6	159
Kia Forte	6	179
Toyota Yaris	5	259

Specifications

Drive. . . . . .FWD
Engine 1.6-liter I4
Transmission . . . . CVT
Tow Rating (lbs.) . . . . –
Head/Leg Room (in.) Cramped-39.8/41.8
Interior Space (cu. ft.). . . . . Very Cramped-90.2
Cargo Space (cu. ft.) Cramped-14.9
Wheelbase/Length (in.) 102.4/175.4

Price Range

Price Range	Retail	Markup
S MT	$11,990	6%
S Plus	$13,990	6%
SV	$15,580	6%
SL	$17,140	6%

Porsche Macan

Ratings—10 Best, 1 Worst

Combo Crash Tests	—
Safety Features	7
Rollover	1
Preventive Maintenance	3
Repair Costs	1
Warranty	6
Fuel Economy	2
Complaints	9
Insurance Costs	8
OVERALL RATING	—

Porsche Macan

Porsche Macan

At-a-Glance

Status/Year Series Started Appearance Change/2015
Twins . . . . –
Body Styles . . . . SUV
Seating 5
Anti-Theft Device . Std. Pass. Immobil. & Active Alarm
Parking Index Rating . . . . Hard
Where Made. . . . . Leipzig, Germany
Fuel Factor:. . . . .
  MPG Rating (city/hwy) . . . . .Very Poor-17/23
  Driving Range (mi.) Short-381
  Fuel Type. . . . . .Premium
  Annual Fuel Cost . . . . Very High-$2087
  Gas Guzzler Tax . . . . .No
  Greenhouse Gas Emissions (tons/yr.). . Average-6.6
  Barrels of Oil Used per year High-15.0

How the Competition Rates

Competitors	Rating	Pg.
BMW X5	6	100
Cadillac XT5	5	110
Lexus RX	5	196

Price Range

	Retail	Markup
Base	$47,500	11%
S	$54,400	11%
GTS	$67,200	11%
Turbo	$76,000	11%

Safety Checklist

Crash Tests:
  Frontal . . . .–
  Side . . . .–
Airbags:
  Torso . . Standard Front & Rear Torso from Seat
  Roll Sensing. . . . . .Yes
  Knee Bolster . . . . .Standard Front
Crash Avoidance:
  Collision Avoidance . . . . . .Optional CIB & DBS^
  Blind Spot Detection . . . . Optional
  Lane Keeping Assist . . . . Optional^
  Backup Camera . . . . Optional*
  Pedestrian Crash Avoidance . . . . None
General:
  Auto. Crash Notification . . . . None
  Day Running Lamps . . . . Standard
Safety Belt/Restraint:
  Dynamic Head Restraints . . . . None
  Adjustable Belt. . . . . .Standard Front

^Warning feature does not meet government standards.
*Backup camera does not meet government standards.

Porsche Macan

Specifications

Drive. . . . . .AWD
Engine 3.0-liter V6
Transmission . . . . 7-sp. Automatic
Tow Rating (lbs.) Low-4409
Head/Leg Room (in.) . . . .–
Interior Space (cu. ft.). . . . .–
Cargo Space (cu. ft.) Average-17.7
Wheelbase/Length (in.) 110.5/184.3

Ratings—10 Best, 1 Worst

Combo Crash Tests	5
Safety Features	2
Rollover	1
Preventive Maintenance	9
Repair Costs	10
Warranty	2
Fuel Economy	1
Complaints	4
Insurance Costs	8
OVERALL RATING	**4**

Ram 1500

Ram 1500

Safety Checklist

Crash Tests:
Frontal . . . . Poor
Side . . . . Good
Airbags:
Torso . . . Standard Front Pelvis/Torso from Seat
Roll Sensing. .Yes
Knee Bolster . . . . None
Crash Avoidance:
Collision Avoidance . . . . None
Blind Spot Detection . . . . None
Lane Keeping Assist . . . . None
Backup Camera . . . . Optional
Pedestrian Crash Avoidance . . . . None
General:
Auto. Crash Notification . . . . None
Day Running Lamps . . . . Standard
Safety Belt/Restraint:
Dynamic Head Restraints . . . . None
Adjustable Belt . . . . .Standard Front

^Warning feature does not meet government standards.
*Backup camera does not meet government standards.

At-a-Glance

Status/Year Series Started. Unchanged/2009
Twins . . . . –
Body Styles . . . . Pickup
Seating 5/6
Anti-Theft Device .Std. Pass. Immobil. & Opt. Pass. Alarm
Parking Index Rating . . . . .Very Hard
Where Made. . . . . Warren, MI / Saltillo, Mexico
Fuel Factor:. . . . .
MPG Rating (city/hwy) . . . . .Very Poor-13/19
Driving Range (mi.) Short-394
Fuel Type . . . . .Regular
Annual Fuel Cost . . . . Very High-$2128
Gas Guzzler Tax . . . . .No
Greenhouse Gas Emissions (tons/yr.)Very High-12.0
Barrels of Oil Used per year . . . . . . .Very High-22.0

Ram 1500

How the Competition Rates

Competitors	Rating	Pg.
Chevrolet Silverado	5	119
Ford F-150	8	141
Toyota Tundra	–	258

Price Range

Price Range	Retail	Markup
Tradesman Reg. Cab 2WD	$26,295	4%
SLT Quad Cab 2WD	$34,595	6%
Sport Crew Cab 4WD	$43,895	9%
Laramie Longhorn Crew Cab 4WD	$52,695	10%

Specifications

Drive. 4WD
Engine 5.7-liter V8
Transmission . . . . 6-sp. Automatic
Tow Rating (lbs.) . . . . Very High-8807
Head/Leg Room (in.) Cramped-41/41
Interior Space (cu. ft.). Roomy-116.6
Cargo Space (cu. ft.) . . . . Very Roomy-57.5
Wheelbase/Length (in.) 140.5/229

Ratings—10 Best, 1 Worst

Combo Crash Tests	—
Safety Features	1
Rollover	3
Preventive Maintenance	4
Repair Costs	4
Warranty	3
Fuel Economy	9
Complaints	1
Insurance Costs	5

OVERALL RATING —

Smart ForTwo

Smart ForTwo

At-a-Glance

Status/Year Series Started	Unchanged/2016
Twins	—
Body Styles	Coupe
Seating	2
Anti-Theft Device	Std. Active Immobil. & Pass. Alarm
Parking Index Rating	Very Easy
Where Made	Hambach, France
Fuel Factor:	
MPG Rating (city/hwy)	Average-34/39
Driving Range (mi.)	Very Short-278
Fuel Type	Premium
Annual Fuel Cost	Low-$1114
Gas Guzzler Tax	No
Greenhouse Gas Emissions (tons/yr.)	Very Low-4.1
Barrels of Oil Used per year	Low-9.1

How the Competition Rates

Competitors	Rating	Pg.
Fiat 500	2	134
Mini Cooper	5	214
Mitsubishi Mirage	3	217

Price Range

Price Range	Retail	Markup
pure	$14,650	8%
passion Coupe	$17,490	8%
Prime Cabriolet	$19,900	8%
Proxy Cabriolet	$20,900	8%

Safety Checklist

Crash Tests:
- Frontal .... −
- Side .... −

Airbags:
- Torso . . . Standard Front Pelvis/Torso from Seat
- Roll Sensing.............................. No
- Knee Bolster ....Standard Front

Crash Avoidance:
- Collision Avoidance .... Warning Only Standard
- Blind Spot Detection .... None
- Lane Keeping Assist .... None
- Backup Camera.................... Optional*
- Pedestrian Crash Avoidance .... None

General:
- Auto. Crash Notification.............. None
- Day Running Lamps .... None

Safety Belt/Restraint:
- Dynamic Head Restraints .... None
- Adjustable Belt..................... None

^Warning feature does not meet government standards.
*Backup camera does not meet government standards.

Smart ForTwo

Specifications

Drive	RWD
Engine	1.0-liter I3
Transmission	5-sp. Automatic
Tow Rating (lbs.)	—
Head/Leg Room (in.)	Cramped-39.7/41.2
Interior Space (cu. ft.)	Very Cramped-45.4
Cargo Space (cu. ft.)	Very Cramped-7.8
Wheelbase/Length (in.)	73.5/106.1

Ratings—10 Best, 1 Worst

Combo Crash Tests	5
Safety Features	8
Rollover	3
Preventive Maintenance	4
Repair Costs	6
Warranty	3
Fuel Economy	6
Complaints	10
Insurance Costs	—
OVERALL RATING	**6**

Subaru Crosstrek

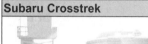

Subaru Crosstrek

At-a-Glance

Status/Year Series Started	Unchanged/2013
Twins	—
Body Styles	SUV
Seating	5
Anti-Theft Device	Std. Pass. Immobil. & Active Alarm
Parking Index Rating	Very Easy
Where Made	Gunma, Japan
Fuel Factor:	
MPG Rating (city/hwy)	Poor-26/34
Driving Range (mi.)	Long-462
Fuel Type	Regular
Annual Fuel Cost	Low-$1109
Gas Guzzler Tax	No
Greenhouse Gas Emissions (tons/yr.)	Average-6.2
Barrels of Oil Used per year	Average-11.4

How the Competition Rates

Competitors	Rating	Pg.
Jeep Renegade	2	176
Kia Sorento	6	183
Nissan Juke	2	224

Price Range

	Retail	Markup
Base	$21,595	5%
Premium MT	$22,395	5%
Limited	$25,095	6%
Hybrid Touring	$29,995	5%

Safety Checklist

Crash Tests:
Frontal	Average
Side	Poor

Airbags:
Torso	Standard Front Pelvis/Torso from Seat
Roll Sensing	Yes
Knee Bolster	Standard Driver

Crash Avoidance:
Collision Avoidance	Optional CIB & DBS
Blind Spot Detection	Optional
Lane Keeping Assist	Warning Only Optional
Backup Camera	Standard
Pedestrian Crash Avoidance	Optional

General:
Auto. Crash Notification	Operator Assist.-Fee
Day Running Lamps	Standard

Safety Belt/Restraint:
Dynamic Head Restraints	None
Adjustable Belt	Standard Front

^Warning feature does not meet government standards.
*Backup camera does not meet government standards.

Subaru Crosstrek

Specifications

Drive	AWD
Engine	2.0-liter I4
Transmission	CVT
Tow Rating (lbs.)	—
Head/Leg Room (in.)	Roomy-39.8/43.5
Interior Space (cu. ft.)	Average-97.5
Cargo Space (cu. ft.)	Average-22.3
Wheelbase/Length (in.)	103.7/175.2

Ratings—10 Best, 1 Worst

Combo Crash Tests	6
Safety Features	9
Rollover	3
Preventive Maintenance	4
Repair Costs	7
Warranty	3
Fuel Economy	3
Complaints	5
Insurance Costs	3
OVERALL RATING	**4**

Subaru Forester

Subaru Forester

At-a-Glance

Status/Year Series Started	Unchanged/2014
Twins	–
Body Styles	SUV
Seating	5
Anti-Theft Device	Std. Pass. Immobil. & Active Alarm
Parking Index Rating	Easy
Where Made	Lafayette, IN

Fuel Factor:

MPG Rating (city/hwy)	Poor-24/32
Driving Range (mi.)	Long-430
Fuel Type	Regular
Annual Fuel Cost	Low-$1193
Gas Guzzler Tax	No
Greenhouse Gas Emissions (tons/yr.)	Average-6.6
Barrels of Oil Used per year	Average-12.2

How the Competition Rates

Competitors	Rating	Pg.
Hyundai Tucson	6	165
Mazda CX-5	3	200
Toyota RAV4	6	254

Price Range

Price Range	Retail	Markup
2.5i MT	$22,595	6%
2.0 XT Touring	$24,295	6%
2.5i Premium AT	$25,995	6%
2.5i Touring	$31,295	7%

Safety Checklist

Crash Tests:

Frontal . . . . .Poor
Side . . . . Good

Airbags:

Torso . . . Standard Front Pelvis/Torso from Seat
Roll Sensing. . . . . .Yes
Knee Bolster . . . . Standard Driver

Crash Avoidance:

Collision Avoidance . . . . . . Optional CIB & DBS
Blind Spot Detection . . . . Optional
Lane Keeping Assist . . . . Optional
Backup Camera . . . . Standard
Pedestrian Crash Avoidance . . . . Optional

General:

Auto. Crash Notification . . . Operator Assist.-Fee
Day Running Lamps . . . . Standard

Safety Belt/Restraint:

Dynamic Head Restraints . . . . None
Adjustable Belt. . . . . .Standard Front

^Warning feature does not meet government standards.
*Backup camera does not meet government standards.

Subaru Forester

Specifications

Drive	AWD
Engine	2.5-liter I4
Transmission	CVT
Tow Rating (lbs.)	Very Low-1500
Head/Leg Room (in.)	Very Roomy-41.4/43
Interior Space (cu. ft.)	Roomy-113.1
Cargo Space (cu. ft.)	Very Roomy-34.4
Wheelbase/Length (in.)	103.9/180.9

Subaru Impreza   Compact

Ratings—10 Best, 1 Worst

Combo Crash Tests	—
Safety Features	9
Rollover	—
Preventive Maintenance	4
Repair Costs	7
Warranty	3
Fuel Economy	7
Complaints	—
Insurance Costs	1
OVERALL RATING	**—**

Subaru Impreza

At-a-Glance

Status/Year Series Started. . . . . All New/2017
Twins . . . .—
Body Styles . . . . Sedan, Hatchback
Seating 5
Anti-Theft Device . Std. Pass. Immobil. & Active Alarm
Parking Index Rating . . . . Easy
Where Made. Gunma, Japan
Fuel Factor:. . . . .
  MPG Rating (city/hwy) . . . . .Very Poor-20/27
  Driving Range (mi.) Average-419
  Fuel Type. . . . . .Regular
  Annual Fuel Cost . . . . .Average-$1424
  Gas Guzzler Tax . . . . .No
  Greenhouse Gas Emissions (tons/yr.). . Average-6.5
  Barrels of Oil Used per year High-15.0

How the Competition Rates

Competitors	Rating	Pg.
Dodge Dart	4	132
Mazda Mazda3	8	202
Mitsubishi Lancer	4	216

Price Range

	Retail	Markup
Base Sedan MT	$18,295	5%
Premium Hatchback AT	$21,595	5%
Limited Sedan	$22,595	5%
Sport Limited Hatchback	$23,595	6%

Subaru Impreza

Safety Checklist

Crash Tests:
  Frontal . . . .—
  Side . . . .—
Airbags:
  Torso . . .Standard Front Pelvis/Torso from Seat
  Roll Sensing. . . . . .Yes
  Knee Bolster . . . . Standard Driver
Crash Avoidance:
  Collision Avoidance . . . . . . Optional CIB & DBS
  Blind Spot Detection . . . . Optional
  Lane Keeping Assist . . . . Optional
  Backup Camera . . . . Standard
  Pedestrian Crash Avoidance . . . . Optional
General:
  Auto. Crash Notification . . . Operator Assist.-Fee
  Day Running Lamps . . . . Standard
Safety Belt/Restraint:
  Dynamic Head Restraints . . . . None
  Adjustable Belt. . . . . .Standard Front

^Warning feature does not meet government standards.
*Backup camera does not meet government standards.

Subaru Impreza

Specifications

Drive. . . . . .AWD
Engine 2.0-liter I4
Transmission . . . .-
Tow Rating (lbs.) . . . .—
Head/Leg Room (in.) . . . .—
Interior Space (cu. ft.). Average-100
Cargo Space (cu. ft.) . . . . .Very Cramped-12
Wheelbase/Length (in.) 105.1/182.1

Ratings—10 Best, 1 Worst

Combo Crash Tests	10
Safety Features	8
Rollover	8
Preventive Maintenance	1
Repair Costs	8
Warranty	3
Fuel Economy	6
Complaints	3
Insurance Costs	1
OVERALL RATING	**6**

Subaru Legacy

Subaru Legacy

At-a-Glance

Status/Year Series Started. Unchanged/2015
Twins . . . . –
Body Styles . . . . Sedan
Seating 5
Anti-Theft Device . Std. Pass. Immobil. & Active Alarm
Parking Index Rating . . . . Average
Where Made. . . . . Lafayette, IN
Fuel Factor: . . . .
  MPG Rating (city/hwy) Poor-26/36
  Driving Range (mi.) . . . . Very Long-550
  Fuel Type . . . . Regular
  Annual Fuel Cost . . . . Low-$1085
  Gas Guzzler Tax . . . . No
  Greenhouse Gas Emissions (tons/yr.). Low-6.0
  Barrels of Oil Used per year Average-11.0

How the Competition Rates

Competitors	Rating	Pg.
Ford Fusion	6	145
Kia Optima	9	180
Mazda Mazda6	8	203

Price Range	Retail	Markup
Base	$21,995	6%
Premium	$23,995	6%
Limited	$28,840	6%
3.6R Limited	$31,640	7%

Safety Checklist

Crash Tests:
  Frontal . . . . Very Good
  Side . . . . Very Good
Airbags:
  Torso . . . Standard Front Pelvis/Torso from Seat
  Roll Sensing. . . . . Yes
  Knee Bolster . . . . None
Crash Avoidance:
  Collision Avoidance . . . . . . Optional CIB & DBS
  Blind Spot Detection . . . . Optional
  Lane Keeping Assist . . . . Optional
  Backup Camera . . . . Standard
  Pedestrian Crash Avoidance . . . . Optional
General:
  Auto. Crash Notification . . . Operator Assist.-Fee
  Day Running Lamps . . . . Standard
Safety Belt/Restraint:
  Dynamic Head Restraints . . . . None
  Adjustable Belt. . . . . Standard Front

^Warning feature does not meet government standards.
*Backup camera does not meet government standards.

Subaru Legacy

Specifications

Drive. . . . . AWD
Engine 2.5-liter I4
Transmission . . . . 6-sp. Automatic
Tow Rating (lbs.) . . . . –
Head/Leg Room (in.) Roomy-40/42.9
Interior Space (cu. ft.). Roomy-104.6
Cargo Space (cu. ft.) Cramped-15
Wheelbase/Length (in.) 108.3/188.8

Ratings—10 Best, 1 Worst

Combo Crash Tests	10
Safety Features	8
Rollover	2
Preventive Maintenance	1
Repair Costs	10
Warranty	3
Fuel Economy	7
Complaints	3
Insurance Costs	1
OVERALL RATING	**7**

Subaru Outback

Subaru Outback

At-a-Glance

Status/Year Series Started	Unchanged/2015
Twins	–
Body Styles	Wagon
Seating	5
Anti-Theft Device	Std. Pass. Immobil. & Active Alarm
Parking Index Rating	Average
Where Made	Lafayette, IN
Fuel Factor:	
MPG Rating (city/hwy)	Poor-25/33
Driving Range (mi.)	Very Long-519
Fuel Type	Regular
Annual Fuel Cost	Low-$1149
Gas Guzzler Tax	No
Greenhouse Gas Emissions (tons/yr.)	Average-6.4
Barrels of Oil Used per year	Average-11.8

How the Competition Rates

Competitors	Rating	Pg.
Mazda CX-5	3	200
Volkswagen Jetta	5	263
Volkswagen Tiguan	1	265

Price Range

	Retail	Markup
Base	$25,645	5%
Premium	$27,695	6%
Limited	$32,390	7%
3.6R Limited	$34,995	7%

Safety Checklist

Crash Tests:
Frontal . . . . Very Good
Side . . . . Very Good

Airbags:
Torso . . . Standard Front Pelvis/Torso from Seat
Roll Sensing. . . . . Yes
Knee Bolster . . . . None

Crash Avoidance:
Collision Avoidance . . . . . . Optional CIB & DBS
Blind Spot Detection . . . . Optional
Lane Keeping Assist . . . . Optional
Backup Camera . . . . Standard
Pedestrian Crash Avoidance . . . . Optional

General:
Auto. Crash Notification . . . Operator Assist.-Fee
Day Running Lamps . . . . Standard

Safety Belt/Restraint:
Dynamic Head Restraints . . . . None
Adjustable Belt. . . . . Standard Front

^Warning feature does not meet government standards.
*Backup camera does not meet government standards.

Subaru Outback

Specifications

Drive	AWD
Engine	2.5-liter I4
Transmission	6-sp. Automatic
Tow Rating (lbs.)	Very Low-2700
Head/Leg Room (in.)	Roomy-40.8/42.9
Interior Space (cu. ft.)	Roomy-108.1
Cargo Space (cu. ft.)	Very Roomy-35.5
Wheelbase/Length (in.)	108.1/189.6

Ratings—10 Best, 1 Worst

Combo Crash Tests	10
Safety Features	10
Rollover	10
Preventive Maintenance	5
Repair Costs	5
Warranty	10
Fuel Economy	10
Complaints	1
Insurance Costs	5
OVERALL RATING	**10**

Tesla Model S

At-a-Glance

Status/Year Series Started	Unchanged/2015
Twins	–
Body Styles	Sedan
Seating	5
Anti-Theft Device	Std. Passive Alarm Only
Parking Index Rating	Hard
Where Made	Fremont, CA
Fuel Factor:	
MPG Rating (city/hwy)	Average-88/90
Driving Range (mi.)	Very Short-208
Fuel Type	Electricity
Annual Fuel Cost	Very Low-$472
Gas Guzzler Tax	No
Greenhouse Gas Emissions (tons/yr.)	Very Low-4.1
Barrels of Oil Used per year	Very Low-0.2

How the Competition Rates

Competitors	Rating	Pg.
Cadillac XTS	9	111
Chevrolet Impala	7	117
Chrysler 300	2	128

Price Range

Price Range	Retail	Markup
60 kWh	$68,000	6%
75 kWh	$74,500	6%
90D kWh	$89,500	6%
P100D kWh	$134,500	6%

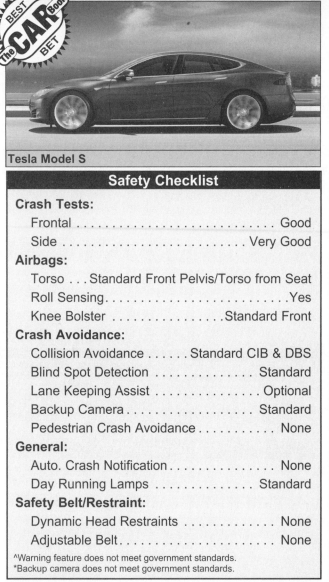

Tesla Model S

Safety Checklist

Crash Tests:
Frontal . . . . Good
Side . . . . Very Good

Airbags:
Torso . . . Standard Front Pelvis/Torso from Seat
Roll Sensing . . . . Yes
Knee Bolster . . . . Standard Front

Crash Avoidance:
Collision Avoidance . . . . . . Standard CIB & DBS
Blind Spot Detection . . . . Standard
Lane Keeping Assist . . . . Optional
Backup Camera . . . . Standard
Pedestrian Crash Avoidance . . . . None

General:
Auto. Crash Notification . . . . None
Day Running Lamps . . . . Standard

Safety Belt/Restraint:
Dynamic Head Restraints . . . . None
Adjustable Belt . . . . None

^Warning feature does not meet government standards.
*Backup camera does not meet government standards.

Tesla Model S

Specifications

Drive	AWD
Engine	Electric
Transmission	CVT
Tow Rating (lbs.)	–
Head/Leg Room (in.)	Cramped-38.8/42.7
Interior Space (cu. ft.)	Cramped-94
Cargo Space (cu. ft.)	Roomy-31.6
Wheelbase/Length (in.)	116.5/196

Ratings—10 Best, 1 Worst

Combo Crash Tests	—
Safety Features	10
Rollover	10
Preventive Maintenance	5
Repair Costs	5
Warranty	10
Fuel Economy	10
Complaints	—
Insurance Costs	5
OVERALL RATING	**—**

Tesla Model X

Tesla Model X

At-a-Glance

Status/Year Series Started . . . . All New/2017
Twins . . . . –
Body Styles . . . . SUV
Seating 7
Anti-Theft Device . . . . Std. Passive Alarm Only
Parking Index Rating . . . . Very Hard
Where Made. . . . . –
Fuel Factor: . . . .
  MPG Rating (city/hwy) Average-89/90
  Driving Range (mi.) . . . . Very Short-238
  Fuel Type . . . . Electricity
  Annual Fuel Cost . . . . Very Low-$470
  Gas Guzzler Tax . . . . No
  Greenhouse Gas Emissions (tons/yr.). Very Low-0.2
  Barrels of Oil Used per year . . . . Very Low-0.0

How the Competition Rates

Competitors	Rating	Pg.
Audi Q5	3	90
BMW X5	6	100
Cadillac XT5	5	110

Price Range

	Retail	Markup
75 kWh	$88,800	6%
90D kWh	$98,800	6%
P100D kWh	$138,800	6%

Safety Checklist

Crash Tests:
  Frontal . . . . –
  Side . . . . –
Airbags:
  Torso . . . Standard Front Pelvis/Torso from Seat
  Roll Sensing. . . . . Yes
  Knee Bolster . . . . Standard Front
Crash Avoidance:
  Collision Avoidance . . . . . . Standard CIB & DBS
  Blind Spot Detection . . . . Standard
  Lane Keeping Assist . . . . Optional
  Backup Camera . . . . Standard
  Pedestrian Crash Avoidance . . . . None
General:
  Auto. Crash Notification . . . . None
  Day Running Lamps . . . . Standard
Safety Belt/Restraint:
  Dynamic Head Restraints . . . . None
  Adjustable Belt . . . . None

^Warning feature does not meet government standards.
*Backup camera does not meet government standards.

Tesla Model X

Specifications

Drive. . . . . AWD
Engine . . . . Electric
Transmission . . . . CVT
Tow Rating (lbs.) . . . . –
Head/Leg Room (in.) Roomy-41.7/41.2
Interior Space (cu. ft.). Roomy-120
Cargo Space (cu. ft.) Roomy-26
Wheelbase/Length (in.) 116.7/198.3

Ratings—10 Best, 1 Worst

Combo Crash Tests	1
Safety Features	5
Rollover	1
Preventive Maintenance	9
Repair Costs	3
Warranty	2
Fuel Economy	1
Complaints	9
Insurance Costs	8
OVERALL RATING	**2**

Toyota 4Runner

Toyota 4Runner

Safety Checklist

Crash Tests:
Frontal . . . . Very Poor
Side . . . . Poor

Airbags:
Torso . . . Standard Front Pelvis/Torso from Seat
Roll Sensing. . . . . .Yes
Knee Bolster . . . . .Standard Front

Crash Avoidance:
Collision Avoidance . . . . None
Blind Spot Detection . . . . None
Lane Keeping Assist . . . . None
Backup Camera . . . . .Standard*
Pedestrian Crash Avoidance . . . . None

General:
Auto. Crash Notification . . . Operator Assist.-Fee
Day Running Lamps . . . . Standard

Safety Belt/Restraint:
Dynamic Head Restraints . . . . . .Standard Front
Adjustable Belt. . . . . .Standard Front

^Warning feature does not meet government standards.
*Backup camera does not meet government standards.

At-a-Glance

Status/Year Series Started. Unchanged/2006
Twins . . . . –
Body Styles . . . . SUV
Seating 5/7
Anti-Theft Device . . . . Std. Passive Immobil. Only
Parking Index Rating . . . . Average
Where Made. . . . . Tahara, Japan
Fuel Factor:. . . . .
MPG Rating (city/hwy) . . . . .Very Poor-17/21
Driving Range (mi.) Average-428
Fuel Type. . . . . .Regular
Annual Fuel Cost . . . . .High-$1734
Gas Guzzler Tax . . . . .No
Greenhouse Gas Emissions (tons/yr.)Very High-10.0
Barrels of Oil Used per year . . . . . . .Very High-18.3

How the Competition Rates

Competitors	Rating	Pg.
Buick Enclave	6	103
Chevrolet Tahoe	5	123
Ford Expedition	7	139

Price Range	Retail	Markup
SR5 2WD	$33,510	9%
SR5 Premium 4WD	$38,065	9%
Trail Edition Prem 4WD	$39,095	9%
Limited 4WD	$43,860	9%

Toyota 4Runner

Specifications

Drive. 4WD
Engine 4.0-liter V6
Transmission . . . . 5-sp. Automatic
Tow Rating (lbs.) Low-4700
Head/Leg Room (in.) Cramped-39.3/41.7
Interior Space (cu. ft.). . . . . Very Roomy-128
Cargo Space (cu. ft.) . . . . .Very Cramped-9
Wheelbase/Length (in.) 109.8/190.2

Toyota 86 Compact

Ratings—10 Best, 1 Worst

Combo Crash Tests	—
Safety Features	3
Rollover	10
Preventive Maintenance	4
Repair Costs	5
Warranty	2
Fuel Economy	7
Complaints	—
Insurance Costs	1
OVERALL RATING	**—**

Toyota 86

Toyota 86

At-a-Glance

Status/Year Series Started. Unchanged/2017
Twins . . . .–
Body Styles . . . . .Coupe
Seating 4
Anti-Theft Device . . . . Std. Passive Immobil. Only
Parking Index Rating . . . . Easy
Where Made. Gunma, Japan
Fuel Factor:. . . . .
MPG Rating (city/hwy) Poor-25/34
Driving Range (mi.) . . . . .Very Short-375
Fuel Type . . . . .Premium
Annual Fuel Cost . . . . .Average-$1416
Gas Guzzler Tax . . . . .No
Greenhouse Gas Emissions (tons/yr.). . Average-6.4
Barrels of Oil Used per year Average-11.8

How the Competition Rates

Competitors	Rating	Pg.
Buick Cascada	—	102
Mazda MX-5	—	204
Nissan 370Z	—	220

Price Range

Price Range	Retail	Markup
Coupe MT	$26,255	5%
Coupe AT	$26,975	5%

Safety Checklist

Crash Tests:
Frontal . . . .–
Side . . . .–
Airbags:
Torso . . .Standard Front Pelvis/Torso from Seat
Roll Sensing. . . . . .Yes
Knee Bolster . . . . .Standard Front
Crash Avoidance:
Collision Avoidance . . . . None
Blind Spot Detection . . . . None
Lane Keeping Assist . . . . None
Backup Camera . . . . None
Pedestrian Crash Avoidance . . . . None
General:
Auto. Crash Notification . . . Operator Assist.-Fee
Day Running Lamps . . . . Standard
Safety Belt/Restraint:
Dynamic Head Restraints . . . . None
Adjustable Belt. . . . . None

^Warning feature does not meet government standards.
*Backup camera does not meet government standards.

Toyota 86

Specifications

Drive. . . . . .RWD
Engine 2.0-liter I4
Transmission . . . . 6-sp. Automatic
Tow Rating (lbs.) . . . .–
Head/Leg Room (in.) . . . . Very Cramped-37.1/41.9
Interior Space (cu. ft.). . . . . Very Cramped-76.5
Cargo Space (cu. ft.) . . . . Very Cramped-6.9
Wheelbase/Length (in.) 101.2/166.7

Ratings—10 Best, 1 Worst

Combo Crash Tests	8
Safety Features	10
Rollover	7
Preventive Maintenance	6
Repair Costs	4
Warranty	2
Fuel Economy	4
Complaints	6
Insurance Costs	8
OVERALL RATING	**7**

Toyota Avalon

At-a-Glance

Status/Year Series Started	Unchanged/2013
Twins	–
Body Styles	Sedan
Seating	5
Anti-Theft Device	Std. Pass. Immobil. & Alarm
Parking Index Rating	Hard
Where Made	Georgetown, KY

Fuel Factor:

MPG Rating (city/hwy)	Poor-21/31
Driving Range (mi.)	Average-418
Fuel Type	Regular
Annual Fuel Cost	Average-$1313
Gas Guzzler Tax	No
Greenhouse Gas Emissions (tons/yr.)	High-7.5
Barrels of Oil Used per year	High-13.7

How the Competition Rates

Competitors	Rating	Pg.
Cadillac XTS	9	111
Chevrolet Impala	7	117
Ford Taurus	4	148

Price Range

Price Range	Retail	Markup
XLE	$33,250	11%
XLE Premium	$36,450	11%
XLE Touring	$37,650	11%
Hybrid Limited	$42,550	11%

Toyota Avalon

Safety Checklist

Crash Tests:

Frontal	Average
Side	Very Good

Airbags:

Torso	Std. Fr. & Rear Pelvis/Torso from Seat
Roll Sensing	Yes
Knee Bolster	Standard Front

Crash Avoidance:

Collision Avoidance	Optional CIB & DBS
Blind Spot Detection	Optional
Lane Keeping Assist	Optional
Backup Camera	Standard
Pedestrian Crash Avoidance	Optional

General:

Auto. Crash Notification	Operator Assist.-Fee
Day Running Lamps	Standard

Safety Belt/Restraint:

Dynamic Head Restraints	None
Adjustable Belt	Standard Front

^Warning feature does not meet government standards.
*Backup camera does not meet government standards.

Toyota Avalon

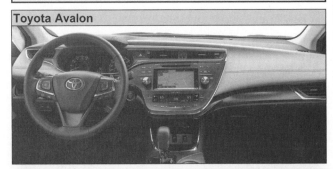

Specifications

Drive	FWD
Engine	3.5-liter V6
Transmission	6-sp. Automatic
Tow Rating (lbs.)	Very Low-1000
Head/Leg Room (in.)	Cramped-37.6/42.1
Interior Space (cu. ft.)	Average-103.63
Cargo Space (cu. ft.)	Cramped-16
Wheelbase/Length (in.)	111/195.3

Toyota Camry

Ratings—10 Best, 1 Worst

Combo Crash Tests	7
Safety Features	10
Rollover	6
Preventive Maintenance	6
Repair Costs	4
Warranty	2
Fuel Economy	7
Complaints	9
Insurance Costs	5
OVERALL RATING	**8**

Toyota Camry

Toyota Camry

At-a-Glance

Status/Year Series Started........ Unchanged/2012
Twins ....–
Body Styles ....Sedan
Seating 5
Anti-Theft Device .Std. Pass. Immobil. & Opt. Pass. Alarm
Parking Index Rating .... Average
Where Made....................Georgetown, KY
Fuel Factor:................................
  MPG Rating (city/hwy)............ Poor-25/35
  Driving Range (mi.) .... Very Long-488
  Fuel Type ....Regular
  Annual Fuel Cost .... Low-$1124
  Gas Guzzler Tax ....No
  Greenhouse Gas Emissions (tons/yr.).. Average-6.4
  Barrels of Oil Used per year Average-11.8

How the Competition Rates

Competitors	Rating	Pg.
Ford Fusion	6	145
Honda Accord	9	152
Subaru Legacy	6	239

Price Range

	Retail	Markup
LE	$23,070	9%
XSE	$26,310	10%
XLE Hybrid	$30,140	9%
XLE V6	$31,370	10%

Safety Checklist

Crash Tests:
  Frontal .... Average
  Side .... Good
Airbags:
  Torso . . .Std. Fr. & Rear Pelvis/Torso from Seat
  Roll Sensing........................Yes
  Knee Bolster ....Standard Front
Crash Avoidance:
  Collision Avoidance ......Optional CIB & DBS^
  Blind Spot Detection .... Optional
  Lane Keeping Assist ....Warning Only Optional
  Backup Camera.................... Standard
  Pedestrian Crash Avoidance .... Optional
General:
  Auto. Crash Notification . . . Operator Assist.-Fee
  Day Running Lamps .... Standard
Safety Belt/Restraint:
  Dynamic Head Restraints .... None
  Adjustable Belt...............Standard Front

^Warning feature does not meet government standards.
*Backup camera does not meet government standards.

Toyota Camry

Specifications

Drive.....................................FWD
Engine 2.5-liter I4
Transmission .... 6-sp. Automatic
Tow Rating (lbs.) ....Very Low-0
Head/Leg Room (in.) Cramped-38.8/41.6
Interior Space (cu. ft.)................ Average-102.7
Cargo Space (cu. ft.) Cramped-15.4
Wheelbase/Length (in.) 109.3/190.9

Ratings—10 Best, 1 Worst

Combo Crash Tests	5
Safety Features	9
Rollover	5
Preventive Maintenance	9
Repair Costs	8
Warranty	2
Fuel Economy	8
Complaints	10
Insurance Costs	3
OVERALL RATING	**8**

Toyota Corolla

Toyota Corolla

At-a-Glance

Status/Year Series Started Appearance Change/2014
Twins .... –
Body Styles .... Sedan
Seating 5
Anti-Theft Device .... Std. Passive Immobil. Only
Parking Index Rating .... Easy
Where Made.................... Princeton, IN
Fuel Factor:...................................
MPG Rating (city/hwy).............Poor-27/36
Driving Range (mi.) Short-402
Fuel Type...........................Regular
Annual Fuel Cost ....Low-$1060
Gas Guzzler Tax ....No
Greenhouse Gas Emissions (tons/yr.).....Low-5.8
Barrels of Oil Used per year Average-10.6

How the Competition Rates

Competitors	Rating	Pg.
Ford Focus	6	144
Honda Civic	8	153
Nissan Sentra	5	231

Price Range	Retail	Markup
L	$18,500	6%
LE	$18,935	8%
LE Eco	$19,335	8%
XSE	$22,680	8%

Safety Checklist

Crash Tests:
  Frontal .... Poor
  Side .... Good
Airbags:
  Torso . . . Standard Front Pelvis/Torso from Seat
  Roll Sensing.........................Yes
  Knee Bolster .... Standard Driver
Crash Avoidance:
  Collision Avoidance ...... Optional CIB & DBS^
  Blind Spot Detection .... None
  Lane Keeping Assist .... Standard
  Backup Camera.................... Standard
  Pedestrian Crash Avoidance .... Optional
General:
  Auto. Crash Notification . . . Operator Assist.-Fee
  Day Running Lamps .... Standard
Safety Belt/Restraint:
  Dynamic Head Restraints .... None
  Adjustable Belt...............Standard Front

^Warning feature does not meet government standards.
*Backup camera does not meet government standards.

Toyota Corolla

Specifications

Drive.......................................FWD
Engine 1.8-liter I4
Transmission .... 4-sp. Automatic
Tow Rating (lbs.) ....Very Low-0
Head/Leg Room (in.) Cramped-38.3/42.3
Interior Space (cu. ft.)................. Average-97.5
Cargo Space (cu. ft.) ....Very Cramped-13
Wheelbase/Length (in.) 106.3/182.6

Toyota Corolla iM | Compact

Ratings—10 Best, 1 Worst

Combo Crash Tests	—
Safety Features	5
Rollover	7
Preventive Maintenance	10
Repair Costs	8
Warranty	2
Fuel Economy	8
Complaints	—
Insurance Costs	5
OVERALL RATING	**—**

Toyota Corolla iM

Toyota Corolla iM

At-a-Glance

Status/Year Series Started	All New/2017
Twins	—
Body Styles	Hatchback
Seating	5
Anti-Theft Device	Std. Passive Immobil. Only
Parking Index Rating	Very Easy
Where Made	Tsutsumi, Japan
Fuel Factor:	
MPG Rating (city/hwy)	Poor-28/36
Driving Range (mi.)	Long-436
Fuel Type	Regular
Annual Fuel Cost	Very Low-$1037
Gas Guzzler Tax	No
Greenhouse Gas Emissions (tons/yr.)	Low-4.7
Barrels of Oil Used per year	Average-10.6

How the Competition Rates

Competitors	Rating	Pg.
Mazda Mazda3	8	202
Mitsubishi Lancer	4	216
Volkswagen Jetta	5	263

Price Range

Price Range	Retail	Markup
Hatchback MT	$18,750	8%
Hatchback AT	$19,490	8%

Safety Checklist

Crash Tests:
Frontal . . . . —
Side . . . . —

Airbags:
Torso . . . Standard Front Pelvis/Torso from Seat
Roll Sensing . . . . Yes
Knee Bolster . . . . Standard Driver

Crash Avoidance:
Collision Avoidance . . . . . . Optional CIB & DBS
Blind Spot Detection . . . . None
Lane Keeping Assist . . . . None
Backup Camera . . . . Standard
Pedestrian Crash Avoidance . . . . None

General:
Auto. Crash Notification . . . Operator Assist.-Fee
Day Running Lamps . . . . Standard

Safety Belt/Restraint:
Dynamic Head Restraints . . . . None
Adjustable Belt . . . . Standard Front

^Warning feature does not meet government standards.
*Backup camera does not meet government standards.

Toyota Corolla iM

Specifications

Drive	FWD
Engine	1.8-liter I4
Transmission	CVT
Tow Rating (lbs.)	
Head/Leg Room (in.)	Cramped-39.7/41.7
Interior Space (cu. ft.)	Cramped-90.4
Cargo Space (cu. ft.)	Average-20.8
Wheelbase/Length (in.)	102.4/170.5

Toyota Highlander

Ratings—10 Best, 1 Worst

Combo Crash Tests	9
Safety Features	9
Rollover	3
Preventive Maintenance	8
Repair Costs	1
Warranty	2
Fuel Economy	2
Complaints	10
Insurance Costs	8
OVERALL RATING	**7**

Toyota Highlander

Toyota Highlander

At-a-Glance

Status/Year Series Started Appearance Change/2014
Twins . . . . –
Body Styles . . . . SUV
Seating 7/8
Anti-Theft Device .Std. Pass. Immobil. & Opt. Pass. Alarm
Parking Index Rating . . . . Hard
Where Made . . . . Princeton, IN
Fuel Factor: . . . .
  MPG Rating (city/hwy) . . . . Very Poor-18/24
  Driving Range (mi.) Short-389
  Fuel Type . . . . .Regular
  Annual Fuel Cost . . . . .High-$1590
  Gas Guzzler Tax . . . . .No
  Greenhouse Gas Emissions (tons/yr.) High-9.0
  Barrels of Oil Used per year High-16.5

How the Competition Rates

Competitors	Rating	Pg.
Buick Enclave	6	103
Chevrolet Traverse	6	124
Nissan Pathfinder	2	228

Price Range	Retail	Markup
LE I4 FWD	$29,990	10%
LE Plus AWD	$35,355	10%
Limited AWD	$41,875	10%
Hybrid LTD Platinum	$50,485	10%

Toyota Highlander

Safety Checklist

Crash Tests:
  Frontal . . . . Good
  Side . . . . Very Good
Airbags:
  Torso . . . Standard Front Pelvis/Torso from Seat
  Roll Sensing . . . . .Yes
  Knee Bolster . . . . Standard Driver
Crash Avoidance:
  Collision Avoidance . . . . . . Optional CIB & DBS
  Blind Spot Detection . . . . Optional
  Lane Keeping Assist . . . . Standard
  Backup Camera . . . . Standard
  Pedestrian Crash Avoidance . . . . Optional
General:
  Auto. Crash Notification . . . Operator Assist.-Fee
  Day Running Lamps . . . . Standard
Safety Belt/Restraint:
  Dynamic Head Restraints . . . . None
  Adjustable Belt . . . . .Standard Front

^Warning feature does not meet government standards.
*Backup camera does not meet government standards.

Specifications

Drive . . . . .AWD
Engine 3.5-liter V6
Transmission . . . . 6-sp. Automatic
Tow Rating (lbs.) . . . . .Very Low-2000
Head/Leg Room (in.) . . . . Very Roomy-40.7/44.2
Interior Space (cu. ft.) . . . . Very Roomy-144.9
Cargo Space (cu. ft.) Cramped-13.8
Wheelbase/Length (in.) 109.8/191.1

Ratings—10 Best, 1 Worst

Combo Crash Tests	5
Safety Features	8
Rollover	7
Preventive Maintenance	9
Repair Costs	5
Warranty	2
Fuel Economy	10
Complaints	6
Insurance Costs	5
OVERALL RATING	**7**

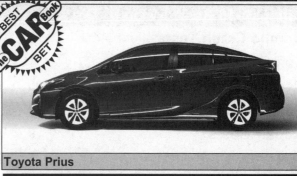
Toyota Prius

Toyota Prius

Toyota Prius

Safety Checklist

Crash Tests:
Frontal . . . . Average
Side . . . . Average
Airbags:
Torso . . . Standard Front Pelvis/Torso from Seat
Roll Sensing. . . . . .Yes
Knee Bolster . . . . Standard Driver
Crash Avoidance:
Collision Avoidance . . . . . . Optional CIB & DBS
Blind Spot Detection . . . . Optional
Lane Keeping Assist . . . . Optional
Backup Camera . . . . Standard
Pedestrian Crash Avoidance . . . . Optional
General:
Auto. Crash Notification . . . Operator Assist.-Fee
Day Running Lamps . . . . Optional
Safety Belt/Restraint:
Dynamic Head Restraints . . . . None
Adjustable Belt. . . . . .Standard Front

^Warning feature does not meet government standards.
*Backup camera does not meet government standards.

At-a-Glance

Status/Year Series Started. Unchanged/2016
Twins . . . . –
Body Styles . . . . Hatchback
Seating 5
Anti-Theft Device . . . . Std. Passive Immobil. Only
Parking Index Rating . . . . .Very Easy
Where Made. . . . . .Tsutsumi, Japan
Fuel Factor:. . . . .
MPG Rating (city/hwy) Average-54/50
Driving Range (mi.) . . . . Very Long-589
Fuel Type . . . . .Regular
Annual Fuel Cost . . . . .Very Low-$619
Gas Guzzler Tax . . . . .No
Greenhouse Gas Emissions (tons/yr.). Very Low-2.8
Barrels of Oil Used per year . . . . Very Low-6.3

How the Competition Rates

Competitors	Rating	Pg.
Chevrolet Volt	–	126
Ford C-MAX	5	136
Nissan Leaf	4	225

Price Range

	Retail	Markup
Two	$24,685	6%
Three	$26,735	7%
Four	$29,135	7%
Four Touring	$30,015	7%

Toyota Prius

Specifications

Drive. . . . . .FWD
Engine 1.8-liter I4
Transmission . . . . CVT
Tow Rating (lbs.) . . . . –
Head/Leg Room (in.) . . . . Very Cramped-34.4/42.3
Interior Space (cu. ft.). Cramped-93.1
Cargo Space (cu. ft.) Roomy-24.6
Wheelbase/Length (in.) 106.3/178.7

Toyota Prius C

Ratings—10 Best, 1 Worst

Combo Crash Tests	3
Safety Features	3
Rollover	5
Preventive Maintenance	9
Repair Costs	9
Warranty	2
Fuel Economy	10
Complaints	10
Insurance Costs	5
OVERALL RATING	**7**

Toyota Prius C

Toyota Prius C

Safety Checklist

Crash Tests:
Frontal . . . . Poor
Side . . . . Very Poor

Airbags:
Torso . . . Standard Front Pelvis/Torso from Seat
Roll Sensing. . . . . No
Knee Bolster . . . . Standard Driver

Crash Avoidance:
Collision Avoidance . . . . . . Optional CIB & DBS
Blind Spot Detection . . . . None
Lane Keeping Assist . . . .Warning Only Optional
Backup Camera . . . . Optional
Pedestrian Crash Avoidance . . . . None

General:
Auto. Crash Notification . . . Operator Assist.-Fee
Day Running Lamps . . . . Standard

Safety Belt/Restraint:
Dynamic Head Restraints . . . . None
Adjustable Belt. None

^Warning feature does not meet government standards.
*Backup camera does not meet government standards.

At-a-Glance

Status/Year Series Started. Unchanged/2013
Twins . . . . —
Body Styles . . . . Hatchback
Seating 5
Anti-Theft Device . . . . . .Optional Pass. Immobil. Only
Parking Index Rating . . . . .Very Easy
Where Made. . . . . .Iwata, Japan
Fuel Factor:. . . . .
MPG Rating (city/hwy) Average-53/46
Driving Range (mi.) . . . . Very Long-471
Fuel Type . . . . .Regular
Annual Fuel Cost . . . . .Very Low-$650
Gas Guzzler Tax . . . . .No
Greenhouse Gas Emissions (tons/yr.). Very Low-3.6
Barrels of Oil Used per year . . . . Very Low-6.6

How the Competition Rates

Competitors	Rating	Pg.
BMW i3	—	97
Chevrolet Spark	6	121
Nissan Leaf	4	225

Price Range	Retail	Markup
One	$19,560	5%
Two	$20,360	6%
Three	$21,785	7%
Four	$24,495	7%

Toyota Prius C

Specifications

Drive. . . . . .FWD
Engine 1.5-liter I4
Transmission . . . . CVT
Tow Rating (lbs.) . . . . —
Head/Leg Room (in.) Cramped-38.6/41.7
Interior Space (cu. ft.). . . . . Very Cramped-87.4
Cargo Space (cu. ft.) Average-17.1
Wheelbase/Length (in.) 100.4/157.3

Ratings—10 Best, 1 Worst

Combo Crash Tests	7
Safety Features	6
Rollover	4
Preventive Maintenance	9
Repair Costs	6
Warranty	2
Fuel Economy	10
Complaints	9
Insurance Costs	5
OVERALL RATING	**8**

Toyota Prius V

Toyota Prius V

At-a-Glance

Status/Year Series Started	Unchanged/2013
Twins	–
Body Styles	Wagon
Seating	5
Anti-Theft Device	Std. Passive Immobil. Only
Parking Index Rating	Easy
Where Made	Tsutsumi, Japan

Fuel Factor:

MPG Rating (city/hwy)	Average-44/40
Driving Range (mi.)	Very Long-501
Fuel Type	Regular
Annual Fuel Cost	Very Low-$766
Gas Guzzler Tax	No
Greenhouse Gas Emissions (tons/yr.)	Very Low-4.3
Barrels of Oil Used per year	Very Low-7.8

How the Competition Rates

Competitors	Rating	Pg.
Chevrolet Volt	–	126
Ford C-MAX	5	136
Nissan Leaf	4	225

Price Range

Price Range	Retail	Markup
Two	$26,675	7%
Three	$28,060	7%
Four	$29,695	7%
Five	$30,935	7%

Safety Checklist

Crash Tests:
Frontal	Poor
Side	Very Good

Airbags:
Torso	Standard Front Pelvis/Torso from Seat
Roll Sensing	Yes
Knee Bolster	Standard Driver

Crash Avoidance:
Collision Avoidance	Optional CIB & DBS
Blind Spot Detection	None
Lane Keeping Assist	Warning Only Optional
Backup Camera	Standard
Pedestrian Crash Avoidance	None

General:
Auto. Crash Notification	Operator Assist.-Fee
Day Running Lamps	Standard

Safety Belt/Restraint:
Dynamic Head Restraints	None
Adjustable Belt	Standard Front

^Warning feature does not meet government standards.
*Backup camera does not meet government standards.

Toyota Prius V

Specifications

Drive	FWD
Engine	1.8-liter I4
Transmission	CVT
Tow Rating (lbs.)	–
Head/Leg Room (in.)	Cramped-39.6/41.3
Interior Space (cu. ft.)	Average-97.2
Cargo Space (cu. ft.)	Very Roomy-34.3
Wheelbase/Length (in.)	109.4/182.3

Ratings—10 Best, 1 Worst

Combo Crash Tests	7
Safety Features	9
Rollover	3
Preventive Maintenance	5
Repair Costs	3
Warranty	2
Fuel Economy	4
Complaints	9
Insurance Costs	8
OVERALL RATING	**6**

Toyota RAV4

Toyota RAV4

At-a-Glance

Status/Year Series Started	Unchanged/2013
Twins	–
Body Styles	SUV
Seating	5
Anti-Theft Device	Std. Passive Immobil. Only
Parking Index Rating	Easy
Where Made	Woodstock, Ontario / Tahara, Japan

Fuel Factor:

MPG Rating (city/hwy)	Poor-22/29
Driving Range (mi.)	Short-392
Fuel Type	Regular
Annual Fuel Cost	Average-$1307
Gas Guzzler Tax	No
Greenhouse Gas Emissions (tons/yr.)	Average-7.2
Barrels of Oil Used per year	High-13.2

How the Competition Rates

Competitors	Rating	Pg.
Ford Escape	7	138
Honda HR-V	5	156
Hyundai Tucson	6	165

Price Range

	Retail	Markup
LE FWD	$24,910	7%
XLE FWD	$26,830	7%
Limited AWD	$33,230	7%
Platinum AWD	$36,150	7%

Safety Checklist

Crash Tests:

Frontal	Average
Side	Very Good

Airbags:

Torso	Standard Front Pelvis/Torso from Seat
Roll Sensing	Yes
Knee Bolster	Standard Driver

Crash Avoidance:

Collision Avoidance	Optional CIB & DBS
Blind Spot Detection	Optional
Lane Keeping Assist	Optional
Backup Camera	Standard
Pedestrian Crash Avoidance	Optional

General:

Auto. Crash Notification	Operator Assist.-Fee
Day Running Lamps	Standard

Safety Belt/Restraint:

Dynamic Head Restraints	None
Adjustable Belt	Standard Front

^Warning feature does not meet government standards.
*Backup camera does not meet government standards.

Toyota RAV4

Specifications

Drive	AWD
Engine	2.5-liter I4
Transmission	6-sp. Automatic
Tow Rating (lbs.)	Very Low-1500
Head/Leg Room (in.)	Roomy-39.8/42.6
Interior Space (cu. ft.)	Average-101.9
Cargo Space (cu. ft.)	Very Roomy-38.4
Wheelbase/Length (in.)	104.7/179.9

Toyota Sequoia

Ratings—10 Best, 1 Worst

Combo Crash Tests	—
Safety Features	5
Rollover	2
Preventive Maintenance	6
Repair Costs	3
Warranty	2
Fuel Economy	1
Complaints	8
Insurance Costs	10
OVERALL RATING	**—**

Toyota Sequoia

Toyota Sequoia

At-a-Glance

Status/Year Series Started	Unchanged/2008
Twins	–
Body Styles	SUV
Seating	8
Anti-Theft Device	Std. Pass. Immobil. & Alarm
Parking Index Rating	Very Hard
Where Made	Princeton, IN

Fuel Factor:

MPG Rating (city/hwy)	Very Poor-13/17
Driving Range (mi.)	Short-384
Fuel Type	Regular
Annual Fuel Cost	Very High-$2218
Gas Guzzler Tax	No
Greenhouse Gas Emissions (tons/yr.)	Very High-12.8
Barrels of Oil Used per year	Very High-23.5

How the Competition Rates

Competitors	Rating	Pg.
Buick Enclave	6	103
Chevrolet Suburban	4	122
Ford Expedition	7	139

Price Range

Price Range	Retail	Markup
SR5 2WD	$44,965	10%
Limited 2WD	$53,755	10%
Limited 4WD	$56,980	10%
Platinum 4WD	$64,720	10%

Safety Checklist

Crash Tests:
- Frontal . . . . –
- Side . . . . –

Airbags:
- Torso . . . Standard Front Pelvis/Torso from Seat
- Roll Sensing. . . . . .Yes
- Knee Bolster . . . . .Standard Front

Crash Avoidance:
- Collision Avoidance . . . . None
- Blind Spot Detection . . . . Optional
- Lane Keeping Assist . . . . None
- Backup Camera . . . . Standard
- Pedestrian Crash Avoidance . . . . None

General:
- Auto. Crash Notification . . . Operator Assist.-Fee
- Day Running Lamps . . . . Optional

Safety Belt/Restraint:
- Dynamic Head Restraints . . . . None
- Adjustable Belt . . . . Standard Front & Rear

^Warning feature does not meet government standards.
*Backup camera does not meet government standards.

Toyota Sequoia

Specifications

Drive	4WD
Engine	5.7-liter V8
Transmission	6-sp. Automatic
Tow Rating (lbs.)	Average-7100
Head/Leg Room (in.)	Very Cramped-34.8/42.5
Interior Space (cu. ft.)	–
Cargo Space (cu. ft.)	Average-18.9
Wheelbase/Length (in.)	122/205.1

Toyota Sienna   Minivan

Ratings—10 Best, 1 Worst

Combo Crash Tests	6
Safety Features	8
Rollover	4
Preventive Maintenance	3
Repair Costs	2
Warranty	2
Fuel Economy	2
Complaints	4
Insurance Costs	5
OVERALL RATING	**2**

Toyota Sienna

Toyota Sienna

At-a-Glance

Status/Year Series Started. Unchanged/2004
Twins . . . . –
Body Styles . . . . .Minivan
Seating 7/8
Anti-Theft Device .Std. Pass. Immobil. & Opt. Pass. Alarm
Parking Index Rating . . . . Hard
Where Made. Princeton, IN
Fuel Factor:. . . . .
  MPG Rating (city/hwy) . . . . .Very Poor-18/25
  Driving Range (mi.) Average-412
  Fuel Type. . . . . .Regular
  Annual Fuel Cost . . . . .High-$1566
  Gas Guzzler Tax . . . . .No
  Greenhouse Gas Emissions (tons/yr.). High-8.6
  Barrels of Oil Used per year High-15.7

How the Competition Rates

Competitors	Rating	Pg.
Honda Odyssey	8	157
Kia Sedona	7	182
Nissan Frontier	–	223

Price Range	Retail	Markup
L FWD	$29,750	8%
SE FWD	$36,110	8%
XLE Premium FWD	$39,505	9%
LTD Premium AWD	$47,310	9%

Safety Checklist

Crash Tests:
  Frontal . . . . Average
  Side . . . . Average
Airbags:
  Torso . . .Standard Front Pelvis/Torso from Seat
  Roll Sensing. . . . . .Yes
  Knee Bolster . . . . Standard Driver
Crash Avoidance:
  Collision Avoidance . . . . . . Optional CIB & DBS
  Blind Spot Detection . . . . Optional
  Lane Keeping Assist . . . . None
  Backup Camera . . . . Standard
  Pedestrian Crash Avoidance . . . . None
General:
  Auto. Crash Notification . . . Operator Assist.-Fee
  Day Running Lamps . . . . Optional
Safety Belt/Restraint:
  Dynamic Head Restraints . . . . . .Standard Front
  Adjustable Belt. . . . . Standard Front & Rear

^Warning feature does not meet government standards.
*Backup camera does not meet government standards.

Toyota Sienna

Specifications

Drive. . . . . .FWD
Engine 3.5-liter V6
Transmission . . . . 6-sp. Automatic
Tow Rating (lbs.) Low-3500
Head/Leg Room (in.) Cramped-41/40.5
Interior Space (cu. ft.). . . . . Very Roomy-164.4
Cargo Space (cu. ft.) . . . . Very Roomy-39.1
Wheelbase/Length (in.) 119.3/200.2

Toyota Tacoma

Ratings—10 Best, 1 Worst

Combo Crash Tests	1
Safety Features	5
Rollover	4
Preventive Maintenance	9
Repair Costs	5
Warranty	2
Fuel Economy	2
Complaints	5
Insurance Costs	5
OVERALL RATING	**2**

Toyota Tacoma

Toyota Tacoma

At-a-Glance

Status/Year Series Started........ Unchanged/2016
Twins . . . . –
Body Styles . . . . Extended Cab
Seating 4
Anti-Theft Device . . . . . Opt. Pass. Immbobil. & Alarm
Parking Index Rating . . . . Very Hard
Where Made . . . . . San Antonio, TX / Tijuana, Mexico
Fuel Factor: . . . .
  MPG Rating (city/hwy) . . . . Very Poor-19/23
  Driving Range (mi.) Long-435
  Fuel Type . . . . Regular
  Annual Fuel Cost . . . . High-$1565
  Gas Guzzler Tax . . . . No
  Greenhouse Gas Emissions (tons/yr.) . . Average-7.3
  Barrels of Oil Used per year High-16.5

How the Competition Rates

Competitors	Rating	Pg.
Chevrolet Colorado	3	113
Nissan Frontier	–	223

Price Range

Price Range	Retail	Markup
SR Access Cab 2WD	$24,120	7%
SR5 Access Cab 2WD	$26,205	7%
SR5 Dbl Cab 4WD V6	$34,705	8%
TRD Sport Dbl. Cab 4WD V6	$35,315	8%

Safety Checklist

Crash Tests:
  Frontal . . . . Very Poor
  Side . . . . Very Poor
Airbags:
  Torso . . . Standard Front Pelvis/Torso from Seat
  Roll Sensing . . . . Yes
  Knee Bolster . . . . Standard Front
Crash Avoidance:
  Collision Avoidance . . . . None
  Blind Spot Detection . . . . Optional
  Lane Keeping Assist . . . . None
  Backup Camera . . . . Standard
  Pedestrian Crash Avoidance . . . . None
General:
  Auto. Crash Notification . . . Operator Assist.-Fee
  Day Running Lamps . . . . Standard
Safety Belt/Restraint:
  Dynamic Head Restraints . . . . . . Standard Front
  Adjustable Belt . . . . Standard Front

^Warning feature does not meet government standards.
*Backup camera does not meet government standards.

Toyota Tacoma

Specifications

Drive 4WD
Engine 2.7-liter I4
Transmission . . . . 6-sp. Automatic
Tow Rating (lbs.) Low-3500
Head/Leg Room (in.) Roomy-39.7/42.9
Interior Space (cu. ft.) . . . . Very Cramped-57.5
Cargo Space (cu. ft.) . . . . Very Roomy-33.5
Wheelbase/Length (in.) 127.4/212.3

Ratings—10 Best, 1 Worst

Combo Crash Tests	—
Safety Features	7
Rollover	1
Preventive Maintenance	6
Repair Costs	5
Warranty	2
Fuel Economy	1
Complaints	9
Insurance Costs	8
OVERALL RATING	—

Toyota Tundra

Toyota Tundra

At-a-Glance

Status/Year Series Started Unchanged/2007
Twins . . . . —
Body Styles . . . . Pickup
Seating 5/6
Anti-Theft Device . Std. Pass. Immobil. & Opt. Pass. Alarm
Parking Index Rating . . . . Very Hard
Where Made . . . . San Antonio, TX
Fuel Factor: . . . .
  MPG Rating (city/hwy) . . . . Very Poor-13/18
  Driving Range (mi.) Short-392
  Fuel Type . . . . Regular
  Annual Fuel Cost . . . . Very High-$2171
  Gas Guzzler Tax . . . . No
  Greenhouse Gas Emissions (tons/yr.) High-8.9
  Barrels of Oil Used per year . . . . Very High-20.6

How the Competition Rates

Competitors	Rating	Pg.
Chevrolet Silverado	5	119
Ford F-150	8	141
Ram 1500	4	235

Price Range

	Retail	Markup
SR Reg. Cab 2WD 5.7 V8	$30,400	8%
SR5 Dbl. Cab 4WD 5.7 V8	$36,150	8%
Limited Crew Max 4WD 5.7 V8	$44,195	8%
1794 Edition Crew Max 5.7 V8	$50,030	8%

Safety Checklist

Crash Tests:
  Frontal . . . . Very Poor
  Side . . . . –
Airbags:
  Torso . . . Standard Front Pelvis/Torso from Seat
  Roll Sensing . . . . Yes
  Knee Bolster . . . . Standard Front
Crash Avoidance:
  Collision Avoidance . . . . None
  Blind Spot Detection . . . . Optional
  Lane Keeping Assist . . . . None
  Backup Camera . . . . Standard
  Pedestrian Crash Avoidance . . . . None
General:
  Auto. Crash Notification . . . Operator Assist.-Fee
  Day Running Lamps . . . . Standard
Safety Belt/Restraint:
  Dynamic Head Restraints . . . . None
  Adjustable Belt . . . . None

^Warning feature does not meet government standards.
*Backup camera does not meet government standards.

Toyota Tundra

Specifications

Drive 4WD
Engine 5.7-liter V8
Transmission . . . . 6-sp. Automatic
Tow Rating (lbs.) . . . . Very High-10000
Head/Leg Room (in.) Cramped-39.7/42.5
Interior Space (cu. ft.) . . . . –
Cargo Space (cu. ft.) . . . . Very Roomy-67.1
Wheelbase/Length (in.) 145.7/228.9

Toyota Yaris

Ratings—10 Best, 1 Worst

Rating	
Combo Crash Tests	3
Safety Features	2
Rollover	4
Preventive Maintenance	10
Repair Costs	10
Warranty	2
Fuel Economy	8
Complaints	10
Insurance Costs	1
OVERALL RATING	**5**

Toyota Yaris

Toyota Yaris

At-a-Glance

Status/Year Series Started. Unchanged/2012
Twins . . . . –
Body Styles . . . . Hatchback
Seating 5
Anti-Theft Device . . . . Std. Passive Immobil. Only
Parking Index Rating . . . . .Very Easy
Where Made. . . . . .Iwata, Japan
Fuel Factor:. . . . .
  MPG Rating (city/hwy) Average-30/36
  Driving Range (mi.) . . . . Very Short-360
  Fuel Type. . . . . .Regular
  Annual Fuel Cost . . . . Very Low-$994
  Gas Guzzler Tax . . . . .No
  Greenhouse Gas Emissions (tons/yr.). Low-5.6
  Barrels of Oil Used per year Low-10.3

How the Competition Rates

Competitors	Rating	Pg.
Chevrolet Sonic	9	120
Kia Rio	5	181
Nissan Versa	2	233

Price Range

Price Range	Retail	Markup
L 2 Door MT	$15,250	4%
L 4 Door AT	$16,375	4%
LE 4 Door	$17,285	4%
SE 4 Door	$18,000	5%

Safety Checklist

Crash Tests:
  Frontal . . . . Poor
  Side . . . . Poor
Airbags:
  Torso . . . Standard Front Pelvis/Torso from Seat
  Roll Sensing. . . . . No
  Knee Bolster . . . . Standard Driver
Crash Avoidance:
  Collision Avoidance . . . . . . Optional CIB & DBS
  Blind Spot Detection . . . . None
  Lane Keeping Assist . . .Warning Only Optional^
  Backup Camera . . . . None
  Pedestrian Crash Avoidance . . . . None
General:
  Auto. Crash Notification . . . Operator Assist.-Fee
  Day Running Lamps . . . . Optional
Safety Belt/Restraint:
  Dynamic Head Restraints . . . . None
  Adjustable Belt. . . . . None

^Warning feature does not meet government standards.
*Backup camera does not meet government standards.

Toyota Yaris

Specifications

Drive. . . . . .FWD
Engine 1.5-liter I4
Transmission . . . . 4-sp. Automatic
Tow Rating (lbs.) . . . . –
Head/Leg Room (in.) Cramped-39.3/40.6
Interior Space (cu. ft.). . . . . Very Cramped-85.1
Cargo Space (cu. ft.) Cramped-15.6
Wheelbase/Length (in.) 98.8/155.5

Ratings—10 Best, 1 Worst

Combo Crash Tests	—
Safety Features	3
Rollover	5
Preventive Maintenance	9
Repair Costs	10
Warranty	2
Fuel Economy	9
Complaints	—
Insurance Costs	5
OVERALL RATING	**—**

Toyota Yaris iA

Toyota Yaris iA

At-a-Glance

Status/Year Series Started. . . . . All New/2017
Twins . . . . –
Body Styles . . . . .Sedan
Seating 5
Anti-Theft Device . . . . Std. Passive Immobil. Only
Parking Index Rating . . . . .Very Easy
Where Made. . . . . Salamanca, Mexico
Fuel Factor:. . . . .
MPG Rating (city/hwy) Average-32/40
Driving Range (mi.) Average-408
Fuel Type . . . . .Regular
Annual Fuel Cost . . . . .Very Low-$917
Gas Guzzler Tax . . . . .No
Greenhouse Gas Emissions (tons/yr.). Very Low-4.1
Barrels of Oil Used per year Low-9.4

How the Competition Rates

Competitors	Rating	Pg.
Fiat 500	2	134
Ford Fiesta	3	142
Hyundai Veloster	5	166

Price Range

Price Range	Retail	Markup
Sedan MT	$15,950	4%
Sedan AT	$17,050	4%

Safety Checklist

Crash Tests:
Frontal . . . . –
Side . . . . –
Airbags:
Torso . . . Standard Front Pelvis/Torso from Seat
Roll Sensing. . . . . .Yes
Knee Bolster . . . . None
Crash Avoidance:
Collision Avoidance . . . . None
Blind Spot Detection . . . . None
Lane Keeping Assist . . . . None
Backup Camera . . . . Standard
Pedestrian Crash Avoidance . . . . None
General:
Auto. Crash Notification . . . Operator Assist.-Fee
Day Running Lamps . . . . Standard
Safety Belt/Restraint:
Dynamic Head Restraints . . . . None
Adjustable Belt. . . . . .Standard Front

^Warning feature does not meet government standards.
*Backup camera does not meet government standards.

Toyota Yaris iA

Specifications

Drive. . . . . .FWD
Engine 1.5-liter I4
Transmission . . . . 6-sp. Automatic
Tow Rating (lbs.) . . . . –
Head/Leg Room (in.) Cramped-38.2/41.9
Interior Space (cu. ft.). . . . . Very Cramped-85.9
Cargo Space (cu. ft.) Cramped-13.5
Wheelbase/Length (in.) 101.2/171.7

Ratings—10 Best, 1 Worst

Combo Crash Tests	3
Safety Features	1
Rollover	7
Preventive Maintenance	5
Repair Costs	4
Warranty	5
Fuel Economy	6
Complaints	5
Insurance Costs	1
OVERALL RATING	**1**

Volkswagen Beetle

At-a-Glance

Status/Year Series Started	Unchanged/2012
Twins	–
Body Styles	Hatchback, Convertible
Seating	4
Anti-Theft Device	Std. Pass. Immobil. & Alarm
Parking Index Rating	Very Easy
Where Made	Hai Phong, Vietnam
Fuel Factor:	
MPG Rating (city/hwy)	Poor-25/33
Driving Range (mi.)	Average-407
Fuel Type	Regular
Annual Fuel Cost	Low-$1149
Gas Guzzler Tax	No
Greenhouse Gas Emissions (tons/yr.)	Average-6.5
Barrels of Oil Used per year	Average-11.8

How the Competition Rates

Competitors	Rating	Pg.
Kia Forte	6	179
Mazda Mazda3	8	202
Nissan Sentra	5	231

Price Range

	Retail	Markup
S Coupe AT	$19,795	4%
SE Coupe AT	$22,450	4%
SE R-Line Coupe AT	$27,095	4%
SEL R-Line Convertible AT	$36,050	4%

Volkswagen Beetle

Safety Checklist

Crash Tests:
Frontal . . . . Poor
Side . . . . Poor

Airbags:
Torso . . . . Standard Front Torso from Seat
Roll Sensing . . . . No
Knee Bolster . . . . None

Crash Avoidance:
Collision Avoidance . . . . None
Blind Spot Detection . . . . Optional
Lane Keeping Assist . . . . None
Backup Camera . . . . Optional
Pedestrian Crash Avoidance . . . . None

General:
Auto. Crash Notification . . . Operator Assist.-Fee
Day Running Lamps . . . . Standard

Safety Belt/Restraint:
Dynamic Head Restraints . . . . None
Adjustable Belt . . . . None

^Warning feature does not meet government standards.
*Backup camera does not meet government standards.

Volkswagen Beetle

Specifications

Drive	FWD
Engine	1.8-liter I4
Transmission	6-sp. Automatic
Tow Rating (lbs.)	–
Head/Leg Room (in.)	Cramped-39.4/41.3
Interior Space (cu. ft.)	Very Cramped-85.1
Cargo Space (cu. ft.)	Cramped-15.4
Wheelbase/Length (in.)	100/168.4

Volkswagen Golf

Ratings—10 Best, 1 Worst

Combo Crash Tests	5
Safety Features	6
Rollover	5
Preventive Maintenance	3
Repair Costs	8
Warranty	5
Fuel Economy	7
Complaints	2
Insurance Costs	3
OVERALL RATING	**4**

Volkswagen Golf

At-a-Glance

Status/Year Series Started Appearance Change/2015
Twins . . . .–
Body Styles . . . . Hatchback
Seating 5
Anti-Theft Device . . . . . . Std. Pass. Immobil. & Alarm
Parking Index Rating . . . . Easy
Where Made. . Wolfsburg, Germany / Puebla, Mexico
Fuel Factor:. . . . .
  MPG Rating (city/hwy) Poor-26/36
  Driving Range (mi.) Short-392
  Fuel Type. . . . . .Regular
  Annual Fuel Cost . . . . Low-$1085
  Gas Guzzler Tax . . . . .No
  Greenhouse Gas Emissions (tons/yr.). . Average-6.2
  Barrels of Oil Used per year Average-11.4

How the Competition Rates

Competitors	Rating	Pg.
Buick Verano	10	107
Mazda Mazda3	8	202
Nissan Sentra	5	231

Price Range

	Retail	Markup
S Hatchback AT	$20,995	4%
S Sportswagon AT	$22,680	4%
SE Sportswagon AT	$27,030	4%
SEL Sportwagon AT	$29,970	4%

Safety Checklist

Crash Tests:
  Frontal . . . . Average
  Side . . . . Average
Airbags:
  Torso . . . Standard Front Pelvis/Torso from Seat
  Roll Sensing. . . . . .Yes
  Knee Bolster . . . . None
Crash Avoidance:
  Collision Avoidance . . . . Optional CIB
  Blind Spot Detection . . . . Optional
  Lane Keeping Assist . . . . Optional
  Backup Camera . . . . Standard
  Pedestrian Crash Avoidance . . . . None
General:
  Auto. Crash Notification . . . Operator Assist.-Fee
  Day Running Lamps . . . . Standard
Safety Belt/Restraint:
  Dynamic Head Restraints . . . . None
  Adjustable Belt. . . . . .Standard Front

^Warning feature does not meet government standards.
*Backup camera does not meet government standards.

Volkswagen Golf

Specifications

Drive. . . . . .FWD
Engine 1.8-liter I4
Transmission . . . . 6-sp. Automatic
Tow Rating (lbs.) . . . .–
Head/Leg Room (in.) . . . . Very Cramped-38.4/41.2
Interior Space (cu. ft.). Cramped-93.5
Cargo Space (cu. ft.) Average-22.8
Wheelbase/Length (in.) 103.8/167.5

Ratings—10 Best, 1 Worst	
Combo Crash Tests	7
Safety Features	3
Rollover	6
Preventive Maintenance	5
Repair Costs	5
Warranty	5
Fuel Economy	8
Complaints	6
Insurance Costs	3
OVERALL RATING	**5**

Volkswagen Jetta

Volkswagen Jetta

Volkswagen Jetta

At-a-Glance

Status/Year Series Started.	Unchanged/2011
Twins . . . .–
Body Styles . . . . .Sedan
Seating. 5
Anti-Theft Device	Std. Pass. Immobil. & Alarm
Parking Index Rating . . . . .Easy
Where Made. . . . . .Puebla, Mexico
Fuel Factor:. . . . .
MPG Rating (city/hwy). Poor-28/39
Driving Range (mi.) Long-465
Fuel Type. . . . . .Regular
Annual Fuel Cost . . . . .Very Low-$1006
Gas Guzzler Tax . . . . .No
Greenhouse Gas Emissions (tons/yr.). Very Low-4.6
Barrels of Oil Used per year Low-10.3

How the Competition Rates

Competitors	Rating	Pg.
Ford Focus	6	144
Nissan Sentra	5	231
Toyota Corolla	8	248

Price Range	Retail	Markup
S MT	$17,895	4%
S AT	$18,995	4%
SE AT	$21,995	4%
SEL AT	$24,995	4%

Safety Checklist

Crash Tests:
Frontal . . . . Average
Side . . . . Very Good
Airbags:
Torso . . .Standard Front Pelvis/Torso from Seat
Roll Sensing. . . . . .Yes
Knee Bolster . . . . None
Crash Avoidance:
Collision Avoidance . . . . None
Blind Spot Detection . . . . Optional
Lane Keeping Assist . . . . None
Backup Camera . . . . .Standard*
Pedestrian Crash Avoidance . . . . None
General:
Auto. Crash Notification . . . Operator Assist.-Fee
Day Running Lamps . . . . Standard
Safety Belt/Restraint:
Dynamic Head Restraints . . . . None
Adjustable Belt . . . . .Standard Front

^Warning feature does not meet government standards.
*Backup camera does not meet government standards.

Volkswagen Jetta

Specifications

Drive. . . . . .FWD
Engine 1.4-liter I4
Transmission . . . . 6-sp. Automatic
Tow Rating (lbs.) . . . .–
Head/Leg Room (in.) . . . . Very Cramped-38.2/41.2
Interior Space (cu. ft.). Cramped-94.1
Cargo Space (cu. ft.) Cramped-15.7
Wheelbase/Length (in.) 104.4/183.3

Ratings—10 Best, 1 Worst

Combo Crash Tests	5
Safety Features	3
Rollover	7
Preventive Maintenance	5
Repair Costs	3
Warranty	5
Fuel Economy	7
Complaints	3
Insurance Costs	3
OVERALL RATING	**3**

Volkswagen Passat

At-a-Glance

Status/Year Series Started Unchanged/2012
Twins . . . . –
Body Styles . . . . .Sedan
Seating 5
Anti-Theft Device . . . . . . Std. Pass. Immobil. & Alarm
Parking Index Rating . . . . Average
Where Made. . . . . Chattanooga, TN
Fuel Factor:. . . . .
  MPG Rating (city/hwy) Poor-25/38
  Driving Range (mi.) . . . . Very Long-547
  Fuel Type . . . . .Regular
  Annual Fuel Cost . . . . Low-$1091
  Gas Guzzler Tax . . . . .No
  Greenhouse Gas Emissions (tons/yr.) Low-5.0
  Barrels of Oil Used per year . . . . Very Low-0.0

How the Competition Rates

Competitors	Rating	Pg.
Acura TLX	9	84
Ford Fusion	6	145
Volvo S60	10	266

Price Range	Retail	Markup
S 1.8T	$22,440	4%
R-Line 1.8T	$23,975	4%
SE 1.8T	$25,495	4%
SEL Premium 1.8T	$30,995	4%

Volkswagen Passat

Safety Checklist

Crash Tests:
  Frontal . . . . .Very Poor
  Side . . . . Very Good
Airbags:
  Torso . . . Standard Front Pelvis/Torso from Seat
  Roll Sensing. . . . . .Yes
  Knee Bolster . . . . None
Crash Avoidance:
  Collision Avoidance . . . . None
  Blind Spot Detection . . . . Optional
  Lane Keeping Assist . . . . None
  Backup Camera . . . . .Standard*
  Pedestrian Crash Avoidance . . . . None
General:
  Auto. Crash Notification . . . Operator Assist.-Fee
  Day Running Lamps . . . . Standard
Safety Belt/Restraint:
  Dynamic Head Restraints . . . . None
  Adjustable Belt. . . . . .Standard Front

^Warning feature does not meet government standards.
*Backup camera does not meet government standards.

Volkswagen Passat

Specifications

Drive. . . . . .FWD
Engine 1.8-liter I4
Transmission . . . . .6-SP. Automatic
Tow Rating (lbs.) . . . . –
Head/Leg Room (in.) Cramped-38.3/42.4
Interior Space (cu. ft.). Average-102
Cargo Space (cu. ft.) Cramped-15.9
Wheelbase/Length (in.) 110.4/191.9

Ratings—10 Best, 1 Worst

Combo Crash Tests	1
Safety Features	2
Rollover	2
Preventive Maintenance	3
Repair Costs	5
Warranty	5
Fuel Economy	3
Complaints	3
Insurance Costs	8
OVERALL RATING	**1**

Volkswagen Tiguan

Safety Checklist

Crash Tests:
Frontal . . . . .Very Poor
Side . . . . Poor

Airbags:
Torso . . . Standard Front Pelvis/Torso from Seat
Roll Sensing. . . . . .Yes
Knee Bolster . . . . None

Crash Avoidance:
Collision Avoidance . . . . None
Blind Spot Detection . . . . None
Lane Keeping Assist . . . . None
Backup Camera . . . . .Standard*
Pedestrian Crash Avoidance . . . . None

General:
Auto. Crash Notification . . . Operator Assist.-Fee
Day Running Lamps . . . . Standard

Safety Belt/Restraint:
Dynamic Head Restraints . . . . None
Adjustable Belt . . . . .Standard Front

^Warning feature does not meet government standards.
*Backup camera does not meet government standards.

Volkswagen Tiguan

At-a-Glance

Status/Year Series Started. Unchanged/2009
Twins . . . . –
Body Styles . . . . SUV
Seating 5
Anti-Theft Device . . . . . . Std. Pass. Immobil. & Alarm
Parking Index Rating . . . . Average
Where Made. . . . . .Puebla, Mexico
Fuel Factor:. . . . .
MPG Rating (city/hwy) . . . . .Very Poor-21/26
Driving Range (mi.) Short-389
Fuel Type. . . . . .Premium
Annual Fuel Cost . . . . Very High-$1749
Gas Guzzler Tax . . . . .No
Greenhouse Gas Emissions (tons/yr.). High-7.8
Barrels of Oil Used per year High-14.3

How the Competition Rates

Competitors	Rating	Pg.
Ford Escape	7	138
Lexus NX	6	194
Toyota RAV4	6	254

Price Range	Retail	Markup
S FWD	$24,995	4%
SEL	$34,500	4%
Sport 4Motion	$34,580	4%
SEL 4Motion	$36,475	4%

Volkswagen Tiguan

Specifications

Drive. . . . . .FWD
Engine 2.0-liter I4
Transmission . . . . 6-sp. Automatic
Tow Rating (lbs.) . . . . .Very Low-2200
Head/Leg Room (in.) . . . . Very Cramped-39.1/40.1
Interior Space (cu. ft.). Cramped-95.4
Cargo Space (cu. ft.) Roomy-23.8
Wheelbase/Length (in.) 102.5/174.5

Ratings—10 Best, 1 Worst

Combo Crash Tests	8
Safety Features	7
Rollover	8
Preventive Maintenance	5
Repair Costs	7
Warranty	8
Fuel Economy	7
Complaints	7
Insurance Costs	8
OVERALL RATING	**10**

Volvo S60

Volvo S60

At-a-Glance

Status/Year Series Started	Unchanged/2011
Twins	–
Body Styles	Sedan
Seating	5
Anti-Theft Device	Std. Pass. Immobil. & Active Alarm
Parking Index Rating	Average
Where Made	Torslanda, Sweden
Fuel Factor:	
MPG Rating (city/hwy)	Poor-25/37
Driving Range (mi.)	Very Long-521
Fuel Type	Regular
Annual Fuel Cost	Low-$1102
Gas Guzzler Tax	No
Greenhouse Gas Emissions (tons/yr.)	Average-6.2
Barrels of Oil Used per year	Average-11.4

How the Competition Rates

Competitors	Rating	Pg.
Acura TLX	9	84
Audi A6	6	88
Subaru Legacy	6	239

Price Range

	Retail	Markup
T5 FWD	$34,150	6%
T5 Premier AWD	$38,300	6%
T6 Platinum FWD	$43,300	6%
T6 R-Design Platinum AWD	$47,700	6%

Safety Checklist

Crash Tests:
Frontal . . . . Very Good
Side . . . . Poor

Airbags:
Torso . . . Standard Front Pelvis/Torso from Seat
Roll Sensing . . . . Yes
Knee Bolster . . . . None

Crash Avoidance:
Collision Avoidance . . . . . . Std. CIB & Opt. DBS
Blind Spot Detection . . . . Optional
Lane Keeping Assist . . . . Optional
Backup Camera . . . . Optional*
Pedestrian Crash Avoidance . . . . Optional

General:
Auto. Crash Notification . . . Operator Assist.-Fee
Day Running Lamps . . . . Standard

Safety Belt/Restraint:
Dynamic Head Restraints . . . . None
Adjustable Belt . . . . Standard Front

^Warning feature does not meet government standards.
*Backup camera does not meet government standards.

Volvo S60

Specifications

Drive	FWD
Engine	2.0-liter I4
Transmission	8-sp. Automatic
Tow Rating (lbs.)	–
Head/Leg Room (in.)	Cramped-39.3/41.9
Interior Space (cu. ft.)	Cramped-92
Cargo Space (cu. ft.)	Very Cramped-12
Wheelbase/Length (in.)	109.3/182.5

Ratings—10 Best, 1 Worst

Combo Crash Tests	—
Safety Features	7
Rollover	7
Preventive Maintenance	3
Repair Costs	7
Warranty	8
Fuel Economy	7
Complaints	1
Insurance Costs	8

OVERALL RATING   —

Volvo V60

Volvo V60

At-a-Glance

Status/Year Series Started	Unchanged/2015
Twins	—
Body Styles	Wagon
Seating	5
Anti-Theft Device	Std. Pass. Immobil. & Active Alarm
Parking Index Rating	Average
Where Made	—

Fuel Factor:

MPG Rating (city/hwy)	Poor-25/37
Driving Range (mi.)	Very Long-521
Fuel Type	Regular
Annual Fuel Cost	Low-$1102
Gas Guzzler Tax	No
Greenhouse Gas Emissions (tons/yr.)	Average-6.2
Barrels of Oil Used per year	Average-11.4

How the Competition Rates

Competitors	Rating	Pg.
Lincoln MKZ	5	199
Subaru Outback	7	240
Volkswagen Jetta	5	263

Price Range

	Retail	Markup
T5 FWD	$36,150	6%
T5 Premier FWD	$38,100	6%
T5 Platinum FWD	$41,750	6%
T6 R-Design Platinum AWD	$49,200	6%

Safety Checklist

Crash Tests:

Frontal	−
Side	−

Airbags:

Torso	Standard Front Pelvis/Torso from Seat
Roll Sensing	Yes
Knee Bolster	None

Crash Avoidance:

Collision Avoidance	Std. CIB & Opt. DBS
Blind Spot Detection	Optional
Lane Keeping Assist	Optional
Backup Camera	Optional*
Pedestrian Crash Avoidance	Optional

General:

Auto. Crash Notification	Operator Assist.-Fee
Day Running Lamps	Standard

Safety Belt/Restraint:

Dynamic Head Restraints	None
Adjustable Belt	Standard Front

^Warning feature does not meet government standards.
*Backup camera does not meet government standards.

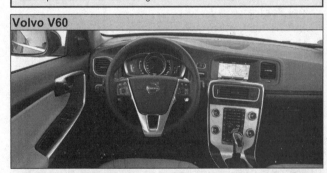

Volvo V60

Specifications

Drive	FWD
Engine	2.0-liter I4
Transmission	8-sp. Automatic
Tow Rating (lbs.)	Low-3500
Head/Leg Room (in.)	Cramped-38.7/41.9
Interior Space (cu. ft.)	Cramped-92
Cargo Space (cu. ft.)	Roomy-28
Wheelbase/Length (in.)	109.3/182.5

Ratings—10 Best, 1 Worst

Combo Crash Tests	—
Safety Features	6
Rollover	1
Preventive Maintenance	5
Repair Costs	7
Warranty	8
Fuel Economy	5
Complaints	—
Insurance Costs	10
OVERALL RATING	**—**

Volvo XC60

Volvo XC60

At-a-Glance

Status/Year Series Started	All New/2017
Twins	–
Body Styles	SUV
Seating	–
Anti-Theft Device . Std. Pass. Immobil. & Active Alarm	
Parking Index Rating	Average
Where Made	Ghent, Belgium
Fuel Factor:	
MPG Rating (city/hwy)	Poor-23/30
Driving Range (mi.)	Very Long-475
Fuel Type	Regular
Annual Fuel Cost	Low-$1255
Gas Guzzler Tax	No
Greenhouse Gas Emissions (tons/yr.)	Low-5.8
Barrels of Oil Used per year	Average-12.7

How the Competition Rates

Competitors	Rating	Pg.
Audi Q5	3	90
BMW X3	7	99
Lexus RX	5	196

Price Range	Retail	Markup
T5 FWD	$36,600	6%
T5 Platinum AWD	$45,650	6%
T6 R AWD	$46,950	6%
T6 R Platinum AWD	$51,050	6%

Safety Checklist

Crash Tests:
Frontal . . . . –
Side . . . . –

Airbags:
Torso . . . Standard Front Pelvis/Torso from Seat
Roll Sensing . . . . Yes
Knee Bolster . . . . None

Crash Avoidance:
Collision Avoidance . . . . . . Std. CIB & Opt. DBS
Blind Spot Detection . . . . Optional
Lane Keeping Assist . . . . Warning Only Optional
Backup Camera . . . . Optional*
Pedestrian Crash Avoidance . . . . Optional

General:
Auto. Crash Notification . . . Operator Assist.-Fee
Day Running Lamps . . . . Standard

Safety Belt/Restraint:
Dynamic Head Restraints . . . . None
Adjustable Belt . . . . Standard Front

^Warning feature does not meet government standards.
*Backup camera does not meet government standards.

Volvo XC60

Specifications

Drive	FWD
Engine	2.0-liter I4
Transmission	5-sp. Automatic
Tow Rating (lbs.)	Low-3500
Head/Leg Room (in.)	Cramped-39.1/41.2
Interior Space (cu. ft.)	Average-98.6
Cargo Space (cu. ft.)	Roomy-30.8
Wheelbase/Length (in.)	109.2/182.8

Ratings—10 Best, 1 Worst

Combo Crash Tests	—
Safety Features	4
Rollover	5
Preventive Maintenance	7
Repair Costs	7
Warranty	8
Fuel Economy	5
Complaints	5
Insurance Costs	10
OVERALL RATING	—

Volvo XC70

Volvo XC70

At-a-Glance

Status/Year Series Started	Unchanged/2008
Twins	—
Body Styles	Wagon
Seating	5
Anti-Theft Device	Std. Pass. Immobil. & Active Alarm
Parking Index Rating	Hard
Where Made	Torslanda, Sweden
Fuel Factor:	
MPG Rating (city/hwy)	Poor-23/31
Driving Range (mi.)	Very Long-481
Fuel Type	Regular
Annual Fuel Cost	Low-$1239
Gas Guzzler Tax	No
Greenhouse Gas Emissions (tons/yr.)	Low-5.7
Barrels of Oil Used per year	Average-12.7

How the Competition Rates

Competitors	Rating	Pg.
BMW X5	6	100
Lexus RX	5	196
Subaru Outback	7	240

Price Range	Retail	Markup
T5 FWD	$37,100	6%
T5 Premier FWD	$40,550	6%
T5 Platinum AWD	$47,175	6%
T5 Classic Platinum AWD	$48,175	6%

Safety Checklist

Crash Tests:
Frontal . . . . –
Side . . . .–

Airbags:
Torso . . . Standard Front Pelvis/Torso from Seat
Roll Sensing. . . . . No
Knee Bolster . . . . None

Crash Avoidance:
Collision Avoidance . . . . . Standard CIB & DBS^
Blind Spot Detection . . . . Optional
Lane Keeping Assist . . . .Warning Only Optional
Backup Camera . . . . Optional*
Pedestrian Crash Avoidance . . . . Optional

General:
Auto. Crash Notification . . . Operator Assist.-Fee
Day Running Lamps . . . . Standard

Safety Belt/Restraint:
Dynamic Head Restraints . . . . None
Adjustable Belt . . . . .Standard Front

^Warning feature does not meet government standards.
*Backup camera does not meet government standards.

Volvo XC70

Specifications

Drive	FWD
Engine	2.0-liter I4
Transmission	8-sp. Automatic
Tow Rating (lbs.)	
Head/Leg Room (in.)	Cramped-38.8/41.9
Interior Space (cu. ft.)	Very Roomy-134.9
Cargo Space (cu. ft.)	Very Roomy-33.3
Wheelbase/Length (in.)	110.8/190.5

Ratings—10 Best, 1 Worst

Combo Crash Tests	—
Safety Features	10
Rollover	1
Preventive Maintenance	4
Repair Costs	7
Warranty	8
Fuel Economy	4
Complaints	1
Insurance Costs	8

OVERALL RATING   —

Volvo XC90

At-a-Glance

Status/Year Series Started Unchanged/2015
Twins . . . . –
Body Styles . . . . Wagon
Seating 7
Anti-Theft Device . Std. Pass. Immobil. & Active Alarm
Parking Index Rating . . . . Hard
Where Made. . . . . Torslanda, Sweden
Fuel Factor: . . . .
  MPG Rating (city/hwy) . . . . . .Very Poor-22/26
  Driving Range (mi.) Long-444
  Fuel Type. . . . . .Premium
  Annual Fuel Cost . . . . .High-$1701
  Gas Guzzler Tax . . . . .No
  Greenhouse Gas Emissions (tons/yr.) . . Average-6.3
  Barrels of Oil Used per year High-14.3

How the Competition Rates

Competitors	Rating	Pg.
Buick Enclave	6	103
Chevrolet Tahoe	5	123
Toyota 4Runner	2	244

Price Range

Price Range	Retail	Markup
T5 Momentum FWD	$43,950	1%
T5 R-Design FWD	$49,350	6%
T6 Inscription AWD	$55,400	6%
T8 R-Design Hybrid AWD	$70,000	6%

Volvo XC90

Safety Checklist

Crash Tests:
  Frontal . . . .–
  Side . . . .–
Airbags:
  Torso . . . Standard Front Pelvis/Torso from Seat
  Roll Sensing. . . . . .Yes
  Knee Bolster . . . . Standard Driver
Crash Avoidance:
  Collision Avoidance . . . . . Standard CIB & DBS^
  Blind Spot Detection . . . . Standard
  Lane Keeping Assist . . . . .Standard^
  Backup Camera . . . . .Standard*
  Pedestrian Crash Avoidance . . . . Standard
General:
  Auto. Crash Notification . . . Operator Assist.-Fee
  Day Running Lamps . . . . Standard
Safety Belt/Restraint:
  Dynamic Head Restraints . . . . None
  Adjustable Belt. . . . . .Standard Front

^Warning feature does not meet government standards.
*Backup camera does not meet government standards.

Specifications

Drive. . . . . .AWD
Engine 2.0-liter I4
Transmission . . . .
Tow Rating (lbs.) Low-5000
Head/Leg Room (in.) Cramped-38.9/40.9
Interior Space (cu. ft.). Roomy-119.6
Cargo Space (cu. ft.) Cramped-15.8
Wheelbase/Length (in.) 117.5/194.8

So you're cosidering an electric vehicle? You're not alone! A recent survey by the Consumer Federation of America found that about one-third of potential car buyers would consider an EV. So it's no surprise that 16 major auto manufacturers have 25 new electric vehicles on the market with choices ranging from subcompacts to the luxury laden Tesla. While they're still more expensive than the corresponding gas powered vehicles, EV prices are on the way down and their benefits may warrant the added expense.

Energy from electricity is something we are all familiar with and, in fact, take for granted. We live in a plug-in world where most electrically powered products are extraordinarily convenient and highly functional. Imagine every night doing the same thing with your car as you do with your cell phone—simply plugging it in for the power it needs the next day. And then getting into a nearly silent, clean running car that glides effortlessly out of your driveway and likely has faster pickup than your gas powered car.

While there are a number of environmental reasons for buying an electric vehicle, the simplicity of operation, quiet ride, high tech feel and responsive performance are also major benefits. When you consider the complexity of a gasoline powered engine (most of us can't even identify the items under the hood!) and associated maintenance costs, the simplicity of electric power is refreshing, understandable, and very reliable. Owners of EVs report very low maintenance costs as there's very little to maintain.

SHOULD I EVEN CONSIDER AN ELECTRIC?

The big question most consumers have about EVs is: will I run out of power at the worst time possible—or anytime! Who hasn't needed a flashlight or tried to make a cell phone call only to find the battery is dead. In addition, many of us find it hard to imagine that the same type of engine that runs our blender, sewing machine or drill could possibly power a car! Finally, will I easily be able to plug this thing in at home? These concerns often dissuade people from looking further into the purchase of an electric vehicle.

The fact is, according to a recent analysis of consumer readiness for electric vehicles, 42% of car buyers meet the typical driving patterns, charging needs, and model preferences of the electric vehicles already on the market. Of households, 56% have access to charging, 95% transport 4 or fewer passengers, 79% don't require hauling, and 69% drive less than 60 miles on weekdays, well within the range of most battery-electric vehicles. Bottom-line, there's an excellent chance that an EV will meet your driving needs.

WHAT ARE MY CHOICES?

EVs come in various sizes, styles and price ranges. In addition, there are various types of EVs. The industry is trying to settle on acronyms to describe the different types, but here's a simple overview:

All Electric:

BEVs (Battery Powered Electric Vehicles) simply have a battery and an electric motor which powers the car. They are the simplest and "purest" form of electric vehicle. Because they depend solely on battery power, the battery systems have to be large which increases the cost of these vehicles. In addition to charging up at home, there are a growing number of publically available charging stations (over 15,000 to date) in shopping centers, employee parking lots, and along the highway. The range of these vehicles is from 62-238 miles per charge.

Electric with Built-In Charging Systems:

EREVs (Extended Range Electric Vehicles) have a gas powered auxiliary power source, that can recharge the battery if you run low on power before getting home or to a charging station. They tend to have smaller batteries and depend on the auxiliary gas powered recharger in place of a larger battery. The battery range on these vehicles is from 53-81 miles. There are only two vehicles in this category and they are a bit different from each other. The BMW i3 has an auxiliary gas engine that simply recharges the battery; it does not power the vehicle. The Chevy Volt has a gas engine that can both recharge the battery and run the vehicle. At various times both the electric motor and gas motor will power the Volt. With the auxiliary recharging engines, the range is 150 miles for the BMW i3 and 420 miles for the Chevy Volt. When the Volt reaches about 37 mph, the gas engine kicks in regardless of the state of the battery.

Dual Electric and Gasoline Vehicles:

PHEVs (Plug in Hybrid Electric Vehicles) have both an electric and gasoline motor which power the wheels at separate times. They are different from the now common hybrid vehicles, because you can plug them in to recharge. If your daily mileage is low, then these can be used like exclusively electric vehicles. Because the gasoline engine will kick in when the battery depletes, the range of these vehicle is similar to gasoline powered vehicles. The electric range is 11-27 miles per charge and the gasoline engine range is 330-550 miles.

WHAT ABOUT CHARGING?

There are three basic types of charging systems, two of which will work in your home.

Level 1: This is the simplest and least expensive system to set up in your home. All you need is a dedicated circuit (nothing else being used on the circuit) and a common household outlet. Level 1 charging is the slowest method because it uses standard 120 volt household current. Your electric vehicle will come with a Level 1 charging cord that you plug into a regular household outlet. The cord comes with a control box which monitors charging. Typically, it will take about an hour to get 4.5 miles of range. Complete charging times range from 3 to 57 hours.

Level 2: This requires a dedicated 240 volt circuit, the same one you would need for an electric dryer or other large appliance. First, your home has to have 240 electrical service (all newer homes will) and second, if there is not a readily available line, it will have to be run to where it is needed from the circuit breaker box. Not only will this require an electrician, but if walls or ceilings are disturbed, carpentry, drywall and painting may also be necessary. In addition, once the circuit is available, you will need a special device to plug into the circuit which monitors the electrical charge to the car. Depending on features, these devices can range from $500-$2500. Before these costs scare you off, it is worth investigating the actual cost (you may be lucky enough to have a circuit box in your garage or very close) and determine if your utility company will offer any financial assistance (many do as they want to sell you more electricity). In addition, you need to consider the fact that this installation will save you hundreds of dollars in gasoline costs as well as being much more convenient than going to a gas station to refuel. Typically an hour's charging will provide 24 miles of driving. Complete charging times range from 1.5 to 12 hours.

Level 3 or DC Fast Charge: This feature enables the car to be connected to a public charging station, many of which have very fast charging systems. This is great if you have an EV and your office provides charging stations or you're on the road and find one on the highway or in a shopping center. You can get up to 40 miles of range with just 10 minutes of charging. Overall charging times can be as low as 20 minutes.

One of the issues the industry is struggling with is a universal plug. There are three types of fast charge plugs, one of which is proprietary to the Tesla. Tesla does offer adaptors that can be used in the various types of outlets. If you are planning to charge your vehicle at work, be sure to check out the DC fast charge plug before you buy. Final Note: Because EVs are so quiet, pedestrians may not hear them coming so the government is considering requiring some type of added noise making capacity. When driving an EV use care when around pedestrians.

FOLLOWING IS *THE CAR BOOK'S* SNAPSHOT GUIDE TO THE 2017 EVs:

This is a very basic guide to many of the key features on today's EVs. It's important to take a good, long test drive in order to make a selection that best meets your needs and to get the details behind the features that are really important to you.

You'll find the following items in the EV snapshot:

Range: The first number is how far you can go on a single charge on just battery power. The second number shows the range with auxiliary power. In some cases that auxiliary power just recharges the battery, in other cases it powers the wheels just like a gas engine. In addition to the estimated range, we have provided two comparative ratings. The first rating is the total electric range which includes the range added with an auxiliary recharging engine. The second includes the range with the auxiliary engine that directly powers the wheels. This range is compared to the range of standard gasoline engines. The ratings for electric and electric + auxiliary vehicles range compares just these vehicles. Beware, driving with a "lead foot" and using heat and air conditioning will reduce your range.

Charging Time: This is the total time for a complete charge using Level 1 and Level 2 systems. We did not include the DC fast charging time because there is significant variation in the power of public stations.

MPGe: This is the equivalent of the traditional gasoline miles per gallon converted to electricity (thus the small 'e' at the end). While it is not actually miles per gallon, it gives you a way to compare the efficiency of EVs with gas powered vehicles. We've presented the 'combined' mileage rating which combines highway and city driving. The rating following the estimate compares the mileage with all other electric vehicles running on just battery power.

Introduction: This is the year the vehicle was first introduced. The longer the production time, the more likely the manufacturer is to have worked out any bugs. On the other hand, more recent introductions will contain more sophisticated technology and safety features.

Price: This is the manufacturer's suggested retail price

which gives you a general idea of EV pricing. It's important to check for federal and local rebate programs and to comparison shop. Car pricing is notoriously variable and that's no different for EVs. To get the best price consider using the services of the non-profit CarBargains program (page 68).

Size Class/Seating: This provides a general idea of the size of the car. Most consumers compare vehicles within the same size class.

On Board Charger: The greater the KW (kilowatt) rating, the faster the charger. In addition we indicate which vehicles have DC Fast Charging (Level 3) built-in which enables you to take advantage of speedy (and sometimes free) public charging facilities.

Auxiliary Power/MPG: This indicates whether or not (and what kind) of auxiliary power the vehicle may have. There are two types—engines that recharge the battery and engines that drive the wheels. For electric vehicles with auxiliary engines that power the car, we've included the EPA combined MPG estimate. The rating following the estimate compares the mileage with all other gasoline powered vehicles in *The Car Book*. See the descriptions on pages 271-272.

Crash Test Rating: Not all EVs have been crash tested. This tells you which one's were crash tested and how they performed using *The Car Book's* rating system based on government's tests. (See page 19.)

Safety Features: Safety has become critically important to today's car buyer, so we've identified 3 key safety features and indicated if the EV has those features. AEB stands for *Auto-

matic Emergency Braking* – this system automatically applies the brakes if a collision is imminent. We do not indicate, here, if the vehicle has other forms of automatic braking technologies such as brake assist or forward crash warning. *Rear Cameras* have become one of the best ways to avoid the tragic consequences of hitting a small child as well as serve as a wonderful parking assistant. *Lane Assist* moves you back into your lane if you're drifting. We do not indicate if the car simply provides a warning.

Warranty: Warranties vary so here's how the car's overall warranty stacks up in comparison with all other warranties.

Battery Warranty: Electric vehicle batteries are relatively new products and critical to the car's operation. As such, you want to be sure that your *battery* comes with a good, long warranty.

Interior Space/Cargo Space: This is another indication of the car's size. The ratings are relative compared to all of the vehicles in the *The Car Book*.

Parking Index: This rating takes into consideration the vehicle's key dimensions and determines an estimate for 'ease of parking' compared to other models. This is a general guide and no substitute for a good long test drive.

Sales: This indicates the total sales for the 2016 version of the vehicle indicating the general popularity of the EV.

For more complete information on many of these vehicles, please see the corresponding vehicle on the car ratings pages.

Audi A3 Plug-in Hybrid

Introduction:	2016
Range:	17 mi.– Short/Aux. Power–430 mi.–Long
Charging Time:	Lvl. 1 (8 hrs.)–Fast/Level 2 (2.5 hrs.)–Fast
MPGe:	Electric-86–Low

On Board Charger:	3.3 kW
Auxiliary Power/MPG:	Yes (PHEV)/MPG-39–Very High
Crash Test Rating:	—
Safety Features	AEB–Yes*; Rear Camera–Yes; Lane Asst–Yes*
Warranty:	4 years/50,000 mi.
Battery Warranty:	8 years/100,000 mi.
Size Class/ Seating:	Compact/5
Interior/Cargo Space:	89 cf–Vry. Cramped/13.6 cf–Cramped
Parking Index:	Easy
Sales:	3,973
Price	$37,900 (MSRP)
Notes:	*Indicates optional feature

BMW i3

Introduction:	2014
Range:	114 mi.–Vry. Long/Aux. Pwr.–150 mi.–Vry. Short
Charging Time:	Lvl. 1 (10 hrs.)–Fast/Lvl. 2 (3 hrs.)–Fast
MPGe:	Elec.-124–Vry. High

On Board Charger:	7.4 kW; DC fast charge optional
Auxiliary Power/MPG:	All Electric (w/opt. Gas Recharging it becomes an EREV)
Crash Test Rating:	–
Safety Features	AEB-Yes; Rear Camera-Yes; Lane Asst-No
Warranty:	4 years/50,000 mi.
Battery Warranty:	8 years/100,000 mi.
Size Class/ Seating:	Subcompact/4
Interior/Cargo Space:	83.1 cf–Vry. Cramped/2.8 cf–Vry. Cramped
Parking Index:	Very Easy
Sales:	16,377
Price	$43,600 (MSRP)/$47,450 w/battery ext.
Notes:	

BMW X5 xDrive Plug-in Hybrid

Introduction:	2016
Range:	14 mi.–Vry. Short/Aux. Power–540 mi.–Vry. Long
Charging Time:	Lvl. 1 (3.7 hrs.)–Vry. Fast/Lvl. 2 (2.7 hrs.)–Fast
MPGe:	Electric-56–Very Low

On Board Charger:	3.5 kW
Power:	Yes (PHEV)/MPG-24–Average
Crash Test Rating:	—
Safety Features	AEB–Yes*; Rear Camera–Yes*; Lane Asst–No
Warranty:	4 years/50,000 mi.
Battery Warranty:	8 years/100,000 mi.
Size Class/ Seating:	Medium SUV/5
Interior/Cargo Space:	cf– /34.2 cf–Very Roomy
Parking Index:	Very Hard
Sales:	6,268
Price	$63,045 (MSRP)
Notes:	*Indicates optional feature

Chevrolet Bolt

Introduction:	2017
Range:	238 mi.–Vry. Long
Charging Time:	Lvl. 1 (51 hrs.) Vry. Slow/Lvl. 2 (9 hrs.) Vry. Slow
MPGe:	119–Very High

On Board Charger:	7.2 kW; DC fast charge optional
Power:	No
Crash Test Rating:	–
Safety Features	AEB-No; Rear Camera-Yes; Lane Asst-No
Warranty:	3 years/36,000 mi..
Battery Warranty:	8 years/100,000 mi.
Size Class/ Seating:	Subcompact/5
Interior/Cargo Space:	95 cf.–Cramped/16.9 - Average
Parking Index:	Very Easy
Sales:	0
Price	$36,620 (MSRP)
Notes:	

Chevrolet Spark EV

On Board Charger:	3.3 kW; DC fast charge optional
Power:	All Electric
Crash Test Rating:	–
Safety Features	AEB-No; Rear Camera-Yes; Lane Asst-No
Warranty:	3 years/36,000 mi.
Battery Warranty:	8 years/100,000 mi.
Size Class/ Seating:	Subcompact/4
Interior/Cargo Space:	86.3 cf–Vry. Cramped/9.6 cf–Vry. Cramped
Parking Index:	Very Easy
Sales:	4,242
Price	$25,995 (MSRP)
Notes:	Only available in Maryland, California and Oregon

Introduction:	2013
Range:	82 mi.–Long
Charging Time:	Lvl. 1 (20 hrs.)–Slow/Lvl. 2 (<7 hrs.)–Vry. Slow
MPGe:	119–Very High

Chevrolet Volt

On Board Charger:	3.6 kW
Power:	Yes (PHEV)/MPG-42–Very High
Crash Test Rating:	-
Safety Features	AEB-Yes*; Rear Camera-Yes; Lane Asst-Yes*
Warranty:	3 years/36,000 mi.
Battery Warranty:	8 years/100,000 mi.
Size Class/ Seating:	Compact/5
Interior/Cargo Space:	90 cf–Vry. Cramped/10.6 cf–Vry. Cramped
Parking Index:	Easy
Sales:	32,261
Price	$33,120 (MSRP)
Notes:	*Indicates optional feature

Introduction:	2011
Range:	53 mi.–Short/Aux. Pwr.–420 mi.–Avg.
Charging Time:	Lvl. 1 (13 hrs.)–Avg./Lvl. 2 (4.5 hrs.)–Avg.
MPGe:	Elec.-106–Avg.

Fiat 500e

On Board Charger:	6.6 kW
Auxiliary Power/MPG:	All Electric
Crash Test Rating:	–
Safety Features	AEB-No; Rear Camera-Yes*; Lane Asst-No
Warranty:	4 years/50,000 mi.
Battery Warranty:	8 years/100,000 mi.
Size Class/ Seating:	Subcompact/2
Interior/Cargo Space:	71.6 cf–Vry. Cramped/7 cf–Vry. Cramped
Parking Index:	Very Easy
Sales:	9,689
Price	$31,800 (MSRP)
Notes:	*Indicates optional feature

Introduction:	2013
Range:	87 mi.–Long
Charging Time:	Lvl. 1 (<24 hrs.)–Vry. Slow/Lvl. 2 (<4 hrs.)–Avg.
MPGe:	116–Vry. High

Ford C-Max Energi

On Board Charger:	3.3 kW
Auxiliary Power/MPG:	Yes (PHEV)/MPG-38–Very High
Crash Test Rating:	–
Safety Features	AEB-No; Rear Camera-Yes; Lane Asst-No
Warranty:	3 years/36,000 mi.
Battery Warranty:	8 years/100,000 mi.
Size Class/ Seating:	Midsize/5
Interior/Cargo Space:	99.7 cf–Avg./19.2 cf–Avg.
Parking Index:	Average
Sales:	12,944
Price	$31,770 (MSRP)
Notes:	

Introduction:	2013
Range:	20 mi.–Vry. Short/Aux. Pwr.–550 mi.–Vry. Long
Charging Time:	Lvl. 1 (7 hrs.)–Fast/Lvl. 2 (2.5 hrs.)–Fast
MPGe:	Elec.-88–Low/

Ford Focus Electric

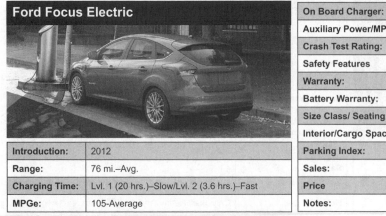

Introduction:	2012
Range:	76 mi.–Avg.
Charging Time:	Lvl. 1 (20 hrs.)–Slow/Lvl. 2 (3.6 hrs.)–Fast
MPGe:	105-Average

On Board Charger:	6.6 kW
Auxiliary Power/MPG:	All Electric
Crash Test Rating:	Front-Good;Side-Average;Overall-Average
Safety Features	AEB-No; Rear Camera-Yes; Lane Asst-No
Warranty:	3 years/36,000 mi.
Battery Warranty:	8 years/100,000 mi.
Size Class/ Seating:	Compact/5
Interior/Cargo Space:	90 cf–Vry. Cramped/14.2 cf–Cramped
Parking Index:	Easy
Sales:	2,065
Price	$29,170 (MSRP)
Notes:	Limited Availability

Ford Fusion Energi

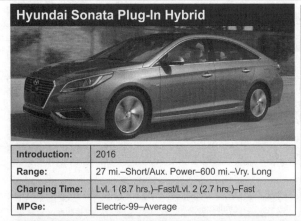

Introduction:	2013
Range:	20 mi.–Vry. Short/Aux. Pwr.–550 mi.–Vry. Long
Charging Time:	Lvl. 1 (7 hrs.)–Fast/Lvl. 2 (2.5 hrs.)–Fast
MPGe:	Elec.-88–Low

On Board Charger:	3.3 kW
Auxiliary Power/MPG:	Yes (PHEV)/MPG-38–Very High
Crash Test Rating:	Front-Very Good;Side-Poor;Overall-Good
Safety Features	AEB-Yes*; Rear Camera-Yes; Lane Asst-No
Warranty:	3 years/36,000 mi.
Battery Warranty:	8 years/100,000 mi.
Size Class/ Seating:	Midsize/5
Interior/Cargo Space:	102.8 cf–Roomy/8.2 cf–Vry. Cramped
Parking Index:	Average
Sales:	20,404
Price	$33,900 (MSRP)
Notes:	*Indicates optional feature

Hyundai Sonata Plug-In Hybrid

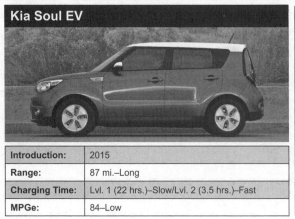

Introduction:	2016
Range:	27 mi.–Short/Aux. Power–600 mi.–Vry. Long
Charging Time:	Lvl. 1 (8.7 hrs.)–Fast/Lvl. 2 (2.7 hrs.)–Fast
MPGe:	Electric-99–Average

On Board Charger:	3.3 kW
Auxiliary Power/MPG:	Yes (PHEV)/MPG-40–Very High
Crash Test Rating:	—
Safety Features	AEB-No; Rear Camera–Yes; Lane Asst–No
Warranty:	5 years/60,000 mi.
Battery Warranty:	10 years/100,000 mi.
Size Class/ Seating:	Midsize/5
Interior/Cargo Space:	106.1 cf–Roomy/9.9 cf–Vry. Cramped
Parking Index:	Easy
Sales:	3,020
Price	$34,600 (MSRP)
Notes:	*Lifetime battery warranty for original owner

Kia Soul EV

Introduction:	2015
Range:	87 mi.–Long
Charging Time:	Lvl. 1 (22 hrs.)–Slow/Lvl. 2 (3.5 hrs.)–Fast
MPGe:	84–Low

On Board Charger:	6.6 kW; DC fast charge optional
Auxiliary Power/MPG:	All Electric
Crash Test Rating:	—
Safety Features	AEB-No; Rear Camera-Yes; Lane Asst-Yes
Warranty:	5 years/60,000 mi.
Battery Warranty:	8 years/100,000 mi.
Size Class/ Seating:	Compact/5
Interior/Cargo Space:	97.1 cf–Avg./18.8 cf–Avg.
Parking Index:	Very Easy
Sales:	2,257
Price	$31,950 (MSRP)
Notes:	Limited availability

Mercedes-Benz B-Class

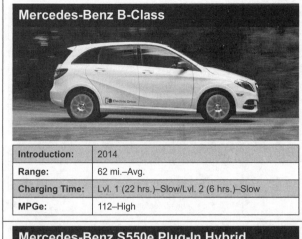

Introduction:	2014
Range:	62 mi.–Avg.
Charging Time:	Lvl. 1 (22 hrs.)–Slow/Lvl. 2 (6 hrs.)–Slow
MPGe:	112–High

On Board Charger:	10 kW
Auxiliary Power/MPG:	All Electric
Crash Test Rating:	–
Safety Features	AEB-Yes; Rear Camera-Yes; Lane Asst-No
Warranty:	4 years/50,000 mi.
Battery Warranty:	8 years/100,000 mi.
Size Class/ Seating:	Midsize/5
Interior/Cargo Space:	—/21.6 cf–Avg.
Parking Index:	Very Easy
Sales:	2,272
Price:	$39,900 (MSRP)
Notes:	

Mercedes-Benz S550e Plug-In Hybrid

Introduction:	2016
Range:	14 mi.–Vry. Short/Aux. Power–450 mi.– Long
Charging Time:	Lvl. 1 (4.5 hrs.)–Vry. Fast/Lvl. 2 (2 hrs.)–Vry. Fast
MPGe:	Electric–58–Very Low

On Board Charger:	3.3 kW
Auxiliary Power/MPG:	Yes (PHEV)/MPG–26–Average
Crash Test Rating:	—
Safety Features	AEB–Yes; Rear Camera–Yes; Lane Asst–Yes*
Warranty:	4 years/50,000 mi.
Battery Warranty:	8 years/100,000 mi.
Size Class/ Seating:	Large/5
Interior/Cargo Space:	112 cf–Roomy/13.9 cf–Cramped
Parking Index:	Very Hard
Sales:	624
Price:	$95,650 (MSRP)
Notes:	*Indicates optional feature

Nissan Leaf S

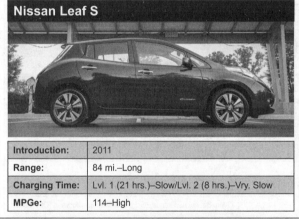

Introduction:	2011
Range:	84 mi.–Long
Charging Time:	Lvl. 1 (21 hrs.)–Slow/Lvl. 2 (8 hrs.)–Vry. Slow
MPGe:	114–High

On Board Charger:	3.6 kW; DC fast charge optional
Auxiliary Power/MPG:	All Electric
Crash Test Rating:	Front-Very Poor;Side-Very Poor;Overall-Very Poor
Safety Features	AEB-No; Rear Camera-Yes; Lane Asst-No
Warranty:	36 years/36,000 mi.
Battery Warranty:	8 years/100,000 mi.
Size Class/ Seating:	Compact/5
Interior/Cargo Space:	92.4 cf–Cramped/24 cf–Avg.
Parking Index:	Very Easy
Sales:	26,605
Price:	$29,010 (MSRP)
Notes:	

Nissan Leaf SV/SL

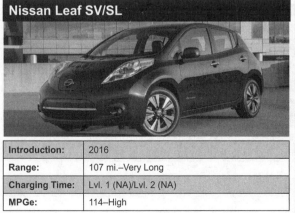

Introduction:	2016
Range:	107 mi.–Very Long
Charging Time:	Lvl. 1 (NA)/Lvl. 2 (NA)
MPGe:	114–High

On Board Charger:	6.6 kW; DC fast charge optional
Auxiliary Power/MPG:	All Electric
Crash Test Rating:	Front-Very Poor;Side-Very Poor;Overall-Very Poor
Safety Features	AEB-No; Rear Camera-Yes; Lane Asst-No
Warranty:	36 years/36,000 mi.
Battery Warranty:	8 years/100,000 mi.
Size Class/ Seating:	Compact/5
Interior/Cargo Space:	92.4 cf–Cramped/24 cf–Avg.
Parking Index:	Very Easy
Sales:	26,605
Price:	$34,200/$36,790 (MSRP)
Notes:	

Porsche Cayenne S E-Hybrid

Introduction:	2015
Range:	14 mi.–Vry. Short/Aux. Pwr.–480 mi.–Vry. Long
Charging Time:	Lvl. 1 (11 hrs.)–Fast/Lvl. 2 (3.6 hrs.)–Fast
MPGe:	Elec.-47–Vry. Low

On Board Charger:	3.6 kW
Auxiliary Power/MPG:	Yes (PHEV)/MPG-22–Poor
Crash Test Rating:	–
Safety Features:	AEB-Yes*; Rear Camera-Yes*; Lane Asst-Yes*
Warranty:	4 years/50,000 mi.
Battery Warranty:	8 years/100,000 mi.
Size Class/ Seating:	Midsize SUV/5
Interior/Cargo Space:	—/20.5 cf–Avg.
Parking Index:	Hard
Sales:	2,223
Price:	$77,200 (MSRP)
Notes:	*Indicates optional feature

Porsche Panamera S E-Hybrid

Introduction:	2013
Range:	16 mi.–Vry. Short/Aux. Pwr.–540 mi. –Vry. Long
Charging Time:	Lvl. 1 (>11 hrs.)–Fast/Lvl. 2 (2.3 hrs.)–Vry. Fast
MPGe:	Elec.-51–Vry. Low

On Board Charger:	3.6 kW
Auxiliary Power/MPG:	Yes (PHEV)/MPG-25–Average
Crash Test Rating:	–
Safety Features:	AEB-Yes*; Rear Camera-Yes*; Lane Asst-Yes*
Warranty:	4 years/50,000 mi.
Battery Warranty:	8 years/100,000 mi.
Size Class/ Seating:	Large/5
Interior/Cargo Space:	—/11.8 cf–Vry. Cramped
Parking Index:	Very Hard
Sales:	703
Price:	$96,100 (MSRP)
Notes:	*Indicates optional feature

Smart forTwo Electric Drive

Introduction:	2011
Range:	68 mi.–Short
Charging Time:	Lvl. 1 (13 hrs.)–Avg./Lvl. 2 (6 hrs.)–Slow
MPGe:	107–Avg.

On Board Charger:	3.3 kW
Auxiliary Power/MPG:	All Electric
Crash Test Rating:	–
Safety Features:	AEB-No; Rear Camera-Yes*; Lane Asst-No
Warranty:	4 years/50,000 mi.
Battery Warranty:	8 years/100,000 mi.
Size Class/ Seating:	Subcompact/2
Interior/Cargo Space:	45.4 cf–Vry. Cramped/7.8 cf–Vry. Cramped
Parking Index:	Very Easy
Sales:	1,720
Price:	$25,000 (MSRP)
Notes:	Offers Battery Assurance Plus, a battery rental program; *Opt. feature

Tesla Model S

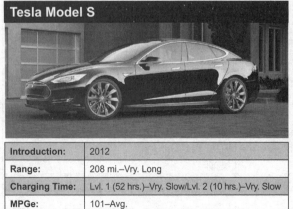

Introduction:	2012
Range:	208 mi.–Vry. Long
Charging Time:	Lvl. 1 (52 hrs.)–Vry. Slow/Lvl. 2 (10 hrs.)–Vry. Slow
MPGe:	101–Avg.

On Board Charger:	11 kW; DC fast charge optional
Auxiliary Power/MPG:	All Electric
Crash Test Rating:	Front-Good;Side-Very Good;Overall-Very Good
Safety Features:	AEB-Yes; Rear Camera-Yes; Lane Asst-Yes
Warranty:	4 years/50,000 mi.
Battery Warranty:	8 years/100,000 mi.
Size Class/ Seating:	Large/5
Interior/Cargo Space:	94 cf–Cramped/31.6 cf–Vry. Roomy
Parking Index:	Hard
Sales:	43,666
Price:	$68,000 (MSRP)
Notes:	

Tesla Model X

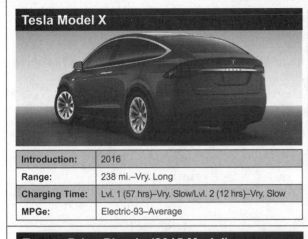

Introduction:	2016
Range:	238 mi.–Vry. Long
Charging Time:	Lvl. 1 (57 hrs.)–Vry. Slow/Lvl. 2 (12 hrs.)–Vry. Slow
MPGe:	Electric-93–Average

On Board Charger:	10 kW
Auxiliary Power/MPG:	None
Crash Test Rating:	—
Safety Features	AEB–; Rear Camera–Yes; Lane Asst–
Warranty:	4 years/50,000 mi.
Battery Warranty:	8 years/unlimited
Size Class/ Seating:	Mid-Size/7
Interior/Cargo Space:	–/–
Parking Index:	Vry. Hard
Sales:	16,829
Price:	$88,800 (MSRP)
Notes:	

Toyota Prius Plug-in (2015 Model)

Introduction:	2012
Range:	11 mi.–Vry. Short/Aux. Pwr.–540 mi.–Vry. Long
Charging Time:	Lvl. 1 (3 hrs.)–Vry. Fast/Lvl. 2 (1.5 hrs.)–Vry. Fast
MPGe:	Elec.-95–Low

On Board Charger:	6.6 kW
Auxiliary Power/MPG:	Yes (PHEV)/MPG-50–Very High
Crash Test Rating:	Front-Poor;Side-Average;Overall-Poor
Safety Features	AEB-Yes; Rear Camera-Yes; Lane Asst-No
Warranty:	3 years/36,000 mi.
Battery Warranty:	8 years/100,000 mi.
Size Class/ Seating:	Midsize/5
Interior/Cargo Space:	93.7 cf–Cramped/21.6 cf–Avg.
Parking Index:	Very Easy
Sales:	42,345
Price:	$29,990 (MSRP)
Notes:	On hold.

Volvo XC90 Plug-in Hybrid

Introduction:	2016
Range:	14 mi.–Vry. Short /Aux. Pwr.–350 mi.–Vry. Short
Charging Time:	Lvl. 1 (7 hrs.)–Fast/Lvl. 2 (2.5 hrs.)–Fast
MPGe:	Electric-53–Very Low

On Board Charger:	3.5 kW
Auxiliary Power/MPG:	Yes (PHEV)/MPG-25– Average
Crash Test Rating:	5 stars
Safety Features	AEB–Yes; Rear Camera–Yes; Lane Asst–Yes
Warranty:	4 years/50,000 mi.
Battery Warranty:	4 years/50,000 mi.
Size Class/ Seating:	Midsize SUV/7
Interior/Cargo Space:	103.8 cf–Roomy/15.4 cf–Cramped
Parking Index:	Hard
Sales:	1,931
Price:	$68,100 (MSRP)
Notes:	

VW e-Golf

Introduction:	2015
Range:	83 mi.–Avg.
Charging Time:	Lvl. 1 (20 hrs.)–Slow/Lvl. 2 (4 hrs.)–Avg.
MPGe:	116–Vry. High

On Board Charger:	7.2 kW; DC fast charge standard
Auxiliary Power/MPG:	All Electric
Crash Test Rating:	–
Safety Features	AEB-Yes*; Rear Camera-Yes; Lane Asst-No
Warranty:	3 years/36,000 mi.
Battery Warranty:	8 years/100,000 mi.
Size Class/ Seating:	Compact/5
Interior/Cargo Space:	93.5 cf–Cramped/22.8 cf–Avg.
Parking Index:	Easy
Sales:	6,962
Price:	$28,995 (MSRP)
Notes:	*Indicates optional feature